CONTENTS

2

What Is SQL? *39*

3

SQL Server Structure *73*

MICROSOFT CERTIFIED SYSTEMS ENGINEER SERIES

10.10. 73.105

JEFFRY BYRNE

MCSE:
ADMINISTERING
MICROSOFT® SQL
SERVER™ 7

Prentice Hall PTR, Upper Saddle River, NJ 07458
http://www.phptr.com/phptrinteractive

Editorial/Production Supervision: *Nicholas Radhuber*
Acquisitions Editor: *Jeffrey Pepper*
Marketing Manager: *Dan Rush*
Manufacturing Manager: *Alexis Heydt*
Cover Design: *Talar Agasyan*
Cover Design Direction: *Jerry Votta*
Series Design: *Gail Cocker-Bogusz*

Prentice Hall books are widely used by corporations and government agencies for training, marketing, and resale.

The publisher offers discounts on this book when ordered in bulk quantities. For more information, contact Corporate Sales Department, Phone: 800-382-3419; fax: 201-236-7141; email: corpsales@prenhall.com or write Corporate Sales Department, Prentice Hall PTR, One Lake Street, Upper Saddle River, NJ 07458.

Printed in the United States of America

10 9 8 7 6 5 4 3 2 1

ISBN 0-13-086863-9

Prentice-Hall International (UK) Limited, *London*
Prentice-Hall of Australia Pty. Limited, *Sydney*
Prentice-Hall Canada Inc., *Toronto*
Prentice-Hall Hispanoamericana, S.A., *Mexico*
Prentice-Hall of India Private Limited, *New Delhi*
Prentice-Hall of Japan, Inc., *Tokyo*
Prentice-Hall (Singapore) Pte. Ltd., *Singapore*
Editora Prentice-Hall do Brasil, Ltda., *Rio de Janeiro*

4

Microsoft SQL Server Components   *121*

PART TWO

Installation and Configuration   *147*

PART THREE

Planning and Managing Security   *215*

Security   *217*

PART FOUR

Working with Database Files *267*

Managing Your Database Files *269*

What Is Data Integrity? *279*

11

Data Consistency and Concurrency   *303*

12

Managing Database Space   *317*

20

Creating and Using Schedules 449

PART NINE

Publishing Data On the Web 471

21

Your Data and the Web 473

PART THIRTEEN

Managing Replication and Distributed Transactions   *525*

Replication Management   *527*

MCSE: Administering Microsoft® SQL Server™ 7 has been written to enhance your own knowledge on the subject and to prepare you for the MCSE exam on this topic.

This book has been written so that all of the required aspects of the exams, and the three courses available are covered in one place. The exam is written to ensure that you have a good working knowledge of SQL Server™ 7 system administration, but this book takes the view that this is only a minimum requirement. All of the topics that are required by the exam are covered and have been expanded so that you will have a good working knowledge of system administration for SQL Server 7 when you are done.

WHO THIS BOOK IS FOR

By selecting this book, you have shown that you are interested in SQL Server 7 system administration and that you are probably planning on taking the MCSE: Administering Microsoft® SQL Server 7.0 exam 70-028, and passing it the first time. This exam is one of several available to you as electives towards the Microsoft Certified Systems Engineer certification. There are other electives that you can take, but this is one of the more interesting topics and is in great demand.

In writing this book, I assume that you are not interested in just the minimum knowledge required to pass an exam. You will take away with you a firm foundation for taking on the job of an SQL Server 7 system administrator and will be able to install and work with your own database. We all know that many people can pass tests without being able to do the job. You will be able to do the job when you have completed this book.

Topics that are specific to the MCSE exam are called out throughout the book, ensuring that you do not miss anything.

WHAT YOU'LL NEED

In order to prepare properly for this exam, and to be able to really follow the examples in the book, you need your own computer that meets the minimum requirements for installation and operation of SQL Server 7. You will also then need a copy of the program CD.

You may either have access to a copy from your company, have purchased it on your own, or you can obtain an evaluation copy. As of this writing, the evaluation CD of SQL Server 7 is still available at Microsoft's Web site at http://www.microsoft.com/sql. This same evaluation copy has been made available at many of the Microsoft seminars held throughout the country over the last many months.

The evaluation copy has the advantage that is either free or cost only the shipping and handling fee. It does come with a limited time license and usually expires 120-days after installation.

HOW THIS BOOK IS ORGANIZED

This book is divided into 13 different parts. Each of these parts consists of one or more chapters and covers a major segment of the MCSE testing curriculum.

Part One: Microsoft SQL Server Overview
This part introduces SQL Server and how it fits into the client/server scheme. SQL Server's various structures and components are also discussed.

Part Two: Installation and Configuration
In this part you will learn to install SQL Server. Once the application has been installed, the various configuration options and how to use them are shown.

Part Three: Planning and Managing Security
This part covers all of the necessary aspects of security. This includes the creation of users, groups, roles, and whether to use Windows NT or SQL Server authentication modes.

Part Four: Working with Database Files

Here you will learn to create and manage database files and database space. You will also learn about data integrity and ensuring that information remains consistent, while also ensuring concurrency for the maximum number of users.

Part Five: Transferring Data

In this part you will learn how data can be transferred into and out of an SQL Server database. You will see how the bulk copy program and the Data Transformation Services are used to help you in these tasks.

Part Six: Backing Up a Database

This part covers the basics of why and how to back up a database. The topics of creating different types of backup devices and how they are used.

Part Seven: Restoring Databases

Here you learn the second half of backing up data—how to restore it from the backup device into a usable format.

Part Eight: Monitoring SQL Server Performance

In this part you will see how to monitor the performance of SQL Server and where improvements can be made in the system configuration.

Part Nine: Automating Tasks

Here you learn to use the SQL Server Agent service to create automatic tasks, events, and create and use schedules. These tasks will simplify your life as a system administrator to a very large extent.

Part Ten: Publishing Data on the Web

This part covers the uses of the Web Assistant Wizard and the stored procedures used to create web pages from data contained in the database.

Part Eleven: Beginning Replication

In this part you will learn the basics of replication: what it is and how it may be used.

Part Twelve: Planning a Replication Strategy

Here you will learn to plan a replication strategy for a business. What is the best model or models for the type of data that needs to be replicated. You also learn how to setup the various partners involved in replication: Publishers, Distributors, and Subscribers.

Part Thirteen: Managing Replication and Distributed Transactions
This part covers how to ensure that your replication strategy is doing what you expect and then how to use Distributed Transactions over a group of servers.

Appendix: Chapter Review Answers
The Appendix contains all of the answers to the review questions at the end of each chapter.

CONVENTIONS USED IN THIS BOOK

There are several simple conventions used throughout this book to help you distinguish between text, figures, examples, and code.

Those sections that deal directly with MCSE testing topics will be found underneath an MCSE heading and are numbered throughout the chapters.

All figures and tables are numbered and captioned so that you can quickly see what is being shown.

Examples and steps that you are to follow in an example are all numbered consecutively. Many of the figures will follow along with a step to show you exactly what you should be doing.

```
Code, Transact-SQL statements, and stored procedures are
all shown in a monospaced type face, like this.
```

ABOUT THE CD-ROM/COMPANION WEB SITE

This book contains a CD-ROM and includes access to a companion Web site.

On the CD-ROM in a folder named SAMPLES are three files that are used in several of the examples. The first file, "Inventory.txt," is used by the bulk copy program as a data source. The second file, "Inventorydb.fmt," is a text file that can be used by the bulk copy program as a format file. You will create one just like it in one of the examples, and this is included as a comparison. The last file, "NWExport.mdb," is a Microsoft Access™ file. It is used as a data source in an example on transferring data from an external database.

The remaining information on the CD-ROM is a computer-based training course from CBT Systems. This course is titled "Microsoft® SQL Server™ 7.0: Core Server Architecture and Features." This course can be installed on your hard disk or run from the CD. To begin the installation, place the CD in your drive and type D:\setup.exe from the Run option on the Start menu. This assumes that your CD-ROM drive is designated as the "D" drive. This course is a $225.00 value and is included free of charge with the purchase of this book.

Microsoft SQL Server Overview

In this first module, the theory and uses for Microsoft SQL Server are discussed. You will learn what SQL Server can be used for, and what is required to install the application. You will be able to describe the various supporting systems required or used by Microsoft SQL Server, and how it interacts with its operating system.

An Overview of Microsoft SQL Server

In selecting this book, you have shown your determination to learn the most you can about Microsoft® SQL Server™ and the role of the System Administrator. Microsoft SQL Server is the best selling database for the Windows NT market. Microsoft SQL Server is a *relational database management system* (RDBM). A relational database management system is one that allows you to store information in tables, each containing very specific information. The information contained in the tables can then be related to information contained in other tables. For example, a Customer table contains information about customers, while the Orders table has information about orders by customers. Both of these tables contain relationships between them so that you can link information about various orders to the customer who placed the order.

It is one-half of the client/server equation and is often referred to as the back-end program. The front-end, or client program is often a custom-designed application, or it can be a stand-alone database program that you can buy off the shelf, such as Microsoft Access.

Microsoft SQL Server uses a version of SQL called Transact-SQL.

In this chapter, you will learn what Microsoft SQL Server is, and how it can best fit into your client/server schema. SQL is an abbreviation for *Structured Query Language* and is often pronounced as "sequel.".

MCSE 1.1   Microsoft SQL Server and Windows NT

Microsoft SQL Server operates on the Windows NT operating system. Windows NT is available for several platforms. Unlike most relational database systems available, Microsoft SQL Server works completely in conjunction with its operating system. This tight integration allows it to make use of many of the operating system services and features that other databases are not able to do.

SQL Server 7.0 supports installation on a variety of platforms, including Windows NT Server, Windows NT Workstation, and Windows 95/98 platforms. SQL Server 7.0 can be run not only on a server class machine, but on a stand-alone desktop, notebook computers, and multiprocessor (SMP) servers supporting up to 16 processors and massive amounts of memory and disk space. Windows NT support is further restricted to only Intel® x86 and Pentium™ processor systems, or to Digital Equipment Corporation's Alpha™ processor systems. Earlier versions of SQL Server included support for both the MIPS™ and Power PC™ platforms, but this is not carried forward to version 7.0.

Integration at this level allows SQL Server to use NT security features and use the features available in its disk subsystem.

Windows NT Subsystems

There are several Windows NT subsystems that can be configured to operate with SQL Server. The primary subsystem that directly affects the performance of a database server is the disk subsystem. Windows NT includes software RAID support. You can easily set NT to provide RAID 0, 1, or 5 support to your database.

SQL Server 7.0 has been further enhanced to take greater advantage of the NT file system. In earlier versions of SQL Server, the database files were stored in database devices not operating system files. With the advent of SQL Server 7.0, databases are now stowed on an operating system file. This allows you to now create a new database without first having to create the database device and then create the database within the device. SQL Server 7.0 files can automatically expand as the database grows. This eliminates the need to increase the size of a database device with an ALTER statement.

Windows 95/98

You can now use Windows 95/98 as a base operating system. Previously, a Windows 95 machine could be a client only. Beginning with SQL Server 7.0, you can now create a Windows 95/98 server for the use of a small workgroup. You can also perform a stand-alone installation on a Windows 95/98 machine for use in testing applications. A Windows 95/98 SQL Server installation must still meet the minimum hardware requirements for SQL Server 7.0.

Client/Server and Microsoft SQL Server

The earliest database servers were mainframe systems. Many database servers are still mainframes and, while fast and powerful, are and always have been very expensive. They also require a dedicated MIS staff to program and maintain them. This means that every request for information from another department must be written down and given to the MIS department. Then, they determine if the information is available in the mainframe database, how to query that database, and finally how to format the report for the departmental customer. Each of these steps takes time and costs the organization money, and if each department is billed for the additional expenses needed, they may decide to make critical business decisions based on incomplete information instead of paying for another potentially expensive report. Figure 1-1 illustrates a mainframe connected to several dumb terminals and printers. All applications and data are stored on the mainframe.

Conversely, the personal computer/local area network (PC/LAN) has been very attractive for many small businesses and departmental computing needs. Many departments in an organization have found that they can provide for their own information needs by building an application with a com-

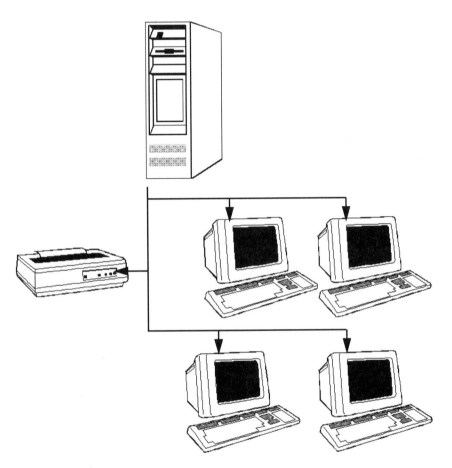

Figure 1–1 *Only text-based information is sent to the terminals or printers.*

mercially available database or spreadsheet in a very short amount of time and for relatively little money. Remember in most businesses the cost involved in creating an application for your department will be charged to your departmental budget by the MIS department. Using a departmental application may eliminate much of the time and cost involved in this process. Instead of sending a request to the MIS department, waiting for them to interpret your request, deciding how to get the information, building an application or query, and then transmitting the resulting data set back to you, you can do it yourself.

This laissez-faire form of construction of the PC/LAN system has been both its greatest asset and its greatest liability. While allowing individuals and departments access to needed information quickly, it has led to widespread redundant and incompatible information systems. This may seem like a contradiction in terms, but is assuredly not. Large organizations—though this can also happen in small organizations—will find that the same basic information is being stored in many different departments. Each department's information is similar, but stored in different formats, in different programs, and even on different operating systems. Each of these problems can require much expensive programming and conversion time so that the departments can share each other's data. It is also a great waste of money and computer resources that can be better used in other ways. Figure 1-2 illustrates a simple client/server LAN system.

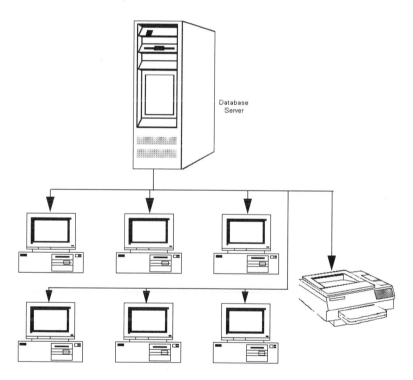

Figure 1–2 *The client/server LAN system has become greatly relied on as the network of choice for many businesses due to cost and ease of use.*

Client/server systems bridge the gap between mainframe systems and PC/LAN-based systems. Instead of keeping all of the processing power on only the mainframe, or distributing all processing power to each individual user, client/server systems share the processing responsibilities. The server RDBM stores virtually all of the data and retains much of responsibility for the basic database structure. You can institute quite strict centralized control over data integrity, administration, and security. Storing data in a central server enables the database administrator to easily perform backups of data and periodic maintenance of both data and server. Each client provides his or her own application—the front-end—information required by the client application that is forwarded from the server to the client. This sharing allows the server to concentrate on what it does best: storing data, ensuring its security, and providing requested data. The client can then handle such processor-intensive functions as complex user interfaces—for example, a graphical user interface, on-screen representations of forms and queries, and local calculations.

The glue that binds the client and the server is the *Structured Query Language* (SQL). Unlike most file-sharing LAN database management systems (DBMS) that respond to a query by delivering large quantities of unnecessary data—usually the entire file—the client/server will deliver only the specific information requested in the query. This helps to make SQL a more efficient manager of your information system. Both the server's database engine and the client applications use SQL to communicate with each other. The client application sends a SQL query to the server. The server then interprets the query by processing it through a procedure called *optimization*. The query optimizer will decide the fastest method of obtaining the information requested. Finally, the data is forwarded to the requesting application. This procedure places a greater portion of the processing burden on the server where the data resides than in earlier file-share systems. The client workstation then can work with a smaller subset of the real data, resulting in less network traffic and less processing for the workstation CPU.

One of the most powerful features of Microsoft SQL Server is its ability to manage data integrity. By having the server manage the integrity of your data, you don't have to rely on the many different programmers of varying abilities who created the many applications used in each department. While you can use the integrity checking available within an application, you do not have to rely wholly on it. With Microsoft SQL Server, you can guarantee the integrity and consistency of the information in your database across the entire LAN.

Why Use SQL Applications?

All office-automation computer programs can be considered an application of some type: word processor, spreadsheet, database, or desktop publishing. These programs are designed to automate specific tasks; for example, typing a letter or creating an invoice. With a word processing application, you can easily create complex documents and then edit, reformat, and finally print them without having to draft them in longhand or retype long sections of a document.

SQL applications are, by nature, information-oriented and may include accounts payable, payroll, sales, weather data, patient records, purchasing, customer and vendor data, and almost any other aspect related to the information needs of the business or institution collecting the data. Most SQL applications are designed to simplify the management of data collection and storage for a business, but there are several reasons for using an SQL client/ server application.

Ease of Use

Most client/server applications are very easy to use. They provide an intuitive interface, often showing an on-screen representation of a commonly used paper form. Therefore, salespeople who may be used to filling out a sales order form will see a familiar form on their screen when they use their sales order application. The client application then automatically updates the server database containing the actual data, using the SQL language. In addition to an easy-to-use screen form, the salesperson often doesn't have to look up information about a customer or items to be sold. The application will provide pop-up lists so that the salesperson only has to select a customer from a list and then choose items for sale from another list. This helps to ensure consistency in the company database by eliminating duplicate information, or selling items for the wrong price. With a few simple keystrokes or clicks on a mouse the form can be completed, filed away in the server application, and then printed for the customer.

With the addition of user-friendly, on-screen forms in the front-end application, the productivity of a salesperson, buyer, or inventory clerk may increase dramatically at the same time improving accuracy of the company's records and accounting information.

Simplify Systems

Many business systems do not follow the client/server model. While they may use some aspects of office automation in their business for certain jobs, the degree of integration that a front-end client application and Microsoft SQL Server as the back-end can provide does not exist. Let's look at a typical transaction chain for almost any business.

A customer calls in an order, which is received by a salesperson. This order is written down on an order pad. The salesperson may have to add up a total for the customer using a hand calculator. The completed handwritten order is then placed in an out basket for the order entry clerk. This person takes the orders and enters them into a computer. This computer then sends the order down to the warehouse, where a picking ticket is printed. The warehouse worker to pull the order uses the picking ticket. Once the order has been pulled, the picking ticket is typed into a packing list and a copy is forwarded to accounts receivable and inventory control. The accounts receivable clerk enters the quantities ordered and picked, along with the pricing information, to create an invoice, checks the customer's credit information, and enters this information into the customer's account file. At the same time, the inventory control clerk must adjust the inventory file to reflect the reduction for the items sold.

This typical system involves at least seven different transactions and six different people. Errors can be made at any point along this chain, and the system requires the same data to be entered and re-entered at each transaction point. While the usage and format of the information may vary from transaction to transaction, each transaction consists of only a few distinct information pieces: customer, part, quantity, and sales price.

Looking at this chain from a client/server viewpoint, you can easily see that almost all of these redundant transactions can be eliminated or reduced. With a client/server application, the order is entered only once;the application then takes care of all of the remaining transactions automatically. The order entry clerk takes the customer's order and enters it using an on-screen form. This application automatically displays a list of customers, items to be sold, and displays a total for the customer. If there are hold flags due to credit problems on this customer, they can be flagged to the order taker's attention at this point. The application then updates the customer file with any changes, updates the inventory, prints the picking list at the warehouse, generates an invoice, adds the sale to the customer's accounts receivable file, and informs the buyer if an item falls below a specified on-hand level.

Each transaction may be handled by a different front-end client application but by a single back-end SQL server database. This consolidation of data with the SQL server helps to ensure both data integrity and its security. Later in Chapter 11, "Data Consistency and Concurrency," you will see how a series of transactions can be placed against multiple servers and databases. Each application allows the user to work with their own representation of the same basic data, but the information needs only to be entered into a single application. Figure 1-3 shows how the information flows through these transactions from an original order to the completed shipment and billing cycle.

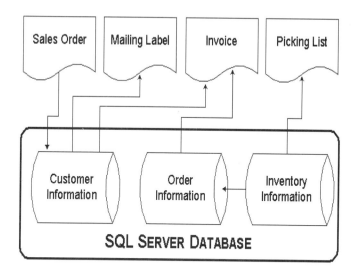

Figure 1–3   *By using a server-based database you can easily reduce many redundant transactions within a business. Each of the different front-end applications meet the needs of each department involved with the transaction.*

Enforcement of Business Procedures

Business procedures can include many things, but with Microsoft SQL Server business procedures, usually called *rules*, they principally have to do with what data is allowed into a field—these types of procedures or rules help to ensure the accuracy and integrity of the data. By building a database with well-designed integrity features, you can help enforce data input accuracy and enforce other types of rules. As often as possible, use server-based rules to enforce integrity rather than granting this job to a client application. When you allow the client to exclusively perform data validation checks, you can open the Pandora's Box of potential data integrity problems. You can not always be sure that different client applications will validate data in the same way, especially different vendors' applications. While there is usually no problem with allowing a client application to perform some validation/integrity functions, your database application should be performing the final data validation before it is saved to a table.

For example, a business often will want to be sure goods and services have been received or performed before payment of a vendor's invoice. Good accounting controls require that the person who orders goods and services—the purchaser—is not the same person who writes the checks that pay the vendor's invoices, and neither of these people should actually receipt for the goods and services. With a Microsoft SQL Server database you can easily provide these controls. The application will not allow a check to be cut for an invoice if a purchase order hasn't already been created and receipt of the goods isn't verified. This is not to say that even good database controls can not be circumvented.

With a well-designed application you can eliminate many of the repetitive, low-skill jobs that are often required of skilled workers. A purchaser can spend more time on the important tasks of qualifying vendors and reviewing products, rather than laboriously typing purchase orders. An accounts payable clerk can quickly approve payments and print checks instead of checking a receiving file against each invoice and then writing out a check. At the same time, you can help to eliminate many of the potential inaccuracies that occur when too great a reliance is placed on unnecessary hand checking of paperwork.

Building Custom Applications

Many front-end packages you can purchase are equipped with a generic group of business rules and procedures that may or may not fit your individual needs. Some applications make allowances for this, permitting you to make changes to these procedures, while others may require you to contract for expensive programming changes by the software publisher. While many of these off-the-shelf programs can work for you, they will often require you to make changes to the way that you do business, instead of the program fitting your own business requirements.

By using any one of a variety of front-end applications, you can build your own customized applications to meet your own specific business rules and needs. Front-end applications can be created using a high-end programming language such as Visual C++™, PowerBuilder™, and even Visual Basic™, or alternatively you can build an application with a database program such as Microsoft Access™. Web-enabled database applications can be created using a package such as Microsoft Visual InterDev™. Each option has its own advantages and disadvantages. The ability to create powerful application products in less time not only reduces the development costs of a system, but enables the organization to open new markets, to enhance its customer service, and to strengthen its competitiveness.

Cost Factors

The final factor in the decision to create a client/server system is its cost. Many client/server systems are being created to replace legacy mainframe systems, which are expensive to maintain, or as an alternative to new mainframe systems of a similar type. The up-front costs of a mainframe are compounded by its high annual maintenance costs. Many companies that are considering "downsizing" or "rightsizing" are driven to the client/server model for the possible cost savings.

Many businesses are already investing in a corporate LAN or WAN system for many reasons, most often for some type of office automation: document sharing, telephony, group fax and modem sharing, and video-conferencing. With a LAN/WAN already in place, adding a client/server system doesn't place a great deal of additional cost—in dollars or network traffic—on a business. This assumes that the existing system is not already so overloaded that it cannot support the additional load and traffic imposed by the new application.

It is critical that you understand what a client/server system can do for your organization so that you can intelligently inform management and obtain realistic goals. Many database programmers have met the goals they believed were set by management, but failed in management's eyes because of a difference in expectations.

MCSE 1.2 Multiprocessing Versus Multithreaded

Client/server database architecture comes in two basic flavors: *multiprocessing* and *multithreaded*. Each has their proponents and detractors. Microsoft SQL Server uses a multithreaded basis for its architecture.

Multiprocessing systems are distinguished by having multiple executable programs running at the same time. Generally, when a new user logs into the system, an entire set of executable programs is launched—this is known as starting an *instance*. These types of systems typically use more system resources than multithreaded engines.

The multithreaded engine, on the other hand, is a single-process system. Microsoft SQL Server is a multithreaded database engine. Instead of each user starting his or her own instance, a single process is started when Microsoft SQL Server is launched and each user has his or her own unique thread. This architecture requires dramatically fewer resources than a multi-process system.

Multiprocess Systems

The multiprocess database engine uses a system of executable applications that perform the necessary client query work. As each user logs onto the database, they are actually starting his and her own separate instance of the programs. In order to coordinate all of the users working with the same data files, other global coordinator tasks are used to schedule resources for each instance that is open.

The most popular of the multiprocess SQL database engines is Oracle Corporation's® Oracle Server™. As a user logs onto the system a new Oracle instance is started. The queries that the user generates are passed to this instance from the front-end program they are using. The instance coordinates with other executable programs and returns the results to the user. These other common executable programs manage file and record locks, write log files, and commit updated files to the disk files. As shown in Figure 1-4, each time another user logs onto the database a new instance is started along with its associated executable programs, each requiring more system resources.

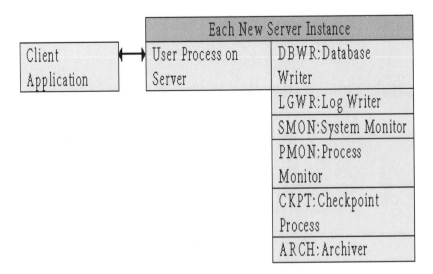

Figure 1–4   *Each instance started by a new user requires many system resources to be duplicated for each user because of the way processes are allocated on a per-user basis.*

The multiprocess database engine has been used for many years and was among the first of the multiuser databases. Both multiprocess and multithreaded servers can provide for scalability with the addition of more CPUs and memory to the physical machine.

Multithreaded Systems

The multithreaded database takes responsibility for managing multiple users itself instead of assuming that the operating system will handle user management. The multithreaded engine is more conservative with available system resources than is the multiprocess system. When the multithreaded engine is started, only a single instance of the program is begun. As new users log onto the database each is given a thread. This thread is the pipe through which all of the user queries and instructions are passed to the database engine and through to the operating system.

Microsoft SQL Server uses native Win32 operating threads, not simulated threads in the database kernel as do other multithreaded engines. These native threads run in their own protected memory space and have preemptive scheduling by the Microsoft Windows NT Server operating system kernel. This type of multithreading ensures that a single corrupt thread can no longer crash an application; instead, this thread can be trapped and isolated.

Microsoft SQL Server has a maximum pool of 1024 worker threads and a default setting of 255 worker threads. If the number of concurrent users does not exceed the number of worker threads in the pool, then each user is assigned to a thread. If the number of concurrent workers exceeds the number of worker threads, then pooling will occur. Pooling means that as a user completes a task their thread is assigned to the next user who has requested access to the database. The minimum setting is 10 threads. The Open Data Service is responsible for administering the pool of worker threads for client processes.

The worker thread parameter can be configured using the Enterprise Manager window or using the stored procedure `sp_configure`. The worker thread parameter is a dynamic configuration option; this means that any change made is effective immediately. Any configuration setting that is not dynamic is considered a static option and does not take effect until the next time that SQL Server is stopped and then started again. Changing these settings will be fully discussed later in Chapter 6, "Configuration Options." Figure 1-5 illustrates how native Win32 threads interact with the Windows NT operating system.

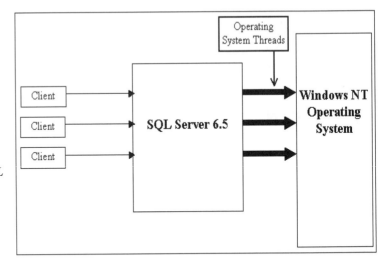

Figure 1–5 *Microsoft SQL Server uses native Win32 threads from the Microsoft Windows NT Server operating system.*

Microsoft SQL Server has different memory requirements depending upon what you intend to do with the particular system. In previous versions of SQL Server, available memory was a static configuration option.

SQL Server 7.0 treats memory as a dynamic resource, allocating what it needs from the available physical memory. This will also be discussed in detail in Chapter 6. The following list shows general guidelines for several types of SQL Server databases.

- Systems used primarily for the development of SQL Server applications can be run with 16MB of RAM, if replication features are not being used.
- Systems used in a production database environment can use as much RAM as you want, or can afford, to make available.
- Systems that will be used in replication must have a minimum of 32MB of RAM on the system and a minimum of 16MB dedicated to SQL Server.

With an operating system that can use multiple CPUs, such as Windows NT, SQL Server really begins to shine. Threads can be assigned to use different processors, ensuring the best usage of the number of processor cycles available from all of the CPUs installed. The allocation of threads to processors is supported in SQL Server 7.0 by using the `srv_threadaffinity` parameter with `srv_config`. `srv_config` is included in SQL Server 7.0 for backward compatibility only and will not be included in future versions. It is highly recommended that you recompile all existing Open Data Services applications that will be used with SQL Server 7 with the new Open Data Services header and library files (Srv.h and Opends60.lib).

MCSE 1.3 Networking

The client/server model assumes that the server application—in this case, Microsoft SQL Server—resides in a computer that is set up as a server. This most often means a server running Microsoft Windows NT Server 4.0. Client machines are physically connected to the server through network cabling, network cards, and the appropriate software. All clients must be able to communicate with the server so that SQL queries can be passed to the server and results passed back to the client.

With Microsoft SQL Server you can use the networking abilities of Microsoft Windows NT Server to communicate with a wide variety of clients: PCs, Macintoshes™, UNIX workstations, or NetWare™ clients. Since Microsoft SQL Server uses the native networking abilities of its host operating system, Microsoft Windows NT Server, any computer attached to the server can be granted access to the SQL database.

For a detailed discussion on networking and Microsoft NT Server, see *MCSE: Networking Core Essentials,* by Jim Keogh, also in this Prentice Hall series.

Protocol Options

Depending on the client configuration that you must deal with on your network, you have a wide variety of network protocol options that you can use with SQL Server 7.0. The primary restriction is that if you have Windows 95/98 clients connected then you must use TCP/IP to connect to them, as they do not work with Named Pipes.

SQL Server uses the various network libraries to pass network packets back and forth between the server and its clients. These network libraries are installed as dynamic-link libraries (DLLs), performing the necessary communications required for specific interprocess communications (IPCs). The network protocols that you can use are listed in Table 1-1. You can use multiple network libraries when installing SQL Server.

Table 1.1 *Network Protocols and their uses*

PROTOCOL	DESCRIPTION
Named Pipes	Default protocol SQL Server will use. Listens on the standard pipe. Used for pipe connections between a server and clients that support named pipes. A pipe is a section of memory used by a process to pass information to another process.
TCP/IP Sockets	This is the default library when using Windows 95/98 clients. SQL Server uses the default TCP/IP port number 1433. You can change the port number by entering another port during installation. If you use Microsoft Proxy Server over TCP/IP sockets, you will need to enter the proxy server address.
Multiprotocol Net-Library	This option uses the advantages available with Windows NT's Remote Procedure Call (RPC). This library uses most of the IPC devices supported by Windows NT.
NWLink IPX/SPX	This protocol is used when you must communicate through a Novell network. You will need to supply the Novell Bindery service name to register SQL Server on the network.
DECnet	Use this protocol when installing an SQL Server on a DECnet network. You will need to be able to provide the Node ID and Object ID for the attached clients.
AppleTalk ADSP	This is a server-side AppleTalk ADSP library that allows Apple Macintosh clients to connect to the SQL Server using native AppleTalk. You must provide the AppleTalk service object name.
Banyan VINES	Banyan VINES Sequenced Packet Protocol (SPP) is supported by SQL Server over a Banyan VINES IP network, only on an Intel-based platform. You must provide the StreetTalk service name during installation. This uses the form of *servicename@group@org*.

Local Area Networks

SQL Server is easily run across a local area network (LAN). Simply choose the appropriate protocols and ensure that the clients have the necessary logon names and passwords. When using Windows NT Server as the primary server operating system, you can choose to use its own security setup or allow SQL Server to provide its own security.

A LAN setup requires that every client be connected to the local server via a cable or a wireless connection. The most common LAN connection is where each client computer has a network interface card (NIC) installed, along with the appropriate driver software and is connected by a cable to a hub and then to the server. The most commonly used cabling is twisted-pair Ethernet cable. When installing a new network be sure that you use only Category 5 twisted-pair cable. This will ensure that your network will be able to meet the 100Base-TX (100mbs) specifications.

> When using a twisted-pair Ethernet network your cabling will all converge to a hub or switch. A hub is the most common method of connecting your network. A switch is most often used when you have a combination of 10Base-T (10mbs) and 100Base-TX connections. The server is then also connected to the hub completing the circuit. This is one of the most reliable methods of connecting a LAN.

Older LAN schemes may still use coaxial cable—avoid this method if possible. A coax network runs a cable from computer to computer and must be terminated at both ends. You will find that if a single link in the network goes down, the entire network goes down, not just the one computer. A coax network is one of the least expensive to install, but you will find that coax NIC cards are becoming harder to find and you are limited to 10mbs.

Wide Area Networks

A wide area network (WAN) is any group of LANs and stand-alone computers that are all interconnected. Most often a WAN connects several LANs that are located at a distance from each other. A dedicated, permanent communication line is set up between each point enabling high-speed data transfers. These high-speed data connections come in several different flavors and run from relatively expensive to very expensive.

A WAN connection requires some specialized equipment to connect your server to the communications line. Table 1-2 lists some of the commonly used data connections, their transfer rates, and the type of equipment required for each. These data transfer rates are maximums that you can expect and may vary by location, time of day, and other factors. You will quickly find that the higher speed or data rate that you require for your connection, the more expensive the setup charges, equipment, and monthly service charges will be.

Table 1.2 *Network Data Connections and Uses*

Type of Connection	Speed or Data Rate	Equipment
Modem (28.8–56K)	Currently the maximum speed available for modems is 56Kbps download and 33.6Kbps upload. By the time that you read this the 56Kbps standard will be set.	Internal or External modem and a standard telephone connection using twisted-pair wire.
Integrated Services Digital Network (ISDN)	A BRI (Basic Rate Interface) consists of two 64Kbps B channels and one 16Kbps D channel. The two B channels can be combined to provide 128Kbps throughput.	Specialized digital telephone circuit using twisted-pair wire. An Internal or External ISDN terminal adapter.
Dedicated 56K Frame Relay	Maximum of 56Kbps	Will vary depending on your service provider. Usually coaxial or twisted-pair wire.
Fractional T1	From 56Kbps to 1.544Mbps. You can purchase a specific amount of bandwidth or allow a variable rate for higher traffic bursts.	Can be either twisted-pair or coaxial cable
T1	1.544Mbps	Twisted-pair, fiber-optics cable, fiber-optic cable, digital microwave transmission, and other media. Requires CSU/DSU and router.
T3	44.736Mbps	Twisted-pair, fiber-optics cable, fiber-optic cable, digital microwave transmission, and other media. Will also require a CSU/DSU and router.

Internet or Intranet

An Internet or Intranet connection has much in common with a WAN connection. Often the terms are synonymous. Usually a WAN connection is a private connection between two or more related entities. The data connection is created from permanent leased lines between the endpoints of the connection. An intranet or Internet connection can be created using the same equipment and connections that composed your WAN. The primary difference between them is that a company Internet/intranet connection often goes from the local office to a local backbone connection, either a local telephone company or Internet Service Provider.

This connection may act like the WAN connection, but instead of being a single direct line between two points, it is a direct connection only at the local points—from business to telco/ISP. The long distance connection route may and probably will vary each time it is created.

MCSE 1.4   Commonly Used SQL Server Interfaces

Here, SQL Server interfaces refer to the various methods you can use to access data both in and out of an SQL Server. Depending on the specific type of front-end application that you intend to use, and the client base that you have to work with, one or more of the interfaces can be used.

Your choice of interface will depend on several factors: your own expertise in the tool set you are using, your development platform, and your expected client base.

Transact-SQL

Transact-SQL, usually referred to as T-SQL, is the native query language included with SQL Server. This query language can be embedded into a client application, or accessed as a compiled stored procedure. T-SQL can be accessed through several different methods:

- ISQL utility: This utility is used to enter T-SQL statements from the command line. There is a long list of command-line switches available to customize the query. You can use ISQL to run T-SQL statements, system procedures, and script files. It uses the DB-library to communicate with SQL Server.
- OSQL utility: This utility is similar to ISQL except that it uses ODBC to connect to SQL Server instead of the DB-library.
- SQL Server Query Analyzer utility: Formally known as ISQL/w. This graphical version of ISQL has significantly improved the plan view of a query. When entering a query, a color-coded editor is used so that you can easily distinguish between different pieces of your query.

T-SQL is one of the easiest methods to access, add, and change information contained in an SQL Server database. You can also use it to ADD, DROP, and ALTER any SQL Server object. The better you know how to use T-SQL, the better you will be able to implement and design a database. Even if you know how to perform the same function through the GUI interface of the SQL Server Enterprise Manager, your understanding of what is happening behind the scene will be greatly enhanced if you know the T-SQL functions that are being performed.

OLE DB

OLE DB is a newly supported native programming interface for SQL Server 7.0 and the T-SQL language. Microsoft recommends that you use OLE DB to develop data access infrastructures within the Component Object Model (COM) environment since it works at a low-level in the COM environment.

By using OLE DB you gain access to many types of data: SQL data sources, mail stores, Web data, directory sources, and both IMS and VSAM data on mainframes. Each of these is accessible through a set of standard interfaces. You also get a greatly enhanced integration between commercial applications and controls, data providers, and data sources.

When you create an application that makes use of OLE DB it can be placed into one of the following general groups:

- Service Providers process and move data. The DTS Data Pump is an example of a service provider. It furnishes the means by which heterogeneous data sources can import, export, and transform data between each other.
- Data Consumers are applications that interface with an OLE DB object by using or consuming it. An application created with Microsoft Visual Basic that uses an OLE DB connection to an SQL Server database would be considered an OLE DB consumer.
- Data Providers are those applications and objects that provide data to an OLE DB interface. Microsoft includes SQLOLEDB as a native data provider with SQL Server.

When you install SQL Server 7.0, three OLE DB providers are included during the process; OLE DB Provider for ODBC, Microsoft SQL Server OLE DB Provider, and Microsoft OLE DB Provider for Jet. These providers work through the stored procedure `sp_addlinkedserver`. `sp_addlinkedserver` is used in this format with the following arguments.

```
sp_addlinkedserver
{'server','productname','providername',
datasource','location','providerstring'}
```

The several arguments that can be entered in the `sp_addlinkedserver` stored procedures are:

- Server: Enter the name of the linked server to be created. There is no default value.
- Productname: This is the product name of the OLE DB data source to be used as a linked server. It has a default value of NULL.
- Providername: This is a unique, "friendly" name for the OLE DB provider that relates to the data source. This must be a unique name for this OLE DB provider on the current computer, and must be registered with this name in the registry. The default value is NULL.
- Datasource: This is the name of the data source as listed by the OLE DB provider. The data source name is passed as a property value of DBPROP_INIT_DATASOURCE to initialize the OLE DB provider. The default value is NULL.
- Location: This is the location of the database as shown by the OLE DB provider. Location has a default value of NULL and is passed as a value of the DBPROP_INIT_LOCATION when initializing the OLE DB provider.
- Providerstring: This is a specific string given by the OLE DB provider to identify a specific data source. The default value is NULL and is passed to the DBPROP_INIT_PROVIDERSTRING property.

The OLE DB Provider for ODBC enables OLE DB to interface with ODBC data sources. SQL Server Distributed Queries can access all ODBC data sources through the OLE DB Provider for ODBC. Before using this provider you must create the ODBC data source by adding it to the list of ODBC Data Source Names (DSN) with the ODBC applet in the Control Panel. Once the DSN has been created you can link to it by using the stored procedure sp_addlinkedserver. When creating the link between SQL Server and the ODBC data source, use MSDASQL as the *providername* parameter. In this example, a linked server named 'SQLInventory' is created from the ODBC data source named 'SQLInventory.' This ODBC data source points to the database Inventory:

```
sp_addlinkedserver 'SQLInventory',
  ' ', 'MSDASQL', 'SQLInventory'
```

The Microsoft OLE DB Provider for Jet is used to create a connection to a Microsoft Access database. When using this OLE DB provider you can directly query a Microsoft Access database through an SQL Server distributed query. sp_addlinkedserver is also used to create the connection with an Access database.

The third OLE DB interface, Microsoft SQL Server OLE DB Provider has been specifically developed to allow programmers to develop OLE DB consumer applications that will access only SQL Server databases. This OLE DB uses SQLOLEDB instead of the more generic MSDASQL. SQLOLEDB can expose many underlying SQL Server functions, including the creation of new tables for use by the application.

ActiveX Data Objects (ADO) is a new application-level interface for OLE DB. It profits from the infrastructure available through OLE DB. ADO has been created as a wrapper for OLE DB and languages such as Visual Basic, Visual Basic for Applications, Active Server Pages, and Visual Basic Script. It is used primarily in an Internet/intranet environment where you need to minimize the network traffic.

ODBC

Open Database Connectivity, or more simply ODBC, is of a standard definition for an application-programming interface (API). It is used to access both relational databases and indexed sequential access method (ISAM) database. For the purposes of this book, only the relational database aspects of ODBC as it relates to SQL Server will be of concern. ODBC is a native API used when writing Visual Basic, C, and C++ applications that transfer data between an application and the SQL Server database. One of the client utilities installed during the setup of SQL Server is an ODBC driver used to access the SQL Server databases.

When an application uses the ODBC driver to interface with the SQL Server database, it sends a call to the driver. The driver translates the call into the appropriate SQL statements and passes them to SQL Server. The results from these statements are then passed from the server to the ODBC driver and then to the application. While this may seem to be a roundabout method of communicating with a database, it allows a programmer to create an application that can use data from a variety of sources.

ODBC is one of the most commonly used methods of communicating between an application and a back-end database, such as SQL Server. ODBC can be used to access information by many applications in common use today. You can easily import data into a Microsoft Excel spreadsheet by using Microsoft Query and the SQL Server ODBC driver.

Before you can connect to an ODBC-compliant database, you must first add the data source on the client computer. Every client who will access the database through ODBC must have the data source named in their ODBC administrator applet. There are three different types of ODBC data sources that you can create:

- The User DSN are data sources visible only to the Windows 95/98 or Windows NT login account when they were created. They are not available to other users, nor are they always available to applications running as an NT service.

- The System DSN data source are available to all accounts with login rights on the computer. They are also always available to applications running as an NT service.
- The File DSN data source was added with ODBC version 3.0. They are not stored in the system registry but in a special file on the client computer.

Before setting up the data source name in the ODBC administrator applet, you must first install the ODBC driver that will be related to the DSN. Each ODBC driver should have its own installation procedure. Once it is installed, you will be able to see it within the ODBC administrator on the Drivers tab.

Microsoft English Query

Microsoft English Query is a new development tool available on the SQL Server installation CD-ROM. It is designed to give a user the ability to query your database in English. The Microsoft English Query interprets the user question into appropriate T-SQL statements and syntax, eliminating the need for a local user to learn how to create complex queries.

Microsoft English Query is not a replacement for the serious application builder. It is designed for the end user to create a relatively complex query. Not all questions submitted by a user will result in either an answer or an incomplete result. Microsoft English Query's limited English language base can be the cause of some queries that do not yield expected results. You can also have problems due to poor application or database design—not that this is a problem for Microsoft English Query alone.

A Microsoft English Query application is built on a knowledge base about the database called a *domain*. The domain should include everything that is known about the database, its tables, columns, joins, indexes, and constraints. The process of creating the knowledge domain can also be thought of as teaching Microsoft English Query how to use the database. While it already understands many terms in the English language, it does not know how these words relate to specific tables and columns in your database. The process is very much like that of teaching a new member of your development staff how your database works, and where everything is in each table, how the tables are related, and what kinds of records are stored in the tables. Once they have a basic understanding of your database, they can begin to be productive members of your team. The same is true for

Microsoft English Query; it must be given a learning period before someone on your staff can create a productive query.

The first half of the learning process is accomplished once the domain knows the basic physical structure of the database. You must next include all of the *semantic* knowledge about *entities* and their relationships. An entity is any object that is referred to in a query by a noun (a person, place, or thing). Examples of entities are employees, products, vendors, and price. Within an English Query application tables are known as major entities, while minor entities are often essential columns within a table. Other columns that are important for answering questions, but not as important as a minor entity are called *traits*. A trait would consist of columns from a table that help to describe some aspect of a minor or major entity. For example, the marital status of an employee is a trait—it helps to describe the entity employee.

Relationships describe how entities and traits interact with each other. Relationships between entities can be described in short, declarative sentences like, "Employees earn salaries" or "Products are sold to customers." Relationships are expressed in one or more *phrasings*. A phrasing is how a relationship is described in English. Two ways to phrase a relationship are, "Products are purchased from vendors" and "Vendors sell products to the company."

MCSE 1.5   Fundamentals of Database Building

The creation of an SQL Server database should be a carefully thought-out process. Your creation process will be much more successful if you have a good idea of what you are constructing before you actually begin creating your first database. Begin the process by gathering information about your database.

- What is it used for?
- What current information systems will it replace?
- What information is currently stored, and in what fashion or media?
- How is the data now retrieved?
- How do the users want to interact with the information?
- What kind of reporting does management want?
- How can the data be divided into tables within the database?

These and many other questions should be fully answered before you begin the actual process of creating a fully functional database. It is much easier to know what you are building and why than it is to have to alter tables, indexes, and data records later. The answers to these questions will come from the current information systems and from the people who use them. Be sure that you interview those users who now perform the day-to-day functions that the new database will replace or enhance. Be sure that you talk to management and find out what their needs and expectations are. You do not want to spend many valuable hours designing and testing a system only to find that it does not meet the expectations of management.

Once you have gathered the necessary information it is time to identify the kind of information you will be storing. This is the point where you need to identify the most important objects that your database will be managing. The object can be either a tangible or intangible thing. A tangible object may be a person or a product, while an intangible object may be a transaction or a time period. The primary objects in the database will usually be stored within their own table.

Now that the objects have been identified, it is time to analyze and how it all relates. This process is called *modeling* the database. This step is vital because it will help you to identify possible relationship problems early on in the design phase. If you see a relationship problem here, you can create the necessary objects to remove the problem. Modeling can be done with pencil and paper, a word processor or spreadsheet, or a specialized data-modeling program. However you choose to work, be sure that you keep your model up to date as you build the database. You will find that it is simpler to refer to your current model than to try and untangle a series of relationships when something does not work like you expected.

It is now time to dissect your table objects. How is the information about each major object gathered and how does it need to be referred or referenced? These questions will give you clues as to how you must divide the object into discrete information types. These will later become the columns of the table. Discrete data pieces can commonly be categorized into one of these types:

- Tangible data such as employee names, products, and vendor names come from a source outside of the database.
- Category data classifies or groups data rows. Data in these columns is usually limited to one of a few responses.
- Identifying information is used to provide a unique identity to each record stored in the table. Convention states that these columns will often have either 'id' or 'number' in their name such as, product_id, vendor_number, or social_security_number.
- Relational or referential columns are used to create a link between information in one table to the information stored in another. For

example, a table about invoices will have links to customers, order details, employees, and products.

You can now identify what relationships will need to be created and how the tables will be linked in your database. One of the greatest strengths of the relational database is the ability to link data from one table to the information stored in another. These relationships are what enable you to create a database without massive amounts of information being duplicated throughout the database.

Finally, you must identify the processes that are involved in the information flow. How is data to be loaded, retrieved, updated, and deleted? Identifying this flow will help you to create the actual user interface to your database.

As you can see, planning the design of an SQL Server database can be a lengthy and involved process, but much depends on the uses for the final product. A simple, single-user database will probably not go into as much detail as a database being created for a large multinational stock brokerage. The keys to planning a database are few:

- Gathering information from users, current information processes, and management.
- Identifying the key objects that will become database tables.
- Model the database so that you can visually view the database concept.
- Analyze the model and identify the information types for each object.
- Identify the relationships between objects.
- Identify the information flow throughout the database.

The time that is required to complete the necessary planning of a database is usually in direct proportion to its final complexity. If you are creating a database that will be used to process many financial transactions every second, you can expect that your planning will be long and extensive. A modeling document for such a database could easily run to several hundred pages as you detail the database, its tables, the relationships, data types, constraints, default values, and the many other details that exist in a complex relational database.

The Relational Database

A *relational database management system* (RDMS) is a system of information that is stored in tables. These tables are linked by a series of relationships.

These links are composed of relationships between a set of data in one table and a corresponding set of data in another table.

As you begin to design your database, you must first understand the data that will be stored in it. Ask yourself these and as many other questions that you can think:

- What kind of information will you be storing?
- Is the data static and never changing, or is it dynamic and constantly being updated?
- How are records now kept, and how are they accessed?
- Does each record currently have a unique identifying characteristic which you can use?
- How can the information within each record be broken down into fields?

As you begin to answer these questions, you will come to have an understanding about the information that you will be working with, and how that information is used by the people who must use it every day. This process helps you to understand the logical design necessary for your database.

Once you are familiar with the data that you will be working with, you will start to see relationships between different pieces of the data. Some of the best database designers will use diagrams to illustrate the relationships between different pieces. As you become even more intimate with the data, you will be able to see how and why different pieces of related data will be placed into separate tables.

The logical design is not necessarily the best database design. The final physical database design, the one that you will use when actually building the tables and columns that your data will be stored in may be different than your initial logical design. Many database design shops feel that once the logical database design has been diagrammed on paper, it is set in stone. Do not become so wedded to a design that you cannot change it when necessary.

The final physical database design should focus on three things:

- The integrity of the data contained in it.
- Creating a structure that allows your users easy access to the data.
- Performance or speed.

The physical database design should help to facilitate the consistency and integrity of the data that is stored within its tables. While this is a requirement most often seen as most important to the database designer or database administrator, users tend to look at things a little differently. To the end users, the most important things are usually speed and access. Often, the end user wants the ability to browse tables and access data in a free-form type of format. Finally, the success or failure of a particular database is often based on the speed of data updates and retrieval—if the database appears to be slow, you can bet that the user coalition will be back demanding speed increases, or a completely new system.

These criteria are what will be used to test your mettle as a database designer. These three criteria—consistency/integrity, performance/speed, and ease of access—tend to be mutually exclusive. By meeting one set of criteria, you will have a tendency to take away from one or both of the others. How well you balance each will be your final test.

What Is a Relational Database?

A relational database has already been described as a group of tables that are linked by relationships. A good relational database is a collection of data that is organized into tables. Each table uses a unique primary key column whose value points to one and only one row. The data contained in separate tables is related to one another through the use of the primary keys of one table being related to the foreign key column of another table. This system of relationships is used to give you easy access to the information that it contains.

Relationships are created between tables through fields that contain data common to both. Most relationships are created using special field constraints called *Primary* and *Foreign* key fields. By definition, a primary key field is unique in a table and all of the data in the table can be automatically indexed, or sorted, by this field. You can not use a NULL value in a primary key field. A foreign key is a field whose values match those of the primary key in another table. A foreign key field can use a NULL value. By creating your database with tables that are linked together using the relationships created with primary and foreign key fields, you can easily divide information between tables in a logical manner.

By dividing your information into discrete tables, you will begin the creation process of a database that will be less prone to errors and duplication of information. A relational database can be a very efficient means of storing and retrieving data. Unlike a flat-file database, where you must search through the entire file for specific data, in a relational database you can use the SQL language to define what you are specifically looking for. SQL will then return a result set to you with the data that meets the criteria you stated in the SQL query statement.

For example, Figure 1-6 is a list of the fields in three tables. Because each table has a field in common with one of the other tables, SQL can create a result set across multiple tables through this common field.

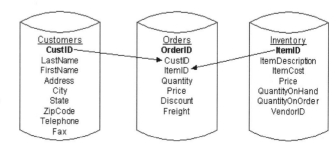

Figure 1–6 *Here you can see how three tables are related through the use of common fields.*

The Customers table uses the CustID field as its primary key. All customer records are indexed on this field and no records can have a NULL value in this field. The Orders table uses the CustID field as a foreign key, so that the two tables can be linked together. The Inventory table uses the ItemID field as a primary key, and again, the Orders table also uses this field as a foreign key so that it can be linked to the Inventory table.

The Normalized Database

As a database is designed, you work towards a *normalized* relational database system. A normalized database must meet several conditions:

- All *entities* (tables) are made up of *attributes* (columns/fields) that define *properties* (datatypes) about each *row* (records) contained within the entity.
- Each row of a table defines a single event or item.
- Each row is uniquely identified through the use of the *primary key.*
- The primary key can be made up of a single column or multiple columns.
- Primary key values can not be null.

One of the characteristics of a normalized database is that it will contain many more numerous *narrow* tables. A table is considered narrow when it has few columns; conversely, a table is considered wide when it has many columns, most often containing data that is repeated throughout many rows. Figure 1-7 shows an unnormalized database.

This unnormalized Customer Database contains several flaws common to databases designed by someone new to the concept.

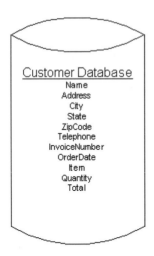

Figure 1–7 *This unnormalized database will contain many duplicated rows, one for each item ordered. Several of the columns should be broken out into separate tables, and calculated columns, such as Total, should not be included.*

- There is no single or multiple column primary key.
- The Name field should be divided into First and Last Name fields. This will enable you to search by a customer's last name only.
- Columns that force repeated data, such as the Item column exist. These columns should never be included in this table. They force you to repeat all of the customer information in each new row, one new row for every item they order. Think how many thousands of additional rows can possibly be added to a table.
- The Total column is not a necessary column. It is a calculated value that can be derived from columns that already exist.

```
(((Quantity * Price) for each item ordered) +
ShippingCharges for entire order.)
```

By working toward a normalized database, you will reap several benefits. You will reduce the duplicated data, and in so doing, the storage requirements of your database. The level of data integrity will increase several-fold by normalization. The reduction in the duplicated data will help to ensure that mistakes are not made through simple data entry errors.

By creating many tables with a narrow focus on the data entered in them, you can place more rows of data on each storage page in SQL Server. This can help to speed queries and table scans, improving the overall performance of your database.

A simplified, normalized version of this database would look something like Figure 1-8.

There are some disadvantages to completely normalizing a database and they primarily have to do with performance. In some cases you may find

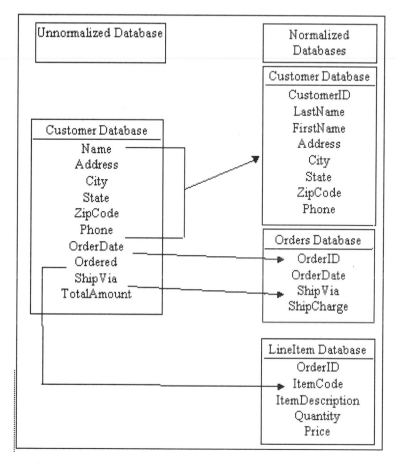

Figure 1–8 *The unnormalized table is now broken down into three normalized tables.*

that your database performance can be substantially increased by denormalizing some portions of the database. Unnormalizing a database should be a planned step and be done only for specific performance increases. Remember, denormalizing a database, and subsequently increasing redundancy in your information, may increase your database performance during queries that require many joins, but you may suffer decreased performance during updates, and will have to plan for greatly increased disk space requirements.

Tables, Columns, and Rows

At its simplest, a database is a collection of information. For a relational database, a table is used as a storage unit for related data of a particular type:

vendors, customers, inventory items, accounts payable, accounts receivable, and so on. You would not have a single table that included information about customers, accounts payable, and inventory items all jumbled together. This would be an inefficient waste of computer resources, and would also be very confusing—this could easily be likened to a filing system where every scrap of paper is placed in any drawer with no thought of possibly having to retrieve a specific page later.

A table is divided into rows and columns, much like a spreadsheet or ledger. A row is often called a *record*, while columns are commonly called *fields*—more specifically, each intersection of a row and column is a single field. Each record contains all of the information available about a specific item, such as a customer, a vendor, or a single inventory item. Each column contains a distinct part of a record, such as a customer's name or address, a product's name, cost, and quantity on hand. In most cases you will find that the database is easier to work with when the information contained in a record is broken down into the smallest logical parts; for example first name, last name, street address, city, state, zip code. Dividing your data into the smallest entities to which they belong is the process of normalizing your database.

As you build your database, you must decide how to break your information into logical groups—these groups will become your tables. As you further divide these groups into their component fields, ask yourself if this piece of information really should go with this group or does it really belong to another table. For example, information about orders does not belong in a customer table, while information about products does not belong in a vendor file.

Device Independence

Microsoft SQL Server shields you from knowing how information is physically stored on a disk. SQL only requires that you know the name of the table(s) in which the information you are looking for is located and the specific columns that should be searched. SQL then decides how and where to find the data, returning a results set to you. This makes using SQL to manage a database much easier than using a programming language, such as C and C++, which are third-generation languages, while SQL is a fourth-generation, or 4GL, language. As a 4GL language, SQL is a step further removed from the hardware of the system than earlier languages. A 4GL language such as SQL Server is device independent because it takes care of all the I/O and storage requirements for you.

Classic programming languages are procedural languages and require you to set out, step by step, exactly what information you are looking for:

- Where it will be physically found on a disk.
- The file name where the data is located.
- Where within the file the data is located.
- Check in the specified field of each record for the specified value.
- When found display or print the selected records as a standard output.

Conversely, with SQL you can issue a simple query statement using your front-end program, or with the SQL Query Analyzer application and display just the selected data, not necessarily the entire record.

Key Points

The key points that you should bring away from this initial overview of SQL Server 7.0 include:

- SQL Server 7.0 can greatly decrease the amount of time necessary in building a back-end database server through its use of intuitive interface and its ability to easily enforce data consistency by building business rules and procedures directly into the database.

- Know the cost factors that are built into your database. Remember, cost factors are not only the budgeted dollars for a project, but also include possible project overruns, end-user training, maintenance, and management expectations.

- That SQL Server 7.0 is a multithreaded system and not multiprocess. The advantages to a multithreaded system are that you do not have to open a new instance of the application for every new user that logs onto the database.

- Understand basic networking topologies and how they may interact with your database application.

- How SQL Server 7.0 interfaces with other applications. By using T-SQL, OLE DB, ODBC, and Microsoft English Query you can build applications that will accomplish the job that the database was designed for.

▲ CHAPTER REVIEW QUESTIONS

▲ Multiple Choice:

1. *Microsoft SQL Server 7 is supported by the following operating systems (choose all that apply):*
    A. Power PC
    B. Microsoft Windows 3.1
    C. Microsoft Windows 95
    D. UNIX
    E. Microsoft Windows NT 3.51
    F. MIPS

2. *SQL Server 7 interprets a query received from a client in a process called:*
    A. Query Interpretation
    B. Parsing
    C. Optimization
    D. Compiling

3. *Database integrity can be _____ with SQL Server 7.*
    A. accurate
    B. consistent
    C. concurrent
    D. Enforced

4. *When proposing a new SQL Server 7 application for a customer, be sure that you know what _____ goals are.*
    A. The application's endusers.
    B. The company's management team.
    C. Your sales goals.
    D. A and B
    E. All of the above

5. *Which of these can be used for SQL Server Interfaces?*
    A. OLE DB
    B. Transact-SQL
    C. ODBC connections
    D. B and C
    E. All of the above

6. *A Transact-SQL can be accessed through*
   A. The SQL Server Query Analyzer
   B. A Basic application
   C. From the command line
   D. All of the above

▲ True or False:

1. *True or False? The ISQL utility does not use an ODBC connection to SQL Server.*

2. *True or False? SQL Server 7 can make use of a custom front-end application to manipulate information.*

3. *True or False? Microsoft SQL Server 7 is almost always used as the front-end in a client/server.*

4. *True or False? SQL Server can communicate with a Windows 95/98 client using the Named Pipes protocol.*

What Is SQL?

Microsoft SQL Server uses a version of the SQL language called Transact-SQL, or T-SQL for short. Transact-SQL is short for Transaction SQL. Standard ANSI-SQL language gives you a method to define and modify or manipulate data. T-SQL extends ANSI-SQL by adding program flow-control devices, such as *if* and *while*, local variables, and other hooks that enable you to write very complex queries, stored procedures, triggers, and other objects that you can build using standard programming techniques.

SQL commands can be divided into three types: Data Definition Language (DDL), Data Manipulation Language (DML), and Data Control Language (DCL). You will use each of these different aspects of T-SQL to build, add data to, and to work with the data in your database. The differences between data definition, manipulation, and control commands are similar to the differences between organization, composition, and regulation.

By using this split between SQL command groups, it is much easier to create a client/server database structure. The system administrator uses DDL commands to create a structure of tables that will remain on the server. The enduser then uses a front-end program created with DML and/or programming code to manipulate the data within the database structure. The system administrator or database owner can use DCL commands to restrict the access to the database objects and the information contained within.

Beginning with SQL Server 7.0, Microsoft has increased the functionality of T-SQL, allowing greater control and flexibility to the application/database programmer. The major new features you can now use throughout T-SQL include:

- A four-part naming scheme for use in distributed queries that allow a four-part database name.

- Information schema views. These new views give you data about system tables independent of those views from the SQL Server metadata. These new views allow older applications to continue to function even when significant changes have been made to the structure of a system table.

- Parallel query execution. This allows queries with access to a system that has multiple processors to execute portions of the query plan run in parallel on different processors.

- Delayed name resolution allows references to be created in batch statements, stored procedures, and triggers, even if the name does not yet exist.

MCSE 2.1   T-SQL and ANSI-SQL

For a client application and the server database engine to communicate with each other, they must use a common language. For many client/server applications it is SQL, and Microsoft SQL Server 7.0 makes greatest use of the version called T-SQL.

ANSI-SQL is a generic term for an SQL language that strictly follows the specifications written for ANSI-92 standards. T-SQL is an ANSI-SQL language, but includes additional commands and functions that are specific to SQL Server.

Standards and Compatibility

T-SQL uses ANSI-SQL as its base and has added extensions that are unique to Microsoft SQL Server. If your application will need to access information from a variety of back-end databases, it is highly recommended that you use ANSI-SQL. If you will be using SQL Server databases exclusively for the backend, then you will be able to make good use of the added SQL extensions in the language.

There are now two SQL standards: ANSI-89 and ANSI-92. The American National Standards Institute (ANSI) published these standards in 1989 and 1992, respectively. The added extensions available through T-SQL provide for additional programming needs and are specific to SQL Server. With SQL Server 7.0, T-SQL moves closer to full compliance with the ANSI-SQL standards by placing emphasis on SQL-92 standards as the preferred SQL dialect. Several inconsistencies that had been noted in earlier versions of SQL Server have been fixed, along with discrepancies between documented and actual SQL behaviors.

Some of the differences between T-SQL and ANSI-SQL include:

- The lists of reserved words. Reserved words are special keywords used by the version of SQL for defining, manipulating, or accessing data. T-SQL and other SQL languages use reserved words to parse SQL statements, and are used as special functions. SQL Server does allow you to use reserved words as object names and identifiers, but you must use them as quoted identifiers. This will be discussed in detail in Chapter 3, "SQL Server Structures."

- SQL Server provides a number of synonyms for the differences in data types between T-SQL and ANSI-SQL. The ANSI-SQL synonym data type is mapped to its T-SQL counterpart; for example, the ANSI-SQL data type *char varying* is mapped to the T-SQL data type *varchar*. This ensures that if you use an ANSI-SQL query, a table using SQL Server data types will recognize it.

The complete list of reserved words is available in the SQL Server Books Online at Building SQL Server Applications\Transact-SQL\Transact-SQL Reference\Reserved Keywords. The reserved word list for ANSI-SQL 92 and ODBC are identical.

MCSE 2.2   Types of SQL Commands

SQL statements can be classified into three broad categories: Data Definition Language, Data Manipulation Language, and Data Control Language. Almost all T-SQL statements will include at least one command. (A SQL command tells the server what action is to be performed by the statement.) SQL commands are also known as *keywords*, and as such are reserved words that have special meaning to Microsoft SQL Server. In this section you will see how several commonly used commands work. The format used with these SQL commands is similar in most versions of SQL databases.

When you are using an SQL program or other type of front-end application, T-SQL commands can be sent to the Microsoft SQL Server in batches. A batch is a group of SQL statements that are sent to the server at one time. Batches can be sent to the server in several ways, the most common being from a front-end application over the network, using ISQL in command mode, or using the Microsoft SQL Server Query Analyzer, or from the SQL Server Enterprise Manager.

Data Definition Language (DDL)

Simply put, the *Data Definition Language (DDL)* concerns all aspects of T-SQL used to create, manage, and drop any data structure that you build within your database. Any SQL statement beginning with CREATE, ALTER, or DROP is a DDL command. DDL statements are used when you are working with the structure of an object, not with the contents of that object. One of the reasons that DDL statements are used is that Microsoft SQL Server does not support the direct manipulation of the system tables by users. These tables are required in order for the database to operate, and so DDL statements are used by the application to shield users from the system tables. Any changes or additions that are made to the system tables are made through the DDL statements. Changes made to any object, such as a database, a table, or an index are reflected in one or more system tables.

Most DDL statements are composed of two elements, the action and the object. The CREATE TABLE statement is composed of an action-CREATE, and the object-TABLE. In order to use these commands you must have permission to create or edit the object you wish to define or redefine—this includes both the object and any properties that it may have. Commonly used DDL commands include:

- CREATE TABLE: This command creates a new table. You must provide the necessary parameters to complete the statement: column names and data types as a minimum.
- CREATE SCHEMA: Creates a schema. A schema is an object that contains the definition of database without the data it contains. Often used by database programmers to create a duplicate of an existing database for testing.
- DROP TABLE: This command drops or deletes a table from a database. Other than the name of the table to be dropped this statement needs no other parameters. A table that is referenced by a FOREIGN KEY constraint by another table cannot be dropped in this way without first dropping the constraint. Only an administrator or the table owner can use this command.
- CREATE VIEW: This command is used to create a view of a table. A view is an excellent tool to restrict data access to only selected columns of a table that are included in the view.
- ALTER TABLE: This command is used to alter the current table definition. You can add or remove columns and constraints, or disable and enable constraints.
- DROP VIEW: This command drops or deletes an existing view. Permission to use this command is available only to the view owner or the system administrator and is not transferable. A view must be explicitly dropped when the table the view refers to is dropped; it is not dropped automatically.

DDL commands and statements are among the first statements that you will need to be able to use—after all, you can't manipulate or control your data until you have a place to put it. In this section you will learn how the CREATE VIEW and DROP TABLE commands are used. Throughout this book, the pubs sample database included with SQL Server will be used for examples and exercises.

Most client/server applications will access DDL statements through the use of the SQL-DMO (SQL Distributed Management Objects) API. This is an automation set compatible with the Win32 COM objects for Windows NT and Windows 95/98 operating systems. An application developer may use SQL-DMO to shield the user from all DDL functions, helping to ensure the integrity of the SQL Server database objects. An application written using SQL-DMO also has an advantage over one that directly accesses the database system tables. Often, when Microsoft builds an upgrade to SQL Server, changes are made to the underlying structure of the system tables. An application that directly accesses the system tables would have to have the sections of code that read or write to these tables rewritten before it would run on the new version of SQL Server. An application that makes use of the SQL-DMO API will not have to be rewritten. Microsoft considers the SQL-DMO, DDL, and system stored procedures to be published interfaces, and tries to maintain backward compatibility for these interfaces.

A system administrator would use a command line interface such as ISQL or the new SQL Server Query Analyzer, or the SQL Server Enterprise Manager and DDL statements to manage database objects.

Data Manipulation Language (DML)

Data Manipulation Language (DML) is the aspect of T-SQL that is used the most often. This part of T-SQL covers any command used to manipulate objects in the database, and more commonly, the data contained in your database. Beginning with Microsoft SQL Server 6.0, there have been several significant enhancements to many of the DML commands available to you. To use these commands you must have permission from the database owner to make changes to the information contained in the tables, or be the system administrator. Most DML commands are run against a table or a view. If a multiple table view is used with an UPDATE query, only one of the tables from the view can be updated. Examples of DML commands include:

- INSERT: Use this command to add a new row of data to a table(s). You must have the necessary permissions on the table. You must include any columns that are required columns in the table.
- SELECT: This is the most commonly used SQL command, and is often a component of larger queries. A SELECT query will return data that meets the criteria for the query. A criteria is not a requirement for a SELECT statement, but a FROM command is. The FROM command tells the SELECT statement where to find the information being sought.
- UPDATE: This command is used to edit or update information that is already in a table. The UPDATE command requires that you include updated information for all columns in a table. A placeholder or a column list must be provided so that the UPDATE query knows where to place the new information. A WHERE condition is used to select the rows that are to be updated.
- DELETE: The DELETE command is used to delete selected rows of information. A WHERE clause is used to specify the rows that will be deleted from the table. If a WHERE clause is not specified then all rows in the table are deleted. This does not delete the table object.

- EXECUTE: This command is most often used to execute a system, extended, or user-defined stored procedure. You do not have to include the EXECUTE command when executing a stored procedure if it is first in a batch. You can also use it to execute a character string within a T-SQL batch statement.

DML statements are used by endusers when retrieving or manipulating data in some way. DML statements will be included in almost any user-interface when the user has to interact with the data stored in a table. If you use the SQL Server Query Analyzer to run a DML query, the SQL Execution Plan option will display the best execution plan for the query.

Data Control Language (DCL)

Data Control Language (DCL) concerns those commands that give access to a database object. Permission to use DCL commands starts with the system administrator, the *sa* login, who can grant permission to use them to the database owner, who is listed within Microsoft SQL Server as the *dbo*. The system administrator can use the highest level of the DCL, having authorization to use any of the database objects, while a database owner can use DCL commands to give access to those objects that they own.

Permissions to objects are granted, denied, or revoked to security accounts. A security account can be any Windows NT account, an SQL Server account, Windows NT Group, or an SQL Server Role. A group or role are very similar in that they are composed of one or more individual accounts. They are most often used to group users together in common groups. You may want to create a group or role for all users who are salespeople and another for customer service. This way you can grant appropriate permissions to many users at once, and not have to apply the same security options to each individual account. Examples of DCL commands are:

- GRANT: This command is used to grant another user permission to use an object. When permission is granted to a user, an entry is made in that user security account. If a role is granted permission to an object, then all members of the role are affected. If there is a permission conflict between a group and a member of a group, then the most restrictive set of permissions takes precedence. A user or role given a permission with the WITH GRANT OPTION has the special permission to grant specified permissions to other security accounts.
- DENY: This command is used to deny permission for a user, group, or role. When used, the specified security accounts cannot inherit permissions on the denied statement.

- REVOKE: This command removes a previously granted or denied permission. Permissions cannot be revoked for system security roles, such as sysadmin. You can also revoke a WITH GRANT OPTION by specifying the GRANT OPTION FOR clause. The affected security accounts still have permissions on the object, but no longer have permission to GRANT access to other security accounts.

The CASCADE option, used with the REVOKE command, cascades the REVOKE command through the chain of security accounts who have been granted or denied permissions by users who used the WITH GRANT OPTION. This option is activated only when revoking permissions from a specified security account.

MCSE 2.3   Commonly Used T-SQL Statements

Almost all T-SQL statements will include at least one command. (An SQL command tells the server what action is to be performed by the statement.) Because DML statements are the most commonly used of the SQL commands, several of these will be discussed in detail in this chapter. SQL commands are also known as *keywords*, and as such are also reserved words that have special meaning to Microsoft SQL Server. In this section you will see how several commonly used commands work. The format used with these commands is similar with most versions of SQL since they concern basic data manipulation tasks of selecting, inserting, updating, and deleting data from a database.

When you are using an SQL program or other type of front-end application, T-SQL commands can be sent to the Microsoft SQL Server in batches. A batch is a group of SQL statements that are sent to the server at one time. Batches can be sent to the server in several ways, the most common being from a front-end application over the network. A database developer or system administrator may also use several other methods of sending SQL statements to the database: ISQL, OSQL, the Microsoft SQL Server Query Analyzer, or from a developmental front-end program.

How to Use T-SQL Statements

SQL Server can accept SQL commands and statements through several different interfaces. In this section we will be concerned with those interfaces directly accessible through SQL Server. T-SQL statements are used to create a query that is sent to and processed by SQL Server. Results may or may not be returned back to the query creator. Results can be anything from a set of rows that meet a SELECT query criteria, or simply a notification that a set of rows have been added to a table, or that no rows have been returned.

Before you can create a query, or any other form of an application, you must have detailed knowledge about the database, its tables, and the columns within the tables. Without this information you have no way of building a query that SQL Server will be able to understand. At a minimum, you must be able to provide the query with three basic pieces of information:

- The items that you want to retrieve or act on. This will be in the form of the select list. You can choose to retrieve all columns of a table, or only selected columns.
- A FROM clause is used to tell SQL Server the names of the tables where the information is stored.
- The WHERE clause provides the conditions used to limit the returned results.

Queries can be used to retrieve information from tables stored in a local SQL Server database, or from remote locations, or other databases such as Microsoft Access. A query that accesses data from a location other than a local database is called a *distributed* query.

T-SQL AND THE COMMAND LINE

SQL Server has two command-line query tools: isql and osql. Both access SQL Server directly from the operating system. There are several command-line options or switches that you can use when you start the utilities, and these options are case-sensitive.

The primary difference between isql and osql are that isql uses DB-Library as its connection, while osql uses the ODBC drivers to communicate with SQL Server. Both allow you to create an interactive SQL session until you specifically terminate the session by issuing either a QUIT or EXIT command. The results from your queries will be formatted and output to the "standard output device," more commonly known as your screen.

When you start the isql or osql utility, SQL Server will check the environment variables and use them if you do not provide a user name, or server name during the startup. If no environment variables have been set, then SQL Server will use the current logon user name and workstation name along with the appropriate security options available to the logon name.

Here, in this first example, the osql utility will be used to query the pubs database.

1. Open the Windows NT command line prompt and enter the following command:

```
osql -U <username> -P <password> -d pubs
```

Replace `<username>` with your own logon name, and replace `<password>` with your own password. You can also use the `-E` option if you use a trusted connection, thus eliminating the need for the `-U` or `-P` options.

2. Press the Enter key to send the osql command to SQL Server. If your logon name and password are correct, you will see a new command line displayed and indicated by `1>`.

3. Enter the following SQL statements. As you come to the end of each line in the query, press the Enter key to begin a new numbered line. The query does not execute until you tell it to.

```
SELECT au_fname, au_lname, phone
FROM authors
WHERE state = 'CA'
```

4. When you are done, you will have a query statement like the one shown in Figure 2-1. You will find that neither the osql or isql utilities are case-sensitive. T-SQL commands are entered in capitals only for easier reading.

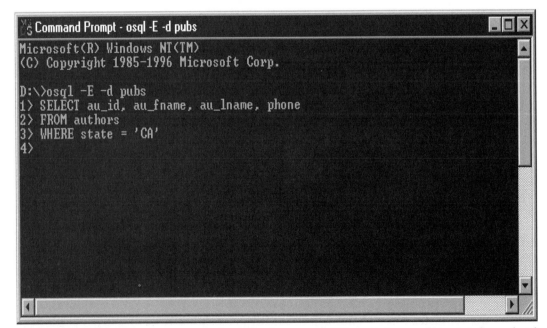

Figure 2–1   *This query statement is shown in the command line window, and is using the osql utili*

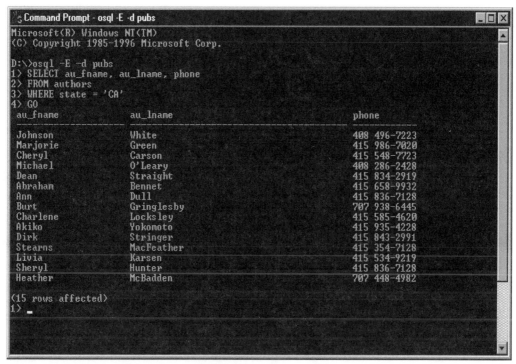

Figure 2–2 *The results set from the SELECT query.*

5. Type the command GO and press the Enter key to execute the query. The results of the query will be displayed on your screen as shown in Figure 2-2.

Notice how the results set from this query are spaced. When using these command-line query tools, the column format takes its settings from the column width setting when the table is created. You can not adjust the column width in this results set.

MICROSOFT SQL SERVER QUERY ANALYZER

The Microsoft SQL Server Query Analyzer replaces ISQL/w as the query tool of choice. Unlike isql and osql, the Query Analyzer provides an extensive set of query analysis tools to its more friendly interface. One change that most users will find very useful is the use of color coding of T-SQL statements, and other query elements. This makes reading and debugging a query much simpler.

Another significant change is that Query Analyzer uses ODBC SQL instead of DB-Library, as did ISQL/w. This is reflective of the widespread acceptance and use of ODBC.

You must expect different results from queries that use ODBC drivers and those that use DB-Library. This is due to the use of ANSI to OEM character translations. Each of these drivers processes these character sets in a slightly different order. Remember, SQL Server Query Analyzer uses ODBC drivers, while isql and ISQL/w for SQL Server version 6.5 use DB-Library.

The Query Analyzer has been much improved over its predecessor. The Plan tab shows much greater detail of each stage of the query execution, its optimization, and use of indexes than did ISQL/w. The Query Analyzer can be accessed from within the SQL Server Enterprise Manager, under the Microsoft Management Console, or as a stand-alone application. This next exercise shows how Microsoft SQL Server Query Analyzer is used.

1. Open Microsoft SQL Server Query Analyzer as shown in Figure 2-3, by doing one of the following:

   • With the Microsoft Management Console open, and SQL Server Enterprise Manager open within it, select Tools from the menu and then choose SQL Server Query Analyzer.

   • Select the Start button on the Task Bar, drilling down through your own menu structure until you come to SQL Server 7 and then SQL Server Query Analyzer on its submenu.

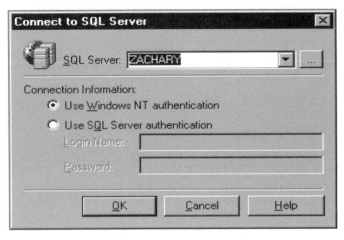

Figure 2–3 *Here you must select the server on which the database you want to query resides.*

2. Select the server that contains the database you want to query. Choose the type of connection that you want or can make to the server and click the OK button.

If you are not sure of the connection type that you can make, ask your network or SQL Server administrator. The first option, "Use Windows NT authentication," is used when Windows NT administers all security for your database. The second option, "Use SQL Server authentication," is used if SQL Server administers its own security. You will need to include your login name and password for this option.

Once you click the OK button, the Microsoft SQL Server Query Analyzer query grid is displayed. Notice the database displayed in the Database combo box is *master*. This is because it is the current default database.

3. Change the database from `master` to `pubs`, by selecting it from the drop-down list box as shown in Figure 2-4. If you do not select the correct database for the query to be run against, it will fail because the tables, columns, and other objects you reference in the query will not be found.

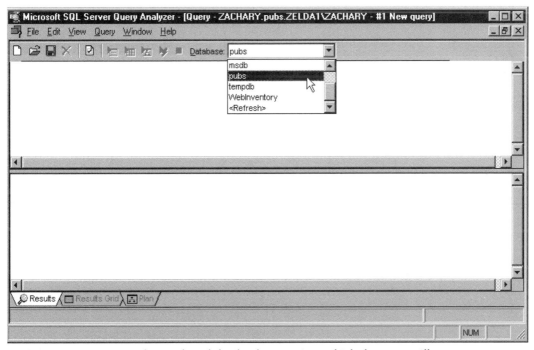

Figure 2–4 *Here you have selected the database against which the query will run.*

SELECT

The `SELECT` command is the most often used of all SQL commands because it is available at any time to retrieve information from your database.

I recommend that you never leave the master database as a default database. By not changing this setting, your end users can easily begin to save their database. This can make it much more difficult to back up the database or to restore it in the event of a hardware failure.

With the SELECT command, in concert with FROM and WHERE commands, you can choose the specific rows of data you need. Microsoft SQL Server will interpret the batch of SQL statements that you send to the server and display the information that you request.

USING A SELECT STATEMENT

Use the Query Analyzer program to create the simple SELECT statement created earlier in this chapter. SELECT for all authors who live in the state of California and display their name and phone number. These records will be selected from the authors' table in the pubs database. Create the SQL statement by following these steps:

1. Open the Query Analyzer program by following the steps in the previous exercise, if the Query Analyzer is not still open. If you are using a trusted connection, your ability to login to Windows NT provides you with your access to SQL Server, if you have been granted appropriate permission.
2. The Results tab is selected by default. Be sure that you have selected the pubs database from the Database list box. Now type the following SELECT statement into the query window.

```
SELECT au_fname, au_lname, state, phone
FROM authors
WHERE state = 'ca'
```

The SELECT command tells Microsoft SQL Server what fields you want displayed in your results set. The next line specifies which tables to look in by using the qualification clause FROM. The final clause is the WHERE condition. The records and fields selected must meet the conditions specified by the WHERE clause as you see in Figure 2-5.

3. Click the Execute Query button, or select Query, Execute from the menu, or press Ctrl+E. Any of these actions will cause Query Analyzer to send the SELECT statement batch to the server. The server will then

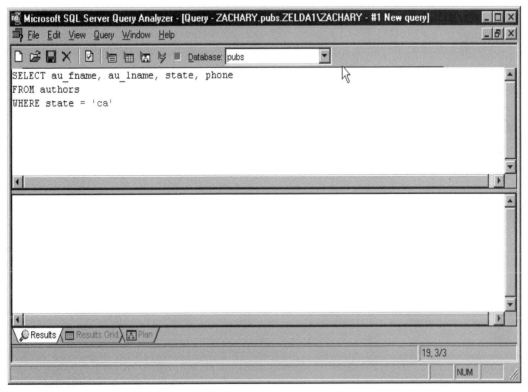

Figure 2–5 *Here is the T-SQL SELECT statement in the Query Analyzer query window.*

 T-SQL is not case-sensitive when you build an SQL statement, if you have selected the normal default settings when installing SQL Server. The keywords are capitalized only so that you can easily distinguish between commands and table, column, and variable names. Query Analyzer also displays various parts of the query in colors. The default colors are blue for commands, black for objects, and red for variables.

return the results set and display it in the lower pane of the Results window as shown in Figure 2-6.

If you use ISQL instead of Query Analyzer, you must end each SQL statement with the GO command. This command tells ISQL that you have completed the statement batch and send it on to the server. The results set output will be displayed on your screen. The GO command is also recognized in Query Analyzer, allowing you to create more complex T-SQL statements

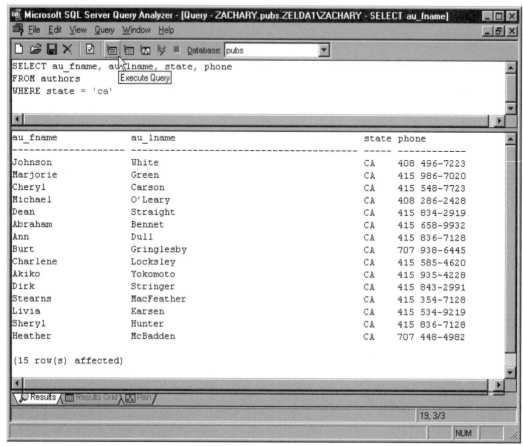

Figure 2–6   *The results of the query are displayed in the lower pane of the query Results window.*

as groups of smaller statements. This is much easier to debug, than is one very long statement without any sort of break.

JOINING TABLES AND SORTING VALUES WITH A SELECT STATEMENT

More often than not, a SELECT query of a single table is of very limited utility. In order to get at the information that you or your users really need, it will require data from more than one table. This requires another T-SQL command?the JOIN command. A JOIN statement tells the T-SQL query optimizer which tables to use in the query, and the specific columns to use in creating the JOIN. This is one of the most powerful features of a RDBMS. Whenever you are drawing data from several tables with a SELECT statement to build a single result set, you are creating a join between the tables. Often the WHERE clause is used to narrow the results set to a specific group of records by specifying multiple conditions within the clause. In this next exercise you will see how this can be done.

1. If the Query Analyzer is still open, return to the upper pane of the Results window. Select the old statement and delete it by pressing the Delete key, then type this new statement:

```
SELECT au_fname, au_lname, title
FROM authors, titleauthor, titles
WHERE authors.au_id = titleauthor.au_id
AND titleauthor.title_id = titles.title_id
AND state NOT LIKE 'ca'
```

This SELECT statement tells Microsoft SQL Server to display all authors and the titles that are associated with them. Notice that there are three tables listed: authors, titleauthor, and titles. This is because there is no direct link between authors and titles—the table titleauthor provides the link used to join the other two tables. The joins are specified by the fields listed in the WHERE clause: au_id joins both authors and titleauthor, while the field title_id joins titleauthor and titles together. Notice how the column names are qualified with both the table and column name, *authors.au_id*. Whenever you refer to a column that exists in more than one table, you must qualify the column name by identifying its table. If you fail to do this the query optimizer will not be able to compile the statement and will return a set of error messages telling you that the references to the column names are ambiguous—in other words, the optimizer can not determine what you are asking for. The last line of the query restricts the output results set to only those authors who do not live in the state of California. Figure 2-7 shows the completed query.

2. This time click the Execute Query Into Grid button to view the resulting data set in the Results window, as shown in Figure 2-8.

3. Notice how the results set has been sorted in standard alphabetical order by the values in column au_lname. You can change the sort order of the results set with the addition of another line in the SELECT statement. Click at the end of the last line of the query and type this line as the fifth line in the query statement, then click the Execute Query Into Grid button:

```
ORDER BY title
```

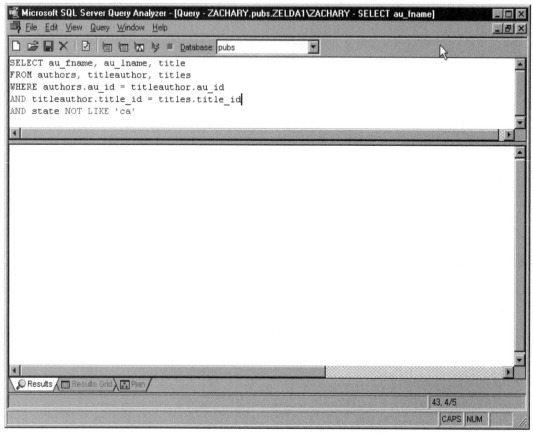

Figure 2–7 *This SELECT query statement links three tables and displays information from two of them.*

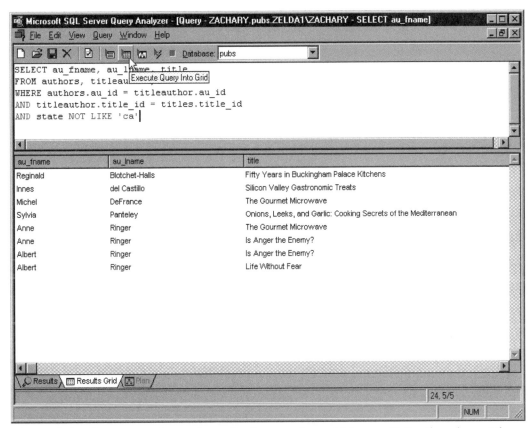

Figure 2–8 *Here you see the results set for the query in a grid format. Notice the column titles and the font change; oftentimes this may be a more readable format.*

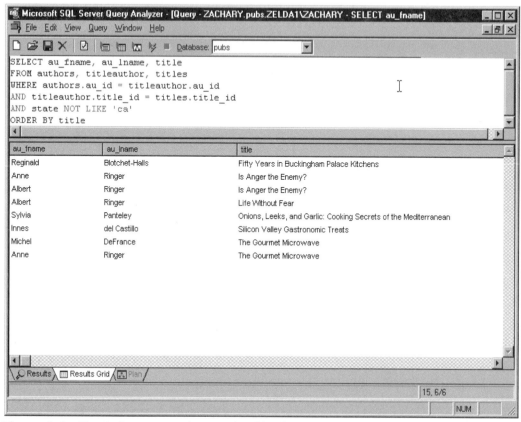

Figure 2–9 *Here is the same results set ordered by the values in the column titles.*

This modified SQL command will cause Microsoft SQL Server to sort the results set by the listed column—title (book title). Figure 2-9 shows the new results set.

CREATING AN ALIAS

As you will have already noticed when displaying a results set, SQL uses the column names as headings for the displayed results set. More often than not, you will find the column names are not the most easily understood headings for columns of data. Unless you were the programmer who created the pubs table, it may take you a moment before you see that the column labeled au_lname means that this column comes from the authors table and contains the last name for each of the authors.

There is an easy way to alleviate this potential problem—by using an *alias*. An alias is used to rename a column in the results set—for example, you may want to rename the au_lname to something easily understood, such as "Last Name." Using an alias to rename a column is quite simple when you are building an SQL statement. In the next exercise you will use an alias to rename the column display. An alias does not affect the actual table in any way. In the next exercise you will see how an alias is used.

1. Click the Query tab in the Query Analyzer window and clear any existing SQL statements by clicking the Remove Current Query Set button. Type the following SQL statement into the window, as shown in Figure 2-10.

```
SELECT au_lname 'Last Name', au_fname 'First Name',
    phone Phone
FROM authors
```

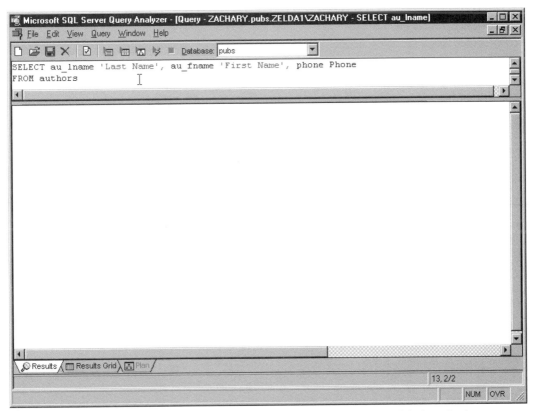

Figure 2–10 *This query statement will display a results set with column labels with alias, or new, names.*

Note You will have noticed that quotation marks are placed around the first two aliases, but not the third one. This is because T-SQL uses the quotations surrounding alias names of more than one word, otherwise it would assume that the first word was the alias while the second was another command. While you can use double quotation marks to indicate the label names, it is regarded as good practice to use single quotation marks when you are using T-SQL reserved words as labels, or in other cases when you do not want them to perform the actions that they would normally.

2. Click the Execute Query button to view the new results set. You should now see a results set much like Figure 2-11.

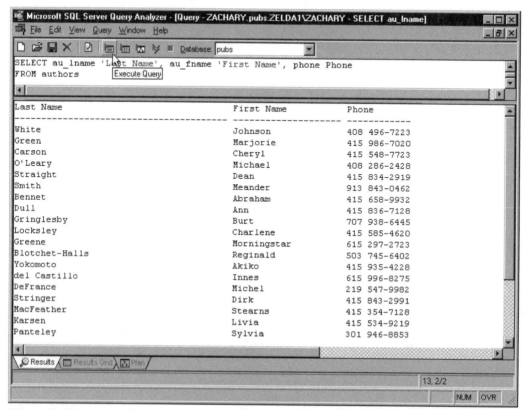

Figure 2–11 *Notice the new column labels displayed at the beginning of the list.*

As you begin your sojourn into SQL, you may forget the necessity of the comma when delineating the column select list. If you do not separate each and every column name with a comma, the following problem will be displayed:

```
QUERY:

SELECT au_lname au_fname FROM authors
RESULTS:
au_fname
--------------------------------------------
White
Green
Carson
...
```

The results set shows a list of names with a column label of au_fname—but is it correct, and what happened to the au_lname column? If you look at the data contained in the authors' table you will find that you have a list of last names, not first names. What has happened is that without the comma separating the two column names, SQL assumes that the second name is to be used as a column alias. Always be sure that you have inserted commas between each name in a select list, whether it be columns or tables.

INSERT

Once you know how to select records from a database you will want to do more. The simplest method to add new rows, or records, to a table is with the INSERT command. INSERT does not require that you fill all of the columns in a table; you can go back later and add additional data or change existing data in any row by using the UPDATE command.

There are other methods for inserting large amounts of data into a table. The BCP utility (Bulk Copy Program) is a special utility that allows you to insert large blocks of new data into an existing table. This procedure is often used when you are converting from an older database system currently in use to a new SQL Server client/server system. You would then use the BCP utility to bulk load data from your old system to the new. SQL Server includes a new utility, Data Transfer Service, that makes transferring information a much simpler task.

When adding new rows you are only required to complete those columns that are designated as key columns, or those that do not allow NULL values. SQL will return an error if a value is not stated for any column that does not allow NULL values, or has not been assigned a default value. You do not have to specify values for columns that use either the *identity* property or *timestamp* datatype. A column with the identity property will automatically be sequentially numbered, while a timestamp datatype will provide an increasing counter with a unique value within the database. A timestamp value will be automatically updated each time a new row is inserted or a value in any column of that row is updated. Follow these steps to see how an INSERT statement is used.

1. Be sure that the pubs database is selected in the Database list box, and then type the following INSERT statement in the upper pane of the Query Analyzer window as shown in Figure 2-12.

```
INSERT jobs
(job_desc, min_lvl, max_lvl)
VALUES
("Sales Rep Intl", 30, 125)
INSERT jobs
(job_desc, min_lvl, max_lvl)
VALUES
("Designer II", 75, 150)
```

Note   The jobs table's first column is job_id. This field is not included in an INSERT statement because it uses an identity property. Microsoft SQL Server will automatically assign a value for this field. For each record that you insert into a table you must repeat the INSERT command, the column list, and the values list.

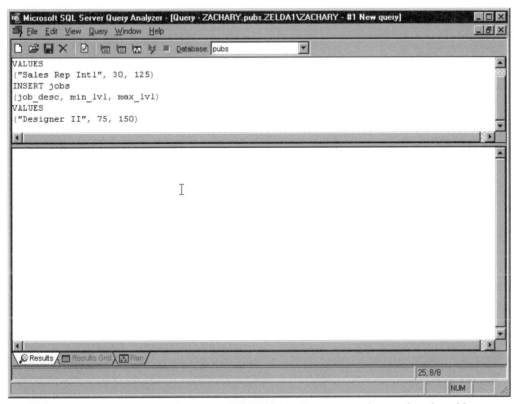

```
VALUES
("Sales Rep Intl", 30, 125)
INSERT jobs
(job_desc, min_lvl, max_lvl)
VALUES
("Designer II", 75, 150)
```

Figure 2–12 *An INSERT SQL statement that adds two new records into the jobs table.*

2. Click the Execute Query button to insert your two new records into the jobs table. For each record successfully added, you will see the statement (1 row(s) affected) listed in the Results pane, and shown in Figure 2-13.

You can omit the column list in an INSERT statement if you provide values for each column—except identity and timestamp columns—in the same order in which the columns occur in the table. If you do accidentally place values in an incorrect order, Microsoft SQL Server may trap the error and display an error message, but only if the statement tries to insert a value incompatible with the column data type—such as an alphanumeric value in an number column. Microsoft SQL Server will not automatically trap two alphanumeric values that are transposed, such as a city and state value. SQL will simply insert the state value into the city column and the city value into the state column. The value inserted into the state column will most likely be truncated to a two-letter value.

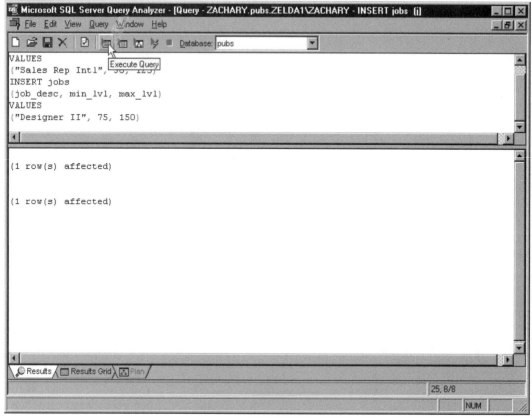

Figure 2–13   *Notice how an INSERT query does not return a list of values as a SELECT query does. You are simply told that the query was successful. If it was not, an error message would be displayed.*

In Chapter 3, "SQL Server Structures" you will learn about rules and triggers, while in Chapter 10, "What Is Data Integrity?" you will learn about referential integrity. All of these can be used to help ensure that errors of this type are caught and allow the user to make corrections before the INSERT is allowed to go through, or is summarily rejected.

UPDATE

The UPDATE statement is used to change values that already exist in a row. For example, if an author already listed in the authors table of the pubs database were to move, you would want to simply update his or her address, not insert a new record for the author.

Common uses for UPDATE statements are to change addresses, telephone numbers, prices, item descriptions, and other information contained in a column. In most cases you must identify a specific record to be updated. Without such an identification Microsoft SQL Server will update every row with the same information. For example, a simple UPDATE SQL statement could be constructed that said:

```
UPDATE authors
SET city = 'San Francisco'
```

This SQL statement is unqualified and would result in changing the city column of all rows to the value "San Francisco." This type of mass update is useful when you need to change the same information for many records. A good example of this type of mass UPDATE would be when the telephone company adds a new area code. If the area code for your company and most or all of its employees changes, you would want to do an unqualified UPDATE. An unqualified UPDATE is fairly uncommon.

Most often you will use an UPDATE SQL statement that is qualified by selecting a specific row(s) to be updated using a WHERE clause. A poorly qualified statement can cause all of the rows, or the wrong rows, to be selected and updated with the new data. In the above statement, you would want to identify a specific author and so could qualify this statement by adding:

```
WHERE au_id = '274-80-9391'
```

With the addition of this WHERE clause, SQL knows exactly which individual row is to be updated with the new information. In the case of a change of city, you will most likely have to change street address, and possibly the phone number also. It is more efficient to tell SQL to change all of these fields with one statement than it is to issue an individual SQL statement to update each column. A complete statement would look like this:

```
UPDATE authors
SET phone = '510-555-1234'
address = '1542 Market St.'
city = 'San Francisco'
state = 'CA'
Zip = '92111'
WHERE au_id = '274-80-9391'
```

Since you are not changing the author's name or contract status you do not have to include these columns.

DELETE

The DELETE statement is used to delete unneeded rows from a table, not to delete information from single columns. SQL allows you to delete rows from only a single table at a time. Generally, a DELETE statement should be a qualified statement, selecting specific rows to be deleted from a table. An unqualified statement, or one that is poorly qualified, can inadvertently delete all of the rows in a table. The following SQL statement can be used to delete all publishers who are not located in the United States:

```
DELETE publishers
WHERE NOT country = 'USA'
```

This query works once you have either deleted all of the records in other tables that are linked to the records to be deleted or have shifted these links to another publisher. In the pubs database, both the employee and the pub_info tables are linked to the publishers table through the pub_id column.

SQL does not allow you to delete records that are *dependent* on values that exist in another table. These other tables are often called *child* tables because they are dependent on a value contained in the *parent* table. These relationships and their uses are discussed fully in Chapter 10, "What Is Data Integrity?"

MCSE 2.4   Transactions and SQL

In Microsoft SQL Server, *transactions* are a set of procedures that must be completed at one time. Once a transaction begins, it must be fully completed or completely undone. All business procedures can be reduced to a series of transactions. For example, Ashley deposits a check for $100 into her checking account that she received from Amber. The bank processes several transactions:

- The bank adds, or debits, $100 to Ashley's checking account.
- A credit of $100 is made against the bank's cash account in favor of Ashley's bank account.
- A debit is made to the bank's cash due account for $100. This is the amount now due to Ashley's bank from Amber's bank.
- When Amber's bank transfers the $100 to Ashley's bank, a credit is made to the cash due account, making the bank balance again.

All of these transactions must be completed so that the bank's books remain in balance. All SQL statements, except a simple SELECT statement, are transactional. Microsoft SQL Server guarantees that a transaction will be completely processed or it will not be processed at all. For example, if you want to increase the price of all business books in the pubs' titles table by 25 percent, you would issue an UPDATE statement:

```
UPDATE titles
SET price = price * 1.25
WHERE type = business
```

If the server goes down after this transaction begins but before it has processed all rows in the titles table, what happens? Once the server comes back up, and before the database is ready for use, Microsoft SQL Server will roll back all incomplete transactions—as if the UPDATE transaction had never been started. This is how Microsoft SQL Server can guarantee that a transaction will be completely processed.

There are only a few basic transaction commands that Microsoft SQL Server uses to decide if an SQL transaction has been started, completed, or should be reversed:

- BEGIN TRANsaction. This statement is used to tell Microsoft SQL Server to group all of the subsequent operations—to begin a transaction.
- COMMIT TRANsaction. This statement tells the server to commit the operations in the current transaction. The transaction is completed and is to be written to the disk.
- ROLLBACK TRANsaction. This statement tells the server to reverse all transaction changes to the previous BEGIN TRAN statement.
- SAVE TRANsaction. This statement allows a user to set a save point within a transaction. If a transaction must meet specified conditions, it can be rolled back to the save point. It must then either be completed with additional SQL statements and a COMMIT TRAN statement, or rolled back to its beginning.

All SQL statements are implicitly begun and committed by the server. This means that you do not have to use BEGIN TRAN and COMMIT TRAN statements around each statement. If you are only processing short statements that are single transaction then a BEGIN TRAN and COMMIT TRAN statement are probably not necessary.

When you do not use a BEGIN and COMMIT TRAN statement in a transaction, Microsoft SQL Server assumes that each transaction has an implicit BEGIN and COMMIT TRAN statement. SQL Server implicitly commits each transaction as it is completed. A transaction such as our earlier bank example, though, should have a BEGIN TRAN and a COMMIT TRAN statement surrounding it. Otherwise it could be possible for only half of the transaction to be completed. For example:

```
implicit BEGIN TRAN
UPDATE customer_account
SET balance = balance - 100
tran_id = 3456
WHERE cust_id = "151545 3456"
implicit COMMIT TRAN

implicit BEGIN TRAN
INSERT bank_cashacct (tran_id, amount, cust_id)
VALUES (3456, 100, "151545 3456")
implicit COMMIT TRAN
```

If the server goes down before the second COMMIT TRAN, then only the first half of this transaction, up to the first COMMIT TRAN, will be written to the disk and the records changed accordingly. The second half of the transaction would be rolled back. Any multiple transaction that should be written to the permanent file at one time should always be start with a BEGIN TRAN and end with a COMMIT TRAN statement. This will ensure that the entire transaction will be written or none of it will be written. This same bank transaction should be written like this:

```
BEGIN TRAN
UPDATE customer_account
SET balance = balance - 100
tran_id = 3456
WHERE cust_id = '151545 3456'
INSERT bank_cashacct (tran_id, amount, cust_id)
VALUES (3456, 100, '151545 3456')
COMMIT TRAN
```

By using a BEGIN TRAN and a COMMIT TRAN statement around the transaction SQL Server guarantees that the entire transaction will be properly written to the permanent disk file. Now the server would automatically roll this transaction back if it were to go down before it was completed.

The ROLLBACK TRAN statement would be used in place of the COMMIT TRAN statement if you wanted to reverse all of the changes that had been made in the transaction since the BEGIN TRAN statement was initiated.

Key Points

In this chapter the following key points were discussed:

- T-SQL is fully compliant with both the SQL-89 and SQL-92 ANSI standards. In addition to full compliance, further extensions have been provided that are specific to SQL Server.
- The differences between T-SQL and ANSI-SQL include modifications to the reserved word lists and the names of data types.
- Data Definition Language (DDL) is used to create, alter, and remove database object. DDL statements include an action and an object.
- Data Manipulation Language (DML) statements are used to add, change, and delete data within a database object.
- Data Control Language (DCL) statements are used to grant, deny, and revoke permissions to security accounts. When conflicts between granted permissions are found for a specific security account, the most restrictive permissions will apply.
- How to use commonly used commands such as SELECT, INSERT, UPDATE, and DELETE.
- How to change the sort order by using the ORDER BY clause, and how to change the names of columns in a results set by using an alias.

▲ CHAPTER REVIEW QUESTIONS

▲ Multiple Choice

1. *SQL commands can be divided into three types:*
   A. Data Definition Language, Data Manipulation Language, and Active Server Pages
   B. Data Manipulation Language, Data Control Language, and Defined Database Language
   C. Active Server Pages, Data Control Language, and Defined Database Language
   D. Data Control Language, Data Manipulation Language, and Data Definition Language

2. *T-SQL reserved words are also known as:*
   A. Special words
   B. Keywords

       C. Restricted Words

       D. Named words

3. *An example of the use of a Data Manipulation Language statement is:*

       A. To manipulate the structure of a data table

       B. Insert new information into a table

       C. Create a view of a table

       D. A and C only

       E. All of the above

4. *Permissions to access or use an object are controlled through the use of:*

       A. Permission Controls (PC) statements

       B. Database Owner (DBO) statements

       C. Data Control Language (DCL) statements

       D. Data Definition Language (DDL) statements

5. *The osql utility formats and sends query results to:*

       A. The default printer

       B. The standard output device

       C. Your monitor

       D. A and C

       E. All of the above

6. *An INSERT statement is used to:*

       A. Copy information from the Clipboard to a table

       B. Adds a new row of data

       C. Inserts a new table

       D. B and C

       E. All of the above.

7. *The initial default database on installing SQL Server is:*

       A. There is no default database

       B. pubs

       C. msdbdefault

       D. master

8. *New features of the SQL Server Query Analyzer include:*

       A. An improved Query Execution Plan view

       B. Execute Query into Grid

C. Perform Index Analysis

D. A and C

E. All of the above

9. *Quotes are used to surround what kind of alias names?*

A. When using a keyword

B. For all alias names

C. When the alias is more than one word

D. A and C

E. All of the above

10. *In a SELECT statement, column names are delimited by a:*

A. Tab

B. Space

C. Comma

D. Semicolon

E. Forward Slash

11. *A transaction can be initiated by using the:*

A. START TRANsaction

B. BEGIN TRANsaction

C. INITIATE TRANsaction

D. EXECUTE

▲ True or False

1. *True or False? Most DDL statements are composed of two elements: the action and the object.*

2. *True or False? You can expect identical results using either DB-Library or ODBC connections.*

SQL Server Structure

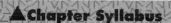
Microsoft SQL Server™ has made a major departure in the structure of a database from its earlier versions. Previously, a database was created on an SQL Server™ logical device. The logical device was in turn built on the operating file system. SQL Server 7.0™ now creates the database directly in an operating system file. This gives you a much greater ability to scale your database as your needs grow.

MCSE 3.1 Creating a Database with SQL Server 7.0

Now that SQL Server databases reside directly in an operating system file, you can eliminate the CREATE DEVICE process when creating a database. A single CREATE DATABASE statement will now create both the database and the operating system file that it will be stored in.

An SQL Server 7.0 database is composed of at least two operating system files. The first required file is the *primary* file and contains all startup information about the database. The primary file may also contain all of the data tables for the database. The second required file is a log file. Each of these files can be used only by a single database. When you create a new database you can create optional files; secondary files can be created to store data and database objects that do not fit in the primary file, and you can create multiple log files. There is only one primary file per database.

During the CREATE DATABASE process, a copy of the model database is included as part of the primary file. The model database includes all of the system tables—also called the *database catalog*—required by SQL Server. You can also update the model database to include any stored procedures, user-defined data types, and other database objects that you want to have included in every new database.

Warning

Updating the model database does not automatically update all of the other currently existing databases. Updates to the model will only be reflected in new databases that you create after the changes have been saved.

The CREATE DATABASE T-SQL statement is formatted as follows. There are several parameters that you can use to customize a new database.

```
CREATE DATABASE db_name
[ON {PRIMARY] (file_specifications) [n secondary files] ]
LOG ON (file_specifications) [n secondary logs] ]
[FOR RESTORE]
(file_specifications)
NAME = Required logical filename
FILENAME = Required operating system filename
SIZE = Optional starting file size
MAXSIZE = Optional maximum file size
[UNLIMITED] allows file growth to available disk space
FILEGROWTH = file growth increments
```

The various arguments and parameters available for use with a CREATE DATABASE statement, in order of normal use, are:

- db_name: This is the name you will use for your database. This must be a unique name within a server. It must also be a valid name within the rules for identifiers.
- ON: This command specifies the actual disk files that will be used to store the data files for the database.
- PRIMARY: This is an optional command. When used, it specifies the file that contains the logical beginning of the database. The system tables will be contained on the primary file. If you do not specify a primary file, the first file listed will be used as the primary.
- Indicates a placeholder. If your database contains additional data files, they will be listed after the primary file. The information required for a primary file is needed for each secondary data file.
- LOG ON: Indicates the beginning of the list of log files that will be used to store the transaction logs. SQL Server will automatically create a log file if you do not use the clause. A default transaction log equal to 25 percent of the total size of all data files will be created.
- FOR RESTORE: This clause is included for compatibility with earlier versions of SQL Server, but has no actual effect in version 7.
- NAME: This parameter is required and specifies the logical name for the file. This name must be unique to the server.
- FILENAME: This parameter specifies the name of the operating system file. You should include the complete path and filename, or the database will be created in the default SQL Server data folder. The file must be contained on the server where SQL Server is installed.
- SIZE: This parameter is used to specify the initial size for the database. The minimum size is 1MB, and the default size is 3MB for data files and 1MB for log files. You can specify a size in either MB (megabytes), or KB (kilobytes).
- MAXSIZE: Use this parameter to specify the maximum size that a data or log file can grow. Again, you can enter this parameter in either MB or KB. If you do not specify the maximum size, SQL Server will allow a file to grow until the disk is full.
- UNLIMITED: Specifically allows the file to grow until the disk is full.
- FILEGROWTH: This parameter is used to select the increment used for file growth. You cannot enter a value for FILEGROWTH that is larger than MAXSIZE. When more space is needed for a file, the size listed here is added to the file. The default value is 256KB and the

minimum is 64KB. Any value entered will be automatically rounded to the nearest 64KB increment.

 While you can use any valid operating system name when creating a new database, Microsoft recommends that you use these extensions: .mdf (primary data file), .ndf (nonprimary data files), and .ldf (log files). This will help to ensure later compatibility for developers.

A couple of simple CREATE DATABASE statement samples are provided here.

The following is a simple CREATE statement with no parameters:

```
CREATE DATABASE test
```

This simple statement will create a primary data file, 3MB in size, and a single log file of 1MB. These will be automatically placed in the same folder that your master database is stored in. The operating system files will be named test.mdf and test.ldf, respectively.

Here is a CREATE statement with a primary data file, one secondary data file, and one log file:

```
CREATE DATABASE Inventory
ON PRIMARY
(NAME = Inventory_P,
FILENAME = 'c:\mssql7\data\Inventory_P.mdf',
SIZE = 20MB,
MAXSIZE = 100MB,
FILEGROWTH = 2MB),
(NAME = Inventory_S1,
FILENAME = 'c:\mssql7\data\Inventory_S1.ndf',
SIZE = 20MB,
MAXSIZE = 100MB,
FILEGROWTH = 2MB)
LOG ON
(NAME = InventoryLog1,
FILENAME = 'c:\mssql7\data\InventoryLog1.ldf',
SIZE = 10MB,
MAXSIZE = 75MB,
FILEGROWTH = 1MB)
```

This CREATE statement creates three operating system files: a primary data file of 20MB, a secondary data file also of 20MB, and a log file of 10MB. Each of these files has been restricted through the use of the MAXSIZE parameter and has a specific size for the increase in file size by using the

FILEGROWTH clause. Note that the log file uses the .ldf extension, but this alone does not make a log file. The LOG ON statement tells SQL Server that the file specifications that follow are log files and not more data files.

If you do not include the LOG ON clause, SQL Server will automatically create the log file for you. The default log will be sized at 25 percent of the total size of all data files that you create.

Compatibility with Earlier Devices

There are a number of compatibility issues that have to be dealt with if you are currently administering databases built on earlier versions of SQL Server. First and foremost, is that you can only directly upgrade databases that were created with either SQL Server version 6 or 6.5. If you are still using version 4.2 databases, you must first upgrade them to 6.5 and then to 7. In earlier versions of SQL Server, you could have multiple databases within a single database device. This is no longer true with SQL Server 7, as you just learned. If you plan to migrate your existing databases to SQL Server 7, the tools are provided that will make the processes less painful. If you plan to keep both new and old databases in place, then you have a different set of issues.

Those of you planning to migrate your existing databases to SQL Server 7 may want to use the SQL Server Version Upgrade Wizard. You also have the option of using the Data Transformation Services to move information from one database to another. Each of these will be discussed in Chapter 14, "Methods of Transferring Data."

Microsoft has tried to ensure that applications using earlier versions of SQL Server will continue to run correctly when upgraded to SQL Server 7. If you have created your own administration or version-specific queries, you will probably have to rewrite them before they will work properly. When you migrate a version 6.X SQL Server database to a version 7 database, they are automatically set with a compatibility level. This will help to ensure that most new features available with SQL Server 7 will run on your converted databases, but those features that require a database created in version 7 will not be allowed to operate on them.

If you have an existing 6.X database that uses any of these features, you may experience some of the following problems during an upgrade:

- An application that uses sp_configure to directly set configuration options, or one that relies on a specific 6.X configuration setting. You will need to rewrite the application so that this is no longer necessary.

- Applications that use SQL-DMO to administer tasks, replication, and device objects will have to be updated. All task objects must be changed to job objects. Applications that use replication-stored procedures must be updated, and all references to 6.X security objects must be updated to version 7 security objects.
- Databases that depend on the physical layout of segments on devices. You will need to rewrite these applications so that they can work with files instead of segments.
- Applications that directly access the system tables without using the provided stored procedures. Rewrite these applications so that they make use of the applicable stored procedures.

There are distinct compatibility problems with running both SQL Server 6.X and SQL Server 7 at the same time. While SQL Server 7 uses the new Microsoft Management Console—or more simply the MMC—you cannot administer a version 6.x database in the console. You can see the SQL Server 6.X in the MMC window, but you cannot perform any administrative functions on it. You will have to use the older SQL Server Enterprise Manager for all administration functions. The MMC will soon be used throughout the Microsoft BackOffice suite of server tools. Due to the inability of the MMC to work with a version 6.X database, you must keep both sets of server tools active.

MCSE 3.2   Database Objects

A database object is the primary container that holds other commonly used user objects such as tables, views, stored procedures, and rules. All of the properties of a single database are contained within the database object. The database owner has primary responsibility for creating all objects that populate their database. Permission can be granted to another user to create, manage, and use the objects within a database.

Before you can create a table or other object in a database, you must first either select an existing database or create a new one. Unlike earlier versions of SQL Server databases are contained within one or more database files, just as a table is contained within a database. Unlike a table, the actual database can be spanned across more than one file—the transaction log portion of the database is always placed on separate files. Databases can be created using the CREATE DATABASE T-SQL statement, or by using the SQL Server Enterprise Manager console. In the previous section of this chapter, you learned how the CREATE DATABASE statement was used. In this section, the Enterprise Manager interface will be used. Create a new database by following these steps:

1. Open the MMC by double-clicking the SQL Server Enterprise Manager icon. Figure 3-1 shows the Enterprise Manager open in the MMC.

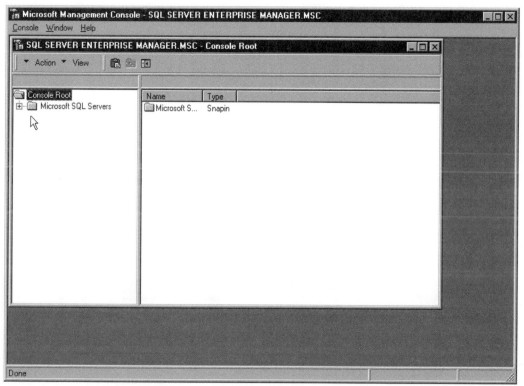

Figure 3–1   *The Microsoft Management Console (MMC) is the primary interface for all Microsoft BackOffice components. SQL Server Enterprise Manager is open inside.*

2. Click on the +(plus sign) beside the server that you want to connect to. This will open the object tree for the selected server and make the connection to it. As you can see in Figure 3-2, a red-horizontal zigzag-line beside the server icon indicates that your connection has been made. If for some reason a connection is refused, SQL Server will display a message box telling you.

3. Place the mouse pointer on the Database icon and right-click. Select the New Database option from the shortcut menu to open the Database Properties dialog box.

Figure 3–2   *A connection has been made to the SQL Server ZACHARY. Notice that the + (plus sign) that you clicked on has changed to a – minus sign.*

4. Type Inventory in the Name text box. This text box takes the place of the NAME = part of the CREATE DATABASE statement.

5. SQL Server automatically enters a default name, based on the name entered in step 4 into the File name and Location columns of the Database files grid. You can override these settings by entering your own file name and location. The first row in the grid is the primary data file. Subsequent rows will be secondary data files.

You can adjust the column widths by placing the cursor on the separator line between the column headers. The cursor will change shape to a vertical bar with a left and right arrow. Simply drag the separator line in the direction you want the column width to go. The separator line to the right side of the column name controls that column's width.

6. Change the Initial size setting if the default setting is too small or large. The File group setting specifies a file group for the data files. Log files are never part of a file group. The file group is another method of handling the administration of similar objects.

7. By checking the Automatically grow file check box you allow the file to grow in the increments indicated in the next step.

8. The File growth option gives you the choice to allow growth by specific amounts by entering that value in the In megabytes box, or by a specific percentage of the database's current size by entering a value in the By percent box. The final database size is determined by selecting either Unrestricted file growth or Restrict file growth and entering a final size value. Figure 3-3 shows what the first part of the Database Properties dialog box should look like.

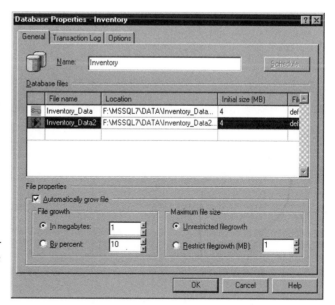

Figure 3–3 *The settings for data files of the new database Inventory are set.*

9. Now click the Transaction Log tab to set up the transaction log file for the new database. As you see in Figure 3-4, SQL Server has already started the process for the new log file. A default transaction log of 25 percent of the total size of all data files is entered as the first transaction log. You can create additional transaction logs if required. You also have the same file growth and limiter parameters that can be set as are available for the data files.

Figure 3–4 *SQL Server makes A default transaction log ready. You can make any adjustments to the settings that you require.*

10. The Options tab contains several options concerning the accessibility of the database, and some settings for the database. Figure 3-5 shows the Options properties available to you.

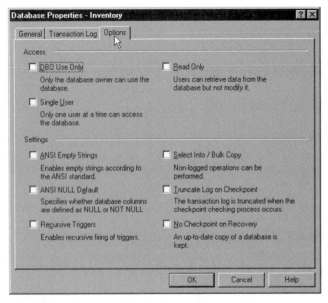

Figure 3–5 *The Options tab of the Database Properties dialog box is used to set accessibility options and certain settings.*

11. Once you have made all of the selections in the Options tab and have set all of the necessary parameters for data and transaction files, you are ready to create the database. Click the OK button and SQL Server will create the database. When the process is complete you will be able to see your new database listed underneath the Database icon.

The alternatives available to you on the Options tab are divided into two major groups: Access and Settings. The Access group has three options:

- DBO Use Only—This option allows only the database owner access to the database. This setting is commonly used when performing bulk copy or Select Into queries.
- Single User—Select this option when you want to restrict access to a database to only one user at a time. This setting is often used on development databases or to diagnose access problems.
- Read Only—Data can be accessed from the database, but not edited.

The Settings group has six options available.

- ANSI Empty Strings—When checked, this option allows empty strings to be entered into a column and not to be treated as a NULL value. An empty string would be a blank space, and must follow the SQL-92 standards.
- ANSI NULL Default—When this option is checked, any new columns created in existing tables or all columns created in a new table will allow NULL values by default. You can override this option on individual columns by removing the checkmark in the Allow Nulls column.
- Recursive Triggers—This option allows a trigger to call itself and refire in response to an update on the table where the trigger is attached.
- Select Into / Bulk Copy—Sets the table for nonlogged operations. Once the nonlogged transactions have been completed, you must back up or dump the database and then turn this option off.
- Truncate Log on Checkpoint—Checking this option allows the transaction log to be truncated each time a checkpoint occurs. Truncating the log means that all committed transactions are removed, and a checkpoint occurs when the transaction log is 70 percent full.
- No Checkpoint on Recovery—When this option is checked and set to ON, then a checkpoint record is not added to the database after it is recovered during SQL Server startup procedures.

File groups are a new object specific to SQL Server 7.0. A file group comprises the operating system files that contain all of the data for a single

SQL Server database. A file group is an object that belongs to the database and can contain the operating system files for a single database. A database can contain more than one file group. When you create a new database, it is created on the file group "default." Once you have created the first default file group, you can add additional file groups.

You can add a new file group to a database through the `CREATE` or `ALTER DATABASE` process. An `ALTER DATABASE` statement such as the one shown here will add a new file group to the pubs database:

```
ALTER DATABASE pubs
CREATE FILEGROUP pubs_data
```

Once you have added a new file group to a database, you will be able to use it for additional database storage. You can place specific database objects on individual files, or you can allow SQL Server to decide how objects will be dispersed through the files.

Tables

Microsoft SQL Server uses two types of tables: *system tables* and *user tables*. Some system tables are stored within each database and are called database catalog (or system) tables, while others known as system catalog (or master system) tables are contained only within the master database. System tables are used by Microsoft SQL Server to keep track of user database objects, including table constraints, permissions, users, groups, and aliases.

Note Whenever you make changes to the system tables you should be sure to back up the master database. This will ensure that your most current changes are available in case of a media failure. If you do not back up the master database, your only option in the unhappy event of a disk crash is to rebuild the master database from the Microsoft SQL Server CD. This will require you to rebuild or reload each of the user databases again so that their information is included in the master database's system tables. you will not be able to use any of the user databases until this possibly lengthy process has been completed. Remember that the system tables in the master database include all of the information about user logins, permissions, database location, and size.

The table is the object that users will become most familiar with and is the storage object for all data. You can have many tables in each database. Tables are generally used to store data of a single type such as: customers, vendors, inventory items, orders, purchases, or purchase line items. Tables can be created to store any type of information. Any user who has been granted the necessary permission by the database owner can create tables in a database. Of course, if you are the system administrator or the database owner you do not need to be granted specific permission to add tables. You can easily add a new user table to an existing database by following these few steps:

1. Click on the +(plus sign) beside the Inventory database in the Enterprise Manager window and open its object list. You can open the New Table dialog box by doing one of the following:

   - Right-click on the Tables icon and select New Table from the shortcut menu.

   - Right-click on the Tables icon and select New, Table from the shortcut menus.

   - Select the Tables icon and then choose Action, New Table from the menu.

   - Select the Tables icon and then click the Add a new button on the toolbar.

2. Unlike previous versions of SQL Server, the name is entered first rather than last. Type `Products` in the Choose Name dialog box as the name for the new table. Click the OK button to continue.

3. Use the table grid to enter the necessary information for each column that will be part of the new table. If the order of the columns is important, be sure that you have a plan before you begin. You can easily delete a column from the grid, but you cannot change the order of the columns. Of course, this does not matter quite so much with a database that is not directly accessed by the end user. Enter the following column information in the indicated position in Table 3.1:

Table 3.1 *Column Information*

Column Name	Datatype	Length	Precision	Scale	Allow Nulls
ProductID	Int	4	10	0	No
ProductName	Varchar	35	0	0	No
QtyOnHand	Decimal	9	18	4	Yes
Cost	Money	8	19	4	Yes
Price	Money	8	19	4	Yes
VendorID	Int	4	10	0	Yes

A checkmark in the box displayed in the Allow Nulls, Identity, and Is RowGuid columns indicates either a Yes or an On setting. Click in the boxes in the Allow Nulls column when you need a Yes response. Figure 3-6 shows the completed table.

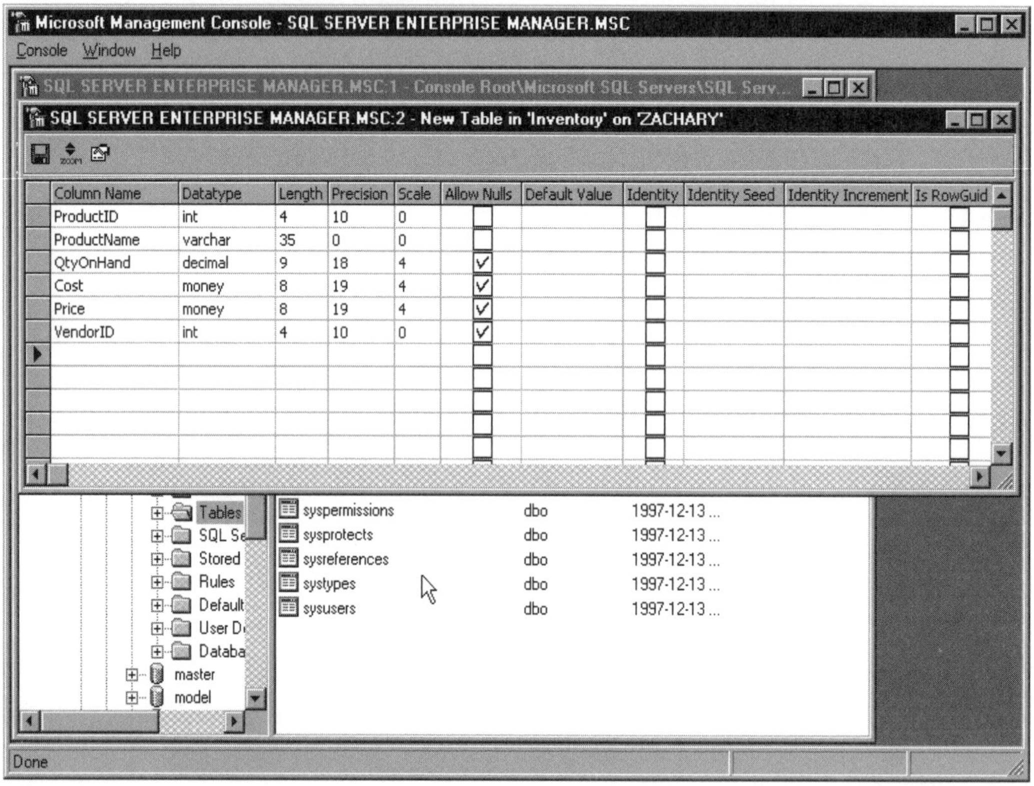

Figure 3–6 *Here the new table grid has been completed with the necessary information.*

When building a new table using the SQL Server Enterprise Manager interface, there are several optional parameters that you can apply during the creation of a new table. Several of these parameters were used while building the Inventory table, but there were several more that were not used. As you created each new column, you will have noticed that some of the values were automatically filled in for you. These default parameters vary depending on the datatype you select for the column. The various parameters available when building a new table include:

- Column Name—This is the value that will be used as the name of the column. You will use this value any time that the column is used in a query, or referred to in any application.

- Datatype—Determines the type of information that will be allowed in the column. For example, if you select a numeric datatype you cannot enter text into the column.
- Length—This is the maximum length of data that can be entered into the column. The default value will vary depending on the selected datatype. You can increase or decrease this value for most datatypes.
- Precision—This value has meaning only when some type of numeric datatype is selected. The value in this column is the maximum number of digits that can be stored in the column.
- Scale—This value is the maximum number of digits displayed to the right of a decimal point. The scale is not defined for any column that uses an approximate floating-point number.
- Allow Nulls—When this column displays a checkmark then the column will allow null values. A null is not equal to a 0 (zero) or blank value. A null value is one that is either unknown or undefined. A primary key column cannot contain a null value and so SQL Server will not allow this property to be changed.
- Default Value—A default value is one that will be automatically entered into a column if no other value is entered. For example, in an employee table you can set a default value for State.
- Identity—Check this column if you want it to be an identity column. Only one column per table can have this property set.
- Identity Seed—This is the first value to be used for an identity column.
- Identity Increment—This is the value SQL Server will use to increment the identity value for each subsequent record added to the table.
- Is RowGuid—When checked, this column is identified as the row global unique identifier column. Only one column per table can be designated the RowGuid column and that column must use the uniqueidentifier datatype. This column can then be used to uniquely identify the row of information in a table.

Some of these values can be changed when editing a table, while others cannot. For example, some datatypes cannot be converted to another datatype, for instance, varchar to money is not an allowed change.

Views

A *view* is a different look at the data contained in a table or a group of related tables. You can create select statements based on views just as you would the table(s) behind the view. Views are often used to create a condensed version, or a window of a table, that can be used by a group of users who do not need access to all of the information contained in the table.

For example, you may want to create a view of a personnel table for someone in the marketing department. A view can be created that will display selected employees, grouped by department or title, and include their education qualifications. You can exclude sensitive information such as salaries and dependent status from the view. To the marketing individual, the view is the same as if they were working with the real data in the table. Views are an excellent method of securing sensitive information from unauthorized access. You can give users access to the view but not to the table behind the view. Other reasons to create and use views could include:

- Allowing customers to browse through inventory tables, but not see your vendor and cost data.
- Use views to preselect data to be exported to another program.
- Create different views for different user groups. This allows users with differing needs and skill levels to work with the same information in their own way.
- A single view can be used that combines information from several tables. This allows a user to view and manipulate data from several tables without having to create, or even know about, the necessary joins needed to combine the information.
- Compiling statistical information about customers or employees.

Like all other objects, a view can be created or dropped, and permission to use the view granted, revoked, and denied. A view can be used to add, delete, or update information in the underlying table, but dropping a view has no effect on the table. A view can be created only in the current database.

You can use the alias function to change the column names displayed in the views result set from those used in the original tables so that they are easier to understand and reference in the view. Here, the au_lname and au_fname columns will be renamed "Last Name," and "First Name," respectively. These names will be used to reference the columns whenever working with this view. When creating a SELECT view, some functions, such as ORDER BY, are not available to you. You can use these functions when you call the view to display the current results set, but not when creating the view.

A view can be created very easily by using the SQL Enterprise Manager window or from the Query Analyzer window. While the end results using either method is the same, their methods of creating the view appear different. In the following steps you will create a new view for the pubs table using Query Analyzer:

1. Open the Query Analyzer application and select the pubs database in the Database text box and type the following:

```
CREATE VIEW Author_Phone_List
AS
SELECT 'Last Name'=au_lname, 'First Name'=au_fname, phone
FROM authors
```

2. Click the Execute Query button to complete the statement. Figure 3-7 shows you both the completed CREATE statement and its results. You will know that you were successful in creating the new view when you see the statement:

```
The command(s) completed successfully.
```

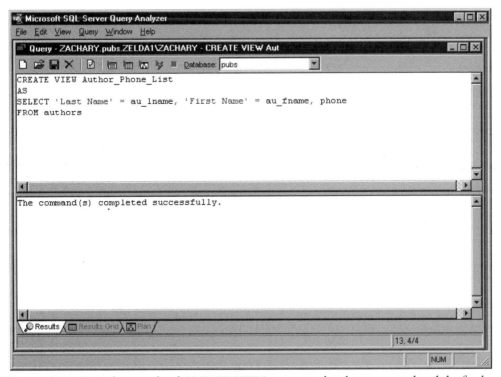

Figure 3–7 *Here the completed CREATE VIEW statement has been executed and the final results displayed.*

Views are an excellent way to allow users access to parts of a table or tables. Each time that the view is accessed a new results set with updated information is displayed; it is not static from the time it is created as a report would be, but is dynamic and always uses the most current information available.

You can also use a view to define a group of rows that will be displayed for a selected user or group. Unlike a table, where you can restrict access to specific columns, with a view you can also restrict access to selected rows. Since the view is based on a query, you can structure it so that only a selected group of rows is displayed in the view.

Permissions to use a view must be specifically granted, revoked, or denied. A user of the table does not automatically inherit permission to use the view.

Database Roles

Database roles have replaced the User Groups as they were used in earlier version of SQL Server. A role allows you to group users by functions and need for access to database objects. When you create a role, you add permissions to use various objects within a database. You can then add users to the role. Any permission that is granted, revoked, or denied to a role is then applied to the user. Using roles to manage permissions is much easier than trying to manage multiple users as they move from job to job and department to department.

When you grant permissions to a role, and then add a user to the role, the most restrictive permissions are applied to the individual user. Roles will be discussed in more detail in Chapter 8, "Security."

Defaults

Instead of using a null value in a column, you can provide a default value that will be automatically inserted if you do not specify a value for the column when adding a new record. Default values are not retroactively applied to rows that already exist in a table. A default value is only inserted when you do not explicitly insert your own value, or null, into the column. Default values are often used for those columns that are often filled in with the same piece of data. For example, if 90 percent of your customers all live in the state of California, you may want to provide the State column with a default value of "CA." Then, whenever a new customer is entered into your database, SQL Server will automatically enter the default value "CA" in the State column for this customer. The data entry clerk can override the default value whenever necessary.

Default values can be set when a table is created or later on by editing the table or using the CREATE DEFAULT statement. A default value set within the table structure is also called a default constraint, while a default created with the CREATE DEFAULT statement creates a default object. When you use the CREATE DEFAULT statement, you must also bind the default value specified to a specific column. This is a separate step and not done automatically. It is recommended that you create default values within the table structure when you create the table, or by altering the table. Default values created in this way become constraints on the specific table and column because they are automatically dropped if the table is dropped, and they incur less overhead. If you have a default value that is rather complex or long, and it is to be applied to several columns, you may then want to use the CREATE DEFAULT statement. This way you do not have to alter several tables and columns. Simply create the default value and then bind it to the necessary tables and columns.

There are many uses for default values in a database. Whenever you have a table with a column that is often filled in with the same value, set a default for the column using that value. Examples include county, state, credit terms, or minimum hourly wage. You can probably think of many other uses for a default value, depending on the database you may be using. For example, the employee table in the pubs database uses four default values, as seen in Figure 3-8.

If a default value or expression is defined for a column it is shown in the Default Value column. Default values are entered enclosed within parentheses (). Notice how the various datatypes are entered; any type of number value is entered within the parentheses, while a char or varchar value will be entered enclosed in single quote marks within the parentheses. The column hire_date uses a different type of default value. The hire_date column uses datetime as a datatype and wants to have the current system date entered into this column. The expression getdate() is enclosed within the parentheses and tells SQL Server to fetch the current date on the servers system clock and enter that value into the column. A user adding a new employee to the table can always override a default value by typing a different value into the column, if they have the appropriate permissions to do so. Default values must be compatible with the datatype of the column. For example, you cannot create a default value of ('CA') in a datetime column. You can easily create your own defaults by entering them into the Default Value column, as seen in Figure 3-8.

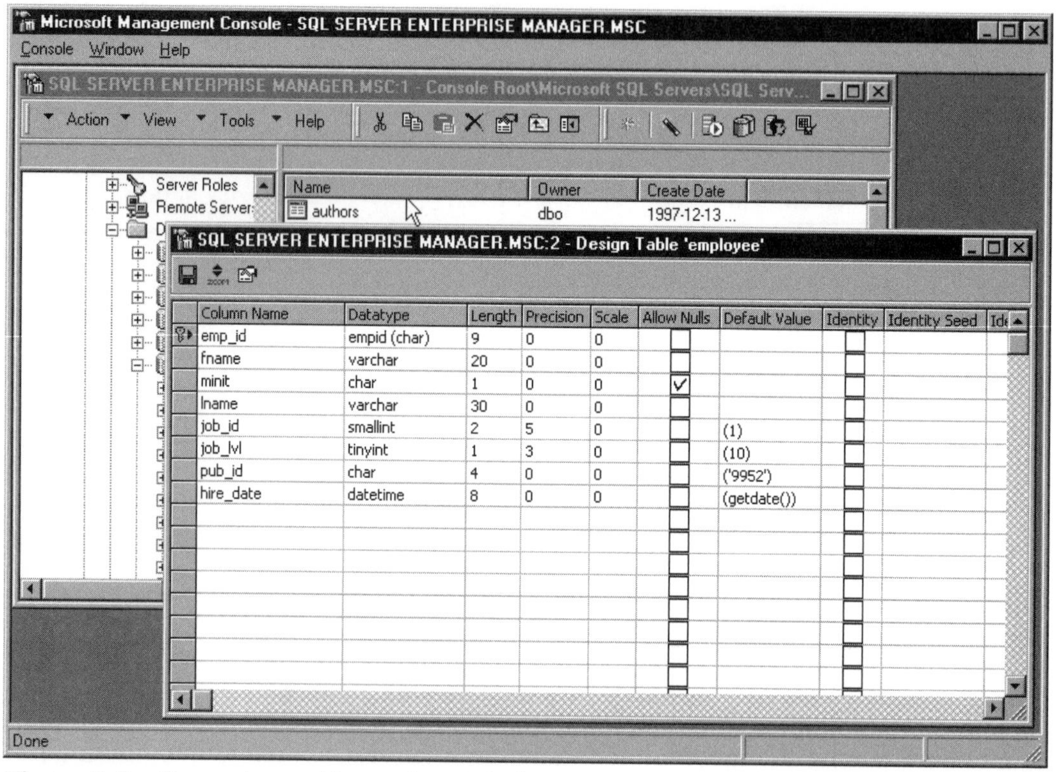

Figure 3–8 *The employee table uses four default values as shown in the column labeled Default.*

The second method you can use to create a default value for a column is through the use of the CREATE DEFAULT statement. A default created using this method is a default object and not attached to a specific table and column until you bind it. Use the CREATE DEFAULT statement like this:

1. Open the Query Analyzer, select pubs in the Database text box and type:

```
/* default publishers country value is "US" */
CREATE DEFAULT def_publ_country
AS 'US'
```

This statement will create a default value of "US" for the country column, once you complete the process of binding the default to a column. If you were creating a default for a numeric datatype, or an expression, do not enclose the default value in quote marks.

2. Execute this statement by clicking the Execute Query button. Figure 3-9 shows both the completed CREATE DEFAULT statement and its results.

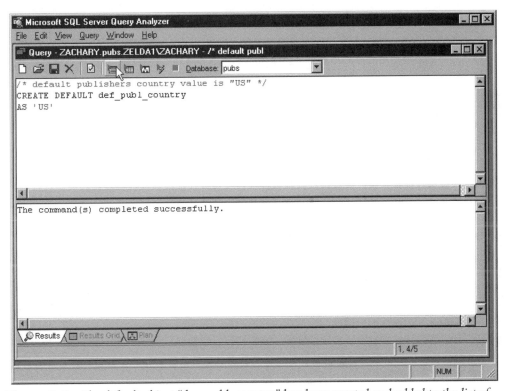

Figure 3–9 *The default object "dep_publ_country" has been created and added to the list of default objects in the pubs database.*

3. Now bind the default value to a specific table and column by using the stored procedure sp_bindefault like this:

```
sp_bindefault def_publ_country, 'publishers.country'
```

Note This example will fail because a default value of "USA" has already been placed on this particular column. You are allowed only one default value per column in a table.

Be sure that you surround the target, 'table_name.column_name' with single quote marks, otherwise SQL Server will assume that you are assigning this default to a user-defined datatype, and not to an existing table and column. Defaults created as shown above are ANSI-SQL defaults that you will be able to port to other ANSI-SQL compatible databases.

Defaults are an excellent method of helping you to ensure that the data entered into a table is consistent and complete. Be sure to use them as necessary, but do not overuse them. Overuse of defaults can lead a data entry clerk to not pay attention to the information being placed in the database. They can become complacent and assume that the data is entered correctly.

Rules

SQL Server uses rules as a device for enforcing data integrity on columns and user-defined datatypes. Rules help to ensure that the data entered into a table is consistent with the requirements of the database. A rule can be created that will ensure that only a specific range of values are entered into a column by restricting allowed values to a specific list of values from another table, or to a selected range such as between 500 and 1000 inclusive.

A rule is a T-SQL condition that defines a data integrity constraint. You can use any of the comparative operators that are allowed in a WHERE clause, but you must use an operator that is allowed with the datatype of the column for which you are creating the rule. For example, you can't use the LIKE operator with a numeric datatype. A rule does not apply to data already existing in the column. Only one rule can be bound to a column at any one time. If you bind a rule to a column that already has a rule bound to it, SQL Server will unbind the original rule and then bind the new rule.

You can use CHECK constraints instead of rules. You can use any number of CHECK constraints on a table or a column.

There are limits to the functions that you can use when applying a rule. Rules can only deal with constant values, SQL Server functions, and edit masks. Rules are applied to data before an INSERT or an UPDATE. This allows SQL Server to check the data against the rules before actually inserting the new data or updating existing data. If the new information doesn't meet the rules, SQL Server will display an error message telling you so. Rules must be given a name with a maximum of 30 characters. This name must be a valid name under the rules for identifiers, and the name must be unique within the database.

Just like default values, rules can be created using the CREATE RULE statement or in the SQL Server Enterprise Manager application. Follow these steps to create a rule:

1. Open the SQL Enterprise Manager window and expand Databases and then pubs. Right-click on Rules object and select New Rule from the shortcut menu, opening the Rule Properties dialog box.
2. Type SSAN in the Name text box. This will become the name for the new rule. In the Text combo type the following:

```
@SSAN LIKE
'[0-9][0-9][0-9]-[0-9][0-9]-[0-9][0-9][0-9][0-9]'
```

This rule will require the user to enter a series of three numbers followed by a dash, two more numbers, another dash, and then four numbers. Any other entry will not be ruled as a valid entry and the INSERT or UPDATE will fail.

3. Click the OK button to add this new rule into the list of rules for this database. Figure 3-10 shows the new rule.

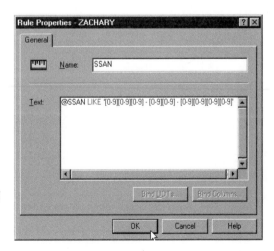

Figure 3–10 *This new rule will require that the entry placed into a column be formatted for a U.S. social security number.*

4. Open the Query Analyzer application and select the pubs database from the Database text box. Type the following query in the upper pane:

```
sp_bindrule SSAN, 'authors.[au_id]'
```

Where sp_bindrule is the stored procedure used to bind a rule to another object, and SSAN is the rule to be bound. The next parameter is the table and column that the rule will be bound to. You must use the syntax shown above to bind the rule to a column or SQL Server will assume that the rule is to bound to a user-defined datatype.

5. Click the Execute Query button to bind the rule to the column.

Figure 3-11 shows the final results of this stored procedure.

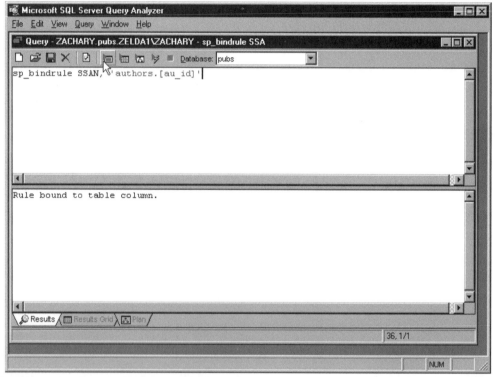

Figure 3–11 *The SSAN rule is now bound to the au_id column in the authors table, and will require the user to enter an author's ID number in a standard U.S. Social Security format.*

Stored Procedures

Stored procedures are database objects that are independent of individual tables, unlike triggers. They are a precompiled set of T-SQL statements and can be built to use parameters passed to them, or to return status, rows, or output arguments back to the client who called the procedure. Stored procedures can call other procedures, or even themselves again, creating very complex systems. Using stored procedures can add significant enhancements to your application.

When you first install SQL Server many stored procedures are also installed. Throughout this chapter you have used several stored procedures. A system stored procedure will begin with the prefix `sp_`. These system stored procedures are stored in the master database and are owned by the system administrator. Some of these procedures can be run from within other databases, but many of them are specific to the master database and are used to perform various maintenance functions. When called from a database other than master, they will act on the tables of the calling database.

You can create your own stored procedures to help speed up processes, to define business rules within the database, and to shield users from the database and its tables. Normally, a user-defined stored procedure will be stored with the database that it was created for. If the stored procedure will be used by other databases, then you can place it in the master and/or model databases. A user-defined stored procedure is more correctly called a user-defined system stored procedure if it:

- is stored in the master database
- is owned by the database owner (DBO)
- its name begins with sp_

Another type of stored procedure is an *extended* stored procedure, some of which are also installed with SQL Server. Extended stored procedures are compiled within a dynamic-link library (DLL) file and are called and used in the same manner that any other stored procedure is used. More than one extended stored procedure may be incorporated within a single dll file. Extended stored procedures can be used to call for and return information from a remote server, all the while being completely transparent to the client.

One reason to create and use stored procedures is that you can improve overall system performance by reducing the network traffic. The client calls to a stored procedure on the server and may pass some additional parameters that are required by the stored procedure. The SQL Server in turn runs the compiled version of the SQL statements and passes the answer or other information back to the client. Instead of having many SQL statements passing back and forth over the network, only the original call, along with any parameters and the results, are passed over the network.

Stored procedures are called by name. If you do not use the stored procedures name as the first word in an SQL statement, you must precede it with the keyword EXECUTE. Writing a stored procedure is a simple process that requires you to give the procedure a unique name, and then to write the SQL statements that are the heart of the stored procedure. The next few steps show you how to build a stored procedure that returns a results set displaying authors and the titles they have written:

1. Open the SQL Enterprise Manager application and drill down to the pubs database. Right click on master and select New, Stored Procedure from the shortcut menus. The Stored Procedures Properties dialog box is now displayed. From this dialog box you can create new procedures and edit existing ones. You can, of course, also use the Query Analyzer program.

2. Replace <PROCEDURE NAME> with the name for your new procedure by typing `au_pub_titles`. Complete the rest of the procedure as follows, and seen in Figure 3-12:

```
CREATE PROCEDURE au_pub_titles AS
SELECT a.au_lname, t.title, p.pub_name
FROM authors a, titleauthor ta, titles t, publishers p
WHERE a.au_id = ta.au_id
AND ta.title_id = t.title_id
AND t.pub_id = p.pub_id
RETURN
```

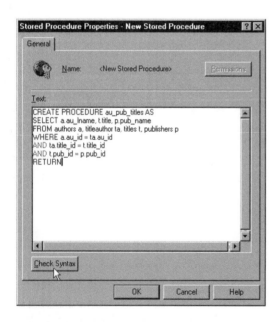

Figure 3–12 *Here you see the completed stored procedure in the Properties dialog box.*

3. Click the Check Syntax button. If your procedure is syntactically correct, you will see a dialog box telling you so. If there is a problem with

the procedure, then the displayed dialog box will indicate where the problem exists.

4. Click the OK button to create the stored procedure. SQL Server does not return anything indicating that it is complete. You can see your new stored procedure by opening the pubs database; display the available stored procedures by clicking on the Stored Procedures icon. In Figure 3-13 you can see the new procedure at the top of the list.

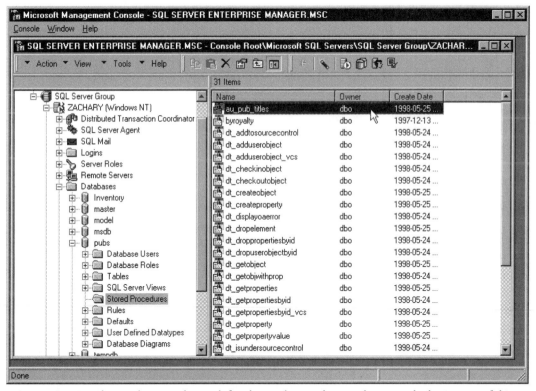

Figure 3–13 *The newly created user-defined stored procedure is shown at the beginning of this list. It is first on the list because it is first in alphabetical order.*

This stored procedure does not contain any code containing variable requiring user input. When you do include such variables you must declare the datatype for the parameter. You can use any of the standard datatypes or any user-defined datatypes if they exist within the database where the stored procedure is created. A simple stored procedure as shown here contains the single parameter `@au_lname`.

```
CREATE PROCEDURE titles_by_author
(@au_lname varchar(40))
AS
SELECT a.au_lname, t.title
FROM authors a, titleauthor ta, titles t
WHERE a.au_id = ta.au_id
AND ta.title_id = t.title_id
AND au_lname LIKE @au_lname
RETURN
```

This stored procedure returns a results set that displays all books by the selected author, along with his or her last name. The variable is declared in the second line of the procedure. Using Query Analyzer this stored procedure would be called like this:

```
titles_by_author <authors_last_name>
```

Simply include the last name of the author for whom you want to see a listing of titles as the parameter <authors_last_name>.

Triggers

Triggers are special stored procedures that automatically activate when a specified condition is met. When the condition for the trigger is met, the trigger fires and the actions required by the trigger are performed. Triggers are most often used for enforcing complex referential integrity that cannot be met by using a set of simple constraints. Remember, constraints act on the table that they are attached to, while a trigger may be activated by the action of a single table but can act across many tables, other databases, and even other servers. Triggers can be created that will execute a DLL within Windows NT, which in turn can access data from other programs, or pass information to other programs.

One example of a trigger is the ability to cascade updates and deletes of primary keys. For example, your vendor ID is created from a combination of zip code and company name, and one of your vendors moves to a new location. The company name probably doesn't change, but the zip code very likely does. You can use a trigger to automatically perform a cascade update that will change the information in all tables that reference the vendor ID for the particular vendor so that they now reference the new vendor ID code. Using a trigger for this operation is much simpler than requiring a data entry clerk to manually go through all of the tables in the database searching for each occurrence of the old vendor ID to update them—very likely missing one or more in the process.

Earlier versions of SQL Server allowed a maximum of three triggers: one each for `INSERT`, `UPDATE`, and `DELETE` statements for a table. Now with SQL Server 7, you can create multiple triggers of each type. If you give a trigger the name of an existing trigger, of the same type, within a table, the new trigger will overwrite the current trigger. Whenever a condition is met that fires a trigger, it is only fired one time for every statement that calls it. This means that if your statement modifies multiple rows of data, you must ensure that your trigger will fire for all the modified rows and not just simply the first or last. A trigger can execute many functions and can be nested up to 16 deep. This means that trigger1 can call trigger2, which in turn can call trigger3, and so forth, with trigger15 finally calling trigger16. The trigger can be constructed such that if all of the actions required by the trigger are not met, then the trigger will roll back the transaction. Be sure any trigger you create that rolls back a transaction sends an error to the user so they know the transaction was not processed.

If your database is using a compatibility level of 65 or lower, then any new trigger of a given type will replace an existing trigger. You can use multiple triggers if you are using a compatibility level of 70 or higher.

There are several SQL statements that cannot be used within a trigger:

- CREATE statements, including the creation of temporary tables
- All ALTER table, database, procedure, view, and trigger statements
- SELECT INTO statements
- All DROP statements
- TRUNCATE table statements
- UPDATE STATISTICS statements
- GRANT, REVOKE, and DENY permissions statements
- LOAD database and log statements
- RECONFIGURE any object statements
- SELECT INTO statements
- DISK INIT and DISK RESIZE statements

SQL Server now allows triggers to be recursively fired. If a trigger is invoked by an `UPDATE` statement for multiple records, it previously acted only on the first record and then terminated. You can now enable Recursive Triggers by using the stored procedure sp_dboption.

When a trigger is fired, it creates two temporary tables: *inserted* and *deleted*. These tables are views of the transaction log and are available only for the duration of the trigger. Once the trigger completes its actions, these views no longer exist. A trigger that contains an INSERT statement stores the rows that are inserted into the table in the *inserted* table, while a DELETE statement stores the rows that are being deleted in the *deleted* table. An UPDATE statement acts if it is a DELETE statement followed by an INSERT statement. Triggers can use the inserted and deleted tables to determine if and how they should proceed with an action. If any member of a nested trigger group does a ROLLBACK TRANSACTION, then no triggers further along in the nested levels will fire.

Triggers like other database objects, require a name, the table to which it will be attached, the actions that will activate it, and what it is to do. Triggers can be created by using the CREATE TRIGGER statement, or from within the SQL Enterprise Manager window. Only the database owner or the system administrator can create or drop a trigger, and these permissions cannot be granted to others. Create a simple trigger that will perform a cascade delete from the titles table to the titleauthor table by following these steps:

1. Open the SQL Enterprise Manager application, drill down to the pubs database, and click on the Tables icon.
2. Right-click on the titles table, select Task, Manage Triggers from the shortcut menus to display the Trigger Properties dialog box. Now type the following trigger in the large window, as shown in Figure 3-14:

```
CREATE TRIGGER delete_titles ON titles
FOR DELETE
AS
IF @@rowcount = 0
RETURN
/* Cascade delete from titles to titleauthor table */
DELETE titleauthor
FROM titleauthor t, deleted d
WHERE t.title_id = d.title_id
IF @@error !=0
BEGIN
PRINT 'Error occurred in deletion in related tables'
ROLLBACK TRAN
END
RETURN
```

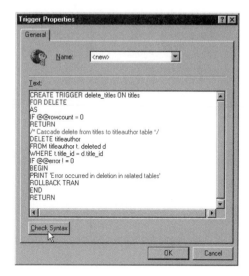

Figure 3–14 *The 'delete_titles' trigger is ready to be saved and bound to the titles table. You can click the Check Syntax button to check your trigger before attempting to save it.*

3. Click the OK button to save the new trigger and bind it to the titles table.

Some things to note about this trigger include:

The first part of the statement creates the trigger, specifying the table to which it is attached and on what it will trigger—delete, insert, or update.

The next part of the statement checks to see if any rows were altered. Remember, the trigger fires even if data was not altered or deleted. With the IF statement IF @@rowcount = 0 is true, then the next action, RETURN, is executed and the trigger action terminates. Otherwise, the trigger continues to the next statement.

The meat of the trigger tells it what to do. In this case, to look at both the titleauthor and deleted tables; if a value for title_id in the deleted table exists in the titleauthor table, then the trigger deletes the corresponding row in the titleauthor table.

The final statements are used to trap errors that may occur. If SQL Server is not able to delete a row from the titleauthor table, then it will return the error message "Error occurred in deletion in related tables," and roll back the transaction. Remember, a trigger is fired from within a transaction. This means that the entire transaction, the deletion of a row in the titleauthor table, and the first part of the transaction when a row was deleted from titles, are all rolled back.

This trigger does not check for any dependencies that may exist between tables. Additional code will have to be written to affect all of the tables that reference the title_id column.

Cursors

What is a cursor? In SQL Server it is not the mouse pointer, or the blinking bar in a word processor. A cursor provides a mechanism that gives you a subset of a results set. When you use a SELECT query on a database, the entire set of rows that meet the requirements of the WHERE condition are delivered. Often in an interactive or client/server networking environment, this possibly large result can be difficult to work with at the client level. A cursor gives you a method of working with a subset of the results set or just a row at a time.

Cursors can be either *dynamic* or *forward only*. A dynamic cursor can scroll through the results set as needed. The FETCH statement will determine the location of the cursor. A forward-only cursor is limited to moving from row to row in a single direction. Each FETCH statement delivers the next row from the results set.

When using a T-SQL cursor it must be explicitly activated with a DECLARE cursor statement. If you do not declare the cursor, then T-SQL will return the entire results set before any other statement is executed. On the other hand, cursors that use OLE DB, ODBC, or ADO can be implicitly opened on any results set returned by an SQL statement. The default settings for these cursors is the same as a T-SQL cursor, but you can implement the cursor by changing any of its default attributes or properties. There are three forms of cursors that you can implement with SQL Server 7:

- T-SQL cursors are implemented with the DECLARE CURSOR statement and used in T-SQL stored procedures, scripts, and triggers. T-SQL cursors are server-based only.
- The API server-based cursors support OLE DB, ODBC, ADO, and DB-Library. When a client requests the cursor, the API transmits it to the server for action by the specific API cursor.

- Client-based cursors are API cursors using the SQL Server ODBC driver, DB-Library dll, or the ADO dll. All the requested results set is cached on the client and then the cursor is implemented against the set.

Cursors are most often used to provide a method for single-row operations to be performed in a results set from a query. Cursors can complement the normal page-lock methods used in most queries when set operations are impractical, though with SQL Server 7's very efficient ability to use row-level locking, cursors are becoming less necessary. With a cursor, you can increase the granularity of your queries by allowing row-level functions, instead of page-level. Data in tables can be updated through a cursor, except in the case of a T-SQL cursor declared with the keyword INSENSITIVE.

Cursors should generally be used only when other methods that use a results set cannot be found. The cursor places a substantial overhead burden on a server's resources.

As all objects that are used in SQL Server, the cursor must be named within a T-SQL statement. Cursors, like other objects, are restricted to the requirements of an identifier. When you create a statement that uses a cursor, the usual procedure will follow this format:

- DECLARE cursor statement. This statement names the cursor and uses a select statement specifying what tables and columns are to be selected for results set this cursor will work with. When using ISQL, Query Analyzer, or SQL Server Enterprise Manager, the statement must be executed by using a GO command before the remaining parts of the statement can use the cursor.
- OPEN statement. This statement opens the declared cursor.
- FETCH statement. The FETCH statement specifies the conditions, if any, that must be met for a rows inclusion into the results set.

- CLOSE statement. This statement closes an open cursor. You must name the cursor that is to be closed.

- DEALLOCATE statement. This final statement removes the data structures created by the DECLARE cursor statement.

A FORWARD ONLY cursor is the default unless specified in the DECLARE CURSOR statement. This means that the cursor, when used with an INSERT statement, begins with the first row in a table and continues forward from row to row throughout the results set. As the cursor moves to a new row, the row is locked and no other user is allowed to update the row. Once the cursor has finished and moved forward to the next row, it can be updated by another user, but the cursor never goes back to look at the updated information, unless you have specifically declared the cursor to be able to scroll through the results set.

You can create a cursor that is able to scroll through a table by using the keyword SCROLL in the DECLARE statement. With the SCROLL keyword, your cursor can scroll both backward and forward, and even move to an absolute row number or specific number of rows from the current row. If data is updated in the underlying table, the next FETCH statement will return an updated results set.

A cursor that is declared with the keyword INSENSITIVE is not able to update the underlying table. When the INSENSITIVE keyword is used, a copy of the selected data is placed into a temporary table. The cursor then acts upon this temporary table. This is an effective method when you are using a cursor for creating a report and only need a snapshot of the current data.

Cursors will be created and declared by using the Query Analyzer. A simple cursor is shown in Figure 3-15, and is built like this:

```
DECLARE cur_author CURSOR

FOR SELECT au_id, au_lname, phone

FROM authors

OPEN cur_author

FETCH NEXT FROM cur_author
```

To view the next row from the results set you only have to issue the FETCH statement again.

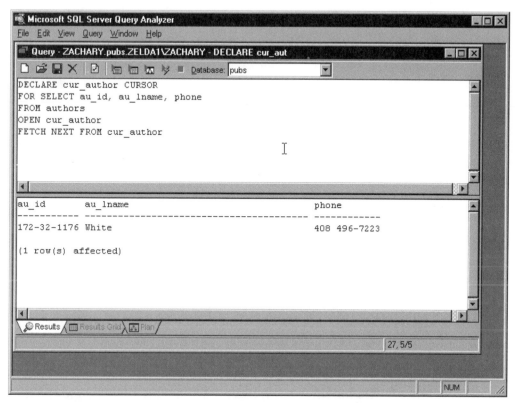

Figure 3–15 *This T-SQL cursor returns a selected group of columns from a table.*

Indexes

An index on a table in an SQL database acts just like any index that you use in everyday life. It is a tool that enables you to quickly search for some specific bit or category of information. An index is a database object used by SQL Server to speed access to data contained in the table. Indexes create a method that SQL can use when performing a SELECT query so that every row does not have to be scanned for records that meet the WHERE clause. There are two types of indexes that you can use: clustered and nonclustered. The SQL query optimizer will decide if an index can be used to increase the speed of the query when it looks at the individual tables and data to be selected.

Indexes can be created that include multiple columns. For example, you could have a table that stores information about the individual line items on all orders. You could not create a unique index on an invoice number column because you can have more than one item sold per invoice and this would cause a conflict. At the same time you could not use an Item ID number either because you would obviously sell the same item to many different customers. This problem is usually alleviated through the use of a combination index using both the InvoiceID and ItemID columns to create a unique index. An index made of one or two columns works well and is often referred to as a *narrow* index. An index made up of three or more columns is called a *wide* index and is not usually recommended. The reason that you do not often see an index of three or more columns is that if a query only makes use of columns B and C, the index will not be used. In a multiple column index, a query looks at the index starting with the first column of the index and moving to the right: column A, then B, and then C. You could reference A and B with a fair likelihood that SQL Server may use the index.

When you create an index, SQL Server places the index on index pages, while the actual data contained in the rows are stored on data pages. An index may consist of several layers of pages, until the lowest level index page points directly to the data page and the rows they contain. A new index can be built by using the CREATE INDEX statement, or by using the SQL Server Manager application. When you first create your indexes, it is better to build the clustered index before the nonclustered index. This ensures that SQL will not have to do the work of sorting and resorting a nonclustered index while the clustered index is being created. The next few steps show you how an index is created:

1. Open the SQL Enterprise Manager window, drill down to the pubs database, then to the Table titles. Right-click on the table titles and select Design Table from the shortcut menu.

2. Right-click the mouse anywhere inside the grid and select Properties from the shortcut menu. You will now see the Properties dialog box for the table. Now click the Index/Keys tab to view the Index sheet for the pubs table, as shown in Figure 3-16.

3. Select the New button on the Index/Keys dialog box. Select the column type from the Column name list box.

4. Type titles_type in the Index name text box. SQL Server inserts a default name that you can use if you want.

5. The Index file group option allows you to place this index on a specific file group for the database. This allows you to store your indexes on a file group other than the default file group.

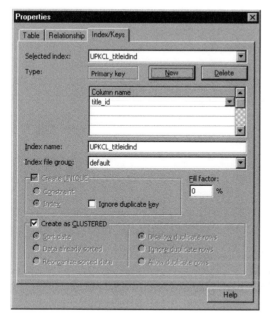

Figure 3–16 *The table Properties dialog box is used to create, remove, and edit indexes within the tables of your databases.*

If you select a second column for the index, notice how the previously selected column is removed from the list box of the available columns. This ensures that you don't accidentally try to use a column twice in a single index.

- The Create UNIQUE option group is used to create a unique Constraint or Index for the selected column(s). If you select Index you also have the option to Ignore duplicate key. This means that when loading information, SQL Server will ignore the insertion of new rows that may violate the unique index rules. You can then change any records that violate this rule and then turn this option off.

- The Create as CLUSTERED option group is used only if this index will be a clustered index. You have several options to go along with a clustered index. You can choose to sort the data as it is entered into the table. You can assume that the data is already sorted in the order necessary, or to reorganize data that is sorted. You can choose to allow, or not allow, duplicate rows, or to ignore duplicate rows.

6. Now click the New button to create the new index, as seen in Figure 3-17.

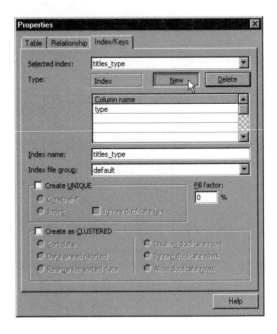

Figure 3–17 *The Manage Indexes dialog box is now complete for the new index being created for this table.*

7. Click the X window close button when you have completed all of the indexes that you need at this time.

Once you have created a clustered index, SQL Server will not allow you to build another clustered index on the table unless you drop it first. Remember, the clustered index causes the rows of data to be physically sorted by the index order so that like values are placed together.

When you create a clustered index on a table be sure that you have the necessary free database space necessary. You will need approximately 120% of the table size in order to create a clustered index. This space enables the table and the index to both exist in the same database while it is being sorted.

CLUSTERED INDEXES

A clustered index means that the data in a table is physically stored in the index's order. There can be only one clustered index per table; after all, you can't force a table to physically order its rows on the disk by two different criteria. A clustered index may have several levels or leaves, with the last leaf being the data pages. Because a clustered index will usually have one or more less leaves than a nonclustered index, it will tend to be faster. Figure 3-18 shows how a clustered index on a column named State can work.

With this clustered index on the state column, SQL Server creates the root page and stores a selected group of values and a set of pointers to the intermediate page, which in turn points to the beginning of each data page in the table. From there, SQL Server will simply scan the page to find the specific data requested. For example, to find the state "Iowa," SQL Server will look first at the root page and find that Iowa must exist between the values Alabama and Maine on the root page. Following the pointer for Alabama brings us to the intermediate page that also begins with the value Alabama. Now scanning through this index page we find that Iowa is after the value Illinois. Following that pointer for Illinois to its data page, SQL Server now scans the data page and finds Iowa. Unlike scanning an entire table, scanning a single page at each step takes very little time.

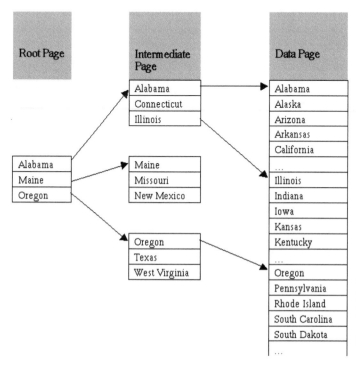

Figure 3–18 *With a clustered index, SQL stores pointers that match the physical sort order of the data. The lowest index level leaf points to the actual data pages.*

NONCLUSTERED INDEXES

The nonclustered index adds an additional step or leaf in the process described above. An additional level of index is required for every row in the table to provide the necessary page pointers. Figure 3-19 shows how a nonclustered index works for finding cities in a table that is clustered by state names.

Figure 3-19 shows how a nonclustered index on a city name in a table that has a clustered index on the state name works. The Root Page is the highest level of the nonclustered index and contains relatively few entries. It is maintained in the table on its own index page and contains pointers to the first entry of each page in the Intermediate Page index level. This next level has more entries and in turn pointers that point to the first item of each page in the Leaf Page index level. The Leaf Page index has one entry for every row in the table. As you add or delete rows in the table index, entries are also added and deleted in the Leaf Page index. This level contains both an entry for each row in the table, and also its row id that consists of both the page and row number for the row it points to.

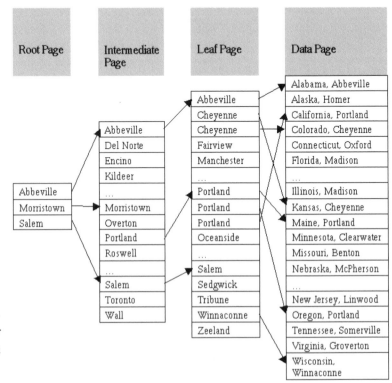

Figure 3–19 *A nonclustered index adds an additional leaf level that keeps track of each individual rrow in a table and its row id.*

Naming Objects

Defining the rules and conventions for identifiers, or more simply *names*, is one of the most important jobs you will have as you create your database schema. Consistency throughout the company database and across servers is very important. By using a consistent naming scheme, you will help to ensure that the foundation used to build your client/server structure will hold together. You want someone who is defining a new database object to be able to easily determine what name to use for the new object, while also ensuring that another user who accesses the object should be able to determine what is stored in it, or what function it will perform.

However you decide to enforce naming standards within your organization, be sure they are consistent across the entire organization. One of the things that you will have to determine is whether to use all uppercase, all lowercase, or mixed-case letters in naming schemes. And whether to use underscores between words, as in *customer_address*, or if a mixed-case convention is better, like *CustomerAddress*. Whatever you and your company decide, be consistent.

Identifiers define the conventions used to name the objects used in SQL Server, such as servers, databases, tables, views, indexes, procedures, triggers, and variables. There are several rules that SQL Server places on naming conventions, and then there are the business rules that you may apply to your own database. The rules that SQL Server places on identifiers are conventions that it requires you to use. You should also set your own naming conventions to be used within your own database.

NAMING RULES

SQL Server has several rules that you are required to follow as you create names for the objects that you create, the servers that you set up, and for any databases you create within a server. The basic rules include the following:

- Names are limited to a maximum of 128 characters.
- The owner of the database can use a name once per object. For example, a single database owner cannot have a stored procedure named min_qty_onhand and at the same time have a constraint also named min_qty_onhand in the same database.
- The first character of a name can be any alphabetic character (a-z or A-Z) or the symbols; @ (at sign), _ (underscore), or # (pound sign). After the first character, you can use any letters, numbers, or the symbols $, #, _.

- The reserved symbols @ and # have specialized meanings when used as the first character of an identifier; the @ symbol denotes a local variable, as you learned in the previous section on stored procedures, while the # symbol means that the named object is a temporary object. An object that begins with a double pound sign "##" is a global temporary object.
- Embedded spaces are not allowed within an identifier, except under the rules of a quoted identifier, which is discussed later in this section.

You should limit the name of a temporary object to a maximum of 29 characters including the #, or ## symbols. SQL Server adds an internal numeric suffix to all temporary objects.

In addition to the rules required by SQL Server, you should consider the following as you set your naming schemes for a production database:

- Do not use a database name for a table name, nor a table name for a column name. While these are strictly legal in SQL Server, it is not good practice.
- Do not use SQL Server reserved words as a name. See the section on "Quoted Identifiers" later in this chapter.
- When naming databases, be sure that your naming scheme can be used by the front-end client. For example, if you have many DOS-based clients the naming scheme should be no longer than eight characters.
- Keep database names short, but descriptive. The name should be descriptive enough that a user or programmer can tell which object they should be using, and not have to consult an object dictionary.
- Standardize your naming schemes. SQL Server is case-sensitive when naming databases.
- Do not use special or hard-to-type characters in a name. After all, you don't want your users or programmers to think about burning you in effigy every time they have to twist their fingers around the keyboard to enter a database name.

AS OBJECT NAMES

Each owner of an object can use a name only once per object, but different owners can use the same object names within the same database. For example, Erik and Casey both have access to the CustomerDB database that is located on the server ZELDA, and have the ability to create new tables within this database. Both Erik and Casey can each create a table named *customer_tbl*. When an object's name is completely qualified it consists of:

```
[[[server].database].owner].object
```

This results in two objects that may appear to have the same name at the lowest level but actually have unique names:

```
ZELDA.CustomerDB.Casey.customer_tbl
ZELDA.CustomerDB.Erik.customer_tbl
```

Those parts of the fully qualified name in the first example that are displayed within the brackets are optional. SQL Server assumes that the default value for owner is the current user, the default value for database is the current database, and the current value for server is the current server. This allows Erik to create a table with the same name that Casey used because the owner name will be different, creating a different qualified name. But if Casey, who is logged into the server ZELDA and into the CustomerDB, wants to access Erik's customer_tbl table, she would have to qualify the table name to *Erik.customer_tbl*. She must, of course, have already been granted permission by Erik as the table's owner to use the table.

QUOTED IDENTIFIERS

The use of quoted identifiers is a feature that was added to Microsoft SQL Server 6.0, aligning its feature set more closely with the current ANSI standards. When using quoted identifiers, use double quotation marks (") or square brackets ([ ]) to indicate keywords within a name—this is called quoted or delimited identifier. While this is acceptable usage as far as the SQL Server's parser is concerned, it is not good practice. Whenever possible, if an object name uses a keyword, reserved word, or standard database terminology that may possibly become a keyword, try finding another word or term that can be used as the identifier. If this is not possible, then use the quoted identifier. Because the keyword *view* is reserved, you must enclose it within the double quotation marks in order to use it as an identifier, hence the name *quoted identifier*. A quoted identifier can be used as follows:

```
CREATE VIEW "view"
(au_lname, au_fname, phone)
AS
SELECT au_lname, au_fname, phone
FROM authors
```

By using the SET command, you can turn SQL Server's ability to use a quoted identifier on or off. By default this setting is on, and you can then use a quoted identifier. If you turn it off, then SQL Server will not be able to see an object that uses a quoted identifier as a name. The above example will fail if you have not turned quoted identifiers on. The SET command must be used at the beginning of each SQL Server session, which will require access to objects that use quoted identifiers. The SET command is used as shown in this example:

```
SET QUOTED_IDENTIFIER on
go
CREATE VIEW "view"
(au_lname, au_fname, phone)
AS
SELECT au_lname, au_fname, phone
FROM authors
go
SET QUOTED_IDENTIFIER off
go
```

You can also use quoted identifiers on standard names without setting QUOTED_IDENTIFIER to on. For example, you can create a table "Employee" and then refer to it as either "Employee" or Employee. If you set QUOTED_IDENTIFIER to on and create the table "Employee" with the double quote marks, you must then always turn QUOTED_IDENTIFIER to on and use the table name "Employee" when referring or using the table.

In either case, creating an object name with QUOTED_IDENTIFIER set to on requires that you turn QUOTED_IDENTIFIER to on for every session when you will be accessing these objects. If you do not, SQL Server will simply treat the object as a literal string when attempting to process the query statement. In other words, the object cannot be found or accessed without first turning QUOTED_IDENTIFIER to on.

If you use the square brackets to delimit an identifier, you do not have to worry about the current setting on QUOTED_IDENTIFIER.

System Catalog

Every DBMS system uses one or more data catalogs (also known as dictionaries), which are used to record information about the various databases and all of the objects within them. This catalog is actually a database about the database. These tables are automatically created when you create the database, and are not normally visible to the user. SQL Server uses these tables to keep information about the database, its tables and other objects, and the users who have access to the database and its objects. These tables are maintained by SQL Server and should not be moved or edited by a user or database owner. Doing so may cause the database to become inaccessible.

The primary system catalog resides in the master database, and is most often referred to as the *system catalog*. There have been significant changes in the system catalog with SQL Server 7. The master database contains views that can be used to emulate older versions of the system catalog, enabling applications and databases that are converted from earlier versions of SQL Server to continue to work properly. This includes information about user logins, current system configuration, allocation and mapping of physical storage, and many other distinct pieces of data.

Each database also contains a subset of the system catalog, often referred to as the *data catalog*. These tables contain information about the specific database in which they reside, and are concerned with items such as replication data, names and properties for each column of every table, information about constraints, and all of the other information that makes this a unique database. Whenever you create a new database, the data catalog is copied from the model database.

Key Points

In this chapter you have learned the following key points to remember:

- How a database is created in SQL Server 7 using either Query Analyzer or the Enterprise Manager.
- How to use various database objects: tables, views, defaults, and rules.
- The use of file groups, and what a data file and log file are.
- Using and creating stored procedures.
- How a trigger can be used and created.
- The use of cursors and what they are and how to create one.
- What an index is and the difference between clustered and nonclustered indexes.
- The rules for naming objects.

▲ CHAPTER REVIEW QUESTIONS

▲ Multiple Choice:

1. *What does the following T-SQL query do?*

   ```
   SELECT s.title_id, s.qty, t.title
   FROM sales s, titles t
   WHERE s.title_id = t.title_id
   AND qty >= 20
   ```

   A. Displays all available sales information for all titles.

   B. Displays title id's, titles, and store names, for stores that have sold more than 20 books.

   C. Displays title id's, titles, and quantity sold if 20 or more books have been purchased by any store.

   D. Displays title id's, titles, and quantity sold of an individual title by a store, is more than 20.

2. *What is true of using stored procedures? (Choose all that apply)*

   A. Stored procedures are automatically recompiled each time they are run and so are faster because they are based on current information.

   B. Stored procedures are compiled once.

   C. Stored procedures use precompiled T-SQL statements.

   D. Stored procedures always require an EXECUTE statement.

3. *If a Log file size is not specified it will be:*

   A. 10MB in size

   B. 25 percent of the size specified for the primary data file

   C. 25MB in size

   D. 10 percent of the size of the data files

   E. 25 percent of the size of the data files

4. *Applications written for SQL Server 6.X that use or depend on which of these features will require rewriting before you upgrade to SQL Server 7. (Choose all that apply).*

   A. Applications that use sp_configure to directly set configuration options.

   B. Applications that rely on configuration settings specific to an SQL Server 6.X.

C. An application that depends on having individual parts residing on a specific physical segment.

D. Applications that directly write to the system tables without the benefit of the stored procedures.

5. *A file group contains:*

A. All of the data files for a database.

B. All of the operating system files containing the data files for selected databases.

C. The data and log files for any database added to the file group.

D. The data and log files for a single database.

6. *How many rules can be bound to a column in a table?*

A. One only.

B. As many as needed.

C. Three

D. One for each datatype.

7. *An EXECUTE statement precedes a stored procedure if:*

A. It follows a WHERE clause.

B. It is not the first statement in a query.

C. It is the first statement in a query.

D. A and B.

E. All of the above.

8. *A wide index is one that:*

A. Is implemented on columns that use a large datatype.

B. Is used on tables that have more than three columns.

C. Covers three or more columns.

D. A and B.

E. All of the above.

9. *A name or identifier must meet which of the following rules?*

A. Be no more than 64 characters in length.

B. A name can only be used once within SQL Server.

C. A database owner can use a name only once within a database.

D. A and C.

E. All of the above.

10. *A database can be set to grow: (Select all that apply).*

A. Not allowed to grow.

B. By a specified percentage.

C. By a specified number of KBs.

D. To a specified maximum size.

▲ True or False:

1. *True or False? A single transaction log is shared by all SQL Server user databases.*

2. *True or False? The ORDER BY clause is used to change the sort order of the first column in the SELECT clause from the default order.*

3. *True or False? A database table can span across any of the data files in the database.*

4. *True or False? If you drop a View the underlying table is also dropped.*

5. *True or False? In SQL Server 7, cursors are the favored method of row-level operations.*

6. *True or False? A database can be set to grow no larger than the available disk space.*

Microsoft SQL Server Components

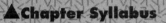
When you install SQL Server, it is tightly integrated with Windows NT and makes use of many of NT's services and processes. This enables SQL Server to dedicate more of its own resources to the performance of its own job. Most other high-end database management systems must provide their own infrastructure because they cannot be sure of what is available from any one specific operating system. This chapter will give an overview of several of the installed components. In addition, there are several components specific to the needs to the system administrator: SQL Mail notification, creating a database maintenance plan, and SQL Server processes.

MCSE 4.1   SQL Mail

SQL Mail™ is a MAPI client service that allows you to configure SQL Server™ to notify specified operators of alerts and events. You can choose the specific alerts and events that will trigger a mail message and who will get it. SQL Server Agent uses the SQL Mail service to make the actual notifications. This is a very good method of ensuring that you as the system administrator are notified when specific alert conditions, or events have happened.

You must set SQL Mail to automatically start when the SQL Server Agent service is started. If the SQL Mail service is not started, then SQL Server Agent will generate an error when it tries to send a mail message. Normally the SQL Mail service works through Microsoft Mail®, but can work in conjunction with any MAPI-enabled mail provider. SQL Server must be set up as an SQL Mail client and you must have a post office available. To successfully use the SQL Mail service, you must first start the local Windows NT Mail™ client, or you will not be able to connect to the mailbox.

The SQL Mail service is normally set to automatically start every time that the SQL Server Agent starts. This is controlled through the Registry entry:

```
HKEY_LOCAL_MACHINE
\SOFTWARE
\Microsoft
\MSSQLServer
\SQLServerAgent
Name: MailAutoStart
Type: REG_DWORD
Data:
```

When the Registry value is set to 1, the default, then SQL Mail will automatically start when SQL Server Agent starts. SQL Mail will not start automatically if the Registry value is set to 0, or if the Registry key does not exist.

Messages sent through SQL Mail are normally very short, telling you about an event or alert, but can also include the output from a query that is set to run when the event or alert is triggered. SQL Mail can send mail to whomever is added to its notification list. Notifications can be sent via e-mail through the MAPI-enabled mail service, or by pager. Pager notifications require some additional setup and will be fully discussed later in Chapter 19, "The SQL Server Agent."

There are some security issues that should be addressed in regard to SQL Mail and the SQL Server Agent Service. By default, the SQL Mail service is set up to run on NT as a Local System service account. This means that there is no user security account associated with the SQL Mail service. This works very well in a pure Windows NT network. If you are configuring SQL Server for a network that consists of multiple network operating systems, you may be forced to create a specific user account for the SQL Mail service and for SQL Server Agent. This is because some network operating systems, such as Microsoft LAN Manager™ and Novel NetWare™ do not allow a Windows NT service using a Local System account to access their shared directories.

SQL Mail can be set up to run with a Microsoft Exchange™ Server postoffice, but there are a few additional hurdles to be jumped. You must have the SQL Server service (MSSQLServer) running with the same user account. You should also have the Exchange Server set up to deliver messages to the mail server, and not to a local folder. If you are having a problem using SQL Mail and Exchange Server together, you will generally find that the problem stems from one of two issues: permissions and the Microsoft Exchange client setup. Most of these problems can be diagnosed by checking each of the following items listed in these steps:

1. Log on to the computer on which SQL Server and SQL Mail are set up, using the administrator account on the local computer normally used to log on to SQL Server. This account should also be a domain account.
2. Verify that the Exchange client, Exchng32.exe, can connect to the Exchange Server and that you can pass mail back and forth.
3. Verify that the Exchange profile used by SQL Mail does not have a Personal Message Store (*.pst) file associated with it. Check this in the Mail and Fax applet in the Control Panel. The only services associated with this profile should be: Microsoft Exchange Server, Personal Address Book, and Outlook Address Book.
4. Check that MSSQLService is set up to use the administrator security account used in step 1 above. This can be checked in the Services applet in Control Panel.
5. Ensure that SQL Server has permission to access the Exchange Server by using the extended stored procedure xp_cmdshell. This stored procedure uses the same permissions used by SQL Mail. From the command line issue the following command, substituting "ExchangeServer" for the name of the computer on which Exchange Server is located:

```
xp_cmdshell "NET USE \\ExchangeServer\IPC$"
```

If the above command fails then you do not have the correct profile set up in the Mail and Fax applet.

When using standard mail, such as Windows NT Mail, most mail errors tend to be either permission or Registry setup problems. If you have problems connecting to NT Mail, then check these items in this order:

1. Check that the logged-on user can successfully connect and send mail using the Mail Client (Msmail32.exe) application.

2. Ensure that the SQL Mail service is either assigned to the Local System account, or to a valid Windows NT user account in the Services applet in Control Panel.

3. Ensure that the login account has Read/Write (RW) permissions on the shared post office folder. If SQL Server is using the Local System account, then the post office folder must grant Read/Write rights to EVERYONE.

Once you have completed these steps, your SQL Mail service should be running. SQL Mail is used to notify the system administrator, or other operators of events and alerts that happen during the course of running a database. Many of these alerts and events are customizable, and you can add new ones.

MCSE 4.2   Database Maintenance Plans

One of the primary aspects of the system administrators job is to plan for disaster recovery. A disaster can be anything from a simple power failure, a disk drive crash, or fire involving your entire building. With a good database backup plan and proper maintenance of the plan you can recover the company information. This subject will be covered in greater detail later in Chapter 16, "Backing Up the Database." You also need to perform the necessary maintenance to the database that is required to help ensure that a disaster or even poor performance is not encountered. Many performance issues: slow data access or updates, or inaccurate information returned from a query, can be almost eliminated by ensuring that your databases are regularly checked for inconsistencies.

SQL Server 6.5 changed dump devices to backup devices on the SQL Server Enterprise Manager tree. SQL Server 7 has made many improvements to the backup utilities so that backup and restore operations are much faster and have a smaller impact on an operating server. In addition to speed improvements, an incremental backup and restore has been added. An incremental backup allows you to back up only those data pages that have changed since the last backup.

Backup devices can be either physical devices or logical devices. A logical device is one whose name is permanently stored in the sysdevices table in the master database. A logical backup device can be referred to by an alias or common name. For example, you can create a logical backup device as BACKUP1 in the sysdevices table, while its physical name is C:\BACKUP-DEV\ACCTNG\BACKUP1.DAT. As you can see, using BACKUP1 is much easier than is the entire physical device name. You can create additional backup devices and use a variety of media types, including disk, tape, optical drives, and removable media.

Note Earlier versions of SQL Server allowed backups or dumps to a diskette. SQL Server 7 no longer supports backups to this media. When performing an upgrade of SQL Server, be sure to remove all references to diskette backups or dumps from the application.

New backup devices can be created by following these steps:

1. From the SQL Enterprise Manager window, select Backup Devices from the tree and right-click to display the shortcut menu. Choose New Backup Device from the shortcut menu.

2. With the Backup Device Properties dialog box you can create either a disk- or tape-based backup device. Type BACKUP1 into the Name text box. Now click the Disk file name option button. See how this name is appended to the location path in the text box below. The backup device name, like all other SQL Server objects, does not have to be an 8.3 format name, but it does have to meet SQL Server's rules for identifiers. If you are not sure of the path for your backup device, simply click on the Locate button (...) to the right of the Disk file name text box. You can then use the Backup Device Location dialog box to select the path through a directory tree structure. In Figure 4-1, notice also how a tape device is listed in the middle text box.

3. Click on the OK button and SQL Server will add the new device to any other Backup Devices shown in the SQL Enterprise Manager tree.

You will learn to use the backup and restore options in Chapters 15, 16, and 17. When creating a tape backup device, the tape drive must already exist on the local machine. SQL Server does not support a networked tape device, but does support a networked disk device. If your only tape drive is located on a different computer than SQL Server, you can back up your data to a disk-based backup device and then copy the backup to the tape device dur-

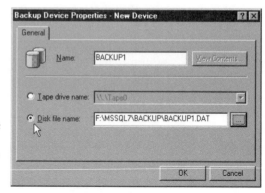

Figure 4–1 *Create a backup device using the New Backup Device dialog box. Backup device names can be no longer than 30 characters.*

ing your normal backup schedule. Other aspects that you need to be concerned with in a database maintenance plan include:

- Ensuring that the database index and data pages are periodically rebuilt using an appropriate FILLFACTOR value. This will help to ensure both that there is room on these pages for new data to be added, and that the current information is evenly spread throughout all of the data and index pages and not clumped among a few.
- Compress the existing data files by removing any empty pages. Pages become empty when you reorganize the index and data pages, or if you delete a large amount of data from the database.
- Update the index statistics on the database. This ensures that the query optimizer has the most current information about the database and the spread of information throughout the tables, ensuring that queries run as fast as possible.
- Internal consistency checks of both data and data pages. This may catch a possible system or software errors that have not yet actually damaged your data.

Each of these tasks can be performed as needed using the tools available in the Enterprise Manager window, or you can set all of these jobs to be automatically scheduled using the Database Maintenance Plan Wizard. This is a feature new to SQL Server 7, and will help to ensure that you do not miss a job, and that it is scheduled properly. The Database Maintenance Plan Wizard must run on a selected SQL Server, not on a Server Group. This wizard is a member of the Management group of wizards. The Database Maintenance Plan Wizard will lead you through a series of dialog boxes that will:

- Let you choose the database the new plan will be used to maintain.
- Choose the data verification tests that will be run and when.
- Update database statistics at selected intervals.

- Determine how often backups should be done, and what backup destination will be used.
- Select a destination folder for the reports that are generated by these jobs.

Once you begin the process of creating a Database Maintenance Plan (DMP) you can select any of the connected SQL Servers on your network, you do not have to set up a new DMP on each server. You can also choose to set up a DMP for selected databases, all databases, all system databases (master, model, and msdb), or all user databases.

After you select the database(s) for which a DMP will be created you will make the selections for data optimization. Figure 4-2 shows you the dialog box used for this process.

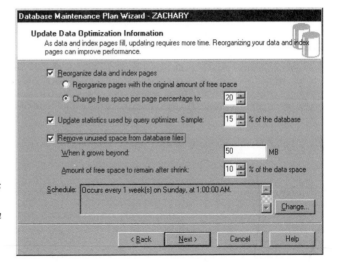

Figure 4–2 *This dialog box is used to choose the various options for data optimization in the DMP.*

- The first option is where you choose how data and index pages will be reorganized. You can choose to reorganize the pages based on their original amount of free space, or to make a specified percentage of the page space free. In this case you see that this has been set to 20 percent of each data and index page will be made free space.
- The next option is where you can choose to update the statistics created for the use of the query optimizer. The better these statistics, the better the decisions made by the query optimizer. If you select this option, then you must also enter how large of a sample will be used for the statistics.
- The third option is whether unused space will be removed from a database or not. If you use this option, then you must also specify how

much unused space can exist before this option is activated, and then how much free space will be left as a percentage of the data space.

• Finally, you can set the schedule for the options you have selected.

In the next DMP dialog box, shown in Figure 4-3, you will select the data integrity tests that will be run. There are three options available here:

• The first option is to perform internal data integrity tests. These tests are sometimes able to catch possible errors before your data is actually damaged. In addition, you can choose to exclude indexes, and/or allow the system to attempt to repair minor discrepancies.

• The second option is to perform database integrity tests. You also have the same two additional selections.

• The final option is to perform these tests before backing up the database or transaction log.

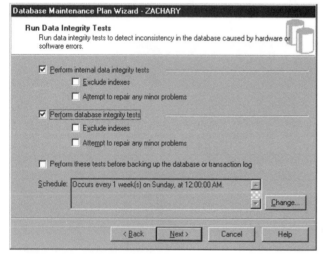

Figure 4–3 *In this dialog box, you choose the integrity tests that will be run, and make any exclusions that you may require.*

The next dialog box is used to specify a backup plan. Here you can choose whether to verify the integrity of the backup after completion, and where the backup will be stored, tape or disk.

In the next dialog box, you choose to backup the transaction logs. You have the same options available to you as in the previous dialog box.

The next dialog box, shown in Figure 4-4, you will select the reports that will be generated, where they will be stored, and how long they will be kept. You can also choose to e-mail the report to a selected operator if you have set up SQL Mail. The report can also be created as an HTML file and stored in a specified directory.

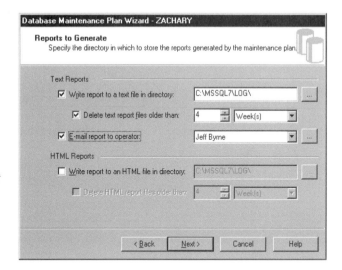

Figure 4–4 *Choose the reports that will be written, where they will be stored, and for how long they will be retained.*

Next you will choose where the maintenance history will be written. They can be written either on the local server or a remote server. The maintenance history is written to the msdb database, and the sysdbmaintplan_history table. You can also choose to send the history to both the local and a selected remote server.

The final dialog box allows you to name the DMP and to review the selections you have made.

Creating a database maintenance plan through the Wizard helps to ensure that you have not missed anything important. You have covered all of the important tasks that need to be done, they are scheduled on a consistent basis, and you have included all of the necessary databases.

Processes

The Windows NT/SQL Server combination is a single-process, multi-threaded database system, unlike many of the earlier client/server incarnations, which were multiprocess servers. There may be many different processes being run at any one time. A process can be either running or sleeping, and come in two varieties: client and server. Client processes are those that have been started from a client system, such as a query. A server process is most often an internal SQL Server process. The *sysprocesses* table contains information about processes that are currently running or sleeping and can be viewed like this:

1. You can view the sysprocesses table by opening the master database and drilling down to Tables.
2. Right-click on the sysprocesses table and select the Open Table option on the shortcut menu. Figure 4-5 shows the sysprocesses table.

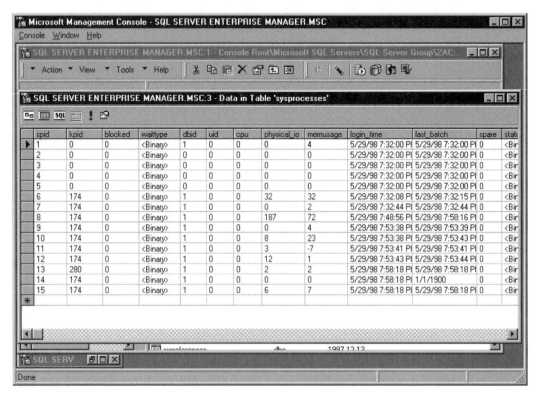

Figure 4–5 *You can see the various processes that are currently being run by SQL Server in the sysprocesses table.*

Every process that is started is automatically assigned a system process ID (SPID). The SPID is stored in the sysprocesses table along with other information about the process. Along with the SPIDs, the following information is also stored:

- The current process status: running, runnable, sleeping, and the like.
- The hostname that started the process. This can be a computer name or an application.
- The SPID of the processes that is blocking this process, if applicable.
- The name of the database to which the processes belongs.
- A command that may be running or waiting for an action.

Each time a user logs into the server, a new client process is started. This process is automatically logged into the sysprocesses table. The server can stop, or kill, a client process at any time. This may be necessary when a client process blocks another process, and for some reason it cannot be terminated at the client end.

When a client logs into SQL Server, it is assigned a Process ID, viewable in the Current Activity's Detail Activity tab. You can see the database to which the process is logged, the user name of the individual who is logged in, the computer from which they logged in, and whether the process is blocked and by which process it is blocked by. This final bit of information can be extremely valuable when deciding if a process needs to be killed. Long-running transactions may need to be terminated if they are preventing the log file from being truncated—potentially causing it to become full and so stopping all transactions from continuing.

A process to be terminated, or killed, can be killed only by the system administrator. The kill command cannot be transferred to another user. The KILL statement should be used only when absolutely necessary, and when you are sure of the process ID of the process to be killed. You cannot kill your own process, nor should you kill the following processes:

- Signal Handler
- Lock Monitor
- Lazy Writer
- CheckPoint Sleep
- RA Manager
- Processes running extended stored procedures "xp"

You can use either the kill statement, or use the kill button in the Current Activity dialog box to terminate a process. To kill a process, follow these steps:

1. Determine the system process ID (spid) number of the process that you want to terminate, by executing the stored procedure sp_who. Open the Query Analyzer, and select the master database.
2. Type sp_who, and click the Execute Query button. Figure 4-6 shows the processes currently running, runnable, or sleeping . In this case there are two runnable and the remainder are sleeping.

The stored procedure sp_who displays a results set that shows you several useful pieces of information. The first is all of the system process IDs currently open, and what their current status is—running, sleeping, or runnable. The next two columns show who is logged to the process, and from what station the process is being run. The next column—blk—now displays

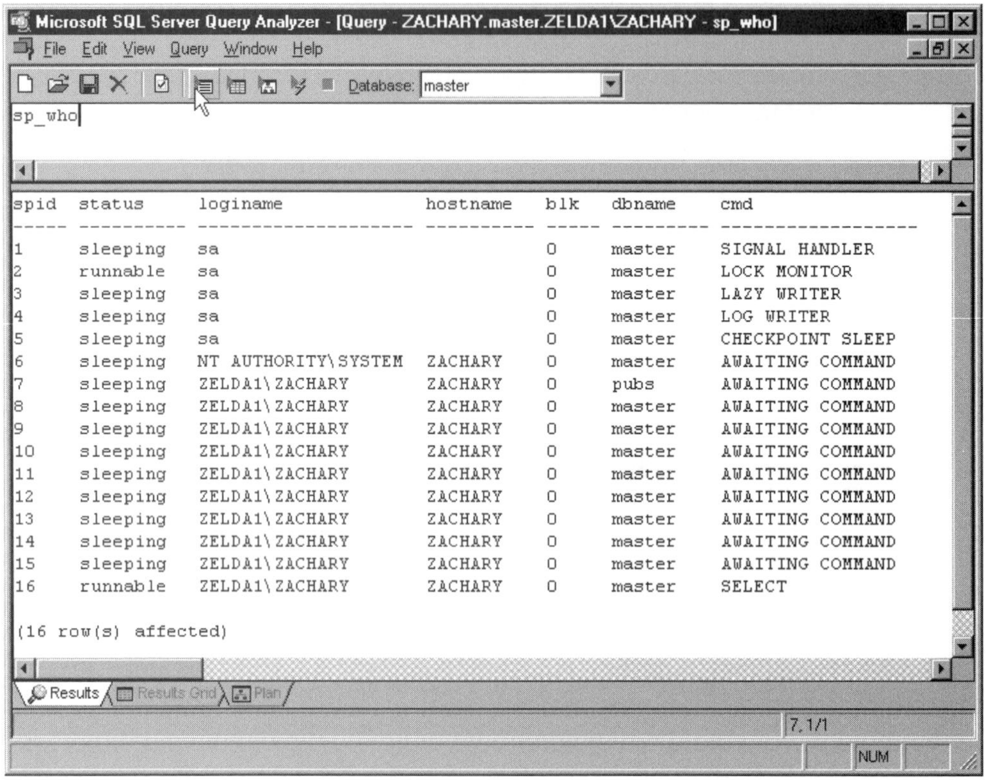

Figure 4–6 *The results set for the sp_who statement. Notice the spid numbers located in the first column. The column widths of the results set have been modified so that you can see the entire set.*

the number 0 for all processes. If a process is blocked by another process, then the blocking processes spid would be displayed in this column. For example, if spid 11 was being blocked by spid 10, then the number 10 would be displayed in the blk column for spid 11. If you, as system administrator, determined that spid 10 was a user process, such as an uncommitted transaction that had failed for some reason, you could terminate the process and allow spid 11 to continue.

3. Clear the previous query by clicking the New Query button and type KILL 7. If you are successful, you will see a message telling you the command completed successfully.

   Follow these steps to kill a process from within the SQL Server Enterprise Manger application:

1. Select the SQL Server that you want to check, and then open the Current Activity window by selecting Tools, Current Activity from the menu.
2. You can terminate a process from any of the tabs, but the Server Activity and Detail Activity are the more useful of the three. Select the process in the window and click the Kill Process button. A confirmation dialog box will be displayed, click the Yes button to kill the process, or the No button to stop the kill process and return to the Current Activity window, as shown in Figure 4-7.

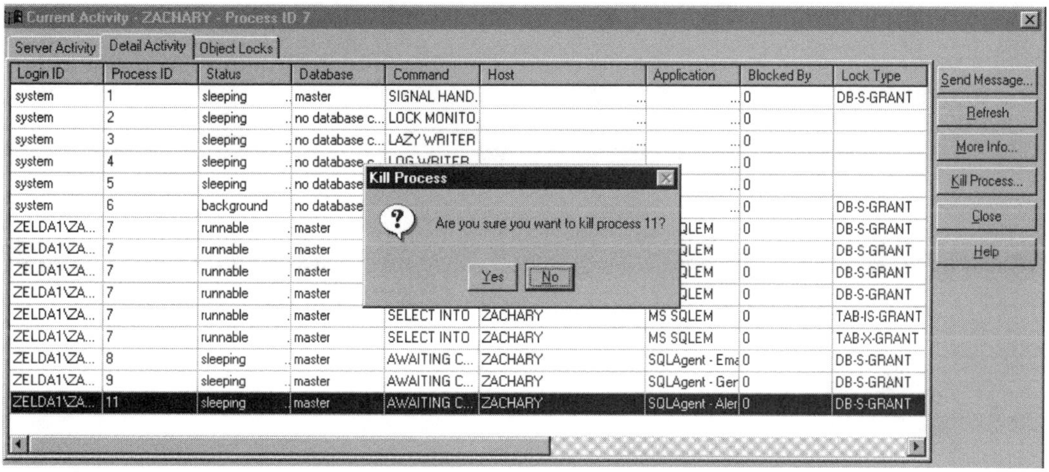

Login ID	Process ID	Status	Database	Command	Host	Application	Blocked By	Lock Type
system	1	sleeping	.. master	SIGNAL HAND.		..	..0	DB-S-GRANT
system	2	sleeping	.. no database c...	LOCK MONITO.		..	..0	
system	3	sleeping	.. no database c...	LAZY WRITER			..0	
system	4	sleeping	.. no database c.	LOG WRITER			..0	
system	5	sleeping	.. no database				..0	
system	6	background	no database				..0	DB-S-GRANT
ZELDA1\ZA...	7	runnable	. master		QLEM	0		DB-S-GRANT
ZELDA1\ZA...	7	runnable	. master		QLEM	0		DB-S-GRANT
ZELDA1\ZA...	7	runnable	. master		QLEM	0		DB-S-GRANT
ZELDA1\ZA...	7	runnable	. master		QLEM	0		DB-S-GRANT
ZELDA1\ZA...	7	runnable	. master	SELECT INTO	ZACHARY	MS SQLEM	0	TAB-IS-GRANT
ZELDA1\ZA...	7	runnable	. master	SELECT INTO	ZACHARY	MS SQLEM	0	TAB-X-GRANT
ZELDA1\ZA...	8	sleeping	. master	AWAITING C...	ZACHARY	SQLAgent - Ema	0	DB-S-GRANT
ZELDA1\ZA...	9	sleeping	. master	AWAITING C...	ZACHARY	SQLAgent - Ger	0	DB-S-GRANT
ZELDA1\ZA...	11	sleeping	. master	AWAITING C...	ZACHARY	SQLAgent - Aler	0	DB-S-GRANT

Kill Process

Are you sure you want to kill process 11?

Yes   No

Send Message...
Refresh
More Info...
Kill Process...
Close
Help

Figure 4–7 *A process about to be killed in the Current Activity window.*

There are several processes that cannot be terminated by using the KILL statement or the Kill Process button in the Current Activity window. System processes such as Mirror Handler, Lazy Writer, Checkpoint Sleep, and RA Manager, and any process running an extended stored procedure, cannot be terminated. As an additional safety factor, SQL Server also does not make the Kill Process button available when a process that should not be killed is selected.

Files

When the setup program is run, five default databases are created. Each of these databases, except pubs, is required for the successful running of SQL Server. Each of these default databases contain their own components and provide their own unique functions. In this section, let's look at these five default databases.

master Database

The master database is where all of the primary system tables reside. This is a required database, and also contains both stored procedures and extended stored procedures. The master database is where all information about the other databases, both user and system are stored. Information about files, and file groups is also included here. The master database is also often called the *data dictionary* or the *system catalog*. Table 4-1 lists some of the more important tables that are unique to the master database.

 Whenever you make changes to the structure of a user or system database, change security features, add to a file group, or anything that is reflected in a system table you should back up the master database. With a current master database you can recreatae a damaged database, without it, you would not have many of the latest changes made to the database. This does not alleviate you from doing back ups of the individual databses and their log files.

Table 4.1 *Primary System Tables in the Master Database*

Table	Description
syscharsets	This table has one row for every character set and sort order that has been defined for use with SQL Server.
sysconfigures	This table has one row for each configuration option that can be set by an individual user.
sysdatabases	This table has one row for each database on SQL Server. The information includes data about the database's name, its owner, current status, and other information that can be used to recover a database.
sysdevices	This table includes one row for each device installed on SQL Server. This encompasses all backup and database devices. Information about some devices is kept only for backward compatibility.
syslanguages	This table contains a row for each language that is known to Microsoft SQL Server. If you are using U.S. English as the only language, then this table will be blank, as SQL Server always has this language available to it.
syslockinfo	All information about current locks held on tables is stored in this table. If the server goes down for any reason, all locks are automatically released.
syslogins	This table contains one row for every authorized SQL Server user account.
sysmessages	This table contains a row for each error or warning message that will be displayed by SQL Server. These error messages are displayed on the users screen.
sysprocesses	This table contains information about both client and server processes currently running on SQL Server.

Table 4.1 *Primary System Tables in the Master Database (Continued)*

Table	Description
sysremotelogins	This table has one row for each user logging in from a remote server, with permission to call stored procedures on this server.
sysoledbusers	This table contains a row for each user and their password for the specific linked server.
sysservers	This table contains a row for each server on which this server can call remote stored procedures.
sysperfinfo	This table contains a representation of the internal performance counters that can be shown through Windows NT Performance Monitors. This is only available if Windows NT is the operating system.

For a complete listing and detailed descriptions of all tables in the master database, see the *System Tables* section in the SQL Server Books Online. Specifically, *Building SQL Server Applications\Transact-SQL\Transact-SQL Reference\System Tables*, on the Contents tab.

model Database

The model database is another database created by the setup program. This database is used by SQL Server as the template on which all new user databases are based. Whenever a new database is created, SQL Server copies the contents of the model and places it onto the primary database file of the new database. A new database can always be larger than the model, but it can never be smaller.

The model database contains all of the system tables that are required for every user database. Table 4-2 lists the more important tables included in the model database, and subsequently every new user database. You can customize the model database so that it will include additional objects that you want to have as part of every table. Remember, if you make a change to the model database, every new database created after saving this change will incorporate these same modifications, so be sure that this is something that you want with every database and not just a modification necessary for a single database. Some commonly added objects that you may want to place in the model database are:

- Logins for users who are to be given access to all new databases.
- Custom user-defined datatypes, rules, defaults, constraints, and stored procedures.

- Default permissions for guest login accounts.
- Base tables used in all production databases.

It is highly recommended that you create and add all of the above options necessary to your own databases, to your model database before you begin to create new user databases. This will ensure that they all have the appropriate customized objects, and you will not have to go back, rechecking and adding objects to databases created earlier.

Table 4.2 *Primary Model Database System Tables*

Tables	Description
syscolumns	Contains a row for each column in every table and view in the database. A row is also included for each parameter in a stored procedure.
syscomments	This table contains a row for every view, rule, default value, trigger, CHECK and DEFAULT constraint, and stored procedure. The *text* column stores the original SQL definition statements for the object.
sysdepends	Contains information about the various dependency relationships between objects.
sysfiles	A row is included for each file in a database.
sysfilegroups	This table stores information about each file group contained in the database.
sysforeignkeys	Contains information about foreign key relationships.
sysindexes	Contains information about each index and table.
sysobjects	Each row has information about each object created in the database. The tempdb also includes a row for each temporary object.
syspermissions	Contains information about the various permissions that have been granted, denied, or revoked for all users, groups, and roles.
sysprotects	Contains information about the security accounts and the permissions applied to them with GRANT and REVOKE statements.
systypes	Contains information about each system and user-defined data type.
sysusers	This table includes information about each Windows NT user, Windows NT group, SQL Server user, and SQL Server role.

msdb Database

The msdb database is created by the setup program and is used by SQL Server as a storage place for task scheduling, event handling, and alert notifications. The msdb database is at the core of the SQL Server task scheduling center. In addition to logging backup and restore events, this database also logs all exception reports. If a problem occurs, it is the msdb database that checks the problem and notifies an operator of the problem. Windows NT cannotify an operator of a problem or possible problem via e-mail or by pager. For a server with a 7X24 uptime requirement, the ability of the server to notify someone of a potential problem can be a lifesaver. Table 4-3 lists some of the more important tables that are unique to the msdb database.

Table 4.3 *Primary System Tables in the msdb Database*

Table	Description
sysalerts	Records a row for each alert. An alert is a message sent in response to an event.
sysjobhistory	Contains information about scheduled jobs that have been executed.
sysjobschedules	This table contains information about jobs that are scheduled to be executed.
sysjobs	Contains details about the jobs that are scheduled for execution.
sysjobsteps	Stores the specific steps involved in a scheduled job.
sysoperators	Contains information about each operator.
sysvolumelabel	Records the incremental volume labels used for backups.

Sample Databases

Both the pubs and Northwind databases are included by SQL Server 7 as sample databases on which most of the examples used in the Microsoft SQL Server documentation are drawn from. You will also see them referred to in almost every book and article you may read about SQL Server. The setup program places them in the same folder as all of the other installed databases.

You can use these databases as a training tool for new users or those users who want to gain more experience with various aspects of SQL Server without using live data. Many objects can be tested using the various tables contained in either the pubs or Northwind database.

Both of these databases are not required databases and can be dropped if no longer needed. If you plan to use them as a learning tool, make a complete backup of the database when you first install SQL Server. Then later, when the next user is in the training program, they can use a fresh copy of the sample database.

The primary difference between these two sample databases is that the pubs database is a relatively simple database. It is a good place to start when you want to begin the task of showing someone how to use SQL Server. The Northwind database is a much more complete database and includes many more aspects of a client/server database than does the pubs database.

tempdb Database

The tempdb database is used for the storage of all temporary objects used by SQL Server and any users. tempdb is a global resource and all users of an SQL Server object have access to it. Whenever a temporary object is created it is stored in the tempdb file. Temporary objects can include temporary tables, stored procedures, and other objects.

Whenever the SQL Server service is stopped, the tempdb file is dropped and then recreated when the service is started again.

Log Files

The SQL Server log file is one of the most important aspects of a DBMS that you will use. Without a log file, maintaining all of the transactions that have occurred since the last write to the permanent disk data file, you could easily lose all of the information that is still stored in memory in the case of a power failure.

In earlier versions of SQL Server the log files were called transaction logs. In SQL Server 7 there must be at least one log file per database. If you do not specifically include the necessary information when you create a database, SQL Server will automatically create a log file for you. SQL Server uses a *write-ahead* log, which means that all transactions are written to the log before they are written to the database itself. This helps to ensure that the log files can be used to recover the database. The log contains a serial listing of all modifications to all objects in the database, and is shared by all users of the database. The log file should always be kept on a separate physical drive from your data files. The reason for this is that if the disk the database files fails, the log files should still be intact and you will be able to recover your database.

You must ensure that the log files are backed up on a regular basis, and that the log is of an adequate size for the number and size of the transactions performed in your databases. If a log file fills up, all further update, delete, and insert activity in any of the databases comes to a halt—if you have specified that the log files cannot grow. A log file can fill up on any database, even the master or tempdb. The space required to keep a log file complete for modifications to a database can be substantial. This is due both to the overhead inherent in the logging procedure, and the data to be logged. When you first create your database, you must specify a size for it. This size figure can be very difficult to estimate at first, causing new administrators to often use a simple percentage of the database size, such as 10 or 25 percent. If you have enough experience with your data, you may be able to create some tests of the data to give you a more reliable number for the size of your log files. If you do not specify a size for the log, SQL Server will create a log file that is 25 percent of the size of all of the combined data files.

The data written to the log files is automatically written to the database when a *checkpoint* is encountered. A checkpoint can occur in three circumstances:

- The database owner or system administrator manually issues a CHECKPOINT command.
- SQL Server executes a CHECKPOINT when the log file cache has reached a specified limit.
- SQL Server executes a CHECKPOINT when the specified *recovery interval* is reached.

A checkpoint forces the log file to write all log pages that have been modified since the last checkpoint to the database device. This ensures that transactions that have been committed will be written to the database. The checkpoint can also force the log file to be truncated, if this option is turned on. When the log is truncated, all log pages whose transactions have all been committed are deleted from the log file. This process helps to ensure that the log file does not become full, stopping additional modifications to the database. An automatic checkpoint is issued by SQL Server approximately every 60 seconds—the actual interval is based upon the recovery interval and the number of transactions added to the log.

The recovery interval is the amount of time you determine that the database can remain down while SQL Server runs its recovery process in the event of an outage. If you determine that you can allow a ten-minute interval to allow SQL Server to recover a database, then set this as the recovery interval. Rmember, in a worst-case basis, the recovery interval is the allowance for each database. If you have 20 databases, a 10-minute recovery equals a possible downtime of almost 3 hours and 20 minutes. Do not set the recovery interval too low either. The checkpoint process adds its own overhead penalty to the server, which will be especially noticeable with a high volume of transactions.

All transaction statements are written to the log file as they are received by the server. When a COMMIT TRANsaction is reached it flushes all of the *dirty* log pages from the log to the disk. A dirty page is a log page that has changed since the last checkpoint. When the COMMIT TRAN statement is reached only those statements that actually change data are written to the database. There is a short, but finite period of time when a transaction exists only in the log file. If a server fails before a transaction has been written to the database, but after the COMMIT TRAN statement has been logged, then the transaction will be rolled forward into the database during recovery. On the other hand, if the transaction has begun but not yet committed, then it will be rolled back during the recovery process.

You may wonder how an uncommitted transaction gets written to the log. The log file works in pages. More than one transaction may be written to a page, especially in multiuser environments. One user can easily overlap another user's transaction statements, causing SQL Server to write both BEGIN TRANscation statements on the same log page. The first user then commits their transaction, but SQL Server writes everything on that page to the log file, potentially creating an uncommitted transaction. Figure 4-8 illustrates how two transactions can be written, logged, committed, and either rolled forward or rolled back.

Unlike many databases, SQL Server allows you to choose a specific date and time through which transactions will be recovered. All transactions that

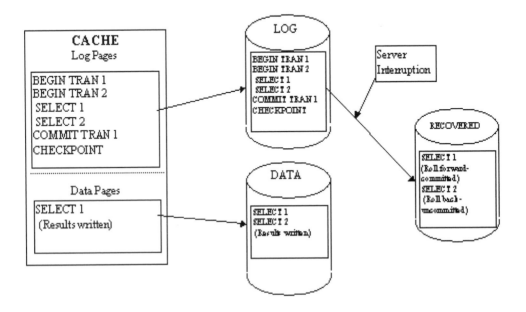

Figure 4–8 *The checkpoint process saves data to the log file as pages. A transaction may be rolled forward or back during recovery, if the server fails.*

occurred after the specified date and time will be rolled back, even if already committed. This recovery applies only to restores from a log file, not to full database or table restores.

Web Files

This feature was new to SQL Server 6.5, and has been further enhanced in SQL Server 7. Now in addition to being able to create Hypertext Markup Language (HTML) documents or web pages, you can also import tabular data from a web site and insert it into a database. You can use the SQL Server Web Assistant to assist you in creating and schedule the creation of web pages and the updating of information already placed on a web page. The Web Assistant is accessed through the SQL Server Enterprise Manager interface. The Web Assistant has been enhanced from its previous version so that it can also post data to and read information from an HTTP or FTP site. Along with enhancements to the Windows Sockets Net-Library to allow connectivity with Microsoft Proxy Server, you can now support secure connections across the Internet. Details about using web pages and the Web Assistant will be discussed later in Chapter 21, "Your Data and the Web."

You can use the Web Assistant with SQL Server 6.5 databases, but not with earlier databases. The Web Assistant is really a front-end for the stored procedure `sp_makewebtask`. This stored procedure can be run from any Windows NT supported platform. There are two additional stored procedures used with generating HTML documents: `sp_runwebtask`, and `sp_dropwebtask`. These three new stored procedures have the following uses:

- `sp_makewebtask` is used to create the task that will produce the HTML document. This is the stored procedure that is run through the Web Assistant interface.
- `sp_runwebtask` is the stored procedure that actually creates the HTML document. When you run this stored procedure, it runs the task specified in the parameters.
- `sp_dropwebtask` is used to drop a previously created web task. You can specify either the task process name or the output file name when using this stored procedure.

The Web Assistant can be used to generate an HTML file as a one-time only or as a regularly scheduled server task. The Web Assistant can make use of SQL Server procedures, queries, and extended stored procedures, enabling you to create a web page that makes use of the most current information available at almost any time.

Using the Web Assistant is a very simple method for creating a web page with information from your database. Some uses for this could be:

- Creating a web page where customers can browse through the items or services you supply and the prices for them.
- Building a web page on which your salespeople can view available inventory.
- Making a web page that can display updatable spec sheets for your products.

 Remember, you can set this task to run as often as necessary. Each time the task runs again, all of the information displayed on your web page is updated with the most current information contained in your database. This has the potential to save a company many thousands of dollars in printing and postage costs. Consider how many color flyers and spec sheets are printed, mailed, and thrown away each year, and how many of these same flyers and spec sheets are out of date by the time they come back from the printer. You can have a completely up-to-date flyer and spec sheet on your web page that your customer can print for themselves if they want a copy, and they have the satisfaction of getting current information about your product.

Key Points

There are several key points that are covered in this chapter. The most important were:

- SQL Mail and its uses as a component to notify designated individuals about selected events.
- The SQL Mail service requires the use of both the SQL Server Agent, and a valid mailbox to send notifications to. Without both of these, the service will not start.
- Creating a database backup device and that it can be either a physical or logical device.
- How to view and distinguish system processes using both the sysprocesses table, and the stored procedure sp_who.
- The uses of the various default database files created when you install SQL Server, including the master database, the model database, the msdb database, the pubs database, the tempdb, and log files.
- The Web Assistant and the stored procedures `sp_makewebtask`, `sp_runwebtask`, and `sp_dropwebtask`. You can schedule the creation of web objects based on a table or database by creating a web job.

▲ CHAPTER REVIEW QUESTIONS

▲ Multiple Choice:

1. *You can use a backup tape from SQL Server 6.5 and load it into an SQL Server 7 database.*

   A. You can only if you are sure to load the full backup and then all transaction log backups.

   B. Only if you load all transaction logs first and then the last full backup.

   C. You cannot load a backup from a tape, only if the backup is on a disk.

   D. You cannot load an SQL Server 6.5 backup into a SQL Server 7 database.

2. *When using SQL Mail in conjunction with Microsoft Exchange Server you must ensure that the SQL Mail profile does not have:*

   A. A network connection

   B. A Personal Message Store (*.pst) file

   C. A Personal Address Book (*.pab) file

   D. Microsoft Exchange Server connection

3. *Which of the following is not a valid Backup Device. (select all that apply)*

   A. A networked disk drive

   B. A networked tape drive

   C. A local disk drive

   D. A local optical disk

4. *Database statistics are used by:*

   A. The SQL Server Agent

   B. The Query Statistical Checker

   C. The Query Optimizer

   D. The Database Optimizer

5. *When creating a Database Maintenance Plan and you choose to remove unused space from the database, then you must also select:*

   A. The amount of unused space that exists before this option is activated in megabytes.

      B. The amount of unused space that exists before this option is activated as a percentage of the used space.

      C. How much free space will remain as a percentage of used space.

      D. How much free space will remain in megabytes.

      E. A and C

      F. B and D

6. *A process can have a status of:*

      A. Running, not running, or sleeping

      B. Running, walking, or still

      C. Running, runnable, or sleeping

      D. Runnable, off, sleeping

7. *Within the Enterprise Manager window, a process can be killed from the:*

      A. Scope Pane

      B. Kill Activity dialog box

      C. Current Activity dialog box

      D. Activity Terminator dialog box

8. *The msdb database is used for the storage of:*

      A. Task scheduling

      B. Event handling

      C. Alert notifications

      D. A and B

      E. All of the above

9. *The recovery interval is:*

      A. The amount of time required to restore a backup

      B. The amount of time to recover a database when SQL Server starts

      C. The amount of time to recover all databases when SQL Server starts

      D. The time it takes the checkpoint process to run

▲ True or False:

1. True or False? You can back up a database using a diskette drive.

2. True or False? SQL Mail can work with any Internet mail client.

3. True or False? Backup Devices are also referred to as Dump Devices in SQL Server 7?

4. True or False? Only the dbo or system administrator can kill a process.

5. True or False? The model database is used by the master database if it needs to recreate itself.

6. True or False? The pubs database is a required database.

7. True or False? SQL Server uses write-ahead log files.

8. True or False? If a log file fills up, SQL Server will automatically back up the file and then truncate it.

Installation and Configuration

In this next module, you will be introduced to how to plan the installation of SQL Server. This will include information about the various operating systems that you can use, and how to go about installing the program. You will then actually install the program. Many of the possible problems that may be encountered are covered and how to go about rectifying the problem will be discussed. Next will be information about the configuration options available and what they can do for you. Finally, this module will be completed with a section on the actually starting and shutdown of SQL Server.

Installing Microsoft SQL Server 7.0

Before you even begin the installation of SQL Server 7™, there are several things that you should accomplish first. After all, it is much easier to get it all right the first time than to have to uninstall a program and reinstall it again.

- Check your disk space. Do you have adequate disk space on the drive that you plan to use for your SQL Server setup? In the previous chapter you learned the minimum requirements.
- Apply any necessary Service Packs before you begin the installation process.
- If you plan to use RAID or disk mirroring as additional database security, set that up before you begin installing.
- What kind of user security are you using? If using Windows NT™ authentication, then be sure that the server that you are installing SQL Server on has access to user accounts through a trust relationship. It is not recommended that you install SQL Server on a Primary or Backup Domain Controller.
- Create the SQL Server Executive service account. Be sure that it can log in as a service.

- Install Internet Explorer 4 on the machine you will be installing SQL Server 7. This is a required program to complete the installation process.

> Service Packs can be downloaded for free from Microsoft's web site, or you can have a CD sent to you for a nominal charge. The Windows NT Service Packs are cumulative, meaning you only have to load the latest, as it will include all of the previous Service Packs. The Microsoft web site for downloads, as of this writing, can be found at http://supportmicrosoft.com/support/downloads.

There are a number of requirements that the system you plan to install SQL Server on must meet before you start the installation process. These requirements fall into two back parts: operating system and hardware.

MCSE 5.1   Operating System Requirements

SQL Server 7™ operates primarily in the Windows NT Server™ environment. However, you can now use Windows 95/98™ for many of the functions previously allowed only to an NT Server. There are three versions of SQL Server available. The version that you choose will depend on the operating system on which the installation is to be done, as shown in Table 5-1.

Table 5.1 *SQL Server Versions*

	Desktop Edition	Server Edition	Enterprise Edition
Operating Systems	Windows 95 Windows 98 Windows NT Workstation 4.0 Windows NT Server 4.0 Windows NT Server Enterprise	Windows NT Server	Windows NT Server Enterprise
Extended Memory Support (>2GB)	No	No	Yes
Failover Support	No	No	Yes
Replication Support	Merge Replication. Subscriber for transaction replication.	Full	Full
CPUs	2	4	32
Database Size	4GB	None	None

Windows NT

When installing SQL Server onto a Windows NT Server or Workstation, you must first install Service Pack 3, the most current version as of this writing. SQL Server 7 will not run on Windows NT 3.51, you must use NT 4. If you are upgrading an existing SQL Server 6.X database, you can do so on a system running Windows NT with Service Pack 3 or later.

Windows 95/98

SQL Server 7 allows the use of the Windows 95/98 operating system as a server environment. Installation and function are the same as the full-server version that runs on Windows NT with the following exceptions: SMP, asynchronous I/O, and integrated security are not supported on Windows 95/98.

Other than these few exceptions, you can implement SQL Server/Desktop Edition, on a Windows95/98 server/workstation and maintain full compatibility with an SQL Server. This is an excellent method for allowing mobile users to maintain connection with the corporate database. By using their own copy of the database for their work, and then replicating back to the corporate database as needed, they can maintain their information.

Hardware Requirements

For the successful installation of SQL Server 7 you must meet several minimum hardware requirements:

- Intel or compatible system (486/33Mhz or better, Pentium, Pentium PRO, Pentium II processor), DEC Alpha AXP, or compatible system.
- A minimum of 90MB of disk space for a compact installation, or 148MB for a typical installation and the SQL Server Books Online. The client management utilities only require at least 50MB. If you are upgrading an existing SQL Server 6.X database, you will need the 148MB for SQL Server 7 plus 11/2 times your existing databases in additional disk space for use during the conversion process.
- A minimum of 32MB of RAM.
- CD-ROM drive.
- Supported network adapter, unless this is a stand alone-setup.

As stated, these are minimum requirements. As with most high-end database products, the bigger and faster the hardware, the better the database will run.

Required User Accounts

Before beginning the installation process, you must create a Windows NT user-account for the MSSQLServer service's use. You can create one more account for the use of the SQLServerAgent service, or they may share the same account. These user accounts will be dedicated to these services, but must be granted "log on as a service" rights.

Creating a new user account is a normal Windows NT function, and may or may not be a procedure that is allowed to the SQL Server System Administrator. This may be assigned to a Network Administrator, or they can be the same person. Creating a new user account only takes a few moments, and is done like this:

1. Open the User Manager for Domains application by selecting Start, Programs, Administrative Tools, and User Manager for Domains.
2. Select User, New User from the menu to display the New User dialog box. Figure 5-1 shows the completed dialog box. Be sure that you enter a password for this account, because it will be granted administrator privileges and must be protected. Also be sure to remove the checkmark from the User Must Change Password at Next Logon.

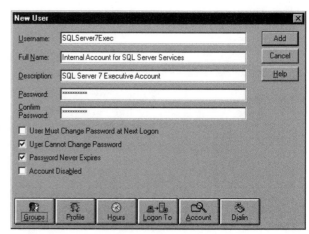

Figure 5–1 *An account for the SQL Executive service's use is being created. The New User dialog box is the first step in this process.*

3. Click the Groups button to open the Group Membership dialog box. Select Administrators from the Not member of list and click the Add button. You should now see a dialog box like the one shown in Figure 5-2. Click the OK button to return to the New User dialog box.

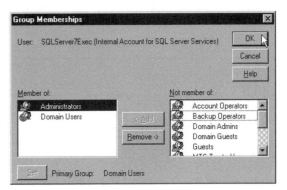

Figure 5–2 *Use the Group Memberships dialog box to select the groups that a user account will be allowed to use. The Administrators group has the greatest range of privileges.*

4. Click the Add button to create the user account, and then the Close button to close the New User dialog box.

5. Select Policies, User Rights from the menu. You must give this account the advanced user rights of logging on as a service.

6. Check the Show Advanced User Rights box at the bottom of the User Rights Policy dialog box.

7. From the Right drop-down list box select Log on as a service, as seen in Figure 5-3.

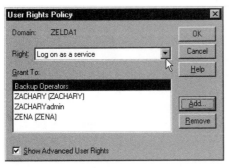

Figure 5–3 *In the User Rights Policy dialog box, the Log on as a service right has been selected. Only those users who have already been granted this right are shown in the Grant To list.*

8. Click the Add button to add the new user account to this list. Only the group accounts are listed in the Names list box. Click on the Show Users button to include individual users in the list box. Scroll down the list until you find the account you just created and select it by clicking on it.

9. To add the account to the Add Names list box you can either click the Add button or double-click the account name. In Figure 5-4 you can see the account now included in the Add Names list. Click on the OK button to return to the User Rights Policy dialog box.

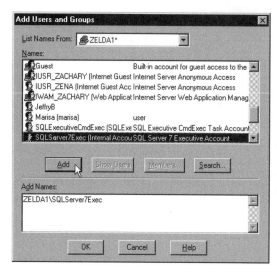

Figure 5–4   *The new administrator account SQLServer7Exec has been added to the lower list box. Once you have completed the next step this service will be able to log in as a Windows NT service.*

10. Click the OK button on the User Rights Policy dialog box, then close the User Manager application.

This is the only required account needed for the installation of SQL Server 7. Once you have a database ready to run you will have to create the necessary user accounts, and possibly additional administrator accounts.

Running the Setup Application

Once you have completed all of the preliminary steps it is time to begin the installation process. SQL Server 7 comes in three versions: Desktop, Standard, and Enterprise, as discussed earlier in this chapter.

The simplest way to install SQL Server is from the computer on which the program is to be installed. This section assumes that this is a new installation and not an upgrade from a 6.X version. This exercises shows the procedure required for a Standard installation.

1. Insert the SQL Server CD-ROM. If your system allows AutoPlay for CDs, the opening screen will be displayed. Otherwise, click on the file Startup.bat. You will see the opening screen as shown in Figure 5-5.

Figure 5–5 *The opening screen is a switchboard allowing you to make several choices about what to do next.*

2. Select the Install SQL Server option from the menu. (Tip: If you have not yet installed Internet Explorer 4.0 then do so now. It is included on the SQL Server CD and can be installed from this switchboard.)

3. Once the SQL Server installation program initializes, the first screen you see will be a simple Welcome screen. Click the Next button to continue.

4. Here you will choose the type of installation, local or remote, as shown in Figure 5-6. The local option allows you to install SQL Server on the machine you are now working on. The remote option allows you to install SQL Server on another machine located on your local area network. Select the Local computer option and click on the Next button.

5. You now have the following three options available to you as you can see in Figure 5-7. Select the first option and click the Next button.

   • Install a new SQL Server and Management Tools: This option installs SQL Server and all of the Management Tools.

   • Install Management Tools only: This option installs only the management tools. Use this selection if you are installing on a client.

   • Work with an existing SQL Server: Use this option to either upgrade a previous version of SQL Server or to change options or rebuild database on an existing SQL Server 7 installation.

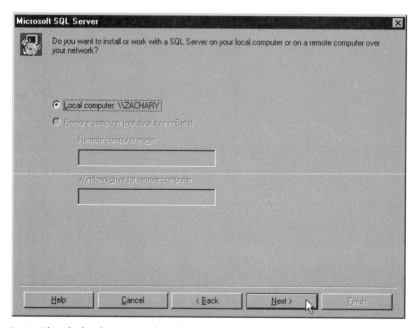

Figure 5–6 *This dialog box is used to choose where SQL Server will be installed—on a remote computer or on the local computer.*

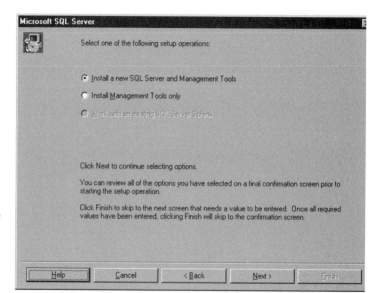

Figure 5–7 *Use this dialog box to choose the type of setup installation you want to do.*

6. Type the information requested in the next dialog box. Only the Name text box is required. Click the Next button to move to the next dialog box. It is recommended that you use the name of the individual who will be responsible for administering the server. The Product ID will be on a sticker on the CD jewel case. This number will be necessary if you attempt to get technical support from Microsoft.

7. In the next dialog box verify that the information you entered in step 6 is correct. If you need to make any changes, click the Back button and make the corrections. Otherwise, click the Next button to move on to the next dialog box.

8. This dialog box is the Software License Agreement. You must agree to the stipulations of this license or you cannot install the software. Read the agreement and then click the I Agree button. Click the Page Down button until you come to the end of the agreement. Once there, the I Agree button will become selectable. Now you can choose the type of installation. You have the following three options available:

   - Typical Installation: This option automatically installs the most common components into a set of default directories

   - Compact Installation: This option installs only the minimum required files to operate SQL Server. This option is recommended only if you are very short on disk space.

   - Custom Installation: This option allows you to make individual selections on a number of various options.

9. Select the Custom Installation option button, and then click the Next button.

10. Select the Do not convert existing SQL Server data at this time option, as seen in Figure 5-8, and then click the Next button.

11. In this dialog box (Figure 5-9), you select the necessary network protocol libraries as required for your own network. Notice that Named Pipes and TCP/IP Sockets have been selected from the six options presented in Figure 5-9 and described here. Click the Next button when you have made your selections. Even if you do not use Named Pipes with your network configuration, it is a required protocol during the setup process. SQL Server can listen on multiple connections at one time. By default, the Multi-Protocol, TCP/IP Sockets, and Named Pipes are selected.

    - Named Pipes: SQL Server always listens on the standard pipe `\\.\pipe\sql\query` for any named pipe connection. Once SQL Server is installed, you can change the pipe name or drop this

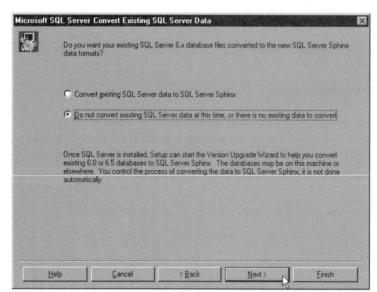

Figure 5–8 *Use this dialog box to choose to convert an existing SQL Server database to SQL Server 7 format.*

support. Windows 95/98 cannot use this protocol and will not be available for an installation on that operating system.

• TCP/IP Sockets: This library is used by SQL Server to listen using Windows Sockets as an IPC method across TCP/IP. An installation on Windows 95/98 will use this as the default network library. You can specify a port that SQL Server will use. The default port 1433 has been

Figure 5–9 *You must choose the necessary Network Protocol Libraries that SQL Server will use to connect to its clients.*

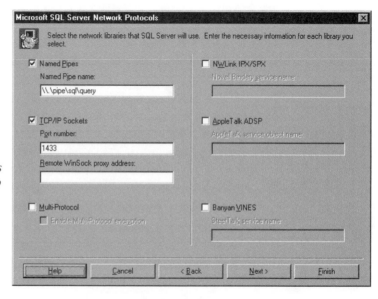

assigned to SQL Server by the Internet Assigned Number Authority (IANA). If you will be using SQL Server to listen on a Microsoft Proxy Server, then include its address in the available text box.

- Multi-Protocol: This library allows communications over the Windows NT Remote Procedure Calls (RPC) facility. Unlike the other network libraries, you do not have to include any additional parameters for this library. The Multi-Protocol library can communicate over most IPC transports supported by Windows NT. As of this writing, only TCP/IP Windows Sockets, NWLink IPX/SPX, and Named Pipes are considered tested and supported.

- NWLink IPX/SPX: Through this library, SQL Server can communicate with Novel SPX clients. When using NWLink IPX/SPX you must provide the Novel Bindery service name to register the SQL Server on the Novell network. The default service name is the name of the computer that SQL Server is installed on.

- AppleTalk ADSP: This server-side network library allows Apple Macintosh clients to connect to the SQL Server using native AppleTalk instead of TCP/IP. You must provide the AppleTalk service object name.

- Banyan Vines: This network library is available only on the Intel platform. SQL Server supports Banyan VINES Sequenced Packet Protocol (SPP) as an IPC method for Banyan VINES IP network protocol. You must provide the StreetTalk service name for this library.

12. Now you must choose a Character Set that SQL Server will use. Be careful in your choice here; you can only change this selection by backing up all of your databases, dropping them, changing the character set, then you may recreate and repopulate them—a very time-consuming process. In Figure 5-10 you see that the default setting, `code page 1252`, is selected. Click the Next button to continue.

A character set refers to a code page containing the ANSI character set. There are 256 upper and lowercase letters, numbers, and symbols in a code page. The normal printable characters are contained in the first 128 and are the same in all of the pages. The next 128 characters, also called the extended characters, are different from set to set. The three most commonly used sets in the United States are:

- Code page `1252`—`ISO Character Set`. This set is also known as ISO 8859-1, Latin 1, or ANSI character set. It is compatible with the character set used by Microsoft Windows and the Windows NT operating systems.

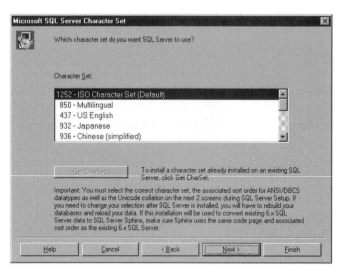

Figure 5–10   *Select an appropriate character set for your database here. Be sure that you select the correct one. Changing the code page later is a laborious process.*

- Code page `850—Multilingual`. This set includes characters used in most of the languages of North and South America, and Europe. This is a good option if you have MS-DOS-based client applications that use the extended character set.

- Code page `437—US English`. This character set is the most commonly used set in the United States, and includes many graphic characters that are not used in database applications. Generally, use code page 1252 unless you have an older application that requires the use of this code page.

13. Now you must choose the sort order that SQL Server will use. Again, this is an important choice and cannot be easily changed later. The sort order you select is how SQL Server will sort a results set in response to a query. Your choices here will vary depending on the character set you selected in the previous dialog box. Figure 5-11 shows that the option `Dictionary order, case-insensitive` has been selected. Other possible choices are described here. Click the Next button to continue to the next dialog box.

   - `Dictionary order, case-insensitive`—this sort order is a simple alphabetical type order, with no distinction made for upper or lowercase letters. Numbers will fall before letters in this type of sort order. You will not be able to predict whether an upper or lowercase letter will appear before its opposite member. You can alleviate some of this problem with the application of business rules on either the server or client-side.

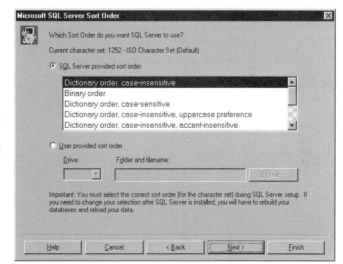

Figure 5–11 *Choose a sort order for SQL Server here. This option will affect all query results sets, and you cannot change your mind without rebuilding and reloading your databases.*

- `Binary`—this sort order will sort values based on their numeric order in the character set.

- `Dictionary order, case-sensitive`—This uses an alphabetical order, but takes the case of a letter into consideration. If you use this selection, then most everything that you do in SQL Server will be case-sensitive, including column and table names.

14. You also have the option of using a custom sort option. Select the User provided sort-order option button, then specify the file containing the necessary information in the text boxes.

15. Now you must choose a sort order for the Unicode data contained in your databases. Unicode data includes the data types nchar and nvarchar. In most cases you will want to choose the same sort order that you selected for your code page data. In Figure 5-12 you see that the General-case-insensitive option has been selected. Click the Next button to go to the next dialog box.

16. Now you must choose the various SQL Server Management Tools that you want to include in the installation. Figure 5-13 shows that all of the tools have been selected for this installation. If you do not want to install a specific tool, remove the checkmark beside it. Click the Next button when you have made any necessary changes.

17. Now select the additional helper applications that you want or don't want to install. If you are running short of disk space, you can choose not to install any of them, but if you are that cramped for space you

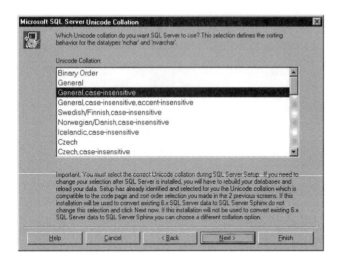

Figure 5–12 *Select a sort order for the Unicode data in your database.*

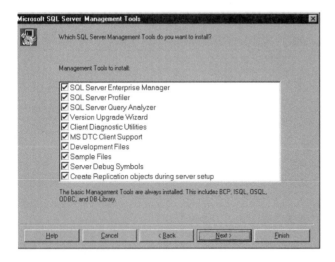

Figure 5–13 *Choose the SQL Server Management Tools necessary for your installation.*

should reconsider installing SQL Server on this machine. Figure 5-14 shows the default selections made. Click the Next button to continue.

18. It is highly recommended that you do install the SQL Server Books Online, at least to run from the CD-ROM. It contains a great deal of useful information. It will, of course, run much faster if installed on the hard disk, and you do not have to make sure that the CD is available each time that you want to use the application.

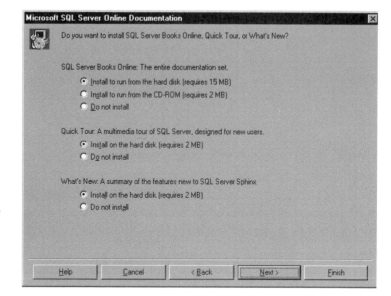

Figure 5–14 *Choose the helper applications that you want to install, and how they will be installed here.*

19. Now choose the drive and location of the folder where SQL Server program will be installed. The default installation chooses the C:drive and a default folder. In Figure 5-15 you see that drive F has been selected and that the default folder remains. Make any necessary changes to the drives and folders required for your own installation. Click the Next button to continue.

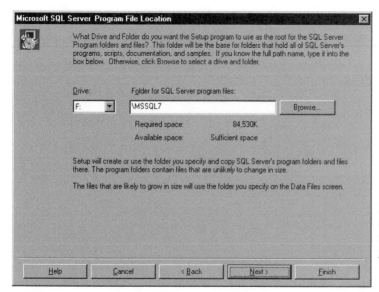

Figure 5–15 *Select the drive and folder where Setup will install the SQL Server program.*

20. Now you must choose the drive and location of the folder where your data files will be located. The default location is the same folder and drive where you have chosen to install the SQL Server program files. A folder will be created for your data files called data in this location. Click the Next button to continue.

21. You must choose the SQL Server Logon Account. In the last chapter you created an account for SQL Server to use. Here is where it will be entered. Figure 5-16 shows the completed options. Click the Next button to move to the next dialog box.

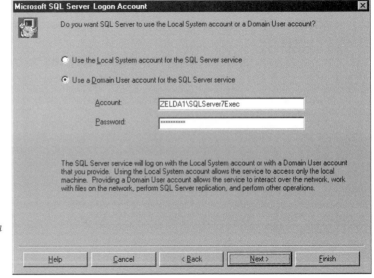

Figure 5–16 *Choose a Logon Account and provide the necessary account name and password if logging on to a Domain account.*

22. If you want this installation of SQL Server to be able to access only the local computer then select the first option button. If you want to allow SQL Server to interact with other computers on the local Domain, then you must choose the second option button and provide the necessary account and password information.

23. Choose whether or not SQL Server service and the SQL Server Agent service will automatically start when Windows NT is booted. Figure 5-17 show that both services will auto start on boot. Click the Next button.

24. Choose a Start menu folder in which SQL Server will be included. The default option is its own folder, Microsoft SQL Server. Click the Next button to continue.

25. You are now at the last dialog box. Use the scroll bar to view the selections that you have made through this process. If you want to change

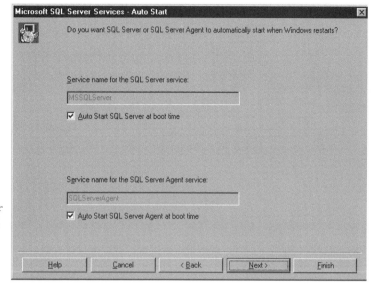

Figure 5–17 *Select which, if any, of the SQL Server services will auto start at boot time.*

any of them, simply highlight them in the list box and click the Change button. You will be immediately jumped back to the dialog box concerning that specific option. Make the necessary changes. You must then click all the way through all of the remaining dialog boxes once again. Figure 5-18 shows some of the current settings. Click the Install Now button to continue.

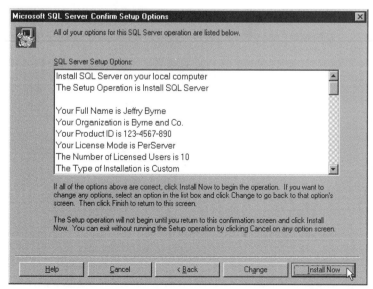

Figure 5–18 *Here the selections made through the install dialog boxes can be rechecked and any corrections made.*

Setup will now proceed with the installation of the SQL Server program. All of the necessary folders will be created, and the files copied to them. When the Setup has completed the installation process you will see one more dialog box telling you that SQL Server is now installed.

26. Click the Exit to Windows button and return to the switchboard.

Full-Text Search Option

When you install SQL Server you have the option to install the optional Full-Text Search sub-component. This is a new feature that enables you to search character-based columns using more than simple equality or LIKE operators. The Full-Text Search option is run as a service under Windows NT and is named MSSearch. This service is not avilable for SQL Server installations on Windows 95/98.

In order to use Full-Text Search, you must not only install the service, but you must specify the tables and columns on which the search will be enabled. you do not simply perform aFull-Text Search on any character-based column. You must also then create a special index that SQL Server uses during a Full-Text Search to find the rows that meet the search criteria.

Full-Text Search is not installed by default. In the previous section of this chapter, you would choose to install this component when you come to the Select Components dialog box. Full-Text Search is a sub-component of SQL Server. You can also add the component to an existing SQL Server 7 installation by simply running the installation application again and specifying the additional component. Figure 5-19 shows the Select Components dialog box with the Full-Text Search option selected.

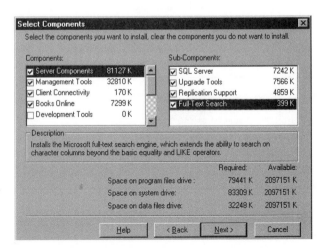

Figure 5–19 *Use the Select Components dialog box to select or unselect components for installation, such as the Full-Text Search option.*

Remember that Full-Text Search runs as a service and needs to be assigned a valid Windows NT user security account in order to run. The simplest method is to use the same security account that you use for the SQL Server Agent service. If you are adding this service after a normal installation, you can set the security account from either the Services applet in the Windows NT Control Panel, or from the Full-Text Search properties dialog box in the Enterprise Manager window.

MCSE 5.2 | Installation Options

You have already seen most of the various options available during the Setup procedure. In this section a few more of the less used options are discussed. These include:

- Installing over the network
- Unattended installations
- The use of installation scripts

Network Installations

Unlike earlier versions of SQL Server you can now perform an installation over the network. This makes it much more convenient in that you do not have to sit in the server room waiting to make all of the necessary choices necessary to the installation. There are two ways that you can install SQL Server through the network: using System Management Server (SMS), or through the Remote Installation option.

If you have System Management Server (SMS) version 1.2 or later installed and in use on your network, SQL Server 7 then includes several files in the root directory of the CD for its use. SMS can be used to greatly automate the installation of SQL Server on several servers at one time. SMS makes use of these files, listed in Table 5-2, that are included to help with an automated installation.

These installation files are text files that you can edit using the text editor of your choice. The Remote Installation is an option that you saw in the previous section in Step 4. By selecting the Remote Installation instead of the Local option you will then be presented with a dialog box asking you to give the name of the server that you will be installing SQL Server.

Table 5.2 *SQL Server SMS Installation files*

File Name	Description
Smssql70.pdf	This is a Package Definition Format (PDF) file used to automate the creation of a SQL Server package in SMS. The package is then distributed and installed on a SMS computer. The PDF file also allows SMS to detect SQL Server on other SMS inventoried computers and report that information to the SMS database.
Sql70ins.cmd	This is a batch file used to detect the hardware platform of the computer. SMS then can run the appropriate version of Setup.
Sql70ins.ini	This script file is used for an unattended setup. You can edit the default settings in this file to specify drive, folders, and other installation options.
Sql70rem.cmd	This batch file detects the hardware platform and then runs the appropriate version of Setup to remove SQL Server in unattended mode.
Sql70rem.ini	This script file is used to complete an unattended removal of SQL Server. The file can be edited to specify the drives and folders where you have actually installed SQL Server.

USING INSTALLATION SCRIPTS

Installation scripts are used for providing SQL Server the necessary parameters for the options during an unattended installation. Without the settings provided by the script, SQL Server will use default settings on all of the installation options. While that may give you a working SQL Server, it may not work in the ways that you need.

In order to run the SQL Server Setup in unattended mode you must start the application from the command line. The command line setup is used like this:

```
setup /t IniFilePath = drive:\path\filename
```

Where the fully qualified file name, including drive and path are inserted in place of "drive:\path\filename." You cannot use a UNC path name, but you can use a redirected path to a network drive. You must have a space on each side of the equal (=) sign. Be sure that you either delete the script file when you have finished using it, or provide the necessary protection for it because it does contain a clear text version of the SQLServerAgent password.

The following sample installation script is very similar to the installation done earlier in this chapter:

```
[Computer]
InstallWhere=Local
[Setup]
Operation=InstallServer
CreateDate=6/30/98
ForceReboot=No
```

```
[Scripts]
CustomScriptList=
CustomScriptPath=
[License]
FullName=
Jeffry Byrne
OrgName=Byrne and Co.
ProductID=123-4567-890
Mode=PerServer
[General]
ConvertExisting=No
ProgramGroup=Microsoft SQL Server Sphinx
[Network]
NetLibList={"SSNMPN70"}
ServerNMPipe=\\.\pipe\sql\query
[CharSet]
CharSet=cpISO
[SortOrder]
SortFileName=nocase.iso
SortConfigValue=52
[Utilities]
Enterprise Manager=Yes
Profiler=Yes
Query Analyzer=Yes
Upgrade Wizard=Yes
Client Diag=Yes
MSDTC Client=Yes
Development Files=Yes
Sample Files=Yes
Debug Symbols=Yes
Create Repl Objects=Yes
[Books]
BooksOnLine=Yes
QuickTour=Yes
WhatsNew=Yes
[ProgramPath]
ProgDrive=C:
ProgFolder=\MSSQL7
[DataPath]
DataDrive=C:
DataFolder=\MSSQL7
[LogonAccountSQL]
LocalSystem=No
UserName=SQLServer
7Exec
UserPassword=password
```

```
[LogonAccountAgent]
LocalSystem=No
UserName=SQLServer7Exec
UserPassword=password
[Services]
AutoServerService=Yes
AutoAgentService=Yes
```

Installing SQL Server Clients Tools

When you install SQL Server the default setup installs all of the client management tools. You can install these tools to a client directly from the SQL Server Installation CD-ROM, or they can be copied onto a shared network drive and installed from there. This, of course, takes a great deal of disk space.

You can also create a network share drive of the CD-ROM drive on the server and install from there. It is a little slower, than a hard-disk drive, but you do not have to later erase the software and folder, and you can use the shared CD-ROM later for other software installations.

Installing the Client Management Tools is an abbreviated form of the complete installation process. Referring back to the section "Running the Setup Application," follow Steps 1 through 4. At Step 5, select the "Install a new SQL Server and Management Tools" option instead of the "Install a New SQL Server."

When installing the tools to Windows 95-based client, you must be sure that there is an autoexec.bat file located in the root directory. If one does not exist, then create one before you try to install the client tools.

Normally all of the Client Management Tools will be selected for installation. You can unselect any of them by removing the checkmark beside their name. The basic Management Tools: BCP, ISQL, OSQL, ODBC, and DB-Library are always installed.

MCSE 5.3 Troubleshooting Setup

During the setup of a complex application like SQL Server 7, you may have various difficulties completing the installation. When you do have an error during the install procedure, be sure to read the dialog box that is displayed; it will give you some clues to the problem.

One of your greatest assets during the troubleshooting sequence is to be methodical. Try not to make several changes to your setup procedure or hardware/software settings and then reinstall—do them one at a time. Unless you can definitely point a finger at several individual items that worked in concert to cause your problems, it is best to take it a step at a time.

If your installation process fails, it will more than likely be due to one of the following:

- A file is currently in use
- Registry errors
- An account name does not exist

If SQL Server Setup tries to write to a file currently in use, it will pause the installation and displays a Critical Error dialog box. If you are installing SQL Server 7 on a machine that currently has an earlier version of SQL Server installed on it, be sure to stop the service before installing the new software. The name of the file causing the problem will be listed in this dialog box. First try clicking the Reset button a couple of times. The application using the file may release it, and if this does not work, then click the Exit Setup button to cancel the installation process. Try to determine what application is using the file and stop the application or service. Then try to reinstall SQL Server.

If an installation fails on a clean Windows NT system with Service Pack 3 installed you may have one of two problems:

Check the Event Log. If you find that ISQL did not log on then the system administrator (sa) password has not been assigned.

If Setup completed successfully, but you were not able to start the application, run regedt32.exe and check the following Registry key:

```
HKEY_LOCAL_MACHINE
\SOFTWARE
\MICROSOFT
\MSSQLServer
\MSSQLServer
\Parameters
SQLArgX -m
```

Look for the key SQLArgX, and if it contains the value "-m" delete it and try to log on to SQL Server again.

If your installation fails part way through the Setup procedure, you should delete the partial installation and rebuild the registry to its state prior to the failed installation. This can be done by running:

```
Setup /t RegistryRebuild = ON
After this has completed, then you must completely remove
the failed installation by running the Setup application
with the following switches set:
Setup /t RemoveAll = WARN
```

Now try to reinstall SQL Server fresh.

Client Connections

If an SQL Server client is unable to connect to the SQL Server you will need to determine what is causing the problem. There are several points that should be checked, including:

- The physical network connection.
- The server name used on the client.
- The network library on the client.
- The port or pipe selected.

The last three of these parameters can be controlled through the Client Configuration Utility, while the first you will need to check with a meter. You will find this as an option on your Start menu, in the Microsoft SQL Server 7 menu. When selected the SQL Server Client Configuration dialog boxis displayed, as seen in Figure 5-20. This utility has three tab buttons available to you.

- *General*: This tab enables you see what servers are connected by which network libraries. The client and the server need to be using the same libraries in order for you to make a successful connection. You can add, remove, or edit connections by clicking the appropriate button.
- *Network Libraries*: This tab lists the network libraries that are currently available to you, and gives you information about the version, filename, and file date of the specific library.
- *DB Library Options*: This tab enables you to see what DB Library options are selected. There are only two options available to you; Automatic ANSI to OEM and Use International Settings. The first allows you to automatically convert ANSI characters to OEM characters. The second option allows the client to use the international settings for things such as dates and currency types.

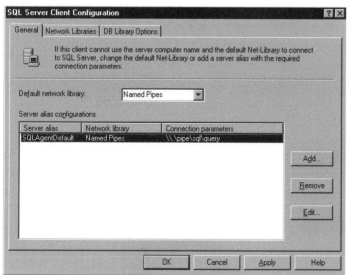

Figure 5–20 *Use the SQL Server Client Configuration utility to set the options necessary for the client to connect to the server.*

When troubleshooting connection problems from the client, be sure to check these settings. More often than not, the problems lie and can be corrected at the SQL Server Client Configuration utility dialog box.

Key Points

In this chapter you have learned these key points:

- The operating system requirements for installing and running SQL Server.
- The hardware requirements for the successful installation of SQL Server.
- Creating a Windows NT user account with administrator privileges and the advanced user right of logging on the system as a user.
- Use a checklist prior to beginning the Setup procedure to help ensure that your installation will proceed smoothly.
- Apply any Service Packs before installation.
- Know where you plan to install the software and that you have adequate room, and the necessary permissions to install the software.
- Choose a licensing option: Per Seat or Per Server.
- Know what type of network libraries you must install. Check with the Network Administrator if you are not sure.
- Select the correct character set/code page and sort orders.

- You can install SQL Server from a shared network drive.
- Use a script if you plan to use an unattended setup.
- Install the Client Management Tools to a client computer.

▲ CHAPTER REVIEW QUESTIONS

▲ Multiple Choice:

1. *SQL Server can be installed on what operating systems (Select all that apply).*
   A. Windows NT Server 4 with Service Pack 1
   B. Windows 95
   C. Windows NT Workstation with Service Pack 3
   D. Windows for Workgroups

2. *The Desktop Edition of SQL Server can run on which platform.*
   A. 486/33 with 48MB of RAM and Windows 95
   B. Pentium 133 with 64MB of RAM and Windows for Workgroup
   C. Pentium 200 laptop with 16MB of RAM and Windows 98
   D. B and C
   E. All of the above

3. *SQL Server uses which network connection during installation?*
   A. TCP/IP port 1433
   B. Named Pipes
   C. Multiprotocol
   D. IPX/SPX

4. *Microsoft recommends which code page for standard installation in the United States.*
   A. Code page 437 - U.S. English
   B. Code page 850 - Multilingual
   C. Code page 1252 - ISO Character Set

5. *An unattended installation of SQL Server makes use of?*
   A. Low-paid network clerk to enter information from a list
   B. An installation script
   C. An installation dll
   D. A command-line module named "unattended"

6. *When installing the Client Management Tools on a Windows-95 based client, you must be sure that there is a _____ file located in the root directory.*

    A. config.sys

    B. autoexec.bat

    C. autoexec.dos

    D. config.sql

7. *The Basic Management Tools that are always installed include which of the following:*

    A. BCP

    B. ODBC and DB-Library

    C. IPX/SPX

    D. ISQL and XSQL

    E. A and B

    F. All of the above

8. *SQL Server can be installed through a network connection by using: (Select all that apply).*

    A. SMS

    B. TCP/IP

    C. An Installation script

    D. Remote Installation option

    E. LAN Installation option

    F. All of the above

9. *Full-Text Search is a_____.(Select all that apply).*

    A. Type of query

    B. Query criteria

    C. NT service

    D. Installed in any SQL Server installation.

10. *Use the SQL Server Client Configuration utility to: (Select all that apply).*

    A. Select an international currency type.

    B. Add a network library.

    C. Edit a network library.

    D. Setup the Master database on the client

11. *The DB Library tab on the Client Configuration utility dialog box enables you to set the default configuration for: (Select all that apply).*

    A. Which DB Library will be used by the client to connect to SQL Server.

    B. The ANSI to OEM automatic conversion

    C. Which network protocol will be used by DB Library

    D. If the International settings will be used.

▲ True and False:

1. *True or False? You cannot change the sort order once you install SQL Server.*

2. *True or False? You can choose not to install any of the Management Tools.*

3. *True or False? The NT service that controls the Full-Text Search is the MS Text Search service.*

4. *True or False? The SQL Server Client Configuration utility must be run from the client workstation.*

5. *True or False? The Windows NT security account used for the SQL Server service must be able to "log on as a service."*

6. *True or False? Unicode collation is a synonym for character set.*

Configuration Options

Other than the everyday tasks of maintaining databases, client access, and other such tasks, a system administrator will attempt to tweak and tune SQL Server™ to improve the performance of the database as a whole. This is not a single procedure, but a continuous process that involves several of SQL Servers subsystems: memory, physical disks, data and log file structures, and queries. In this chapter, database performance has to do with the speed with which your clients can access information contained in an SQL Server database. This can be a very complex topic, with some specialists devoting years to mastering the craft.

This chapter will provide an overview of the subject and some of the steps you can use to improve the performance of your SQL Server database. In the Windows NT™ operating system, much of the memory configuration is done by Windows NT itself in conjunction with the operating system administrator, who may not be the same as you, the SQL Server System Administrator.

Optimizing Memory Usage

How much memory is made available to SQL Server is determined by a number of factors, including:

- How much physical memory is installed in the computer?
- Is the server used for any other purposes, or is it dedicated exclusively to SQL Server's use?
- How much physical disk space is available?
- Will the server be participating as a replication server?

System Memory

As you consider memory, you must consider how Windows NT uses memory and how it allocates that memory for SQL Server to use. Windows NT configures the available memory, reserving approximately the first 12MB to its own operating kernel and services. The amount of memory required by Windows NT will grow as your needs for resources for SQL Server also grow, as Windows NT has to accommodate additional threads, page tables, and other memory needs. The next portion of available memory is available for executable programs, such as SQL Server. The physical memory available to SQL Server is determined by several configuration settings, and the various services that you may have running on your server. The Setup application initially configures SQL Server with a default memory option of zero (0). This setting enables SQL Server to dynamically change its memory requirements based on its own needs and the available resources. You can also hard-set the amount of memory allocated to SQL Server by using the memory option. As an estimate, SQL Server will appropriate 4 to 8MB of memory in servers with less than 32MB of RAM, or 16MB or more in systems with 32MB or more. With the current price of memory today, it is not unreasonable to expect that you should start with at least 64MB in a production server.

Win32 applications, such as SQL Server, can make use of Windows NT's Virtual Memory Manager, allowing the application to make use of virtual memory. Virtual memory is a combination of both physical RAM memory and hard disk space used by the `PAGEFILE.SYS` file. To ensure the best possible performance, SQL Server can lock memory for its own use, potentially causing other applications to receive "out-of-memory" errors. If this does occur, you may need to adjust the amount of memory assigned to SQL Server downward a little. If the server is assigned more work than simply a server for SQL Server, you may have to give less memory than SQL Server optimally wants, unless you add additional RAM to the computer.

The maximum setting is 30,072MB for the memory option regardless of the actual physical memory available.

SQL Server allocates memory into several parts. The first is the part that is used by the SQL Server executable program. This memory is not configurable, nor adjustable. The next part is configurable and is used by SQL Server's kernel and internal structures. The final, and largest part, is the buffer cache. The buffer cache is composed of two parts: procedure and data. The procedure cache holds stored procedures, triggers, views, rules, and defaults. The data cache holds the data that SQL Server believes will be needed next. The size of the procedure cache can be changed, which has the effect of changing the data cache at the same time.

SQL Server provides several tools to help you decide how to tune your server's memory. The primary tools are the SQL Server Performance Monitor and DBCC MEMUSAGE.

DBCC MEMUSAGE will give you a detailed report on how SQL Server is using the cache memory it has been provided. This report is divided into two sections: Buffer Cache and Procedure Cache. DBCC MEMUSAGE can be used from within the Query Analyzer application.

The first part of the report lists the first 20 largest objects, tables, and indexes, which are being held in the buffer cache. If you do not have 20 objects open in the buffer cache, then it will report on the number available. This part of the report will need to be scrolled as it is many columns wide. The listing below is only a partial view of the results. An abbreviated version of the report looks like this:

```
Buffer Cache, Top 20:
     DB Id          Object Id    Index Id   2K Buffers
     1              5            0          187
     1              3            0          41
     1              1            0          21
     5              5            0          20
     1              5            1          10
     1              1            2          9
```

1	99	0	9
2	3	0	8
1	2	0	6
1	6	0	6
1	36	0	4
5	1	0	4
5	2	0	4
5	3	0	4
5	5	1	4
1	6	1	3
2	2	0	3
5	1	2	3
5	99	0	3
1	45	255	2

The final part of the DBCC MEMUSAGE report lists the largest 20 objects stored in the procedure cache, though only four are shown here. If an object has been duplicated in the procedure cache, all of its aspects are lumped together and only listed once in this report. You may often have duplicated objects. A precompiled version of an object is listed as *trees*, while compiled versions are listed as *plans*. You can see trees listed as the last column, while plans are in the next several columns to the right and are not displayed.

```
Procedure Cache, Top 4:
```

	(4 row(s) affected)						
Name	Type	version	Dbid	Objectid	Uid	#trees
	Adhoc statement	0	5	0	0	0
	Adhoc statement	0	5	0	0	0
	Adhoc statement	0	5	0	0	0
CK__authors__au_id __08EA5793	Check	0	5	149575571	1	1

MCSE 6.2   Monitoring and Profiling

SQL Server includes a suite of performance and profiling monitors. Performance monitors track specific, selected indicators over time. The Profiler is used to trace selected objects. These objects can range from security events, locks, transaction statements, and many other aspects of a database.

Performance Monitors

You can also use the SQL Server Performance Monitor to check selected performance statistics. This can be shown as a live graph, allowing you to monitor how well SQL Server is using the resources available to it. You should run these tests while the server is under a normal working load, otherwise you will get results that will probably not be representative of your system.

One of the easiest and least expensive ways to improve the performance of SQL Server is to add additional physical memory. By using SQL Performance Monitor, you can determine if this will actually help in your situation or not. New memory is primarily used by SQL Server as additional buffer cache, which consequently may improve the cache hit ratio. The cache hit ratio is a statistic that shows how often, as a percentage, SQL Server finds the data it needs available in the data cache. The more often, or the higher this ratio, the less often SQL Server has to go and read this information from disk. Since disk reads are many times slower than reading the same information from the data cache, disk reads are much more expensive than are memory reads in terms of performance. The SQL Performance Monitor is used like this:

1. Open the SQL Server Performance Monitor by selecting the Start button, then Programs, Microsoft SQL Server, and then SQL Server Performance Monitor from the Start menu. You will now see the Performance Monitor window displayed in Figure 6-1.

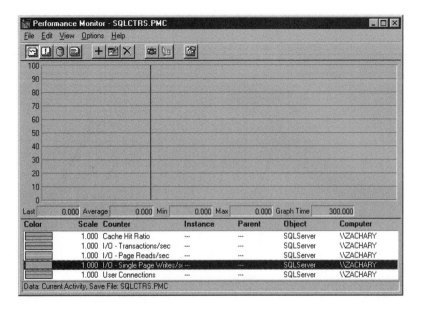

Figure 6–1 *The default SQL Server Performance Monitor and is counters are displayed.*

2. You can add other counters to the Monitor by clicking the Add counter button on the toolbar, select Edit, Add To Chart from the menu, or use the keyboard shortcut Ctrl+I to open the Add to Chart dialog box, as seen in Figure 6-2.

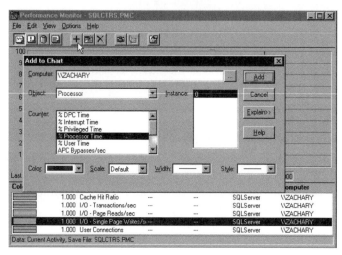

Figure 6–2   *Use the Add to Chart dialog box to select from the many different groups of counters available to the normal Windows NT Performance Monitor.*

3. From the Object list box, leave the default setting of Processor. There are a great many options available here. Select %Processor Time from the list displayed in the Counter list box, then click the Add button. Notice that the Cancel button changes to a Done button. Click it when you have added all of the counters that you currently want to view. Click it now. You will see a new counter at the bottom of the counter legend, as shown in Figure 6-3.

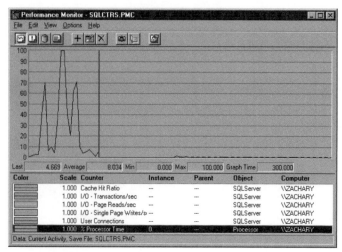

Figure 6–3   *The Page Faults/sec graph is now displayed. This counter can help you to decide if your memory configuration is optimized for SQL Server.*

The Performance Monitor can run in the background so that you can periodically check current statistics. You can display more than one counter at a time on the graph, and you can adjust the frequency at which the Performance Monitor will update the graph. A setting of between 1 and 3 seconds is usually adequate for most statistics. If you want to view the graph over a longer period of time, click the Option button on the toolbar and reset the value for Interval to a greater number of seconds. The value shown in Figure 6-3 for Graph Time is the number of seconds for the Performance Monitor to complete a sweep from one side of the graph to the other. You can also decrease the time interval to values of less than one second, but take note: too short a time interval adds a measure of overhead to the graph. Once you set the time interval too small, such as one-tenth of a second, some of the counters will jump to 100 percent, and you may add a degree of unstability within Windows NT itself, possibly causing a system crash.

You can also adjust the counter scale by selecting the specific counter and double-clicking it. The Edit Chart Line dialog box will be displayed where you can change the line color, style, width, and scale.

The Profiler

The SQL Server Profiler is a new graphical tool you can use to view events. Events that can be monitored are engine events, and can include:

- Security login connections, failures, and disconnections.
- Opening of cursors.
- Lock acqusitions and releases.
- Errors written to the SQL Server error log.
- T-SQL statements such as SELECT, INSERT, UPDATE, and DELETE.
- Remote Procedure Calls (RPC) batch status.

The information captures by the Profiler traces can be captured in a table for later review and analysis. Figure 6-4 displays the Profiler window and shows a login trace. As you can see, there have been three failed login attempts. This is an excellent method to track failed login attempts. The trace records information about the class of the event that triggered the trace, a short text message, the application that originated the event, the NT User Name and SQL User Name of the user triggering the trace, and other data that may be useful in anaylzing an event at a later date.

The Profiler is accessed from the Start menu, or from the Tools menu on the Enterprise Manager, or the Tools option on the Server shortcut menu. If you have not set a trace then you will be presented with a blank window. clicking the New Trace button will display the Trace Properties dialog box

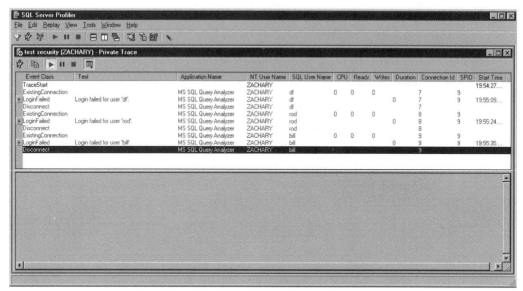

Figure 6–4 *The SQL Server Profiler can be used to create a trace on many types of events, including security failures.*

and enables you to set up a new trace. A new trace must be named, and can be either shared or private. They are set up on a single server, and results can be captured to a file or a table.

Once you have set the new traces name, you can choose from nine event classes on the Event tab. These are the general types of objects that can be used to trigger the trace. Each event class has several specific events that you can select from.

The Profiler window shown in Figure 6-4, displays certain columns of data. You can add or remove columns on the Data Columns tab on the Trace Properties dialog box. This enables you to trace the specific information that you require.

The last tab, Filters, is used to specify criteria that can be used to either include or exclude an event from being captured by the trace. These criteria can be specific applications, connections, database ID's, and other criteria.

Allocating Memory

If you are using the default memory options, and allowing SQL Server to dynamically configure memory, you do not have to worry much about it again. It is always a good idea to periodically check the SQL Server Performance Monitor and verify that everything is in good working order.

In dynamic memory mode, the lazy writer queries the system to determine the current amount of free physical memory available. It then grows or shrinks the buffer cache to ensure that the free physical memory stays at 5MB, plus or minus 200KB at all times. This amount should be enough to ensure that Windows NT does not have to resort to paging. If the free physical memory is less than 5MB, then the lazy writer releases memory from SQL Server to Windows NT. Memory reallocated to the operating system goes on a free list. If the lazy writer finds that there is more than 5MB of available free physical memory, it will recommit the memory to the buffer cache. Memory is recommitted only when the free list is repopulated.

Note Setting the memory option too high may cause the system to have to read from the paging system, while setting it too low will cause poor overall SQL Server system performance because it does not have access to the resources it wants.

If your use of the Performance Monitors has indicated a possible problem that increasing the amount of memory to SQL Server will help, it is a relatively simple process to make these adjustments. As with many things in SQL Server, there are two ways to adjust these parameters: through the use of the SQL Server Enterprise Manager, or by using the Query Analyzer. There are two parameters that have an effect on the amount of memory allocated and how it is allocated: the memory option and the procedure cache. The memory option can be changed using either method, while the procedure cache can only be changed through the Query Analyzer and the stored procedure `sp_configure`. Here, you will use the Query Analyzer and the stored procedure `sp_configure` to change the memory configuration:

1. Open the Query Analyzer application. Be sure that the master database is displayed in the Database list box, and type the following:

```
sp_configure
```

2. Click the Execute Query Into Grid button. As you can see in Figure 6-5, a long list of configurable items appears. Using `sp_configure` without any parameters lets you see all of the standard parameters.

3. Now add to the `sp_configure` statement as shown here.

```
sp_configure 'memory', '32'
EXEC sp_configure
```

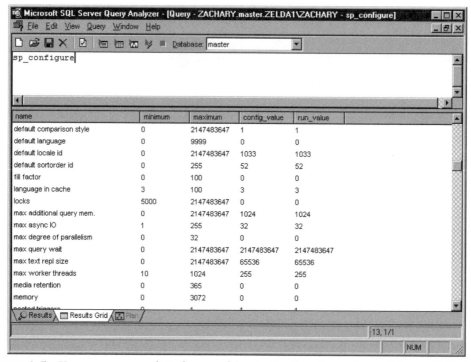

Figure 6–5 *You can now see a list of many of the standard configuration options available in the query results grid. Notice the memory option at the bottom of the list.*

4. You must use the EXEC statement in front of the second `sp_configure` statement because it is not the first statement in the query.

5. Click the Execute Query Into Grid button. You will see a new result set generated as shown in Figure 6-6.

6. This value change indicates that the configured memory value has been set to a specific physical memory size of 32M. Notice that the value in the `run_value` column remains 0. This value comes from the system table syscurconfigs, while the `config_value` comes from the sysconfigure system table. Unless the option that you change is a dynamically configured option, in which case issuing the RECONFIGURE WITH OVERRIDE statement will reset the `run_value` immediately, you must stop and restart SQL Server for a nondynamic option before it will take effect.

There are additional parameters that are considered Advanced options. By default, these options are not displayed—you must specify that these

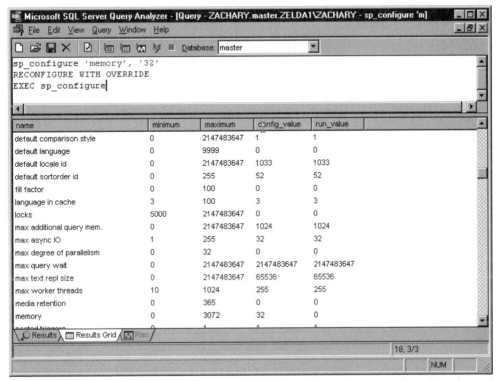

Figure 6–6 *You now see the memory option has been changed from a config_value of 0 to that of 32.*

If you accidentally change the memory option to a value too high for SQL Server to support, it will then default to a dynamic setting, rather than an incorrect one.

options be visible and available for configuration by changing the Show Advanced Options configuration to 1. You would use a statement like this:

```
sp_configure 'show advanced option', '1'
RECONFIGURE WITH OVERRIDE
EXEC sp_configure
```

The procedure cache option has minimum and maximum settings of 1 and 99, respectively. The default values for `config_value` and `run_value` are both set at 30. The procedure cache setting is expressed as a percentage of the remaining memory after SQL Server's basic needs are met.

In the default setting, 30 percent of the remaining memory is allocated to the procedure cache. There is no specific configuration setting for the buffer cache. It is simply the amount remaining after SQL Server gets its bite, and then the procedure cache gets its allocation.

You can also change the memory option parameter through the use of the Enterprise Manager. In this exercise you will reconfigure the memory parameter like this:

1. Open the SQL Enterprise Manager window and right-click on a server icon. Select Properties from the shortcut menu. You can also use the menu bar and choose Action, Properties and display the SQL Server Properties dialog box, as shown in Figure 6-7.

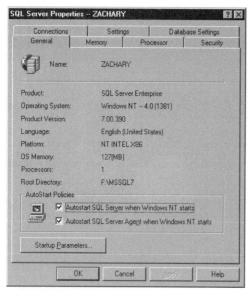

Figure 6–7   *The Server Configuration/Options dialog box is used to change many options and configuration parameters, including memory and procedure cache size.*

2. Click the Memory tab to make adjustments to the total memory configuration. You have four options available:

   • Dynamically configure SQL Server memory: This is the default setting and allows SQL Server to configure its own memory allocation.

   • Use a fixed memory size (MB): When you select this option button, you then select the amount of memory that you want SQL Server to allocate. Allocate memory by dragging your mouse on the slide control. Stay within the green area when you choose the amount of memory to allocate.

- Reserve physical memory for SQL Server: Use this checkbox if you want to allocate the amount of memory you select on the slide bar for the exclusive use of SQL Server. When selected, Windows NT cannot control the swapping of pages from this memory to the page file if another application needs the memory.

- Maximum query memory (KB): This option sets the maximum amount of memory allocated per user for a query execution. The default setting is 1024K (1MB) per user.

3. Click the first option button, Dynamically configure SQL Server memory as you can see in Figure 6-8.

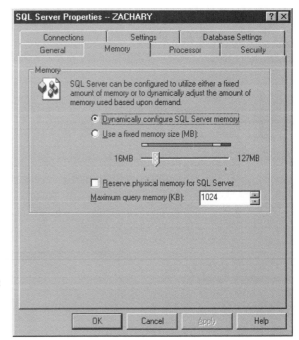

Figure 6–8 *Use the Memory tab of the SQL Server Properties dialog box to change most of the memory configuration options.*

If you inadvertently set an invalid memory configuration (usually by overcommitting memory), SQL Server may not be able to start. you can start SQL Server in a minimum configuration using the -f switch. This is done within Windows NT's Control Panel and the Services applet. The -f switch is used as a startup parameter.

4. Apply your changes to the memory parameter by clicking the OK button. Now stop SQL Server by selecting Action, Stop from the menu, or by using the SQL Server Service Manager application. Click the red light button to stop the server, and then click the green light to restart the server once again. Once the server service has started, close the SQL Server Service Manager. Your new settings will now be in effect.

Always recheck the Performance Monitor statistics after making changes, especially increases to the memory parameter. If you see that the number of page faults increases, then you have allocated too much memory for SQL Server's use and are causing the system to resort to the paging file for data. Causing SQL Server to read from the paging file results in actual disk reads and, consequently, a much slower response time.

MCSE 6.3 Optimizing Disk Performance

Once you have optimized your available memory for SQL Server, you can now look at your disk subsystem. Under most circumstances your I/O system is not as much of a bottleneck as is the actual disk access. The first piece of information you need to know is, do you have one hard disk for SQL Server, or do you have two or more?

The problem with a single disk system is the collision between disk reads requested by a user needing data from a table, and disk writes from the log writer. As a database becomes busier, the potential for collisions between conflicting I/O requests will become more frequent, resulting in slow performance. As a System Administrator, one of your jobs is to periodically check the health of the disk subsystem. Using some of the additional Performance Monitor counters can give you valuable information about the disk I/O your system is producing. One of the goals you should be striving for is the smallest amount of disk activity that you can get. After all, that is one of your slowest I/O processes.

There are not many things that can be done to speed up a hard drive's access speed, short of replacing your drives with faster ones. This can get expensive very quickly. After adding more physical memory to your system, the next easiest and least expensive thing you can do is to separate data and log files, placing them onto separate disks. Even better is to place the files on separate disks, and then to separate the disks with two controllers. By reducing the competition of the log and data files for the narrow access available for I/O access to the relatively slow disk drives, you can help to improve the performance of the entire system.

There are several methods for getting around the problems of optimizing the performance of the disk subsystem. The best option is the use of a Redundant Array of Inexpensive Disks (RAID) subsystem, which will be covered further in Chapter 16, "Backing Up the Database."

The next best option is with the use of software-based disk striping. Windows NT allows you to create stripe sets across several disks. A stripe set allows you to create a single logical volume across several disks. When you use this option Windows NT allows you to create separate partitions on 2 to 32 separate disks, which are then combined as a single volume, as illustrated in Figure 6-9. You cannot place more than one member partition from any stripe set on any one disk. A hard disk may contain more than one partition, each of which is a member of a different stripe set. Then, as a database is read or written to, it is placed as stripes across all of the disks in the set. This form of disk writing and reading provides a relatively inexpensive way to balance the I/O load of a database.

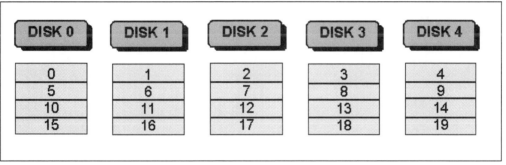

Figure 6–9 *A striped set composed of five disks. As a database is read or written it will be evenly distributed across all of the members of the set.*

An older technique that can be used instead of striped sets is to simply separate the data, index, and log files onto separate drives. The idea behind this is that separating these files onto their own disk will help to balance the I/O load across the several disks. The problem is that it places a greater burden on the system administrator, that of balancing the load. This means that the system administrator must manually adjust the locations of each of these files or segments, and routinely monitor their activity, making additional changes as necessary. Also, as a database becomes larger, or even at different times of the day, the database activity may change. One table may become significantly larger than the table it has been balanced against, or one table may be heavily accessed early in the day, and the second is accessed later in the day, resulting in the uneven load you were trying to eliminate.

MCSE 6.4   The Multithreaded Server

The concept of threads was introduced in Chapter 1. SQL Server uses native Windows NT operating system threads for all work performed.

One of the features to Windows NT and SQL Server is the ability to associate a thread with a specific processor in a Symmetric MultiProcessor (SMP) system with four or more processors. The term used is *processor affinity*. By configuring the affinity mask option, you can select which processors will receive work from specified groups of threads. This also reduces the number of times that the processor cache has to be reloaded. You can also use processor affinity to associate or exclude SQL Server processes from a processor.

By using processor affinity, you can often improve throughput of data by taking worker threads from certain processors that are busy and placing them on processors with unused cycles. In an SMP system, Windows NT uses processor 0 for all I/O processing, so this processor is often very busy. Without thread affinity, many additional processes may be placed on this processor instead of one that has less work, slowing the overall system throughput and degrading performance. Windows NT also places all delayed process calls (DPC), usually associated with the work required by a network interface card (NIC), on the highest numbered processor. If, for example, you have a server with two NICs and eight processors, then one NIC will have its work placed on processor 7, while the second NIC's work will be placed on processor 6. That leaves five processors on which you can balance SQL Server's workload.

Threads are associated with a processor by using the affinity mask option of `sp_configure`. This is an Advanced Option so it is only visible if you set the Show Advanced options to 1 first. The thread affinity mask uses a number 1 in a bit designation for the processor to turn the processor on. A 0 indicates that this processor will not accept input from SQL Server. For example, Table 6-1 shows some of the affinity masks options for a four-processor system: This example of an affinity mask in a four-processor system will set processors 1, 2, and 3 as being available for SQL Server's threads:

```
sp_configure 'affinity mask', 14
```

This system will now pass no-thread requests to processor 0, isolating it for the use of the I/O subsystem.

The Affinity Mask option is only available on SMP systems with more than four processors. Trying to run this stored procedure parameter on a system that does not meet these requirements will result in a message telling you the option is not available and may be an advanced option.

Table 6.1 *Some Processor Affinity Mask Options*

Decimal Value	Binary bit mask	Will allow SQL Server threads on processor
1	00000001	Allows SQL Server threads on processor 0.
3	00000011	Allows SQL Server threads on processors 0 and 1.
6	00000110	Allows SQL Server threads on processors 1 and 2, isolating processor 0 for I/O use, and processor 3 for DPC use.
7	00000111	Allows SQL Server threads on processors 0, 1, and 2, isolating processor 3 for DPC use.
14	00001110	Allows SQL Server threads on processors 1, 2, and 3, isolating only processor 0 for I/O use.
15	00001111	Allows SQL Server threads on all processors.

Key Points

There are several key points covered in this chapter:

- How Windows NT and SQL Server allocate memory resources between them.

- How to use DBCC MEMUSAGE to view statistical information about memory configuration.

- How to use SQL Server Performance Monitor to monitor various statistical information about the server.

- How to use the SQL Server Profiler to audi and record data about selected events.

- How to use `sp_configure` to view and change memory options.

- How to use `sp_configure` to view the Advanced Options.

- How to use the Enterprise Manager to change SQL Server's memory configuration options, including the total memory allocated, or to use dynamic memory options.

- What stripe sets are and how they can be used to optimize disk performance.

- How to set and use thread affinity masks for a multiprocessor system.

▲ CHAPTER REVIEW QUESTIONS

▲ Multiple Choice:

1. *When the SQL Server Setup program is finished, the initial memory configuration is set at:*

    A. 32MB

    B. 12MB

    C. 0MB

    D. 8MB

2. *8MBSQL Server allocates the largest amount of available memory to the:*

    A. Executable programs

    B. Kernel memory

    C. Internal Structures

    D. Buffer cache

3. *Resetting the Memory option in sp_configure to a value too high for SQL Server to support will cause:*

    A. SQL Server will be unable to start

    B. SQL Server will automatically change the value to the maximum value available

    C. SQL Server will default to dynamic mode

    D. SQL Server will crash

4. *If you make an invalid memory configuration and SQL Server is unable to start, which switch would you use in the Services applet for MSSQLServer to attempt a start in a minimum configuration?*

    A. The -min switch

    B. The -m switch

    C. The -f switch

    D. The -x switch

5. *After making a change to the memory configuration, what Performance Monitor statistic may indicate that too much memory has been allocated to SQL Server's exclusive use?*

    A. An increase in the memory faults

    B. An increase in the page faults

    C. A decrease in the SQL Server memory faults

    D. A decrease in the CPU utilization

6. *You can use processor affinity and thread association in a system with how many processors?*

    A. One

    B. Three

    C. Eight

    D. All of the above

7. *In an SMP system, Windows NT uses processor 0 for all:*

    A. Delayed process calls associated with an NIC card

    B. All SQL Server management

    C. All I/O processing

    D. All video support

8. *If you want to check that your memory configuration is working for your particular server, you would use the: (select all that apply)*

    A. SQL Server Performance Monitor.

    B. Windows NT Performance Monitor.

    C. SQL Server Profiler.

    D. The Memory tab on the SQL Server Properties dialog box.

▲ True or False:

1. *True or False? In order to allow SQL Server to manage memory dynamically, you must set the memory configuration option to the Dynamic setting.*

2. *True or False? You can change the size of both the procedure cache and the data cache.*

3. *True or False? The SQL Server Performance Monitor shows monitors that are specific to the health of SQL Server.*

4. *True or False? The SQL Server Profiler produces output that can be captured in either a file or a table.*

5. *True or False? The SQL Server Profiler is used on Server Groups and not specific servers.*

Startup and Shutdown

Before other users can work with a database, SQL Server™ must first be started. If a user tries to log in to the database when the server has been stopped or not yet started, they will get an error telling them that the connection failed.

There are many reasons for shutting down SQL Server: upgrades, full off-line backups, loading a database, or making changes to a database's structure, to name a few. Once SQL Server has been stopped or shut down, it must be started before users can gain access to the information contained in the databases. For certain jobs, such as upgrading the server software, loading a database from a backup and transaction logs, or making changes to the structure of a database, you will need to shut down SQL Server and then restart it in a single-user mode. This ensures that no user can access the database and update records that may be in a state of change. Shutdowns can be scheduled, allowing you to send a message to all users currently logged in, or they can be performed immediately with no warning to users.

197

MCSE 7.1   Starting Microsoft SQL Server

Microsoft SQL Server™ runs as a *service* under Windows NT. As a service, you can control SQL Server's current state from five different places: SQL Server Service Manager, SQL Server Enterprise Manager, command line, Services applet in Control Panel, and the Server Manager. SQL Server has three different normal states:

- Start: When the SQL Server service is started it will respond to requests for information and process queries. This is the normal running state.
- Stop: When an SQL Server service is stopped it does not respond to any requests.
- Pause: When paused, users currently logged on can continue to work normally; queries in process will continue, but no new users can be logged on to the service. If you are currently logged into an SQL Server service that is then paused and you log out, you will not be able to log back in until the service is started again.

Using the Services Applet

In a multiuser DBMS system, the primary purpose for SQL Server, it is a good idea that it starts as an automatic service when the server is booted. If you did not choose the automatic startup option when you ran the Setup program, it can easily be done with a few simple steps. Resetting this configuration is done with the Services applet in the Windows NT Control Panel.

1. Open the Windows NT Control Panel by selecting Start, Settings, Control Panel, and then double-click the Services applet. You will now see the Services dialog box.
2. Scroll down the list box until you come to MSSQLServer. Click the Startup button to display the Service dialog box as seen in Figure 7-1.
3. Click the Automatic option button in the Startup Type group. The logon account should be the same one that you selected when you installed SQL Server. If you want to change the default startup account, you can do so here by selecting any of the following choices.

   - The Automatic option allows the service to start when Windows NT is booted.
   - The Manual option allows the service to be started by a user or a dependent service.

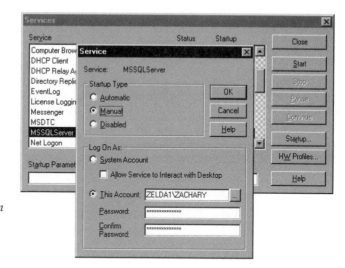

Figure 7–1 *From the Service dialog box you can change how a service will be started and the logon account used.*

- The Disabled option prevents the service from being started by a user or dependent service.

4. Click the OK button when you have completed all of the necessary changes.

5. If the service is not currently started, you can do so from here by clicking the Start button. The other pertinent buttons are:

- Stop: This button will stop the currently selected service. If there are any other services that are dependent on the selected service they will also be stopped.

- Pause: This button allows you to pause a service. When a service is paused, only members of the Administrators group can access the MSSQLServer service. Some other services allow members of the Server Operators group to have access.

- Continue: This button allows a paused service to continue in a normal running manner.

6. Click the Close button once the service has been started and you are ready to leave the Services applet.

Using the SQL Server Enterprise Manager

Unlike the other remaining methods, you can use the SQL Server Enterprise application to change both the current state of the service and also set whether it will auto-start on boot up. As you have already seen in previous chapters, you can make many configuration changes to the way that SQL

Server works from within the Properties sheet for a server. You can also start, stop, or pause the server from the Enterprise Manager. Follow these steps:

1. Open SQL Server Enterprise Manager application. Select the server that you want to work with and right-click on it. Figure 7-2 displays the shortcut menu.

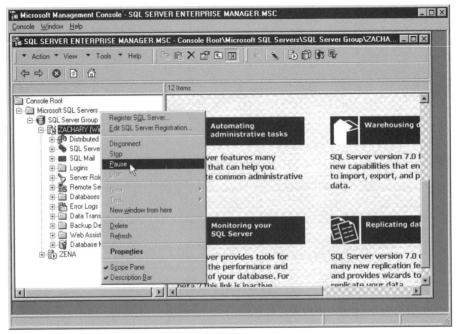

Figure 7–2   *Use the server shortcut menu to start, stop, or pause a server.*

2. Use the Pause or Stop options on this menu for the selected server. If you pause the server, the grayed unselectable Start option changes to a Continue option, allowing you to resume the server's normal state.

3. Select the Properties option from the shortcut menu. Figure 7-3 displays the SQL Server Properties sheet for the selected server.

From the General tab of the SQL Server Properties sheet you can set both SQL Server and SQL Server Agent to autostart on Windows NT boot up. By clicking on the Startup Parameters button you can set various startup options for SQL Server. These will be discussed in detail later in this chapter.

4. Click the OK button when you have completed using the Properties dialog box.

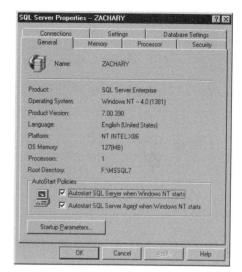

Figure 7–3 *Use the General tab of the SQL Server Properties sheet to set AutoStart policies and startup parameters.*

SQL Server Service Manager

The SQL Server Service Manager is a special application limited to connecting to a server, controlling the selected server's current state and that of its other services, and setting a polling interval. This application is one of the most intuitive ever devised. The icon for the SQL Server Service Manager sits on the task bar at all times, as shown in Figure 7-4. You can easily access the SQL Server Service Manager at any time like this:

Figure 7–4 *Here you can see the SQL Server Service Manager icon beside the clock.*

1. Double-click the SQL Server Service Manager icon to open the application, as shown in Figure 7-5. The current state of the server and service is indicated by which light of the stoplight is lit. You can also see it listed in the indicator bar at the bottom of the dialog box.

2. If there is more than one server, you can select another server from the Server list box. You can also work with other services that may be installed with the selected server. Select a service from the Services list box.

Figure 7–5 *With the SQL Server Service Manager you can easily start, stop, and pause the selected server and service.*

3. Double-click the Pause, or yellow light on the stoplight. Shortly you will see the yellow light lit and the text at the bottom of the dialog box change to indicate the service has been paused. This is shown in Figure 7-6.
4. Double-click the Start/Continue button to resume the server services then close the application.

Figure 7–6 *Here you see the server ZACHARY's service MSSQLServer has been paused.*

Using the Server Manager

Windows NT includes a special utility as one of the Administrative Tools called the Server Manager. This utility is accessed like this:

1. Select Start, Programs, Administrative Tools, Server Manager from the Start menus. This will open the Server Manager application as shown in Figure 7-7
2. Select the server that SQL Server is installed from the list, and then choose Computer, Services from the menu.
3. You now see the Services applet that was discussed earlier in this chapter. Close the applet when you have completed your changes, then close the Server Manager application.

This is simply another method of accessing the same Services applet that you used from the Control Panel.

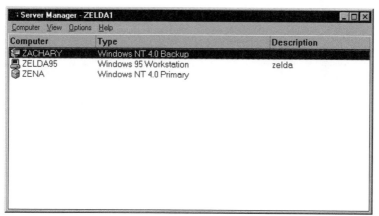

Figure 7–7 *The Server Manager application can be used to control many aspects of the selected computer.*

Using a Command Line Startup

For those of you who still use it, let alone know what it is, the command prompt can be used to start and stop the MSSQLServer service. You can pause and continue the server service from a command prompt only if it has been started as a Windows NT service. At a command line prompt, you will use the NET START and NET STOP commands as shown here.

1. From the Start menu select Programs, Command Prompt.
2. Type the following and then press the Enter key:

```
NET STOP MSSQLServer
```

If the service is stopped successfully, you will see the two lines shown in Figure 7-8 that follow the command you entered

.

3. To start the service again, execute the following command, then close the command prompt window.

```
NET START MSSQLServer
```

As you may already have guessed, pausing and continuing the server service is done with the NET PAUSE and NET CONTINUE commands.

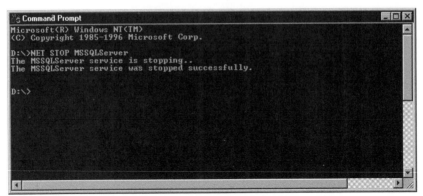

Figure 7–8 *Here you see the MSSQLServer service has been stopped from the command prompt.*

Options for Startup

SQL Server can be started with several options. It can be run in a single-user mode, or in the normal multiuser mode. You have already learned how to start the SQL Server and to set it to run automatically upon system bootup.

The default options set when you first installed SQL Server are stored in the Windows NT Registry and are used every time SQL Server is started, whether as a service, from the command line, or from the SQL Enterprise Manager window. You can also start the SQL Server by doing one of the following:

- Starting the service from the Services applet in the Control Panel.
- Typing `net start mssqlserver` from any command line prompt.
- From an operating system command line prompt running the SQL Server application SQLSERVER.EXE, using the following option switches:
- `-c` Starts SQL Server separately from the Windows NT Service Control Manager, shortening the startup time. SQL Server does not run as a Windows NT service with this switch.
- `-d` This switch must be followed by the fully qualified path for the MASTER database device. This option is useful if the path parameters stored in the Registry are no longer correct.

- `-e` Follow this switch with the fully qualified path for the error log file.
- `-f` Starts SQL Server in a minimum configuration. Often used when resetting options that have prevented the server from starting.
- `-l` Allows you to specify the fully qualified path for the master database log file.
- `-m` Starts SQL Server in a single-user mode. Often used when repairing or upgrading the server software or databases.
- `-n` Causes the Windows NT event log to be bypassed. It is recommended that when this option is selected you use the `-e` switch, or no SQL Server events will be logged.
- `-p` This option lets you specify the level of precision that will be supported by decimal and numeric datatypes. The default setting is a maximum precision of 28. You can specify a precision level from 1 to 38. If no precision level is specified when the -p switch is used, the maximum level of 38 will be used for both decimal and numeric datatypes.
- `-s` Selects an alternate set of startup parameters held under the alternate key name in the Registry. This option can only be run from a command-line prompt.
- `-T` Starts SQL Server with a specified trace flag. A trace flag is used to start the server with nonstandard parameters. This switch should be set using an uppercase T. A lowercase t, while accepted by SQL Server, sets additional internal trace flags used by SQL Server support engineers.
- `-x` Disables SQL Server from keeping both CPU time and cache-hit ratio statistics, and allows maximum performance.

The first two methods start SQL Server as a Windows NT service, while the third method does not. With SQL Server started independently of the Service Control Manager, you cannot use SQL Enterprise Manager to start, stop, or pause SQL Server as a service. Also, all system messages will print in the window used to start SQL Server. All command-line options will take priority over default options set in the Registry. Finally, you must shut down the server before logging off of the Windows NT network.

MCSE 7.3   **Troubleshooting Startup**

Trying to troubleshoot startup problems for SQL Server can be a seemingly overwhelming task. There are so many things that can possibly go wrong.

When you have a problem with SQL Server starting, there are some basic problem-solving tactics to try:

1. Do not panic. Nothing can be worse than the system administrator going around telling everyone that all is lost. Chances are it's not that bad.
2. Check the current state of the MSSQLServer service: started, stopped, or paused.
3. Check the SQL Server error logs.
4. Check the Windows NT Event Viewer logs.
5. Check the output files, *.OUT, in the \MSSQL7\Install folder for any errors.
6. Test the network connections that SQL Server uses.

You have already learned how to check the current state of the MSSQLServer service earlier in this chapter. If the service is stopped, try to start it; if paused continue it. If this works then SQL Server should work normally. If the service stays in a stopped condition, you probably have other problems preventing it from starting.

Using the SQL Server Error Log

SQL Server has its own error log. The current error log and the last six logs are stored in the folder \MSSQL7\Logs. If you have a problem with SQL Server starting after a successful installation, or if your installation failed, your first stop should be the SQL Server error logs. These may give you an indication of what is causing your problem. SQL Server records three types of messages in the error logs:

- Information messages. These provide information about the general condition of the application. For example, "98/06/01 18:48:36:15 spid1Starting up database 'master'" is an information message.
- Warning messages. These are messages about potential problems. For example, "98/06/06 15:10:31:55 kernelinitdata: warning: could not set working set size to 0Kb" is the warning message logged when the memory option is set too large.
- Error messages. These messages are indications of problems that usually require intervention on your part to fix. For example, "98/06/06 15:35:09.67 odsError: 17832, Severity: 18, State: 0." This error occurred when the SQL Server ODBC driver could not be found.

For example, the error message shown above was recorded in the current error log. While the SQL Server started, a connection to the server itself was unable to be established. This was caused because the current SQL Server ODBC driver could not be found by the service. For the example I had renamed it, but it could just as easily be a corrupt or missing file.

The SQL Server error logs are started when SQL Server is started, and the log is closed when the service is stopped. Only the past six logs are kept and are denoted as "errorlog.1, errorlog.2... errorlog.6." The current error log does not have a number designator. The oldest log is 6, and the numbers are rotated each time a new error log is started. If you cannot connect to your SQL Server service, the error logs can be viewed using Notepad. If you do have a good connection, they can also be viewed from within the Enterprise Manager like this:

1. Connect to the server, then click on the + (plus) sign beside it to expand the tree. Do the same on the + sign beside Error Logs, as shown in Figure 7-9.

2. Click on the Current log and it will be displayed in the right-hand window pane as seen here in Figure 7-10.

Figure 7–9 *You can see the current error log and the six archive logs displayed in the tree.*

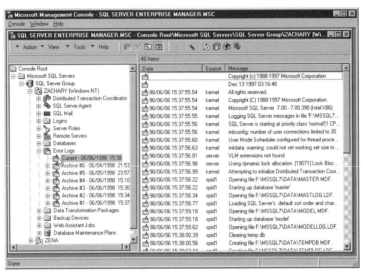

Figure 7–10 *The current log is displayed in the right-hand window pane. You can view any of the logs by clicking on them.*

If you cannot make a connection to SQL Server, or it simply will not start, use Notepad and view the latest errorlog file located at \MSSQL7\Logs. This is the default location; if you have placed your SQL Server application in a different place, then adjust this accordingly.

Using the Windows NT Event Viewer

The Windows NT Event Viewer logs most of the events that also appear in the SQL Server error logs. You will find them in the Application log. Other applications also write to the event log. If you have never used the Event Viewer, you will find that there are three logs that are being written: System, Security, and Application. The Application log will contain any events concerning SQL Server. In this next exercise you will see how the Application log can be used to see what errors may have occurred in the SQL Server application:

1. From the Start menu select Programs, Administrative Tools, Event Viewer.

2. Select Log, Application from the menu. This will display the Application Log. If you already see that the title bar says "Event Viewer–Application…" then you do not have to perform this step.

3. Notice that there are three types of indicator icons to the left of the date. These icons indicate the type of log event:

- A informational event is indicated by the blue icon with the lowercase "i" inside it.
- A warning event is indicated by the yellow icon containing an exclamation point "!".
- An error event is shown by the red icon that looks like a stop sign.

4. The details of the event can be viewed by either double-clicking on a specific event, or selecting it and pressing the Enter key. Figure 7-11 shows the details of a selected error event.

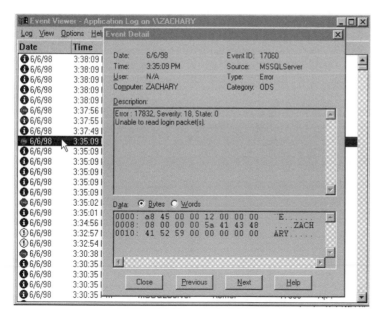

Figure 7–11 *Here you see the details of a selected event in the Event Detail dialog box.*

5. Close the Event Detail dialog box by clicking the Close button, then close the Event Viewer.

The Event Viewer is a good place to go and periodically check on what is happening inside of Windows NT and the various applications that you use.

Viewing the Output Files

When you install SQL Server several output (*.OUT), files are created by the installation scripts. These files can help you to determine what may have gone wrong during an installation. More often than not, the output file that was created last will probably have the information that you may be searching for.

Use Notepad or another text editor and open the output file with the latest creation date and scroll through the text. The output files will be located in the \MSSQL7\Install folder. If you do not see the OUT extension, use NT Explorer and look for files of the type OUT File.

Checking Named Pipes

During the installation procedure SQL Server uses the named pipes protocol. You can use the MAKEPIPE and READPIPE commands to ensure that you can establish communication between a server and a client. The simplest method is described in the next exercise, but you can also perform this same test over a LAN. The only restriction is that both server and client must be Windows NT machines, as Windows 95/98 does not use named pipes.

1. Open a Command Prompt window from the Start menu by selecting Programs, Command Prompt.
2. Type MAKEPIPE at the prompt and press the Enter key to execute the command. You should see a response like that shown in Figure 7-12 in the left-hand window.
3. Open another Command Prompt window on the client, or a second instance on the same server.
4. Type READPIPE /S<*servername*>   /D<*string*>. Replace <servername> with the name of the server you are trying to connect with, and replace <string> with the text string you want to send as a test. There cannot be any spaces in the string or anything after the space will not be sent. The right-hand window in Figure 7-12 shows the client part of the test.

This test shows that the named pipe protocol does work between the server and the client and that this potential problem place is working correctly.

5. Close the pipe by closing the Command Prompt window.

Key Points

In this chapter you have learned to bring SQL Server to an orderly shutdown and restart, and several troubleshooting techniques. Specifically:

- How to manually stop and start SQL Server.
- How to set SQL Server for automatic startup.

Figure 7–12 *Here you can see both the server (left-hand window), and the client (right-hand window). The client has sent a text string to the server, and the server has received it.*

- How to pause the Server before shutting it down.
- How to start, stop, and pause SQL Server from the Command Prompt.
- The five methods of starting and stopping SQL Server service.
- How to use the SQL Server error logs to find errors that may be preventing SQL Server from operating.
- How to use the Application Event Viewer to find SQL Server errors.
- How to view the output files created during installation to find possible problems.
- How to test the connection between a client and server using named pipes.

▲ CHAPTER REVIEW QUESTIONS

▲ Multiple Choice:

1. *SQL Server runs under Windows NT as:*
    A. An application.
    B. A service
    C. A program.
    D. A server

2. *You can control the current state of SQL Server from which of these locations? (Select all that apply).*
    A. The SQL Server Service Manager

B. The command line

C. Services applet in Control Panel

D. File Manager

3. *Which startup option allows the SQL Server service to automatically start when Windows NT is booted?*

A. AutoStart

B. Auto

C. Automatic

D. Nondisabled

4. *A paused SQL Server is indicated in the SQL Server Service Managers dialog box by: (Select all that apply).*

A. A red light

B. A green light

C. A yellow light

D. A message at the bottom of the dialog box

E. A and D

5. *The default options that you set when you install SQL Server are stored in:*

A. The Windows Registry

B. The SQL Server sysdefaultoptions system table

C. The MSSQLServer service startup parameters in the Services applet

D. The SQLSERVER.exe file

6. *The SQL Server error logs can be easily viewed from which of the following? (Select all that apply).*

A. The command-line using Edit

B. Using the Notepad applet

C. The Enterprise Manager

D. All of the above

▲ True or False:

1. *True or False? When SQL Server is paused, all current users must log off immediately.*

2. *True or False? You can always use a command-line prompt to pause or continue the SQL Server service.*

3. *True or False? When SQL Server is started from a command-line with the -c switch, you will not be able to control the server state from the Enterprise Manager.*

4. *True or False? Some of the messages contained in the SQL Server error logs are information messages.*

Planning and Managing Security

Security is an aspect of database management that many system administrators would rather not have to think about, but it is something that we all need to be concerned about. With more and more businesses becoming dependent on their information systems, the potential damage that can be realized through a compromised database management system runs to the millions of dollars annually in the United States alone. Planning and managing your systems security is not a task that you should leave for the last minute, or cut corners on.

Security

Another of the many important jobs of the system administrator is managing the security requirements of the SQL Server™ systems and databases. In the world of the client/server application, controlling who has access to what resources is a very important requirement. Simply controlling who has access to read and write in the database and its tables is only the beginning of controlling security.

Using SQL Server to manage security is not a difficult task, but it is one that should be taken seriously. Having an unauthorized person hacking into your system can be a formula for disaster, especially if they gain access to sensitive information.

MCSE 8.1   Identification and Authentication

The key to any security system is to identify and to control. SQL Server can take this task onto itself, use Windows NT's™ security features, or can mix the two together. In order to use an object contained in an SQL Server database, a user may have to pass through the following four levels of security.

- The Windows NT operating system
- SQL Server application running on Windows NT
- The SQL Server database
- The SQL Server database object

Each of these is a security hurdle, or door, through which a user must pass before being able to gain access to the resources available at that level.

The central theme in using a secure client/server system is the identity of the user. This identity must be maintained throughout a session, regardless of the work they are currently doing. As with any security system, whether it is a computer system, a bank vault, or a store's front door, the security system is only as good as the people who use it. If a trusted individual gives their keys to the front door and their code to the alarm system to another person, they have created a very real breach in the security of that front door. This breach gives the second person access to everything in the store. SQL Server and Windows NT use a system of usernames as a means of identifying a specific individual. The username is the set of keys to the front door; more is required, as shown in Figure 8-1.

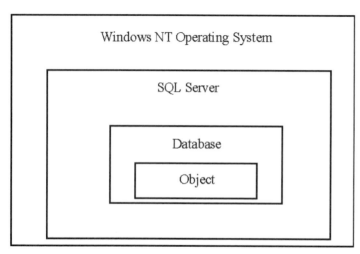

Figure 8–1 *A user must pass through all four levels of security to use an SQL Server database object.*

Usernames are just the first half of the security system. Since the username is simply typed in through a keyboard, how does the computer know that this is really the person who should have access to the information and the applications authorized to the person with this username? The second half of the system is the authentication of the user through the use of passwords. The password is like the alarm code to the building. If a person enters a correct username but an incorrect password, they will not be allowed access to the computer. Usernames must first be created by an individual who is authorized to do so. Depending upon the process in place in your company, and the level of access required, this may be the SQL Server system administrator, the Windows NT system administrator, or the network administrator. These are the people most often charged with this task. Usernames and passwords may also be called log ins.

In addition to controlling access, the username can be used for audit purposes. With most network systems you can view an audit log showing what actions were performed and what files were accessed by an individual username. This can be especially helpful when tracking down unauthorized accesses to a database. Security audits can be logged by turning this feature on during the SQL Server setup procedures; it is one of the options in the "Set Security Options" dialog box. The audit log can then be viewed either in SQL Server's error log, or in the Security log of the Windows NT Event Viewer.

You can create many more levels of security if your specific application needs a very high level of security. In the next several sections, you will become familiar with the various levels of security.

Windows NT Security

The typical client/server system may require that a user have access to more than one operating system in order to run a typical application. For example, a user who is running a client application on their own computer will access the operating system of the computer they are using. The client application may have another security door that must be passed before gaining access to the client application. Then the user will also have to log in to the Windows NT operating system, or other network operating systems to gain access to the server on which SQL Server resides. This simple system requires the use and access of at least three security systems, each with their own requirements and uses. In most business systems, each of these processes will be running on their own individual systems. Few, if any, client/server systems run with both the client application and the SQL Server database engine running on the same computer.

An individual user does not require a Windows NT log in on the host machine where SQL Server resides, unless SQL Server is running on their local computer. The exception to this is that the system administrator, who does need to have access to the Windows NT operating system, also needs to have a valid Windows NT log in.

Windows NT's security requires that a valid username and password be entered before access is granted to any of the system resources. The Windows NT system administrator will set up individual user accounts and log ins, at the same time determining the level of access to various systems resources.

Whenever possible, it is recommended that the Windows NT security system be used over the SQL Server security system. You have many more options available to you—groups, allow or restrict access to resources or folders and files—with this type of security.

SQL Server Security

SQL Server can provide for its own security in networks where a trusted connection is not available. When a user is validated as having a current NT user account, SQL Server assumes the user was correctly identified and the connection is a trusted connection. SQL Server security is tied to the syslog ins system table located in the master database. Any user who cannot be identified with a Windows NT log in account is assumed to come from a non-trusted connection and SQL Server will assume the authentication process.

The syslog ins table is a system table and is located only in the master database. It is used to hold all information about users and their log in identities. Usernames, encrypted passwords, system log in IDs, group memberships, and permissions that have been granted, revoked, or denied are included in this table. Only the system administrator can add, delete, or change information in the syslog ins table.

Whichever type is used, either can be used to grant access to the SQL Server processes. Once in, a wide variety of additional doors can be made available to the user. These doors lead to the databases and applications that have been created. The first door is to their default database. All correctly identified users can be assigned to a default database.

Database Security

Once a user has been authenticated and allowed to log in into SQL Server they must have an account in the databases' security system. A user account can be mapped directly to a Windows NT user account or a Windows NT group account. It can also be mapped to an SQL Server log in account, or to a database role. Once this mapping has been established, a certain level of access is granted to it. The level of access is controlled by the permissions that have been granted to the user or log in. If a user account attempts to perform some function that they do not have the necessary permissions to perform, they will receive a permission error message. This database security level can take several forms, for example:

- Giving the log in ownership of the database. This grants the log in all rights to the database.

- Creating the log in as a guest user.

- Creating an alias. Tells the database to regard the user as a different user log in, and subsequently granting all of the same rights and privileges as those granted to the owner of the alias log in.

- Adding the log in as a new user to the database.

Warning

The guest user log in account has the potential of leaving your security system wide open. The guest user will be discussed in detail later in this chapter. Use caution with the guest user account; it is available to any user who can gain a connection to SQL Server.

Even though a user has been granted log in access to the database, the user still must be granted permission to access each database object. This is the final level of security. To see how permissions are controlled, read the section, "Using the Permissions System," later in this chapter.

In order to be granted access to a database, two lists are checked by SQL Server:

- The sysusers system table is the list of all authorized users of the database. A copy of sysusers is stored in each database and contains all of the users, and their permissions to the various objects located in the database.

- The sysalternates table contains the list of all users who are allowed to log in as an alias. This table is also stored in each database and contains the mappings for users who are allowed to log in using an alias. This table is included only for backward compatibility. SQL Server 7 makes use of the user role in place of an alias.

> You can easily have the log in name for the Windows NT server be the same as the username to a database. It is not requried that they be different, and may actually make the security administration a simpler task. It is also easier on your users to only have to remember one log in name and password.

MCSE 8.2   Selecting the Type of Security

In the context of this book the system administrator refers to the SQL Server system administrator. The system administrator must work closely with the network or Windows NT system administrator in order to make sure that the security of SQL Server is maintained. The first level of security is the responsibility of the network system administrator and he or she will be responsible for creating the initial user accounts and passwords. The system administrator will then be responsible for ensuring that proper log ins receive appropriate access to the correct databases and objects within each database.

How security is implemented is a basic determination that is decided based on the business needs and security requirements of the database owner and the information the database contains. Security of information contained in an SQL Server database depends not only on a system of user log ins and passwords, but also in the physical security of the network, and especially the server where SQL Server resides. A computer system where the server is located in a secure room is safer than one where it is placed in an out-of-the-way closet, or even worse—located beside someone's desk. The same can be said of the network itself. If there is no access to the network from the outside—for example, a modem connection—then it is safe from outside hacking. The physical security of your server and network must be taken into consideration when designing your overall security policies and procedures.

Both Windows NT and SQL Server use a hierarchical security environment. This method simplifies the storage, management, and enforcement of a security system. Within NT, users are managed in groups, while in SQL Server the same function is performed by roles. Instead of managing every individual user on a system, it is much easier to manage groups of users. You will find that your corporate organizational chart will lend itself to being an initial guideline to the creation of security groups and roles. People who have similar functions in the organizational chart at the same level will also have similar security requirements. You will find that this is only a start for the definition of your groups and roles. Some users will not fit neatly into a single category. Many administrative users need to have access to a wide range of information in order to perform their jobs.

There are three security modes from which you can choose—Windows NT Authentication, SQL Server Authentication, and Mixed. In previous versions of SQL Server, Windows NT Authentication was also known as *integrated* security, while SQL Server Authentication was called *standard* security. Each have their own advantages and disadvantages, and will be discussed through the next several sections along with their pros and cons.

Windows NT Authentication

The Windows NT security option allows you to use the Windows NT security log ins and authentication systems for all SQL Server connections. This mode allows only trusted multiprotocol and named pipe's connections to have access to SQL Server. If your system consists of only a Windows NT domain, this is the best choice for security. NT can easily manage all of your security needs. This method of security allows your users to connect to SQL Server without having to supply another log in name and password. This can be especially helpful for those users who have a hard time remembering one log in name and password, let alone several.

By using Windows NT security, SQL Server applications can take full advantage of the security features available from Windows NT. These features include:

- The ability to pass encrypted passwords through the network. Many networks store passwords in an encrypted form at the user's workstation, but send the password to the server in a clear text format. This has the potential of allowing someone to capture a password, and to later log in as an authorized user.
- Using Windows NT groups. Groups allow you to place users into common groups and apply security parameters across all of them at one time.
- The ability to apply permissions to specific folders and files.
- Using password aging. Requires a user to change a password once it has become more than a specified number of days old. The number of days is entered as part of Windows NT's User Manager Domains application, as an Account Policy option. The maximum number of days that can be set is 999, or you can set a password to never expire.

Windows NT security can be used with any trusted connection. Trusted connections can be multiprotocol or named pipes from other Windows NT workstations, Windows for Workgroups, Windows 95, and Microsoft LAN Manager running under either MS-DOS or Microsoft Window's clients. By using the multiprotocol Net-Library, you can also create trusted connections with Microsoft Windows clients using Novell NetWare and running the IPX/SPX protocol. This user will be prompted for a log in when connecting to SQL Server. Clients using other network protocols are not supported as Windows NT trusted connections, and so must be handled using SQL Server standard security.

When Windows NT security is being used, a user is mapped from their trusted connection to a valid SQL Server log in that has been set up for them to a default log in—usually the *guest* log in, or to the system administrator log in if the user has administrator privileges. Once the user has gained access to SQL Server, all additional security is handled by SQL Server itself. This includes user access to a database and to any of the resources or information available in that database.

The most widely recommended way to use Windows NT security with SQL Server is to create at least two security groups within Windows NT and to provide each with the appropriate access to SQL Server. These groups are often named:

- SQLUsers and are assigned all normal user privileges. Assign anyone who needs to have access as a user to this group. They will be able to perform normal UPDATE, SELECT, DELETE, and INSERT functions necessary to their particular job.
- SQLAdmin are assigned administrator duties and privileges and log in as an administrator. The individuals assigned to this group will have all of the privileges and responsibilities of system administrator, and will be able to use the CREATE DATABASES command, add new users, and other such duties.

When using Windows NT security, users and user groups must first be set up within the NT security system. Depending upon your own business situation, this responsibility may belong to another person within your organization. If so, contact them about setting up the necessary accounts for users who need access to SQL Server. Otherwise, set up the accounts by following these few steps:

1. From the Start menu, select Programs, Administrative Tools, and User Manager for Domains application. The User Manager dialog box will be displayed as seen in Figure 8-2. This is where you create user accounts, set permissions to access SQL Server, and access to other Windows NT system resources.

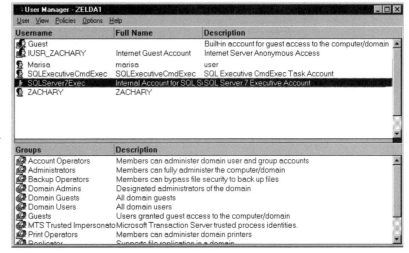

2. Select User, New Local Group from the menu, displaying the New Local Group dialog box. In the Group Name text box type SQLUsers. Move down to the Description text box and type SQL Server User Group. Click the OK button to save the new group.

Your new group will be visible in the list of groups in the lower half of the User Manager window, as shown in Figure 8-3. If you do not see it, then scroll the list until you do. This group will be available to you when you create the individual users who will be assigned to the SQLUsers group.

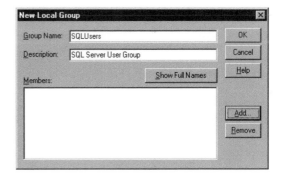

Figure 8–3 *A new user group has been created for those people who will be assigned as SQL Server users.*

3. Select User, New User from the menu, displaying the New User dialog box. Here you can add the user accounts for everyone who will be working within the SQL Server User Group you just created.

If you have already created the users who will be added to this new users group, click the Add button, and then select them from the next dialog box.

Below is a sample of the information that must be supplied and is shown in Figure 8-4:

Username:	egermesin
Full Name:	Eric Germesin
Description:	Member SQLUser group
Password:	(type a password - only asterisks '*' are displayed in the text box)
Confirm Password:	(retype the password for confirmation, exactly as entered in the Password text box)

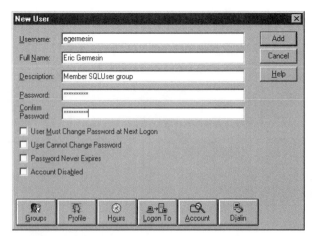

Figure 8-4 *Use the New User dialog box to enter the basic information required for each new user account.*

When entering the initial password you have several options. The default setting User Must Change Password at Next log on allows you as the system administrator to enter a default password for all users, requiring them to change it when they next log in. You can also use the other three options by clicking the checkbox:

- User Cannot Change Password. As it states, a user cannot change this password.

- Password Never Expires. This password will not expire without manually changing this option.

- Account Disabled. Disables the account. This option is often used if you are using the account as a template when creating a number of similar accounts. You may also want to disable an account when a user goes on vacation or on a leave of absence and you do not want to delete the user account.

4. Click the Groups button. You will now see a new dialog box, Group Memberships. Scroll through the Not member of list box until you find the group you just created, SQLUsers, and select it. When you click the Add button, the group will be moved to the Member of list box, as seen in Figure 8-5.

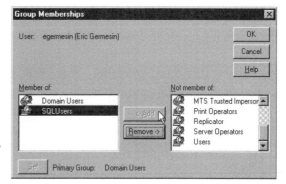

Figure 8–5 *The new user has been added to the SQLUsers group.*

5. If this is the only group that this user is to be added to, then click the OK button, returning to the New User dialog box. If you are done, click the Add button to create the user account and add it to the list of Users, as seen in Figure 8-6, then click the Close button to return to the User Manager window. You will see the new user listed in the upper half of the window. Close this application window unless you plan to add additional groups or users.

Create the SQLAdmin group in the same way you just created the SQLUsers group. If necessary, create log ins for any users who have not yet been added to the Windows NT user list, then add only those users who will have system administrator privileges to this new group.

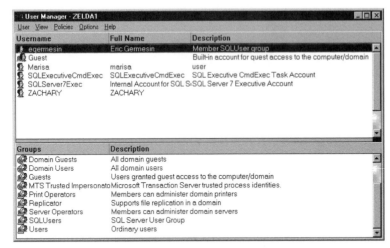

Figure 8–6 *The new user has been added to the Windows NT user list.*

In the New User dialog box there are several additional buttons. Each of these displays another dialog box, allowing you to exercise additional control over the user account:

- Profile: This option is used to set additional user environment profile options. You must create a profile file for the user and then enter the required information into this dialog box. A profile can be used to give each user a customized Windows NT desktop and access to selected resources, including network connections.
- Hours: This option is used to select specific days and hours of the day that this user can log on to the system. This does not restrict them from using their own workstation, but does restrict them from logging on to the server outside of the specified hours. The default setting allows access 7 days per week, 24 hours per day.
- log on To: Here you can choose to allow a user to log on to the server from any workstation, or from a selected workstation. If you choose to allow access from a specific workstation, you can allow the user to log on to the server from any one of eight different workstations. Once you have selected the workstation from which the user can log on, they will not be able to use another person's station to log on to the server.
- Account: Allows you to set an expiration date for the account and determine if the account is a regular user of the domain or a user from an untrusted domain.

Once you, or the Windows NT system administrator, have created and set up all of the necessary groups and user accounts, you have completed the first half of setting up the requisite security processes for SQL Server. Setting up the next half will be discussed later in this chapter in the section "Setting Security Modes."

SQL Server Authentication

The SQL Server Authentication security mode is included for backward compatibility issues and works in conjunction with the Mixed Mode security when a user cannot be authenticated under Windows NT. This form of security is always used when a user from an untrusted domain attempts to log on to the server. Under this security mode, SQL Server manages its own log in authentication process for all users attempting to connect to the server, who have not already been authenticated through Windows NT authentication.

You can force the server to deny all trusted client connections, but this will also restrict the use of applications and features that use forced trusted connections such as SQL Enterprise Manager, and SQL Server's replication features.

When you select standard security mode, SQL Server uses the *syslog ins* table to store a user's log in ID and password. When the user attempts to log in to the server, SQL Server looks for a valid log in ID and password. If one is found, the user is granted access to SQL Server.

Mixed Security

This final security option mixed modes, uses both Windows NT and SQL Server Authentication security modes, depending upon the type of connection the client comes from. This is the default security option when you install SQL Server. Under the mixed security mode, SQL Server will use Windows NT Authentication for all trusted connections. If a connection fails to connect through Windows NT due to not being a valid log in, then SQL Server Authentication will be used, requiring the entry of a valid SQL Server log in.

If the user attempts to log on through any connections other than a trusted one, the user is required to supply a log in ID and password. SQL Server will then use the standard security mode, checking the log in attempt against the valid entries in the *syslog ins* table for authentication.

If your network consists of a combination of Windows NT and another operating system, chances are very good that you will use this form of authentication for your security.

Trusted Connections

Why is a connection trusted or not trusted? SQL Server assumes that a connection that has already been validated by Windows NT and its authentication procedures is a trusted connection. If the connection was not validated through Windows NT's security system, then it is an untrusted connection and must be validated through SQL Server's authentication system.

A trusted connection can only be created over a named pipe or multiprotocol connection. If you have client connections that cannot use one of these protocols, then you must configure your security around a Mixed model.

Both ODBC and DB-Library clients can be configured so that they always request a trusted connection from the server. This enables SQL Server to connect to remote servers as long as it is running on a properly configured Windows NT account that has been granted access to SQL Server.

Setting Security Modes

The various security modes are set from within SQL Server Enterprise Manager. By using the Enterprise Manager you can choose the security mode that best meets your own network needs. In addition to choosing a security mode, you will need to set up users and user groups within SQL Server. Use this next exercise to learn how to set the security mode:

1. Open the SQL Server Enterprise Manager and right-click on the server folder and select Properties from the shortcut menu. The SQL Server Properties dialog box is now displayed. Click on the Security tab to set the security mode that will be used by SQL Server, as shown in Figure 8-7. You can also change the Startup Service Account that SQL Server will use to log on from this tab.

2. You can now choose a security mode to use with SQL Server. Click on the SQL Server and Windows NT option button. Earlier in this chapter you have already created Windows NT security groups to use in the trusted half of your security system. Later in this chapter you will create the user log ins and passwords.

In addition to setting the type of security that you will use with SQL Server, there are two other options that you can set on the Security tab. You can change the Startup Service Account to another log in account, or to a system account. This is the same as the option you used on the Startup dialog box in the Services dialog box when you selected the MSSQLServer service.

The other option is a checkbox labeled "Non-administrators use SQLAgentCmdExec account when executing commands via xp_cmdshell."

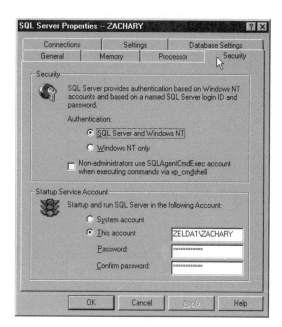

Figure 8–7 *The Security tab of the Server Configuration/Options dialog box is used to set the security mode that SQL Server will use for all user log ins.*

When you grant execute permission to a user, they are able to execute any operating system command at a Windows NT command prompt. This unfortunately means that anyone who can reach the command prompt of the machine running SQL Server can run any command that the SQL Server log on account is able to execute.

By checking the box, you restrict any user who is not a member of the administrator group from executing commands through the `xp_cmdshell`. The `xp_cmdshell` extended stored procedure allows operating system commands that affect SQL Server to be run in the context used by the SQL Server log on account. When you restrict nonadministrators from using the `xp-cmdshell`, their commands will run through the user account that the SQLAgentCmdExec uses to run scheduled tasks for users not in the administrators group.

Unless you have a unique group of people using the databases of your SQL Server system, it is highly recommended that you do restrict nonadministrator users from access to `xp_cmdshell` by checking this box.

MCSE 8.3   Creating Users

When you first install SQL Server, the system administrator (SA) log in is created and becomes the owner of every database and object. This log in bypasses all forms of security checks and therefore has the ability to control anything within SQL Server. You have already learned to create a user and a group under Windows NT. You still need to know how to create users and roles within SQL Server. This is necessary regardless of the security mode you have chosen to use. A user or role within SQL Server defines what access the account will have: what databases, tables, views, procedures, and any other objects that the user account can access or not access. If a log in account is mapped to a Windows NT user account, then a trusted connection can be made, and SQL Server will not attempt to authenticate the account again.

Any users not coming from a trusted Windows NT system cannot be authenticated using the Windows NT system. As the SQL Server System Administrator, you have the responsibility to create log in usernames and passwords for these users. This is accomplished by using SQL Server Enterprise Manager, or through the T-SQL statement `sp_grantdbaccess` for an SQL Server account. In the next several sections of this chapter, you will become familiar with the process of creating and modifying user accounts and then using roles to group users together into similar permission/access roles.

Devising Usernames

The username is the point of entry for all people who want to gain access to SQL Server. When you have decided to use Windows NT of Mixed security, you will have to add at least some, if not all, of the usernames so that SQL Server will recognize the user as being a person authorized to have access to information contained in a database.

When setting up user accounts you must supply SQL Server with several pieces of information, the first being a username. It is highly recommended that you work with your users when devising their usernames. While you must be concerned with the security of your data, you must also ensure that your users can access the databases they must use for their own work. A complex username and password system, while secure, is also prone to human error. Many people have a hard time remembering complex security schemes. They end up forgetting their password or username and require you to rebuild it for them, or they write them down where they can easily prompt themselves—like underneath their keyboard or taped to their monitor.

Creating user accounts within SQL Server Enterprise Manager takes just a few simple steps:

This warning is included for those of you who are either Windows NT or SQL Server administrators. If you forget your own username or password, it is not as simple as rebuilding an account and/or password. Unless there is a backup administrator who still can access the proper applications, recreating your user account will require reinstalling either Windows NT or SQL Server. Needless to say, this affects more people than someone else forgetting their log in. Be careful.

1. Open SQL Server Enterprise Manager application and click the +(plus) sign beside the server that you want to add users to.
2. Right-click on the log ins folder and select New log in from the shortcut menu. Be sure that the General tab is selected. You will see the SQL Server log in Properties dialog box displayed. Enter a name for the user in the Name text box.

   Choose the authentication method that will be used for this user account.

   - Choose the first option Windows NT Authentication if the user has a valid log in account on the local Windows NT network. If this is the case, you must also supply the NT Domain name by selecting it from the drop-down list box. You can also choose to Grant Access or Deny Access to this Windows NT user account. More often than not, you will be granting access. You may want to use the Deny option on a user who is transferred to another department and no longer needs access to the database but who may be transferred back in the near future.

   - The second option, SQL Server Authentication, is for any user without a valid NT log in account, or a user who connects from an untrusted domain or connection. You must supply them with a password at this time.

3. There are two default options that you can set for the new user. The first is the default database the user will use, and a default language.

   - The default Database option allows you to choose a database the user will be placed in when they log in to the server. I recommend that you do change this option from the master database to the database the user will normally work with. In the case of the sample databases it would be pubs.

   - The default Language option allows you to change the language settings for this particular user. This gives the user the option of seeing event messages and dialog boxes displayed in their own language.

Other language options are only available to you if you have purchased the necessary non-English version of SQL Server.

Your new user account will now look much like Figure 8-8. Here a new user from an untrusted connection has been created.

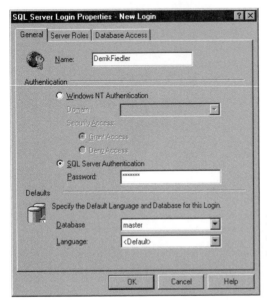

Figure 8–8 *A new user account is set up using the SQL Server log in Properties dialog box. From the General Tab you will begin the process.*

The next tab is the Server Roles tab. The options available here will be discussed in the section on Roles later in this chapter.

4. Now choose the databases that this user will have access to by clicking on the Database Access tab. Click in the check box beside those databases that this user will be permitted to have access. Click the box beside the pubs database. SQL Server will add the user name into the User column. The pubs database has already been set as the default database for this user, but they must still be granted permission to use it. If they are to be allowed access to any other databases, you can check the boxes beside them now. The default database is set in the General tab, but permission to use other databases is granted here.

5. Select the Database Roles for the user in the database selected in the upper list box. A user can have different roles in different databases. All users are always assigned to the public role by default and you cannot remove them from this role. There are several roles that are created when SQL Server is installed and you can assign a user to any or none of them. Figure 8-9 shows the completed Database Access tab for the new user Derrik Fiedler.

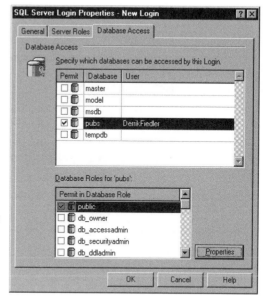

Figure 8–9 *Use the Manage log ins dialog box to add new users to SQL Server. You can also assign a default database and select an alias log in.*

6. Click the OK button to finish the new user account. If you have selected the SQL Server Authentication method, you will now see a Confirm Password dialog box. You must reenter the password that you entered in the General tab before the user will be added to the list of log in accounts. Confirm the password by typing it exactly the same, and click the OK button. If you make a mistake, a warning dialog box will be displayed and you can try again.

7. Click the log ins folder. You should be able to see the new user in the log ins listing.

You can drop a user by selecting the user name from the log in folder and pressing the delete key on your keyboard. You will see a confirmation dialog box asking you if you do want to remove the log in account. Clicking Yes will delete the user account. Clicking No will leave the account.

User names are specific to a domain. If you are working with a network with more than one domain, a user must specify which domain they belong. For example, you have two domains in your company: SALES and ACCOUNTING. SQL Server belongs to the ACCOUNTING domain. Both SALES and ACCOUNTING each have a separate user with username *marisa*. Marisa in the accounting department will be known to the ACCOUNTING SQL Server simply as *marisa*, while the Marisa in sales will be known to the accounting server as SALES_marisa. If most of SQL Server's users belong to one domain in particular, then set it as the default domain.

Passwords

Passwords are used to authenticate a log in. Without a password, anyone who manages to get access to a valid log in can gain access to SQL Server. Passwords are not required for any log in who is either an NT user or group security account. SQL Server trusts these log ins and does not process security information, except for database access and permissions. If the user comes from an untrusted connection, or is not a registered user or a member of an NT group, then you must provide them with a log in name and password.

SQL Server has no minimum requirements for a password, but it is recommended that you try to enforce some form of minimum requirements: no names, no dictionary words, and a minimum length. When creating a password, you can use any printable character, including A–Z, a–z, 1–0. When adding or changing a password, either by using the stored procedure `sp_password`, or in the log ins properties dialog box, the password must be enclosed within quotes if it uses any character other than A–Z, a–z, or 1–0. You cannot change the password for an NT user or group using any method from within SQL Server. This must be done from within NT.

A password can be created when the user log in is created, or it can easily be changed later by using either the SQL Server Enterprise Manager, or with the stored procedure `sp_password`. The syntax for `sp_password` is like this:

```
sp_password oldpassword, newpassword, log in
```

- The argument oldpassword is used to enter the old password that is being replaced. If you are the SA log in, or a member of sysadmin role, you can use NULL in lieu of the original password.
- The newpassword argument is used to enter the replacement password.
- The log in parameter is used only by the SA when replacing another user's password. This tells SQL Server that the password belongs to the specified log in name, otherwise SQL Server would assume the SA was replacing her own password.

To use the Enterprise Manager to set or change a password, simply expand the log ins folder and select the specific log in security account. Double-click it to display the log ins properties dialog box and then add or change the password. After you click the OK button on the dialog box, you will see the confirmation dialog box for the new password. Retype it and then close the dialog box.

You can also use the stored procedure `sp_password` to change an existing password, or add a password like this:

1. Open the Query Analyzer and type the following:

`sp_password NULL, newpassword, DerrikFiedler`

2. Click the Execute button. The results are displayed in Figure 8-10.

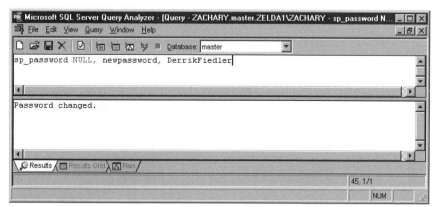

Figure 8–10 *Here you see a password has been changed by the SA for the user*
DerrikFiedler.

Just like log in IDs, a password should be something that a hacker will not immediately guess, but not so difficult that the user will forget it. Hackers will generally tell you that their first guess on a password is the log in name, or the individuals first or last name.

Guest User

The guest user is a special log in that can be created. It will allow anyone access to a database on the server if they do not have an otherwise valid log in. You must expressly create the guest log in if you want it to exist on your server. The purpose behind the guest user is to allow someone who has proper access to SQL Server databases to work within the database before they have been specifically added to a database. The user account is added to a database when you select the database in the SQL Server log ins Properties dialog box on the Database Access tab. The guest log in permissions default to the values given to the public group, unless you place additional specific restrictions.

When a guest log in is created, any user who can log in to SQL Server can also gain access to any database the guest user has been given access to. This log in is added in the same way that you added a user in the previous section. You should be cautious in adding the guest log in to the model database—and it is not recommended. This would allow almost anyone access to any database created after the guest account is added to the model database. This can create a potential hole in your security system.

Using Roles

Roles perform the same function in SQL Server that groups do in Windows NT. SQL Server roles have also replaced the use of user aliases as used in earlier versions of SQL Server. A role allows you to assign all of the various permissions necessary for a set of users. For example, everyone who works in the accounts payable department have to be able to access the same set of database tables, stored procedures, and other database objects. You can set all of these for each of the user log ins one by one—which is very time-consuming, tedious, and prone to mistakes. A better idea is to create a role that you assign all of the necessary permissions, and then add the people in the accounts payable department to the role. If their needs as a group change, you can simply alter the permissions for the role and they will automatically be applied to all members of that role.

When you create a database, there are several roles that are automatically created, but there is one that every user automatically becomes a member of—the *public* role. Every user who is given access to a database is added to the public role. A user can be a member of several roles, but roles do not span over multiple databases. If a user is a member of the Sales role in database1, they do not automatically assume the permissions of the Sales role in database2. The two Sales roles may have similar uses and permissions—they may even be identical—but they are distinct objects. This is in contrast to SQL Server 6.5 and earlier, where a user could belong to only one group at a time. Only the system administrator, the database owner, or any user that belongs to the `db_securityadmin` role can create new roles in a database.

> If you have a Role that can be used by every new database that is created, then create that Role in the model database. Then when each new database is created, that Role will also be created in the new database.

In most production database environments, the role is a natural way to classify categories of users. For example, you have an inventory database that stores information about products, sales, customers, and purchases. Users can be divided into several groups: sales, purchasing, and customer service. Each of these groups of people requires access to some of the information available in your database, all in differing ways. Instead of applying the various permissions to each individual, it would be much easier to create three roles and add the users to the role that best suits their job. For example, you can create three roles, SALES, PURCHASING, and CUSTOMER-SERVICE. The SQL Server Enterprise Manager role is created like this:

1. Open the SQL Server Enterprise Manager application. Expand the database folder in the scope pane. Expand the database in which you will create the new role—in this case the pubs database. Right-click the Database Roles folder and select New Database User from the shortcut menu. You will now see the Database User Properties dialog box.

   You can also reach this same dialog box by right-clicking the database and then selecting New, Database Role from the shortcut menu. You can also select the Database Roles folder, and then select Action, New Database Role from the menu, or by clicking the New button on the toolbar after selecting the Database Roles folder.

2. Type `Purchasing` in the Name text box at the top of the properties dialog box.

   Now you must choose the type of role you are creating. Select the Standard Role. SQL Server security operates at the database level. This meets the needs of almost all applications, but for some extremely complex applications you may want a little more security.

   - The Standard role is the normal database level role security. Standard roles allow you to grant, deny, and revoke permissions as necessary. On the downside, if you have granted a role the permission to read and write a database, it generally means that a member of the role can read and write to the database in almost any manner that they want to. For example, they would be able to use the SQL Server Query Analyzer to query a table for information and update selected data. If a user does not really know how to use T-SQL, they can easily create a poorly designed query that may cause severe performance problems in your database.

   - The Application role allows you to specifically restrict a user of this role from accessing the database in any manner except through the specific application. This way you can restrict all of your users to a front-end application and not bypass it by using another tool. The application role requires a password.

3. To add users to this role, click the Add button. You will see the Add Role Members dialog box displayed as you see in Figure 8-11.

Figure 8–11 *Use the Add Role Members dialog box to select the users who will be added to the new role.*

If you were removing a user from a role, you would select the user in the list box and click the Remove button. This does not delete the role or the user, simply the user's membership in the role. They would retain memberships in any other roles, and the public role.

4. Select the individual users or NT Groups who will become new members of the role. Click the OK button when you have made your selections, as shown in Figure 8-12.

Figure 8–12 *Here you can see the completed Database Role Properties dialog box.*

To select multiple consecutive users in the list you can click on the first and then press and hold the Alt key while clicking the last member of the list. All users between the first and last will be selected. To select multiple nonconsecutive users, press and hold the Ctrl key while clicking on your selections. This will only select the users you click and leave the intervening ones unselected.

5. Click the OK button once you have completed adding users to the role.

You can create users and roles in any order that you want. If you create the roles first, you can easily add the user to the roles membership as you add the new log in account. This is done on the Database Access tab of the SQL Server log in Properties dialog box. When you select a database that the log in has permission to access, the list of database roles is displayed. Any new role that you create for a database will be listed there.

Roles can also be created by using the stored procedure `sp_addrole`. Once a role has been created, you can quickly add accounts to the role using the `sp_addrolemember`. These stored procedures perform the same function as shown in the previous steps. The same restrictions as to who can create new roles apply in this method as they did in the previous. In this next exercise, you will learn to create the role Sales in the pubs database and a user to the role.

1. Open the Query Analyzer application and select the pubs in the Database list box.

2. Enter the following T-SQL statement:

```
sp_addrole 'Sales'
```

The name of the new role must be a valid identifier and must be unique in the sysusers system table of the current database. You can also use an additional argument after the role name for the owner of the new role. This owner defaults to dbo, or must be a user or role in the current database.

3. Click the Execute button. Figure 8-13 shows the results of this successful creation of the new role.

4. Click the Clear Query Window button, and then the Yes button in the confirmation dialog box. Do not worry about the results still displayed in the lower pane of the window.

5. Type this stored procedure in the query window.

```
sp_addrolemember 'Sales', 'DerrikFiedler'
```

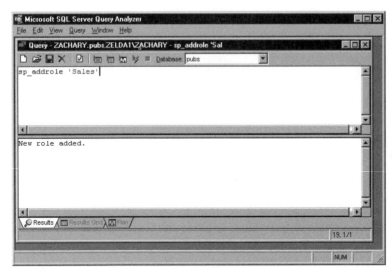

Figure 8–13 *A new role has been added to the pubs database.*

6. Click the Execute button. The results are displayed in Figure 8-14.

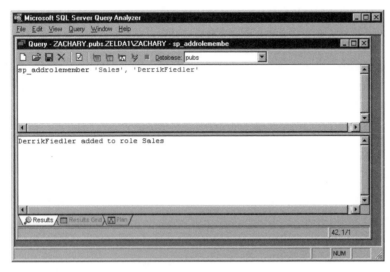

Figure 8–14 *Here you can see the user 'DerrikFiedler' has been added to the role Sales.*

If you were adding an NT User or Group account instead of an SQL Server user account, you would need to preface the username with the domain name. The above statement would read like this:

```
sp_addrolemember 'Sales', 'domainname\DerrikFiedler'
```

The primary difference is that you need to add the NT domain name to qualify the user or group for SQL Server.

Application Roles

Application Roles are used when you wan to implement a set of security standards for all users who access the SQL Server through a specific application. The role's security properties are applied to the user when they log in through the application. A user that has their own permissions, due either to their membership in another role, or through their own account, will have these other permissions inactivated while their are working through the application role.

The application role is an excellent method for restricting the access of a user that accesses your database using a connection that is not readily secured, such as an Internet connection. The application role is activated through the request by the application for access, and the password provided by the application. The password can be embedded within the application, or entered by the user. The embedded password model, allows you to permit another application to manage its own security, and if a user with a certain level of access requests a connection to SQL Server, the application can pass this on through the application role. This is one method by which you can create an Internet transaction, allowing a remote user to connect through a middle application such as Microsoft Transaction Server (MTS). MTS can coordinate the transaction from the user, and pass along the necessary data to SQL Server.

If you are creating an application role, you will not add users to the role. The role becomes active when the user enters the Application Role password. Any other roles that they currently are members of will temporarily be inactivated by the Application Role and its permissions.

The application role only exists within the database, and as such enables the user to access only that database. The only potential problem this may bring, is that the user can gain access to other databases through the *guest* account. If the guest account is active in another database, and has permissions granted to it, the user access those databases and the permissions. If you do not explicitly grant permissions to the guest account, then this potential hole is not available to the application role.

An Owner

Every database and database object has an owner, the user who created it. Some permissions are granted only to an object's owner, while others can be granted by them to another user. An owner must give permission to another user to use their object. Of course, the system administrator, or SA log in, is the implied owner of all objects and can act as the owner of any object.

The system administrator can grant the use of the CREATE DATA-BASE statement to another user. Great care should be taken when granting this permission. In a normal SQL production environment, the ability to use the CREATE DATABASE statement should remain only with those users who are acting as system administrators or developers. Anyone who is given this permission can create a new database, which they are then the default owner of. The ability to create a database also gives the power to use all of the system resources that go along with a database. The database owner or the system administrator can transfer ownership of a database to another user.

When SQL Server is installed, the system administrator, SA log in, is the default owner of all database objects, and remains the owner of the master database. SQL Server will also treat the system administrator as the database owner of any databases he or she uses, regardless of who actually created it.

A database owner is the creator of that database and has full authority to:

- Give access to the database.
- Grant other users permission to create objects.
- Grant permission to others to execute commands and statements on objects.
- Revoke any permission granted.
- Deny a user access to any object.
- Set up and manage roles.
- Assign users to specific roles.

The database owner has essentially system administrator privileges within their own database. Ownership of a database can be transferred to another user. This often occurs when a database passes from a developmental stage to a production stage. Database ownership may also be transferred so that the responsibility for day-to-day management of the database can be carried out by someone other than the system administrator. Only the ownership of a database can be transferred from one user to another: ownership of tables, views, and other objects cannot be transferred.

SQL Server views ownership of database objects as a chain of ownership. Beginning with the database, each object created within the database, and also each object created in the database that depends on another object.

For example, the system administrator gives Derrik permission to create a database, and he creates the Inventory database, and the tables Products, Vendors, and Orders. Derrik is the database owner of Inventory and the three tables. Derrik grants permission to Jenna to create views on the tables, and she creates viewProducts. Jenna as the owner of the viewProducts gives Griffen permission to use the view.

When Jenna creates the view on the Products table, SQL Server only has to check the permissions on the table because the table owner and the database owner are both Derrik. When Griffen attempts to use viewProducts, SQL Server will check permissions not only on the view, but will go back to the table Products and see what permission he has on object.

Ownership of a database can be transferred, or you can allow other users to act as the dbo of a database. The ownership of the master database cannot be transferred, it always belongs to the system administrator. Ownership of any other user database can only be transferred using the stored procedure `sp_changedbowner`. This stored procedure has two possible arguments that you can use:

```
sp_changedbowner 'log in'[,drop_alias_flag]
```

- The argument 'log in' is the new owner of the database and must be currently listed as a log in user in the syslog ins table of the master database. This can be any valid log in who is either a Windows NT user or an SQL Server user. The new owner cannot be a current log in or alias in the table they are taking ownership of.
- The second argument is optional and has only three possible values: True or False, and a default value of NULL. When true or NULL, any alias log ins that have been mapped to the old owner will be mapped to the new dbo. A value of false will drop the mapped aliases entirely.

In order to transfer ownership of a database, you must be either a member of the sysadmin server role, or the `db_owner` database role. You can always add a user to the role of `db_owner` in a database and allow them to function as the database owner without actually transferring ownership. Use `sp_changedbowner` to transfer ownership of the pubs database like this:

1. Open the Query Analyzer and select the pubs database in the Database list box. Type the following statement:

```
sp_changedbowner 'ZELDA1\egermesin'
```

This statement uses a NULL value for the `drop_alias_flag` setting.

This stored procedure acts on the current database so be sure that you have the correct database selected.

2. Click the Execute button on the toolbar. You see the result set in Figure 8-15.

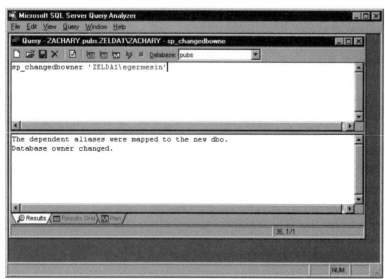

Figure 8–15 *The sp_changedbowner statement is used to change the ownership of a database from the current owner to another user.*

Similar to the `sp_changedbowner` is the stored procedure, `sp_changeobjectowner`. This stored procedure allows you to change the ownership of any other object that exists within the database. The syntax for using this procedure is very much like that of `sp_changedbowner`, except that there is no argument for the `drop_alias_flag`. This stored procedure must be run from within the database where the object exists. You cannot use the master database as the current database and try to change the ownership of a view in the pubs database. This procedure would be used like this:

```
sp_changeobjectowner `object', `owner'
```

The two arguments are used to designate the object whose ownership is to be transferred, and the security account of the new owner. The new owner must be a current valid Windows NT user or group, or an SQL Server user or role. The username must be listed in the sysusers table in the current database.

- The object is the specific database object: table, view, rules, et cetera. If necessary, you can qualify the object's name when more than one user has created an object with the same name—*ownername.objectname*. The qualified ownername is the current owner of the object, not the owner-to-be.

- The owner argument is the name of the new owner of the object.

You cannot drop or delete a security account if the account is the owner of any current object in the database. You must either first drop the object, and then its owner, or change the ownership of the object and then drop the user.

MCSE 8.4   Using the Permissions System

Permissions are a system whereby the system administrator, the owner of a database, or database object give their permission to use objects or commands. Simply put, permissions are the final system of controls over who can use the objects within a database, or select, insert, or delete any of the information contained in the tables. Some permissions cannot be granted, but belong exclusively to the system administrator and other members of the sysadmin role.

The permissions that you can be granted, and those that you can grant depend on your status as a user. As a system administrator you can grant the widest range of permissions, while as a user without ownership of any objects, you will probably not be able to grant any permissions to another user. The exception to this is when you are granted permission on an object and the WITH GRANT clause is used. This allows you to grant the same permission to another user. Permissions can be granted, denied, and revoked to users and groups, not to log in IDs.

When permissions are granted to users, groups, and roles, conflicts can occur. For example, the ADMIN role may be granted permission to SELECT information from the Personnel table. Now George, a member of the ADMIN role is transferred to another department where he still requires most of the permissions available from the ADMIN role, but does not need access to the Personnel table. He can be denied access to the Personnel table. Even though he is still a member of the ADMIN role, the fact that he has been denied access takes precedence. Whenever there is a conflict in permissions, the stricter of the available permissions will take effect.

- The GRANT statement specifically gives the Windows NT or SQL Server user or group, or SQL Server role specific permission to use an object or perform a function.
- The DENY statement specifically prohibits the use of an object or function.

- The REVOKE statement will reverse the effect of either a GRANT or DENY statement.

When permission is granted, a positive entry is made in the sysprotects table. If a permission is denied to a user, a negative entry is placed in the sysprotects. If a permission is revoked, then the negative or positive entry in the sysprotects table is removed. The sysprotects table is a system table, and a copy is maintained in every database. A permission statement that specifies either an NT or SQL Server user security account will affect just that user, while a permission statement that specifies an NT group or SQL Server role will affect all of its members. For most users and groups, permissions for the more commonly used commands and stored procedures are easily granted from within SQL Server Enterprise Manager. You can also use the GRANT, DENY, and REVOKE statements from the Query Analyzer. When a user is granted permission to use an object or command, they do not have the ability to pass it to another user, unless they have been given explicit permission through the use of the WITH GRANT clause.

GRANTing Permission

When using the T-SQL statements to grant, revoke, or deny permissions, there are slight variations in the statement syntax depending on whether you are working with a permission for a statement or an object. Permission granted on a statement allows the grantee to use a T-SQL statement. Permission granted on an object gives the grantee permission to access the specified object. When you are giving or denying permission for an object you can be very specific. For example, if you are granting permission to use the SELECT statement on a table, you can allow the user to select on the entire table, or you can restrict the permission to selected columns. Of course, the simpler and more common method is to create a view and then grant the SELECT permission on the view, not the table. Shown here is the syntax of a GRANT statement for both a statement and an object.

Syntax for GRANT on a statement:

```
GRANT
{ALL [or statement1, statement2, ...n]}
TO {security_account[user, group, or role]}
```

Syntax for GRANT on an object:

```
GRANT
{ALL [or permission1, permission2, ...n]}
[(columnname1, columnname2, ...n]
```

```
ON {table, view, storedprocedure, extendedprocedure}
TO securityaccount, ...n
WITH GRANT OPTION
AS [group or role]
```

The GRANT statement can be a complex statement, and should be used with great care. Whenever possible, use the simpler format in SQL Server Enterprise Manager. When using the GRANT statement, everything inside of [] is either optional, or you will use one or more of the options. The statement arguments are:

One of these options can be used.

- ALL—Grants all permissions available on the object(s) listed in the ON clause. Only a member of the sysadmins role can use the ALL clause when permission is being granted to statements. This is due to the fact that ALL includes the CREATE DATABASE statement.

- *permission1* or *statement1*—Substitute either the specific permission or statement, or a list of permissions or statements that you are granting permission to. Each item in a list must be separated with commas. When granting an object permission, you can optionally name the specific column(s) that the permission is to be applied. You must enclose the column name(s) within a set of parentheses. If you have a list of columns, separate each name with a comma.

- The permissions on objects that can be granted inlcude: SELECT, INSERT, UPDATE, and DELETE.

- Permission on statements, stored procedures, and extended procedures is an EXECUTE permission.

- When specifying permissions for columns, then permissions can be SELECT and/or UPDATE.

- When granting INSERT and UPDATE permission to a user on a table or view, and the FOREIGN KEY constraint has been applied, SQL Server must be able to validate the new information against the data in the referenced foreign key. If the user does not already have SELECT permission on the referenced column or table, you must grant REFERENCE permission on the foreign key column in the referenced table to the user. Without this, every attempt to INSERT or UPDATE a new record will fail. You cannot grant REFERENCE on a system table.

This clause is required when the permission is on an object:

- ON—This clause is used to specify the object(s) over which the permissions being granted will be effective. You can grant permissions to tables, views, stored procedures, and extended procedures.

This clause is required for both objects and statements:

- TO—This clause specifies to whom the permissions are to be granted. You can grant permissions to an NT user or group, or to an SQL Server user or role. When the same permission is being granted to several users/groups/roles, you can include them as a list, separating each by a comma.

- WITH GRANT OPTION—Allows the user granted this permission, or permissions, to grant them to another user. This clause cannot be used with the CREATE DATABASE statement. This clause is optional and should be used with caution.

- AS—This clause is used when the user executing the GRANT statement belongs to several security groups or roles. With the potential of conflicts in available permissions, the AS clause specifies which security account is being used that has the necessary permission to GRANT these permissions. This clause may be required.

In Figure 8-16 you see a GRANT statement being executed in the Query Analyzer application. This statement says that permission is granted to the user DerrikFiedler to select information from the columns au_lname, and au_fname from the view authorsphone. The permission is granted by another user who has permission to act as the database owner.

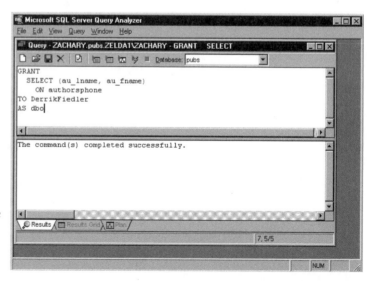

Figure 8–16 *Here you see a SELECT permission is granted to a user. The result sets says the command was successful.*

DENYing Permission

To DENY a permission takes away a previously granted permission to a statement or object or specifically denies a permission available to a group or role. In earlier versions of SQL Server this was done with the REVOKE statement. You can deny permissions from a user, a role, or a group.

An exception to the DENY statement is when a user uses an application role. Remember, when a user activates the application role, all of their existing permissions are temporary inactivated. This includes any permission denials. If the application role requires access to an object or statement that the user has been denied, they will have access to it while in the application role.

If you deny a permission to a user, group, or role, and they are later added to a group or role that does have the denied permission, they will not inherit the new permission. It will remain denied. If a permission has been denied, simply revoking the denial does not mean that the permission has been granted. On the other hand, if you specifically GRANT a permission that has been previously denied, the denial will be revoked and the permission granted in one step. The DENY statement can be used by members of the sysadmin, db_owner, and db_securityadmin roles. Any owner of an object can use the DENY statement on their own object.

Note DENY is a new keyword in SQL Server 7. If you are upgrading an existing application from an earlier version, you may need to change any scripts that use REVOKE to specifically deny access to a permission.

Like the GRANT statement, the DENY statement can also be complex. The syntax for the DENY statement for a statement looks like this:

```
DENY
{ALL [or statement1, statement2, ...n]}
TO {security_account[user, group, or role]}
```

Syntax for DENY on an object:

```
DENY
{ALL [PRIVILEGES] [or permission1, permission2, ...n]}
[(columnname1, columnname2, ...n]
ON {table, view, storedprocedure, extendedprocedure}
TO securityaccount, ...n
[CASCADE]
```

The DENY statements options are very similar to the GRANT statement, with the exception of the last option:

- CASCADE—This option allows you to revoke a permission granted with the WITH GRANT OPTION, and cascades the revoke statement down through all users who have been subsequently granted permission by the user or group whose permission is now being denied.
- PRIVILEGES—This parameter is an optional keyword and included for SQL-92 compatibility.

Be sure that you use the GRANT and DENY statements so that they work the way you intend them. There is no hierarchy for these statements other than one—*the last statement committed is the one that is in effect.* If you deny permissions to a user and then grant them to the public group, the user will also get the permissions since they are a member of the public group. If you are restricting access to specific users, grant all of the required permissions to the group, and then deny any specific permissions from the single user.

Figure 8-17 shows both a completed DENY statement that denies the user DerrikFiedler the use of the select statement on the view authorsphone, and then the attempt to use select in the second query window.

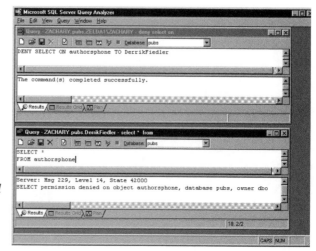

Figure 8–17 *Here you can see both a DENY statement and the results of the users attempt to execute the denied permission.*

REVOKE Permissions

The REVOKE statement has new meaning in SQL Server 7. In past versions of SQL Server the REVOKE statement functioned much the way that the DENY statement now does. In this version of SQL Server the REVOKE statement is used to remove the effect of the last GRANT or DENY statement. This does not mean that if you revoke a denied permission the user has been granted permission to the object or statement. It simply means that they are now no longer denied access and would have whatever permissions are available to them through any role or group memberships.

The syntax of the REVOKE statement is like this:

```
REVOKE
{ALL [or statement1, statement2, …n]}
FROM {security_account[user, group, or role]}
```

Syntax for REVOKE on an object:

```
REVOKE
[GRANT OPTION FOR]
{ALL [or permission1, permission2, …n]}
[(columnname1, columnname2, …n]
ON {table, view, storedprocedure, extendedprocedure}
FROM securityaccount, …n
[CASCADE]
AS [group or role]
```

REVOKE has many similarities to its cousins, GRANT and DENY, in its use and options. The differences include:

- GRANT OPTION FOR: This clause is optional and means that the earlier grant of the WITH GRANT OPTION permission is being revoked. This security account will no longer be able to grant this permission to another user. If just this permission is revoked, the security account retains any other permissions that were granted in the same statement.
- FROM: This keyword takes the place of TO in GRANT and DENY.
- CASCADE: Use this clause any time you are revoking the WITH GRANT OPTION. This causes the revocation to cascade down through all users to whom the permission was granted by this security option.

In Figure 8-18 you can see how the REVOKE statement is used to remove the effect of a denied permission. In Figure 8-17 you saw how the select statement was denied to the user DerrikFielder. In this figure you see how the revocation of that denial now allows him to execute the statement.

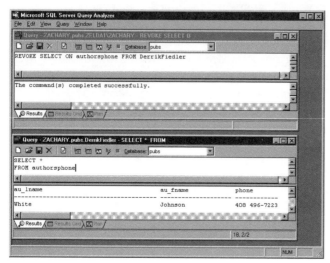

Figure 8–18 *Here you see how the revocation of a denied permission now allows the user to see the information available by selecting from the view.*

Permissions and the SQL Server Enterprise Manager

You can also grant, deny, and revoke permissions from within the SQL Server Enterprise Manager application. The number and types of permissions is more limited than with the GRANT/REVOKE statements, but covers most objects and commands a user needs to access. Permissions can be specified for either users or roles. The only difference between permissions for users and roles is that users are grouped into the Database User folder, while roles are placed in the Database Roles folder. Windows NT groups will appear in the Database Users folder.

OBJECT PERMISSIONS

Object permissions are granted, denied, and revoked at the database level. This is because SQL Server security for objects is based at the database level. Permissions for objects cannot span across multiple databases. Use these steps to grant and revoke permissions inside SQL Server Enterprise Manager:

1. Open the SQL Server Enterprise Manager window and then expand the Database folder in the Scope pane. Expand the specific database to which permissions are to be granted or revoked, in this case pubs, and then click the Database Roles folder. The list of current roles will be dis-

played in the results pane. Double-click the public role to display it in the Properties dialog, box as shown in Figure 8-19.

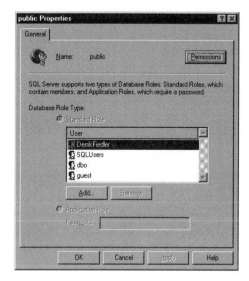

Figure 8–19 *You can set permissions for either roles or users by using their Properties dialog box.*

2. Click the Permissions button to open the Database User Properties. This is the dialog box you will use to grant, revoke, or deny permissions for an object.

3. Scroll down the permissions list until you see the authors table listed. Click the check box in the authors table row in the SELECT column, as seen in Figure 8-20. This grants the SELECT permission to the public role on the authors table.

4. When you have completed making any other necessary changes to the object permission for this user or role, then click the OK button. Use the Apply if you want to apply your current changes immediately. Otherwise they will not take effect until you exit from this dialog box. Close the Properties dialog box.

A permission can be denied by clicking in the applicable check box until you see a red X displayed inside. This means that the permission on this object and action is denied. A permission is revoked by clicking a checkmark or X until the check box is blank. Figure 8-21 shows the authors table row with a granted SELECT permission, a denied INSERT permission, and a revoked or blank UPDATE permission.

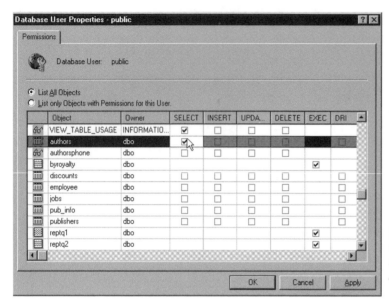

Figure 8–20 *The public role has been granted SELECT permission on the authors table.*

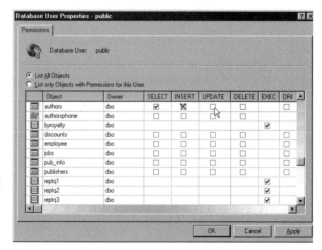

Figure 8–21 *The public role has been granted, and denied permissions on the object table authors.*

STATEMENT PERMISSIONS

You can also change some of the statement permissions from within the SQL Server Enterprise Manager. Only a few of the more commonly used statements are available here, but it is enough for many purposes.

1. Open the Enterprise Manager application and expand the server in the Scope pane. Click on the Databases folder. As you see in Figure 8-22, a listing of the databases on this server is displayed in the results pane.

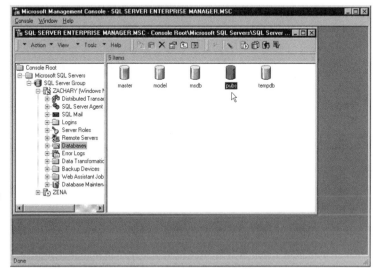

Figure 8–22 *Here you see the databases listed in the results pane of the Enterprise Manager.*

2. Double-click the pubs database icon in the results pane. You will see the pubs Properties dialog box displayed. Click the Permissions tab button as, seen in Figure 8-23.

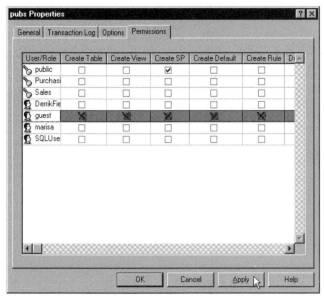

Figure 8–23 *Use the Permissions tab of database Properties dialog box to set permissions on statements.*

3. As you can see here, the guest user has been granted permission on many of these important statements. In Figure 8-24 you see that these permissions have been denied by the red X. Click the Apply button once you have made any other changes necessary to complete setting of your changes. Close the Properties dialog box.

Using the SQL Server Security Wizard

You have already seen that the creation of a new SQL Server log in account, and then access to a database, can be easily performed. The SQL Server Security Wizard can make the process even easier. With the Security Wizard you can:

- Create a new Windows NT or SQL Server log in security account.
- Add the security account to a database.
- Include the security account in one or more of the fixed server roles.

Using the Security Wizard only takes a few easy steps:

1. Open the SQL Server Enterprise Manager application. Choose the Security Wizard by either: Select Help, Wizards from the menu, or by clicking the Run a Wizard button on the toolbar.

2. From the Select Wizard dialog box, choose the Security Wizard, then click the OK button.

3. The first screen you see contains the welcome information and some information about the wizard. Click the Next button.

4. Choose the Authentication mode that the new log in account will use. If the user already has a valid NT user account in a trusted domain, then you can use the Windows NT option; otherwise select the SQL Server option. Click the Next button to move to the next screen.

5. The screen you now see will depend on your choice of Authentication mode. Figure 8-24 shows the screen for Windows NT authentication, while Figure 8-25 shows the SQL Server authentication screen. Click the Next button to continue.

When you select the Windows NT Authentication mode you will use the screen shown above. You must enter a valid NT user or group account into the text box. This must be entered in the format *domainname\user-groupname*. You can then choose to GRANT access to SQL Server for the group or user, or to DENY access.

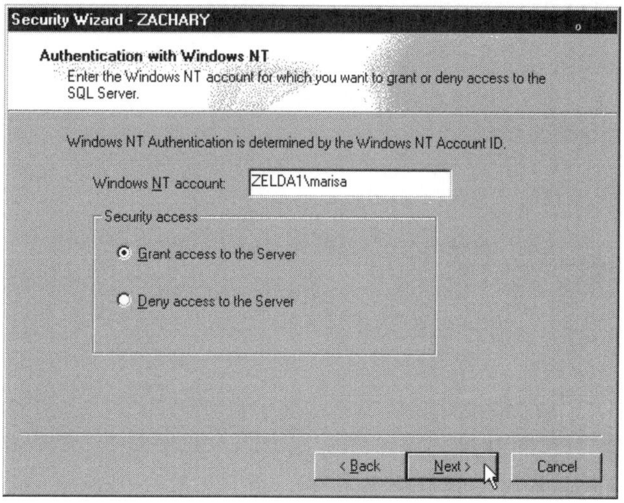

Figure 8–24 *Here you see the Windows NT Authentication mode account screen.*

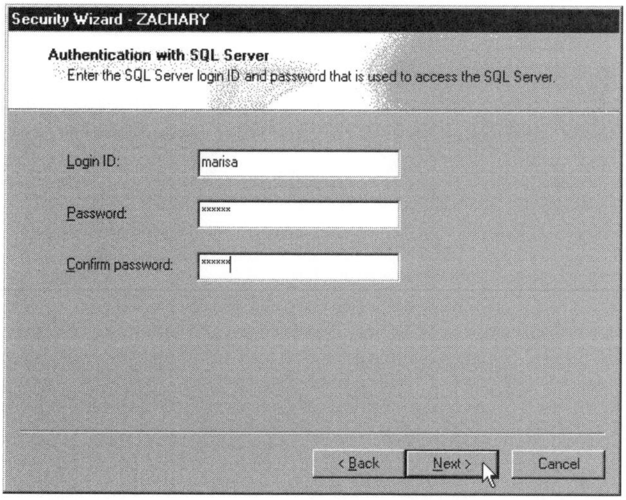

Figure 8–25 *This is the screen you will use when using SQL Server Authentication mode.*

When you choose the SQL Server Authentication mode you will see this screen. Enter the user name and a password, then confirm the password.

6. In this screen you will choose whether this security account will have access to any of the server security roles, as shown in Figure 8-26. These options are normally reserved to someone who needs to have a high level of access. Click the Next button to open the next screen.

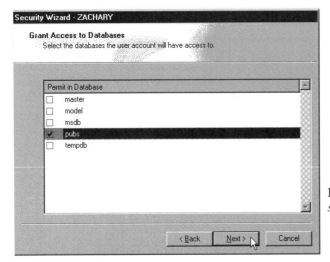

Figure 8–26 *Use this screen to grant server roles to the new security account.*

7. Select the database(s) that the security account will be able to access, as seen in Figure 8-27. This is not the same as selecting a default database. Click the Next button.

8. This screen shows you what options have been granted to the new account. If they are all correct, click the Finish button. If you have made a mistake, click the Back button and correct the error. Figure 8-27 displays the completed entry.

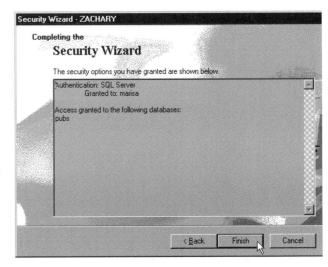

Figure 8–27 *This screen displays a summary of the changes that will be made. Check it, and make any necessary corrections before committing the changes.*

MCSE 8.5   Security Between Linked Servers

In some types of transactions, such as a distributed transaction, servers will share in its completion. One server may record part of the transaction, while the other server records the other part. Or, the transaction may require information from another server before the transaction can be committed. There are several ways for this transaction to be completed, and one method is through linked servers. Linked servers have special security applications.

For a connection to be made between a pair of linked servers, there must be a log in mapping. This mapping is similar to the one used by SQL Server in server to server remote procedure calls (RPC). Instead of the the mapping being done at the receiving server, in a linked server connection, the mapping is done by the sending server. The sending server passes the user name and password to the receving server. You can use the stored procedures `sp_addlinkedsrvlog` in and `sp_droplinkedsrvlog` in to manage these connections, or they can be easily managed within the Enterprise Manager window.

If you are using an exclusive Windows NT authentication mode for your security, you will need to map a local log in name and password that the sending server will pass to the receiving server. This log in must use SQL Server authentication mode. This allows the log in to be authenticated at both ends of the connection. A linked server connection can easily be created within the Enterprise Manager by following these steps:

1. In the console tree window, expand the server group that contains the sending server, and then expand the sending server. Right-click on the Linked Servers icon.

    From the shortcut menu, select New Linked Servr. As shown in Figure 8-28, the Linked Server Properties - New Linked Server dialog box is displayed. You will use this dialog box to create new linked servers, and to edit existing linked server connections. You must either select an existing linked server connection to edit, or create a new one. To create the new linked server connection you must be able to provide the server name, and the type of connection to be used. You can select from either an SQL Server connection, or an OLE DB connection. For the OLE DB connection, you must enter the provider name, and product name for the connection. You also need the name of the data source on the reciever server, and any necessary provider string.

2. Click on the Security tab button to enter the necessary security account information to complete the linked server connection.

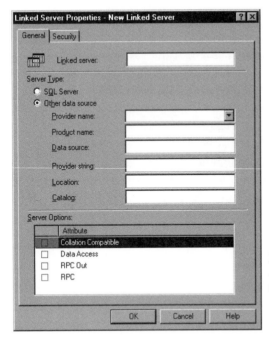

Figure 8–28 *The General tab of the Linked Server Properties dialog box is used to set up the connection.*

3. In order for the linked server connection to log in to the receiving server, you must map an existing security account on the sending server, to a valid account on the receriver. Select the sending server account in the from the combo box, as shown in Figure 8-29.

4. If the local log in account is also valid on the receiving server, then click the Impersonate check box. The log in will then use its own security credentials on the receiving server.

5. If the local log in account cannot or should not use their own credentials, then enter the remote user and password in the next two columns.

If all local log in accounts should use their own security credentials, then click the box at the bottom of the dialog box, and this will be set as the default action.

6. Click the OK button to complete the creation of the linked server and the log in accounts.

In planning the security for linked servers, you must set up the security accounts for the users at both the sending and receiving servers so that they can be properly mapped from one to the other. The security accounts do not

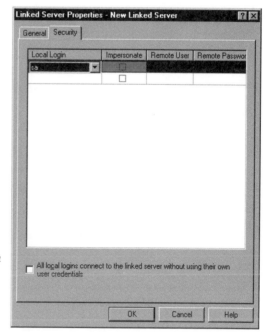

Figure 8–29 *Use the Security tab on the Linked Server Properties dialog box to select an account, and create the log in mapping to the receiving server.*

have to have the same permissions on both ends of the connection, but the user should have the permissions necessary to complete the tasks required by the transaction or connection.

Key Points

Several very important key points about SQL Server security have been made in this chapter.

- How Windows NT and SQL Server identify and authenticate a user log in through the use of usernames and passwords.
- How to choose between integrated, standard, and mixed security modes.
- How to create both a user group and a user log in for Windows NT.
- How to create users, roles, and user log ins for SQL Server.
- How to grant and revoke permissions.
- How to set up the security for a linked server connection.
- And, finally, to use SQL Security Manager with integrated and mixed security.

▲ CHAPTER REVIEW QUESTIONS

▲ Multiple Choice:

1. *The central reason(s) for using a security system on your database is: (Select all that apply).*
   A. To identify the user
   B. To restrict access to authorized personnel
   C. To make it difficult for anyone to use the database
   D. To track a user's movements within the database

2. *A common SQL Server access system consists of: (Select all that apply).*
   A. A log on name
   B. A password
   C. A fingerprint scanner
   D. A retinal scanner

3. *SQL Security must be used when:*
   A. A user is rejected by Windows NT security
   B. The user does not have a trusted connection
   C. The user connects through a network connection, but does not have a Windows NT log in account
   D. A and B
   E. All of the above

4. *User log in information is maintained in the _____ database.*
   A. msdb
   B. master
   C. Each user database
   D. Pubs

5. *A user has a trusted connection when:*
   A. They have been validated by SQL Server.
   B. They have been validated by Windows NT.
   C. They have a direct LAN connection to the SQL Server.
   D. They use a dial-up connection.

6. *A user account should default to _____ database.*
   A. Temporary

B. Master

C. User

D. Pubs

7. *The following users can create new roles in a database. (Select all that apply).*

A. The system administrator

B. The database owner

C. A member of the `db_useradmin` role

D. A member of the `db_securityadmin` role

8. *When granting a permission to a user on an object, the WITH GRANT option is used to:*

A. Allow the user to use the object.

B. Allows the user to give others permission on the object.

C. Makes the user an owner of the object.

D. It depends on the permissions being granted.

9. *When a permission is denied using the DENY statement, a user is:*

A. Denied any access to the SQL Server database

B. Permanently removed as a user

C. Denied the use of the permission

D. Denied use of a permission unless it is granted by their membership in a role

10. *SQL Server allows another application to log in to a database through the use of? (Select all that apply).*

A. Anonymous log in

B. Anonymous role

C. Guest user

D. Application role

11. *When setting up a log in for a linked server connection, you would use which of the following? (Select all that apply).*

A. sp_addlinkedsrvlog in

B. sp_newlinkedsrvlog in

C. Security tab on the Enterprise Manager window

D. Linked Server Properties dialog box

▲ True or False:

1. *True or False? Controlling access to the SQL Server database is an important aspect of the system administrator's responsibilities?*

2. *True or False? Windows NT security is recommended over SQL Server security.*

3. *True or False? The alias is replacing the role in SQL Server security.*

4. *True or False? When setting up the security accounts for a group of users, be sure to make the passwords easy to remember, like their last names.*

5. *True or False? The mixed security mode is the default when SQL Server is installed.*

6. *True or False? If you are a member of the sysadmin role, you can change another users' password with the following command:*

7. *True or False? If a user is a member of a role that has UPDATE permission on a table, logs in through an application that uses an application role that only has SELECT permission on the table, this user can do either.*

8. *True or False? The application role can be used to allow another application to authenticate a user, and then allow the user to gain access to SQL Server.*

9. *True or False? A log in using a linked server connection, automatically has the same permissions on the receiving server as they do on the sending server.*

Working with Database Files

This module covers the topic of working with your database files. Through the next four chapters you will learn the following:

Chapter 9 - "Managing Your Database Files." Here you will learn how SQL Server 7 database files are constructed. The subject of the normalized database will be covered, as will basic relationships.

Chapter 10 - "What is Data Integrity?" This chapter will cover the subject of integrity. What is it and how does it effect your data?

Chapter 11 - "Data Consistency and Concurrency." In this chapter you will learn how SQL Server prevents users from editing the same information at the same time. The subject of locks will be covered in depth.

Chapter 12 - "Managing Database Space." Here the subject of managing database space requirements will be covered. How SQL Server uses disk space, and how it allocates space.

Managing Your Database Files

In this chapter you will be introduced to the topic of managing the files necessary to SQL Server 7™, and how SQL works within this structure. You will see how data is stored and retrIeved, and what you will need to do to access information from other databases.

MCSE 9.1   The Relational Database

In order for a client application and the server database engine to communicate with each other they must use a common language. For Microsoft SQL Server™ that language is *Structured Query Language*, commonly called *SQL*. There are several different versions of SQL, and Microsoft SQL Server uses a version called Transact-SQL. Currently there are two SQL standards: *ANSI SQL-89* and *ANSI SQL-92*. These standards were published by the American National Standards Institute in 1989 and updated in 1992. Transact-SQL meets all of the standards set forth in both ANSI SQL-89 and ANSI SQL-92, and provides extensions for additional programming needs.

In this chapter, you will see how an SQL Server relational database is constructed, and how data is organized within it. SQL Server generally works in a client/server format. SQL Server itself is the server side of the equation, while an application on the connected workstation is the client end. By understanding the database's basic structure, you will more easily understand how Transact-SQL works with it and how a client application should be built.

A *relational database management system*, or RDMS, is a system of information that is stored in tables. These tables are linked by a series of relationships. These links are composed of relationships between a set of data in one table and a corresponding set of data in another table.

As you begin to design your database, you must first understand the data that will be stored in it. Ask yourself these and as many other questions that you can think of about the information that you must deal with.

- What kind of information will you be storing?
- Is the data static and never changing, or is it dynamic and constantly being updated?
- How are records now kept, and how are they accessed?
- Does each record currently have a unique identifying characteristic you can use?
- How can the information within each record be broken down into fields?

As you begin to answer these questions, you will come to have an understanding about the information that you will be working with, and how that information is used by the people who must use it every day. This process helps you to understand the logical design necessary for your database.

Once you are familiar with the data you will be working with, you will begin to find logical relationships between different pieces of the data. Some of the best database designers will use diagrams to illustrate the relationships between different pieces. As you become even more intimate with the data, you will be able to see how and why different pieces of related data will be placed into separate tables.

The logical design is not necessarily the best database design. The final physical database design, the one that you will use when actually building the tables and columns that your data will be stored in, may be different than your initial logical design. Many database design shops feel that once the logical database design has been diagrammed on paper, it is set in stone. Do not become so entranced with a design that you cannot change it when necessary. The final physical database design should focus on three things:

- The integrity of the data contained in it.
- Creating a structure that allows your users easy access to the data.
- Performance or speed.

The physical database design should help to facilitate the consistency and integrity of the data that is stored within its tables. While this is a requirement most often seen as the most important to the database designer or database administrator, users tend to look at things a little differently. To the end users, the most important things are usually speed and access. Often, the end user wants the ability to browse tables and access data in a free-form type of format. Finally, the success or failure of a particular database is often based on the speed of data updates and retrieval—if the database appears to be slow, you can bet that the user coalition will be back demanding speed increases, or a completely new system.

These criteria are what will be used to test your mettle as a database designer. Of course, these three criteria: consistency/integrity, performance/speed, and ease of access tend to be mutually exclusive. By meeting one set of criteria, you will generally have to take something away from one or both of the others. How well you balance each will be your final test.

The Normalized Database

As a database is designed, you try to work towards a *normalized* relational database system—this is the ideal database. A normalized database must meet several conditions:

- All *entities* (tables) are made up of *attributes* (columns/fields) that define *properties* (datatypes) about each *row* (record) contained within the entity.
- Each row of a table defines a single event or item.
- Each row is uniquely identified through the use of a *primary key*.

- The primary key can be made up of a single column or multiple columns.
- The primary key is unique throughout the table.
- Primary key values cannot be a null value.

One of the characteristics of a normalized database is that it will contain many more *narrow* tables. A table is considered narrow when it has few columns; conversely, a table is considered wide when it has many columns, most often containing information that is repeated throughout many rows. The unnormalized Customer Database depicted in Figure 9-1 contains several flaws, common to databases designed by someone new to the concept.

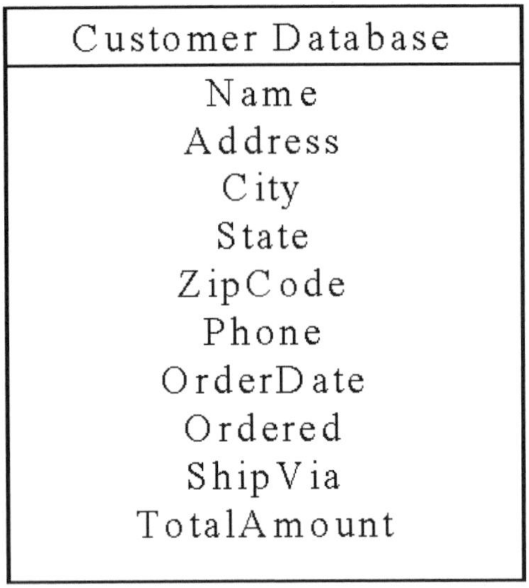

Customer Database
Name
Address
City
State
ZipCode
Phone
OrderDate
Ordered
ShipVia
TotalAmount

Figure 9–1 *This unnormalized database will contain a great deal of duplicated information, such as customer data for each item ordered. There are also several columns that should be broken out into separate tables.*

- There is no single or multiple column primary key.
- The Name field should be divided into First and Last Name fields. This will enable you to search by a customer's last name only.
- Columns that force repeat grouping of information, such as the Ordered and ShipVia columns exist. These columns should never be included in this table. They will force you to repeat all of the customer information in a new row, one new row for every item they order. Think how many thousands of additional rows will probably be added to the table.
- The TotalAmount column is not a necessary column; it is a calculated value that can be derived from columns that already exist:

```
(((Quantity * Price) for each item ordered) +
ShippingCharges for entire order.)
```

By working toward a normalized database, you will reap several benefits. You will reduce the duplicated data, and in so doing, the storage requirements of your database. The level of data integrity will increase severalfold by normalization. The reduction in the duplicated data will help to ensure that mistakes are not made through simple data entry errors. Record processing time, when adding or searching through the database, will be greatly increased. In short, a normalized database can help you by:

- Faster sorting of information
- Faster index creation
- Use of a clustered index on more tables
- Indexes will be narrow, compact, and more useful
- There can be fewer indexes on each table, allowing faster INSERT, UPDATE, and DELETE statements
- Narrower tables will reduce the number of NULL values in columns and increase the consistency of the data

By creating many tables with a narrow focus on the data entered in them, you can place more rows of data on each storage page in SQL Server. This can help to speed queries and table scans, and consequently, improve the overall performance of your database. A simplified, normalized version of this database would look something like Figure 9-2.

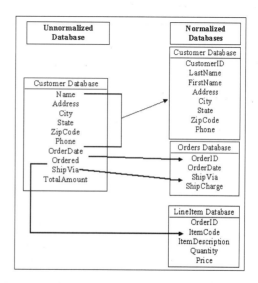

Figure 9–2 *The old, unnormalized database is now broken down into three normalized databases.*

There are some disadvantages to completely normalizing a database, and they primarily have to do with performance. In some cases, you may find that denormalizing some of its tables can substantially increase database performance. Denormalizing a database should be a planned step, and be done only for specific performance increases. Remember, denormalizing a database, and subsequently increasing redundancy in your information, may increase your database performance during queries that require many joins, but you may suffer decreased performance during updates. As already said, the creation of a database is always a series of compromises.

Tables, Columns, and Rows

At its simplest, a database is a simple collection of information. For a relational database, a table is used as a storage unit for data that is of a particular type: vendors, customers, inventory items, accounts payable, accounts receivable, and so on. You would not have a single table that included information about customers, accounts payable, and inventory items, all jumbled together. This would not only be an inefficient waste of computer resources, but would also be very confusing. It can easily be likened to a filing system where every scrap of paper is photocopied many times over so that at least one copy can be found in whatever folder you happen to pull out.

A table is divided into rows and columns, much like a spreadsheet or ledger. A row is often called a *record*, while columns are commonly called *fields*—more specifically, each intersection of a row and column is a single field. Each row contains all of the information—that fits within the table specifications—about a specific item, like a customer, a vendor, or a single inventory item. Each column contains a distinct part of a record, such as a customer's name or address, a product's name, cost, and quantity on hand. In most cases you will find that the database is easier to work with when the information contained in a record is broken down into the smallest logical parts; for example, first name, last name, street address, city, state, zip code. Dividing your data into the smallest entities to which they belong is the process of normalizing your database. This process will later help you when you create a query to find information contained in the table. For example, a customer name could be entered into one field, or two fields—first name and last name (ignoring middle names now). The table with only single field for a name will be very difficult to search for a customer by last name. This is not impossible, but it is much easier to simply place each into its own column.

As you build your database, you must decide how to break your information into logical groups—these groups will become your tables. As you further divide these groups into their component fields, ask yourself if this piece of information really should go with this group or does it really belong to another table. For example, information about orders does not belong in a customer table, while information about products does not belong in a vendor file.

What Is a Relational Database?

A relational database has already been described as a group of tables that are linked by relationships. A good relational database is a collection of data that is organized into tables. Each table uses a unique primary key column whose value points to one and only one row. The data contained in separate tables is related to each other through the use of the primary keys of one table being related to the foreign key column of another table. This system of relationships is used to give you easy access to the information that it contains.

Relationships are created between the fields in two or more tables that contain data common to both. Most relationships are created using special field constraints called *Primary* and *Foreign* key fields. By definition a primary key field is unique in a table and all of the data in the table can be automatically indexed, or sorted, by this field. You can't use a NULL value in a primary key field. A foreign key is a field whose values match those of the primary key in another table. A foreign key field can use a NULL value. By creating your database with tables that are linked together using the relationships created with primary and foreign key fields, you can easily divide information between tables in a logical manner.

By dividing your information into discrete tables, you will begin the creation process of a database that will be less prone to errors and duplication of information. A relational database can be a very efficient means of storing and retrieving data. Unlike a flat-file database, where you must search through the entire file for specific data, in a relational database you can use the SQL language to define what you are specifically looking for. SQL will then return a result set to you with only the data that meets the criteria you stated in the SQL query statement.

For example, Figure 9-3 is a list of the fields in three tables. Because each table has a field in common with one of the other tables, SQL can create a result set across multiple tables through these common fields.

The Customers table uses the CustID field as its primary key. All customer records are indexed on this field and no records can have a NULL value in this field. The Order table uses the CustID field as a foreign key so that the two tables can be linked together. The Inventory table uses the ItemID field as a primary key, and again, the Order table also uses this field as a foreign key so that it can be linked to the Inventory table.

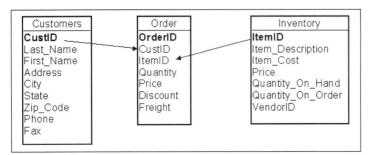

Figure 9–3 *Here you can see how three tables are related through the use of common fields.*

Device Independence

Microsoft SQL Server shields you from knowing how information is physically stored on a disk. SQL only requires that you know the name of the table(s) in which the information you are looking for is located in and the specific columns that should be searched. SQL then decides how and where to find the data, returning a results set to you. This makes using SQL to manage a database much easier than using a programming language, such as C and C++, which are third-generation languages, while SQL is a fourth-generation, or 4GL, language. As a 4GL language, SQL is a step further removed from the hardware of the system than earlier languages. A 4GL language such as SQL Server is device independent because it takes care of all the I/O and storage requirements for you.

Classic programming languages are procedural languages and require you to set out, step by step, exactly what information you are looking for:

- Where it will be physically found on a disk
- The file name where the data is located
- Where within the file the data is located
- Check in the specified field of each record for the specified value
- When found, display or print the selected records as a standard output

Conversely, with SQL you can issue a simple query statement using your front-end program, or through the Query Analyzer to display just the selected data, not necessarily the entire record.

Key Points

Several key points were illustrated in this chapter, including:

- The ideal database should be a normalized database; at the same time realize that this is an ideal and not always a make realistic application.
- Tables are the primary data storage entity within a database and each table is made up of rows and columns.
- A narrow, normalized table will help to ensure the consistency and accuracy of your data.
- Relationships between tables are created through primary and foreign key constraints.

▲ CHAPTER REVIEW QUESTIONS

▲ Multiple Choice:

1. *A normalized database is characterized by: (select all that apply)*
   A. Tables with primary key values that permit NULL values
   B. Primary key values are unique
   C. Each row can be identified as unique
   D. Each row can define multiple items

2. *Relationships are created between tables through joins between:*
   A. Relational fields
   B. Primary and secondary key columns
   C. Primary and foreign key columns
   D. Clustered indexes

▲ True or False:

1. *True or False? Diagramming the database is a waste of time.*

2. *True or False? A database containing few, wide tables is considered to be more efficient than one with many, narrow tables.*

3. *True or False? Completely normalizing a database will always result in performance increases.*

4. *True or False? Foreign key columns cannot contain NULL values.*

What Is Data Integrity?

You are now familiar with the structure of Microsoft SQL Server™. In this and the next several chapters you will learn how SQL Server works to help you do your tasks of being a system administrator.

What is data integrity? If you have been working-behind the scenes on databases you will be familiar with the term. The enforcement of the integrity of the data inserted into a database ensures the consistency and quality of the data. For example, enforcing data integrity may mean different things in different tables:

- If all of your customers are U.S. companies or individuals, you can enforce that a five- or nine-digit zip code is used.

- You can require that a city and state be entered before a new customer record will be inserted into the database.

- If a phone number is entered that it is ten digits in length.

- That duplicate employee IDs are not created.

279

- Allow only current products to be sold.
- A valid social security number is entered.

Each of these is an example of some form of integrity enforcement.

What Is Data Integrity?

Maintaining the integrity of the data contained within a database is one of the highest priorities of the database administrator. Data that has been corrupted or is simply inaccurate from poor data entry can cost a business thousands of dollars in lost time and revenue. Data integrity is important at all levels of database usage, from a small, single-user contact manager to a large, multiuser, multiserver, online transaction-processing database. This chapter covers how SQL Server can be used to ensure the accuracy and integrity of your data without depending on a client application to provide this integrity.

There are four basic types of integrity with which you must be concerned: entity, domain, referential, and user-defined. Each of these different types of integrity all work together to ensure that your data remains accurate and whole at all times.

MCSE 10.1   Entity Integrity

Entity integrity is primarily concerned with how Microsoft SQL Server defines each row in a specific table as a unique entity. This form of integrity is usually enforced through some combination of PRIMARY KEY constraints, UNIQUE constraints, and IDENTITY properties. Through the use of these constraints, SQL Server can help to ensure that each row of a table is indeed unique. With this form of integrity, you can be sure that you will not have a customer table full of duplicate customers, once for each time they may have placed an order. Without entity level integrity, you could easily have a table grow to many times the size that it should be and using valuable disk space.

Primary Key Constraint

The primary key constraint is commonly used to ensure entity level integrity. By definition, the primary key constraint is the column, or groups of columns, that are used in a table to uniquely identify a specific row. A primary key constraint can never be null, must always have a unique index, and can contain no more than one primary key constraint per table.

Generally, you will find that it is advantageous to have a primary key column(s) in every table. The only exceptions should be very small tables, twenty rows or less, that are used primarily as lookup tables for sets of values. For example, you may have a discount table with two columns, one containing a discount code and the other containing a discount percentage. A table like this would not necessarily need to have a primary key constraint, but easily could. Because another table references this table, you may find that you get better results if the discount code column was listed as the primary key column for the table.

Primary key constraints can be defined when you first create a table or can be added later using the ALTER TABLE command, or from within the SQL Enterprise Manager window. When a primary key constraint is defined, SQL Server automatically builds a unique index for the column values. If there is no other UNIQUE constraint defined as a CLUSTERED index, SQL Server will build the new primary key index as CLUSTERED, otherwise it will use the NONCLUSTERED index type.

Primary key constraints can be defined at either table level or at column level when you are creating a new table. If your primary key is composed of more than one column, a composite primary key, then the constraint must be defined at the table level. Otherwise, you can define the constraint at a column level. The primary key constraint is applied at the table level only when it is added to an existing table. Remember that the primary key must uniquely identify every row in a table. If you do not have a single column that can do this, then you must either add a new column that can be so used, or you must select several columns that, taken together, can uniquely identify a row.

As a general rule, when using multiple column primary key constraints, try to confine it to no more than three columns, with two being better. You will quickly find that you will lose much of the benefit you gain from a primary key constraint when you update information. SQL Server will have a great deal of information to update, sort, and index with multiple column indexes.

For example, a LAST_NAME column alone cannot be used as a primary key because too many people have the same last names. For a small table, you may be able to get away with using a combination primary key composed of both the LAST_NAME and FIRST_NAME columns. As your table grows, you will inevitably end up with two people with the same first and last names who are unique individuals. To SQL Server they will be the same person and you will not be able to add the second person to your table because they will violate the primary key constraint. Theoretically, you could use LAST_NAME, FIRST_NAME, and STREET_ADDRESS columns, but this will quickly become clumsy and unwieldy. I recommend using street over city or state because it is more likely that your database will have two or more John Smith's who live in Los Angeles, than two John Smith's both living at the same address. The best option is to include a column specifically dedicated as a primary key column (or other entity constraint) in every table where rows need to be uniquely defined.

A primary key constraint, like a unique constraint, is most easily added to a table during the creation process. Both can be added later, but this may involve a great deal of table manipulation before the process is completed. You can use either the SQL Server Enterprise Manager application or the CREATE or ALTER TABLE T-SQL statements. Creating a primary key constraint while building a new table within the Enterprise Manager is a matter of a few mouse clicks:

1. Open the Enterprise Manager application, and then expand the server and database folders in the Scope pane.

2. Right-click on the Tables folder and select New Table from the shortcut menu. Enter a name for the new table in the displayed dialog box and click the OK button.

3. Enter the necessary information for the table: column names, datatypes, and the like. It is not required that you create the primary key column first, but it is generally done. Be sure that you remove any checks in the Allow Nulls column.

4. When you have added the column(s) that will have the primary key constraint bound to it, right-click within the column definition and select Set Primary Key on the shortcut menu. Figure 10-1 shows the column Pri-maryKeyID is a primary key constraint because of the key symbol displayed on the row selector button.

Once you finish the table definition and save it, the primary key constraint will be part of the table definition. A primary key constraint does not have to be a specific datatype, though of course it cannot be a bit or image datatype. The tinyint datatype should not be used unless you are absolutely certain that the range of values for this datatype is adequate for the table's needs.

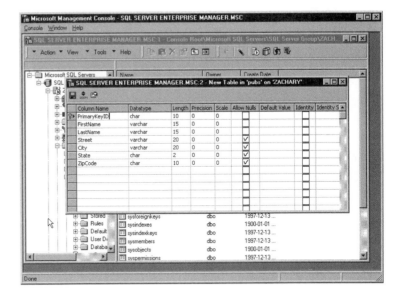

Figure 10–1 *Here you see a column has had a primary key constraint applied to it during the creation of a new table.*

You can alter an existing table's definition to include a primary key constraint, or alter an existing primary key in much the same way. For example:

1. Click on the Tables folder of the pubs database. Right-click on the table discounts and select Design Table from the shortcut menu, opening the table definition in the Design Table window.
2. Right-click on the first row with the column name "discounttype" and select Set Primary Key from the shortcut menu. You will see the primary key symbol placed on the row selector button.

A primary key will be defined for this table as soon as the Save button is clicked.

The primary key constraint can also be included in a table definition when you create a table using the T-SQL statement CREATE TABLE, or to an existing table having the constraint added or dropped by using the ALTER TABLE statement. The CREATE TABLE statement for the sample table created earlier would look like this:

```
CREATE TABLE sample_table
PrimaryKeyIDchar(10)
CONSTRAINT PK_PKID PRIMARY KEY CLUSTERED
FirstNamevarchar(15)NOT NULL
LastNamevarchar(15)NOT NULL
Streetvarchar(20)
Cityvarchar(20)
Statevarchar(2)
ZipCodechar(10)
```

This table will be created with a clustered, primary key constraint named PK_PKID. You can also drop a primary key constraint with an ALTER TABLE statement:

```
ALTER TABLE table_name
DROP CONSTRAINT constraint_name
```

The primary key constraint can also be removed by following steps 1–4 above. After you select the row on which the primary key has been placed, right-click and display the shortcut menu. You will see a checkmark beside Set Primary Key. Simply click on it to remove the constraint. Save the table definition again.

UNIQUE Constraint

The unique constraint is similar in many ways to the primary key constraint with the exception that it does allow null values in the column. The unique constraint can be defined on any column that is not the primary key column, and does not have any rows with duplicate values in the column. You can use a maximum of 249 unique constraints per table. Its primary use is to enforce row-level integrity on nonprimary key columns. If you anticipate having a table that could use that many unique constraints, it is highly recommended that you check to see if the table can be divided into several smaller tables. The use of the UNIQUE constraint ensures that duplicate values will not be entered into the column.

The unique constraint, like the primary key constraint, can be defined at either a table or column level. If the unique constraint is applied to a single column, then it is applied at the column level. Conversely, if the constraint is applied to several columns, as in a composite unique constraint, then it is applied at the table level.

This constraint can be added when you are defining a new table with the CREATE TABLE statement, or you can add or drop it later with the ALTER TABLE command. Like other constraints, you can create and alter them from within the Enterprise Manager application. When you open a table in Design mode, you can open the properties page and add or change constraints. When a constraint is added to an existing table, it is applied only at the table level.

Using the uniqueidentifier Data Type

The uniqueidentifier datatype is a new feature of SQL Server 7. When you use this datatype on a column, a unique 16-byte binary string is created for each row. This datatype is often used when you need to supply a column that will always be able to provide a globally unique identifier (GUID) for all records, often when a table is involved with replication.

The uniqueidentifier must be initialized with a value in one of two ways:

- Using the NEWID() function. This is the simplest method, and you can add this function when you create the column and table.

- Supplying a string constant in a 36 hexadecimal digit format, including the required hyphens (XXXXXXXX-XXXX-XXXX-XXXX-XXXXXXXXXXXX).

As you can see, using the NEWID() function may be in your best interests. The uniqueidentifier datatype can be used in operations of equality (=, <, >, <>) and IS NOT NULL and IS NULL. You are limited to using only these operators with the NEWID() function. You are limited in the constraints and properties of a uniqueidentifier column in that you cannot use the IDENTITY property.

MCSE 10.2 **Domain Integrity**

Domain integrity refers to column level integrity, meaning that the information entered into a column must come from the set of values that are possible for this particular column. With SQL Server 7, domain integrity revolves around DEFAULT, FOREIGN KEY, and CHECK constraints, and NOT NULL settings. In earlier versions you would be more concerned with rules, datatypes, and default values only. Very often, the foreign key constraint is part of the domain integrity, but this will be discussed in detail in the next section. Each column has a fundamental domain that represents the set of all possible valid values. Of course, the domain for some columns and datatypes may be very large indeed.

The DEFAULT constraint

The Default constraint is the preferred replacement for default objects. A default object must be bound to a column or data type before it has any effect on data, while the default constraint when created as part of the table definition is an integral part of the table. It also has the advantage that it is also dropped if and when the table is dropped. On the other hand, the default object is easily used on multiple columns and tables when required. If you are creating a complex default object expression, you may prefer to use the default object so that you only have to create it once. A default constraint cannot be created on a column that uses a timestamp data type, has an identity property, an existing default constraint, or a bound default.

Defaults can be created only on tables in the current database, nor can you combine a CREATE DEFAULT statement with other T-SQL statements in a single batch. A default can be any constant value, or an expression that will evaluate to a constant value. For example, the expression GETDATE() will enter the current date as a default value if no other date is entered into a column that uses this expression as either a default constraint or a bound default object.

Use the CREATE TABLE T-SQL statement when building a new table, or the ALTER TABLE statement when changing an existing table definition to add a default constraint. You have already seen how a table is created earlier in this book. Figure 10-2 displays the employee table in the pubs database where you can see that four default constraints have been used.

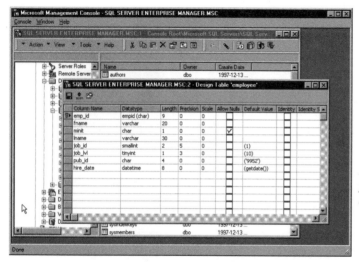

Figure 10–2 *Here you can see the employee table in the pubs database. Notice the four default constraints in the Default Value column.*

Here you see the CREATE TABLE statement that would build a table very much like the employee table in the pubs database. It contains several default constraint statements within it.

```
CREATE TABLE employee
emp_idvarchar(11)
CONSTRAINT PK_empid PRIMARY KEY NONCLUSTERED
fnamevarchar(20)NOT NULL
lnamevarchar(25)NOT NULL
job_idsmallintNOT NULL
DEFAULT 1
job_lvltinyint
DEFAULT 10
pub_idchar(4)NOT NULL
DEFAULT ('9952')
hire_date datetimeNOT NULL
DEFAULT (getdate())
```

The first two default statements simply use a numeric value in a numeric data type column. The third value is a character-based column, and so the default value is enclosed in single quote marks and parentheses. The final default is a function that will return the current date. Functions must also be enclosed within parentheses.

Using the CHECK Constraint

The CHECK constraint is one that is often used. It is an excellent method of ensuring that data entered into a column meets the necessary guidelines. You can set many CHECK constraints for a table. A CHECK constraint could be used for many of the checks that you may have used a rule for in the past, for example:

- To check that a valid social security number is entered.
- To ensure that a positive number is entered in the quantity column for an order.
- To require that a five-digit number is used for a zip code.
- To limit values entered into a column to a specified list.
- To allow only a certain minimum or maximum range of numbers to be entered

The CHECK constraint can be relatively simple, or can be a complex expression that requires the information being entered meet several conditions before being inserted. CHECK constraints are added to a column through the Table Properties dialog box, or by using the CHECK keyword when you create or alter a table.

When replicating a table that uses a **CHECK** constraint, you may need to disable the constraint during replication. If the **CHECK** constraint is specific to the source database, it may prevent new information from being entered into the replicated table at the destination database.

In Figure 10-3 you can see the Properties dialog box for the authors table in the pubs database. On the Table tab you can see the CHECK constraint that has been created on the au_id column. This constraint checks that the information entered into this column are only numbers and formatted as a standard U.S. Social Security Account Number. The constraint has been created so that it does not check any information that already existed in the table prior to its creation. The constraint has been enabled for INSERT and UPDATE queries, and is also enabled for replication.

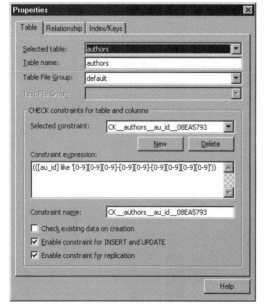

Figure 10–3 *In the authors Properties dialog box you see the CHECK constraint that has been set on the au_id column.*

The same constraint added to the table when it was first created using the CREATE TABLE statement would look like this:

```
CREATE TABLE authors
au_idvarchar(11)NOT NULL
CONSTRAINT UPKCL_auid PRIMARY KEY CLUSTERED
CONSTRAINT CK_authors_auid
CHECK (au_id LIKE
'[0-9][0-9][0-9]-[0-9][0-9]-[0-9][0-9][0-9][0-9]')
```

As you can see in the above example, there are two constraints being placed on the au_id column. The first is the Primary Key constraint, and the second is the CHECK constraint. If this constraint was not to be used during replication, you would include the NOT FOR REPLICATION statement.

Domain Rules

Domain rules refer to those rules specifically bound to a column. Rules are used to help restrict the format of a value entered into a column. For example, a rule can be constructed that restricts values to a specific range of numbers, or to a list of specified items, such as brown, red, green, or Chicago, New York, Portland. You can use only one rule per column.

Rules are often used as a *mask* for data entry of information. A mask requires that data entered into a column follows a specific format. Earlier in Chapter 3, you saw a rule for entering a U.S. social security number.

```
@ssan like '[0-9][0-9][0-9]-[0-9][0-9]-[0-9][0-9][0-9][0-9]'
```

Rules can be created by either using the Manager Rules dialog box from the SQL Enterprise Manager window or by using the CREATE RULE statement. In either case, a rule must be bound to a specific column. The rule can be bound with the sp_bindrule stored procedure, or from the Rule Properties dialog box in the Enterprise Manager. Both methods properly bind the rule to the specified column.

Rules can be dropped using the DROP RULE statement if they are not bound to a column. If you have already bound the rule to a column, you must first unbind the rule with the sp_unbindrule stored procedure.

Datatypes

Datatypes are used within the domain integrity structure as a method of ensuring that data entered in a column is of a specific type. SQL Server has several predefined datatypes you can use when you define a column, and allowances are made for you to create your own specific datatypes.

The selection of the column datatype is extremely important. This will determine the type of data that can be placed in a column, and how long that data can be. Your selections will determine the space utilization of your columns, and will affect the performance, reliability, and manageability of your entire database. Once you choose a datatype for a column, you cannot change it again without first dropping the table and then rebuilding it and reloading the data. Doing this also runs the risk of losing some data if it is not compatible with the new datatype.

Datatypes must be applied to a column when the column is created. If you add a column to an existing table with the ALTER TABLE statement, you can use any datatype except for the **bit** datatype. The reason for this is that a column added to an existing table must be able to support a NULL value, since the rows already in the table will of course have NULL values for the new column. The bit datatype does not allow a default NULL value. Tables 10-1 through 10-5 list the various default system datatypes included with SQL Server.

Table 10.1 *Numeric datatypes*

Datatype/ General Type	Description	Example of Uses
Decimal [(p[,s])],or Numeric [(p[,s])]/ Numeric	These two datatypes are interchangeable, except that only the numeric datatype can be used with an identity column. This datatype stores an exact numeric value between 10^{38}-1 through -10^{38}-1, and will require between 2 and 17 bytes of storage space. The precision p is for the maximum number of digits, both to the left and right of the decimal place that can be stored. The scale s represents the maximum number of digits to the right of the decimal point, and must be equal or less than the value of p.	Use the decimal or numeric datatypes for any column which will be used strictly for number values. Common uses are for quantities, miles traveled, etc.
float[(n)]/ Approximate Numeric	The float datatype is an approximate numeric value. This datatype has a precision of 15 digits, or as specified by n, and is stored in eight bytes. This datatype can include an exponent, and is entered as a negative or positive number X, followed by e or E, followed by another negative or positive integer Y. The number represented is the product of X and 10 raised to the power of the exponent Y.	The float datatype is most often used for those numbers that may have very large ranges but require the same precision, no matter if the number is large or small. Most commonly used for numbers expressed in scientific notation.

Table 10.1 *Numeric datatypes (Continued)*

Datatype/ General Type	Description	Example of Uses
Real/ Approximate Numeric	The real datatype is similar to float. It has a precision of 7 digits, and a storage size of four bytes.	The real datatype is similar to the float datatype except that it has a smaller range and is stored in less space.
Int/ Integer numeric	This datatype stores only whole numbers with a range of -2^{31} through 2^{31}-1 $(-2,147,483,648 - 2,147,483,647)$. It is stored in four bytes.	The int datatype is used when only whole numbers need to be stored. A fractional part of a number cannot be stored.
Smallint/ Integer numeric	This datatype also stores only whole numbers, within the range of -2^{15} to 2^{15}-1 $(-32,768 - 32,767)$. It is stored in two bytes.	The smallint datatype is also used for any whole number within its range. Before using this datatype, be sure that its range will indeed fit all of the anticipated values.
Tinyint/ Integer numeric	This datatype stores whole numbers between 0 and 255, and is stored in one byte.	The tinyint datatype also stores whole number values. Again, be sure that this range will fit the data that will be stored.
Money/ Monetary	This datatype is used to store monetary values. When entering these values, type a dollar ($) sign preceding the value, otherwise SQL Server will assume this is a numeric value with four decimal places. Do not enter commas between numbers in a monetary datatype column. The range of values is from <$922,337,203,685,477.5808> through $922,337,203,685,477.5807. Precision is 0.0001 and is stored in eight bytes. Monetary values are rounded up to the nearest cent when displayed.	The money datatype can be used for most monetary values. Again, be sure that the 4 decimal place precision is adequate. If you are working with stocks and bonds pricing where values are expressed in 1/32s of a dollar ($0.03125), then 4 decimal places is not adequate.
Smallmoney/ Monetary	The smallmoney datatype is similar in all aspects to money, except that it has a range from <$214,748.3648> to $214,748.3647, and is stored in four bytes.	The smallmoney datatype is used where a small range of monetary values are to be stored.

Table 10.2 *Logical datatypes*

Datatype/ General Type	Description	Example of Uses
Bit/ Special	This datatype holds only the integers 1 or 0. Other values can be accepted into the column, but SQL Server will interpret them as 1. A bit datatype is most often used for Yes/No or True/False types of data. This datatype is stored in one byte.	The bit datatype is most often used to store yes/no, true/false types of data.

Table 10.3 *Date datatypes*

Datatype/ General Type	Description	Example of Uses
Datetime/ Date and time	The datetime datatype is stored as two 4-byte integers. The first is the number of days before or after the base date of 1/1/1900, and the second 4-bytes is the number of milliseconds after midnight. Date values must be within the range of 1/1/1753 to 12/31/9999. Time values are accurate to within 3.33 milliseconds. You can enter either or both a date and a time value into a column with this datatype. Date values must be enclosed within single quote marks.	The datetime datatype is used for any column that is used for dates and/or time data. The most common usage is for date values. Use the datetime datatype to capture date information for order dates, ship dates, etc. You can use the value contained in a datetime column in a calculation, such as: add X number of days to the value in the ship date column to get an estimated arrival date.
Small- datetime/ Date and time	This datatype is less explicit than is the datetime datatype. The range of values for this datatype is between 1/1/1900 and 6/6/2079. Time accuracy is to the nearest minute. Date values must be enclosed within single quote marks.	The smalldatetime datatype is used in place of the datetime datatype when precision is not so necessary, or when the more restricted date range is adequate.

Table 10.4 *Character or text datatypes*

Datatype/ General Type	Description	Example of Uses
Char[(n)]/ Character	The char datatype can store a maximum of 255 characters. SQL Server stores the value entered as length n regardless of the actual number of characters entered. A char datatype can be NULL. Use this datatype when the data will be uniformly near the same length. If data entered into a char column is shorter than n, SQL Server will add trailing blanks to the data.	Use the char datatype to store any type of alphanumeric information of a fixed length. Common uses may include customer IDs, product IDs, state abbreviations, and zip/postal codes.
Varchar[(n)]/ Character	This datatype can hold n to 255 characters, and is stored as the actual length of the data entered. Varchar can be NULL, but n must be a number between 1–255.	The varchar datatype is also used to store alphanumeric data. Use this datatype for variable length data such as names, streets, city, and descriptions.
Text/ Text, large	This datatype allows large amounts of text to be added, to approximately 2GB of data. This data is written to a special group of data pages and does not come under SQL Server's normal column limit of 255 characters. This column cannot be used for variables or parameters in a stored procedure, nor can you use this column with an ORDER BY clause.	The text datatype is used for any long text entries. Most often used for long descriptions, telephone notes, or product summaries.

Table 10.5 *Binary datatypes*

Datatype/ General Type	Description	Example of Uses
binary[(n)]/ Binary	The binary datatype can store a maximum of 255 bytes of fixed-length binary data. Regardless of the length of the data you enter into this column, it will be stored as size *n*. You must specify a number from 1–255 bytes as the value for *n*, but you can store 0 (zero) bytes in this column. Use this datatype when you expect that most values will be close to *n* in length.	The binary datatype is used to store binary information in bit patterns, not in hexadecimal format. Characters 0-9, A-F, and a-f can be used. Each binary string group must be preceded by 0x, like 0xAA. A length of 20 indicates that 20 two-character groups can be inputted into this column.
Varbinary [(n)]/ Binary	The varbinary datatype can also be a maximum of 255 bytes, but can be variable in length. Specify *n* between 1–255, as the maximum number of bytes that can be stored in this column. The actual storage space will be the number of bytes entered into the column. Use this datatype when you expect NULL or highly variable length values to be entered.	The varbinary datatype works like the binary datatype, except that you can specify a variable data length for the column.
Timestamp/ Special	This datatype is used by SQL Server and has nothing to do with the system clock. It is used to provide a unique version number for each row. When a row is inserted into a table, the timestamp is entered. Each time the row is updated, the timestamp is also updated by SQL Server.	The timestamp is a special datatype used most often to serialize row updates, enabling you to ensure that your users do not inadvertently update a row after another user has updated it.
Image/ Image	This datatype also allows large graphical files, up to 2GB in size. These files are also stored on a separate group of data pages.	The image datatype is a special datatype that allows you to store images, often used for graphical representations of items, and digitized pictures.

When using the any datatype, if your data exceeds *n* in length, SQL Server will truncate the data without warning. Be certain that your data does not exceed this length, or that the data that is truncated is not crucial to the database, or use a variable length datatype.

When using the datetime datatype, SQL Server allows you to enter a time without a date value. For example, entering a time of 6 A.M. will cause SQL Server to save this value as Jan 1, 1900 6:00:00:000AM. Entering a date/time value in this manner results in a value that will probably be meaningless to most queries. It is unlikely that most people will remember to search for a time value in the year 1900. It is highly recommended that you enter the current date along with a time value. Alternatively, you can create your application so that it will automatically add the current date and include the variable of the time the user enters.

Once a column has been created with a datatype and the table is populated with data, you cannot change the datatype without first dropping the entire table and recreating it. You would then reload all of the data back into the table from the most current backup. With careful consideration of the change in datatype, you may not lose any data.

MCSE 10.3 Referential Integrity

Referential integrity is a key function of a RDMS. By using SQL Server to perform as many of the referential integrity functions as possible, you reduce the possibility of errors in your database being introduced through a poorly written client application. SQL Server can be used to assign primary and foreign key relationships between tables and enforce these relationships before allowing a row to be inserted or updated into a table.

What is Referential Integrity?

Referential integrity is the property whereby all values entered into a foreign key column of one table have a corresponding value located in the primary key column of another table to which they are related. The table that contains the primary key is often called the parent table, while the table with the foreign key is called a child table. A value cannot be entered or changed in the foreign key column of the child table without a corresponding value existing in the parent table's primary key column, but a foreign key can contain a NULL value. For example, titles are related to their authors through the titleauthor table. The relationship is shown in Figure 10-4:

In the authors table the column au_id is the primary key (PK) column, while the titleauthor table uses a composite primary key (CPK) composed of both the au_id and title_id columns, and the titles table uses the title_id col-

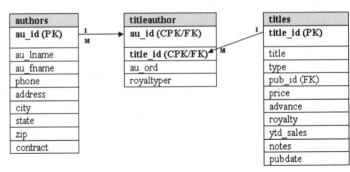

Figure 10-4 *The relationships of primary and foreign key columns are shown between the authors, titleauthor, and the titles tables.*

umn as its primary key. The titleauthor table also contains two foreign key (FK) columns. The au_id column is a foreign key and related to the primary key au_id in the authors table, while the title_id column is a foreign key to the primary key title_id in the titles table. The primary key to foreign key creates the parent/child relations between tables. In the example shown in Figure 10-4, the authors table is a parent table, as is the titles table. The title-author table is a child table to both of the other two. Both the authors and titles table contain a primary key column, which is referenced as a foreign key column in the child table titleauthor. There are three basic relationships that can be defined through the primary/foreign key relations.

• One-to-One	This is a direct relationship between one primary key value ofthe parent table and no more than one related value in the foreign key column of the child table. This relationship is not common in relational databases. An example of this relationship could be found between an employee and her department manager.
• One-to-Many	This relationship is the most commonly found, and exists when, for any single value in the primary key of the parent table, there can be one or more values found in the foreign key of the child table. An example of this relation-SHIP can be found between the publishers table as the parent and the titles table as the child. For every one publisher, they may have many titles that they publish.
• Many-to-Many	This relationship is shown when, for any one row in the parent table, there can be one or more corresponding rows in the child table, and for any row in the child table there can be one or more corresponding rows in the parent table. *This relationship should be avoided because it can yield unpredictable results when querying the two tables.*

You may ask why a direct relationship between authors and titles is not created? The reason for this is that this relationship could easily be a many-to-many relationship. For every author there can be many titles, and for each title there can be many authors. This relationship should be avoided whenever possible because it violates the primary key constraint in the titles table.

For example, the author Jack Smith has written three books: "How to fix a dishwasher," "How to fix a garbage disposal," and "How to fix a washing machine." His wife, Jane Smith, is co-author of the book, "How to fix a washing machine." Without the intervening bridge table, titleauthor, you would have two tables that would look like those in Figure 10-5:

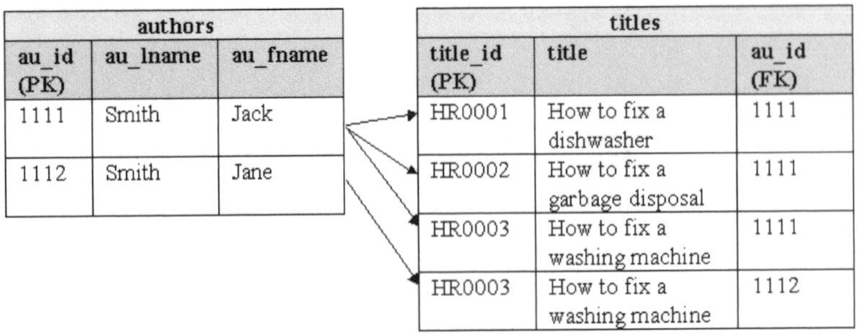

authors		
au_id (PK)	au_lname	au_fname
1111	Smith	Jack
1112	Smith	Jane

titles		
title_id (PK)	title	au_id (FK)
HR0001	How to fix a dishwasher	1111
HR0002	How to fix a garbage disposal	1111
HR0003	How to fix a washing machine	1111
HR0003	How to fix a washing machine	1112

Figure 10–5 *This relationship requires two rows in the titles table for the book, "How to fix a washing machine."*

The many-to-many relationship requires extra rows in one or both tables. As you can see in Figure 10-5, an extra row has been inserted into the table for the book, "How to fix a washing machine." This is an attempt to take into account that there are two authors, and as such violates the primary key constraint by having two rows with the same primary key value. This duplicate entry of information is avoided when the bridge table titleauthor is used. The titleauthor table breaks the many-to-many relationship into two one-to-many relationships. The one-to-many relationship is much easier to use when constructing a query to retrieve selected rows from two or more tables, and does not violate the primary key constraint.

DEFINING PRIMARY/FOREIGN KEYS

Primary and foreign keys are defined for each table when you create the table with the CREATE TABLE statement, or are added with the ALTER TABLE statement. There is one caveat to creating primary and foreign key constraints: you must create the primary key constraint before you can create the foreign key constraint. Understanding this can help to shorten a potentially long frustration cycle. They can also be added to a table from within the SQL Enterprise Manager window. The T-SQL statements for a primary key would look like this:

```
ALTER TABLE authors
au_id varchar(11)
ADD CONSTRAINT au_pk_auid PRIMARY KEY
```

You have the option to make this primary key constraint be a clustered or nonclustered constraint by placing the keyword CLUSTERED or NON-CLUSTERED after the keyword PRIMARY KEY.

The procedure for placing a foreign key constraint is very similar. The T-SQL statements would look like this:

```
ALTER TABLE titleauthor
au_id varchar(11)
ADD CONSTRAINT ta_fk_auid FOREIGN KEY
REFERENCES author(au_id)
```

Again, you add the constraint, name it, and tell SQL Server what kind of constraint you are creating. In the case of the foreign key, you must also tell SQL Server what table and column(s) are being referenced as the primary key.

ENFORCING REFERENTIAL INTEGRITY

By creating a network of primary/foreign key columns, you create a system to enforce the referential integrity of your database. There are two final pieces that will help you to ensure that referential integrity is enforced. They are called:

- *Cascading Delete*: This term refers to the deleting of all records that depend upon a value contained in another table. For example, in an order-entry system if a customer is deleted, then all of their outstanding orders should also be deleted. Otherwise, you may end up trying to ship or post an order as a receivable for a nonexistent customer. The records in the orders table are dependent upon the presence of a corresponding customer.
- *Cascading Update*: This term refers to the ability of the database to automatically change the dependent rows to reflect a change in the parent table. For example, if a customer moves, you may need to change their customer ID. At the same time, you would also want to update all of the customer's outstanding orders, their account in the accounts receivable, and other similar tables with the new customer ID code.

Much of the work done to enforce this form of referential integrity has been confined to triggers in earlier versions of SQL Server. When an action that requires a cascading delete or update occurs, then the trigger would update or delete the referenced records. Beginning with SQL Server 6.5, declarative referential integrity (DRI) can be used in the forms that have been discussed in this chapter. Information about each table is maintained in the system tables: *sysconstraints* and *sysreferences*. SQL Server now uses these tables to maintain the information necessary to enforce DRI for you. As you create PRIMARY, FOREIGN KEY, CHECK, UNIQUE, IDENTITY, and DEFAULT constraints, SQL Server is recording this information in one of these system tables and then using the data to ensure that information recorded in one table meets the requirements of the constraints placed on a column.

If you want to use a trigger to perform cascade updates and deletes, you will need to disable any foreign key constraints for that table.

User-defined Integrity

All forms of integrity checking support the application of a user-defined business rule. User-defined integrity is always based on one of SQL Server's forms of integrity checking, and then enhanced further to support some specific need. You have already learned how to use and create both procedures and triggers. These are often used to enhance the integrity protection available to a database, but much of their abilities have been taken over by DRI.

One of the most commonly used forms of user-defined integrity is the creation of user-defined datatypes. While SQL Server comes with a number of datatypes, there may be business requirements for a datatype with a more precise definition. The user-defined datatype is not really a new datatype, it is only a new way to describe an existing datatype. You can use the stored procedure's `sp_addtype` to create a new datatype definition, and `sp_droptype` to delete a user-defined datatype. You cannot drop a datatype that is currently bound to a column without first dropping the table, then dropping the datatype.

The simplest method to add a new datatype is from within the SQL Enterprise Manager window. Follow these steps to add an additional datatype:

1. Open the SQL Enterprise Manager application and expand the pubs database. Right-click on the User Defined Datatypes icon and select New User Defined Datatype from the shortcut menu. Several user-defined datatypes that are part of the pubs database are already shown. Once you build your own database this dialog box will be empty until you add your first datatype.

2. Enter the following information into the indicated columns, being sure to press the Tab key to move from column to column. Do not use the Enter key. Figure 10-6 shows the User-Defined Datatype Properties dialog box.

   • Type ssan in the Name column for the new datatype.

- In the Datatype column click the list box button and select varchar from the list. This option cannot be changed later.
- Type 11 in the Length column as the maximum number of characters allowed for this datatype. This option cannot be changed without dropping and recreating.
- The Allow Nulls column allows you to choose whether NULL values are allowed for this datatype—it is selected by either clicking it or pressing the Spacebar; a checkmark will be displayed in the column. This option cannot be changed later. Leave it blank for this datatype.
- Select a rule to be applied with this user-defined datatype from the drop-down list box in the Rule column. A rule must already exist to apply it to your new datatype. This option can be added at a later time.
- Select a default definition for this datatype in the Default column if applicable. The default must be created and named before you can select it for use with a user-defined datatype. The default is selected from the list box. This option can be added at a later time.

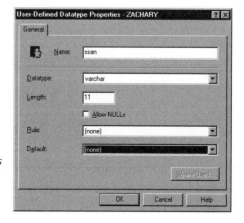

Figure 10–6 *The User-Defined Datatype Properties dialog box makes creating a new datatype a matter of filling in just a few pieces of information.*

3. When you have completed the new datatype, there are two options for you to complete and save it:

- OK. This option saves the new datatype and closes the dialog box.
- Apply Now. This button saves the new datatype and leaves the dialog box open so that you can create another datatype.

4. Click the OK button.

The Where Used button enables you to see where a user-defined datatype has already been used. Both the table and the column will be listed in another dialog box. Figure 10-7 shows the Where Used dialog box for the tid datatype.

Figure 10–7   *Here you see the list of tables and columns where the tid datatype has been used.*

If you decide later to drop a user-defined datatype, simply select it from the list of datatypes in the Results pane of the main window. Select the datatype to be dropped and press the Delete key. The Drop Objects dialog box will be displayed showing you what other objects will be dropped when you delete the selected datatype. By clicking the Show Dependencies button you can see what objects are dependent on this datatype. You can choose to drop all of the objects now, or cancel the deletion. You cannot drop a datatype object that has other objects that are dependent on its existence.

User-defined datatypes can be very useful in helping to enforce the integrity of a database that has many complex business rules. This is the function of each of the various parts of integrity enforcement.

Key Points

In this chapter, you have learned how to ensure entity integrity, domain integrity, and enforce referential integrity. Specifically, you have learned to:

- Use the UNIQUE constraint to enforce integrity on columns that are not primary keys.
- Create and enforce primary key constraints on one or more columns.
- Use domain rules and datatypes to ensure the domains integrity.
- Check or not check new data copied into a table against a CHECK constraint.
- Use referential integrity to help ensure data consistency.

- Create relationships between tables using primary keys and foreign keys in tables.
- Create special user-defined rules, procedures, and triggers to help enforce the integrity of the data in your database.

▲ CHAPTER REVIEW QUESTIONS

▲ Multiple Choice:

1. *What is not an example of data integrity? (select all that apply)*

   A. If all of your customers are U.S. companies or individuals, you can enforce that a five- or nine-digit zip code is used.

   B. If a phone number is entered that it is ten digits in length.

   C. That a customer has given his or her own credit card for a phone order.

   D. Allows only current products to be sold.

2. *A CHECK constraint is often used to: (select all that apply)*

   A. Places a checkmark in a box

   B. Ensures that a valid nine-digit Social Security Number is entered.

   C. Limits values to a selected list.

   D. Ensures that a quantity is entered in a column.

3. *Entity integrity can be enforced through the use of: (select all that apply)*

   A. PRIMARY key constraints

   B. FOREIGN key constraints

   C. UNIQUE constraints

   D. IDENTIFICATION properties

4. *A UNIQUE constraint that is applied to a single column is defined:*

   A. As a single column constraint

   B. At the table level

   C. At the column level

   D. At the constraint level

5. *If you add a new column to an existing table, you must either: (select all that apply)*

    A. Allow NULL values

    B. Not allow NULL values

    C. Use the DEFAULT constraint on the column

    D. Designate the column as NEW

6. *Which datatype cannot be used when adding a column to an existing table? (select all that apply)*

    A. NULL text

    B. Float numeric

    C. Bit

    D. Text Large

7. *Referential integrity is enforced through the: (select all that apply)*

    A. REFERENTIAL INTEGRITY constraint

    B. PRIMARY and FOREIGN key constraints

    C. PRIMARY key and REFERENTIAL INTEGRITY constraint

    D. FOREIGN key constraint and CLUSTERED indexes

▲ True or False

1. *True or False? Entity integrity is used to ensure that a table or other object exists within a database.*

2. *True or False? CHECK constraints are used to verify information before it is entered into a table.*

3. *True or False? The uniqueidentifier datatype can be used in the equality operation IS NULL.*

4. *True or False? If you create a PRIMARY key when you initially define a table, you can allow NULL values, but not if you add the constraint later.*

Data Consistency and Concurrency

In this chapter, you begin to look at the more real-world application of SQL Server™—the multiple-user database. So far, you have really only looked at SQL Server from the point of view of the system administrator. Now, you will look at how SQL Server behaves when more than one user is accessing a database concurrently, all trying to use the same tables, rows, and columns.

The potential problems inherent in a multiple-user scenario are immediately clear. For example, imagine several rental car agencies throughout a city with a big convention just hitting town. There are only a limited number of cars available, and you can see how easy it would be for two agents to try to rent a car to two different people at the same time. You may have one agent at the airport location where the car is physically located, and another agent at the main office taking the toll-free calls. Both can see the same "inventory" in the database. Using SQL Server, how can you ensure that the two agents do not accidentally both book the same car?

Throughout this chapter you will learn how SQL Server can be used to resolve this problem of keeping your data consistent with multiple concurrent users; the complex topic of data consistency will also be covered. How do you resolve the problem of allowing some users to read a database while others are writing to it? The goal of using SQL Server is to allow the maximum number of simultaneous users (concurrency), while maintaining the correctness of your data (consistency).

MCSE 11.1   Statements and Transactions

As you learned earlier in this book, a *statement* is a single T-SQL command, ranging from a simple UPDATE, INSERT, or SELECT statement to very complex statements involving many individual commands and modifying clauses such as WHERE and ORDER BY.

The next step in using T-SQL statements is turning these statements into *transactions*. Transactions consist of one or more T-SQL statements that are sent to the SQL Server by a client application. How much time a transaction takes is dependent on several items, including:

- Whether SQL Server is using the default autocommit, or requires an explicit COMMIT TRANsaction statement. Remember, while SQL Server does write uncommitted transactions to the log and data files, these transactions can and will be rolled back if they are not accompanied by the specific T-SQL statement COMMIT TRAN, in the event of a server failure.
- The actual processing time required by the server's CPU.
- If there are any transactions blocking the transaction and preventing it from being committed.

SQL Server recognizes three forms of transaction modes or settings. The decision on the mode to be used will depend on many factors, and may change with the type of transaction being processed. The types of transaction modes used are:

- Autocommit transactions
- Explicit transactions
- Implicit transactions

New to SQL Server 7 is the default autocommit setting. Autocommit enables SQL Server to commit each transaction if it is completed successfully. A transaction is only rolled back if it generates an error.

Previously, a transaction required a BEGIN TRANsaction statement to explicitly start a transaction, and then a COMMIT TRANsaction to explicitly end the transaction. SQL Server will run in the autocommit mode until a BEGIN TRAN statement is received. This forces the server to shift to an explicit mode. Once the transaction has been committed with a COMMIT TRAN statement, SQL Server will revert to autocommit mode.

The third transaction mode is the implicit transaction mode. Implicit mode must be specifically set for a connection, and then remains in effect until it is returned to the default setting of OFF. When the implicit transaction mode has been set, a new transaction is automatically started when any of the below listed statements is executed:

ALTER TABLE	CREATE	DELETE	DROP
FETCH	GRANT	INSERT	OPEN
REVOKE	SELECT	UPDATE	TRUNCATE TABLE

Once a transaction has begun, it will continue to run until a COMMIT or ROLLBACK statement is issued; only then can a new transaction begin. The next new transaction will start once the next statement from the above list is executed. SQL Server will continue operating in this mode until implicit transaction is turned off. Implicit transaction mode is turned on or off when the following statement is executed:

SET IMPLICIT_TRANSACTIONS [ON/OFF]

Statements sent by separate users to the server do not have to be received at the exact same moment to be considered concurrent. Even when they overlap, there is always the potential for one statement to interfere with the other. In a multiple-user system, you can easily have two people reading the same row, both with the full intention of adding or changing the information contained in that row. As you will come to understand, this is a very important concept. Concurrency can create many potential problems if you are not prepared to resolve them before they begin. Windows NT™, being a multithreaded operating system, automatically serializes each statement as it is received. The serialization of transactions is discussed later in this chapter.

MCSE 11.2   Using Locks for Consistency

SQL Server uses locks in order to ensure data consistency by restricting access, and allows for the maximum concurrency for users by placing the least restrictive lock possible. A lock can come in several forms: exclusive, shared, intent, and update. These locks are over tables, pages, extents, and rows. You will usually find that read transactions acquire shared locks, while write transactions must acquire an exclusive lock. Intent locks can be granted to read transactions when it is the user's intent to update the row. This ensures that another user will not be granted an exclusive lock on the data that the first user intends to update. Additional levels of share and intent locks will be discussed further.

Lock information is maintained in each database in the syslockinfo system table. This table tracks all of the information about what locks have been granted to what resources.

Understanding a Lock

Concurrency issues are solved through the use of locks. SQL Server can hold several different locks, ensuring that the greatest number of users can access the various database tables and rows while providing a level of assurance that data read by one user, with the intent of updating the information, cannot be changed by another user. Once an exclusive lock has been granted to a user, SQL Server holds the lock until a COMMIT TRAN or a ROLLBACK TRAN statement is reached. If a deadlock is detected, one of the deadlocked transactions will have to be terminated with the KILL statement.

SQL Server uses locks to prevent the problems inherent in the example of the car rental agency discussed at the beginning of this chapter. How does SQL Server prevent the rental of a car by two different agents? When the first agent, Casey, queries the database for available cars, she finds a suitable blue mid-size vehicle for her customer. While Casey's query is browsing the database, SQL Server holds an update lock. This lock will allow other users to read the page, but not acquire either an exclusive or another update lock on the page. A second later, Eric queries the database for another customer, and is granted a shared lock on the database. Eric's query also finds that the same blue mid-size car is available. As Eric talks to his customer, Casey finishes her rental agreement and commits a rental transaction. SQL Server grants Casey an exclusive lock and updates the database table by tagging the vehicle as rented and no longer available. If Eric attempts to commit a second rental of this car, it will fail because the selected vehicle has now been tagged as rented. Eric will have to find another car for his customer.

When building an application, you must be careful about allowing a user to create a single transaction statement that updates many rows in many tables. Long running transactions such as this can effectively lock all other users from working in the database until the transaction has completed its actions. By ensuring that transactions are broken into smaller steps, you can help to eliminate this problem.

SQL Server can dynamically adjust the number of locks available, but you can change the total amount of memory resources SQL Server can use. Each lock consumes 96 bytes of system memory that has been allocated to SQL Server. When SQL Server is dynamically adjusting locks, it will normally allocate two percent of allocated memory to the initial pool of locks. As this pool is used, and the locks have not been released, additional memory is allocated to the lock pool. SQL Server will not allocate more than 40 percent of the available memory to lock allocation. If you change the dynamic setting using the lock option with sp_configure, you can allocate a maximum of 50 percent of available memory to the lock pool. Under most circumstances, SQL Server will perform best when dynamic lock allocation is being used.

SHARED LOCKS

In general, SQL Server places a *shared lock* on any operation that does not change or update information, this being the least restrictive lock. Under most circumstances, a shared lock is held only on the page that is currently being read, such as when using a SELECT statement. Once the page has been read, the lock is released. SQL Server can hold many concurrent, shared locks on the same table or same page.

When you use a SELECT statement to view information in a table, you can customize the locking options that SQL Server will place on your query. When you specify the locking option using one of the clauses listed in Table 11-1, it will override any session-level options placed using the SET statement.

Table 11.1 *SELECT statement locking options*

Option clause	Description and effect
HOLDLOCK	Use this clause to hold the shared lock until the transaction has completed. The lock does not automatically release once the page or other object is no longer needed.
NOLOCK	Allows no other shared locks and does not permit exclusive locks. When this clause is used, it is possible to read uncommitted transactions, a set of dirty pages, or information that has been rolled back in the middle of the current read.
PAGLOCK	Requires the use of shared page locks even if SQL Server would have normally escalated a lock to a shared table lock.
READPAST	Allows your query to skip rows that have been locked by another user. This can speed the return of your result set by the query not waiting for a lock to be released. This applies only to transactions using the READ COMMITTED isolation level and only applies to row level locks.

Table 11.1 *SELECT statement locking options (Continued)*

Option clause	Description and effect
ROWLOCK	Requires the use of row level locks instead of another level.
TABLOCK	Uses a shared lock on a table. With this option other users can read the table but are not allowed to gain an exclusive lock to update the table information. This lock is held until the command is complete. This can be combined with the HOLDLOCK clause, in which case the TABLOCK will remain in effect until the entire transaction has been completed.
TABLOCKX	Places an exclusive lock on the entire table. Other users are prevented from reading or updating information in the table. The lock is held until the completion of the transaction.
UPDLOCK	This option gives you an update lock instead of a shared lock. Other users can continue to read information from the table, but they cannot upgrade their locks to an exclusive lock to change information. This guarantees that the data you just read has not been changed when you are ready to update it. This lock remains in effect until command or transaction has been completed.

While a shared lock is held on a page, other more restrictive locks are excluded from being formed. Once one user has a shared lock on a page, another user cannot be granted any form of an exclusive lock—which means that they cannot write to or change the data on that page until the shared lock has been released. A shared lock can be escalated to an update lock, whereby a transaction updates a row. Once the transaction has been completed with a COMMIT TRAN statement, the next user who was trying to acquire an exclusive or update lock will be granted his or her lock.

UPDATE LOCKS

SQL Server uses an *update lock* when the user's intent is to modify the data contained on the page. An update lock is compatible with a shared lock. If an UPDATE transaction plans to make modifications to the data on a page that already is held by a shared lock, the transaction will be granted an update lock. Once all the shared locks have been relinquished, the update lock is promoted to an exclusive lock. Update locks are acquired during the initial read operation, and are held on a page level. Like the SELECT statement, the UPDATE statement can specify some locking options. The descriptions of each of these are listed in Table 11-1. You can use these locking clauses with an UPDATE statement: PAGLOCK, ROWLOCK, TABLOCK, and TABLOCKX.

No other shared locks will be granted while an update lock is held. Update locks are used to prevent one of the common forms of deadlock, which will be discussed later in this chapter. SQL Server services all locks on a first-come first-served basis.

The update lock allows maximum concurrency to your users on the page or table while ensuring a user that no one can change the data they are reading until they have completed their transaction. While the update lock is compatible with shared locks, only one update lock can be held on any one page at a time.

EXCLUSIVE LOCKS

The *exclusive lock* is the most restrictive of all the lock types SQL Server holds. No other user can place any type of lock on a table or page when an exclusive lock has been placed on it. Exclusive locks are used for all transactions that write data to a page; for example, UPDATE, INSERT, and DELETE transactions. Exclusive locks are held for the duration of the transaction and are automatically released once the transaction is completed.

SQL Server cannot grant an exclusive lock until all shared locks have been released. Remember that this is the purpose of the update lock.

INTENT LOCKS

An *intent lock* is placed on a table and tells SQL Server that the transaction intends to place shared or exclusive locks on table resources further down the tree. The use of intent locks can substantially increase the performance of your database. When another transaction wants to acquire an exclusive lock on a table, it simply has to check for table-level intent locks instead of requiring SQL Server to scan the entire table for any shared locks on a row and preventing an exclusive lock. If an intent lock has been granted, then there are transactions with additional locks further down in the table, and as such an exclusive lock cannot yet be granted. The transaction may then try to gain an update shared lock on the table, enabling it to become the next exclusive lock and preventing other shared locks from being placed on the table.

An intent lock can be further categorized as: an intent to share, an intent to gain exclusive, or a share with intent for exclusive.

KEY-RANGE LOCKS

The *key-range lock* is a special lock that is maintained only on the index pages. It is used to help prevent the insertion of phantom records that may occur during the period of time when a transaction reads a set of records and then tries to update them. During this period another transaction attempts to insert or update the records, causing a phantom record to appear in the second half of the first transaction.

The use of the key-range lock places a lock on the index rows that covers the range of records selected in the first part of the transaction. If another transaction attempts to insert a new record or delete or update an existing record into that range, the transaction will be blocked until the first transaction has been completed and releases the key-range lock. The key-range lock helps to ensure the serializability of the transaction is sustained.

LOCK ESCALATION

The subject of *lock escalation* is concerned with how much of a table is held by the lock, and when a lock changes from a row lock to a page lock or another higher-level lock. SQL Server can create locks that will cover a row, a range of rows, a page, an extent, a table, or even an entire database. The finer the granularity, the less real estate is covered by the lock. SQL Server will automatically escalate lock granularity from row to page to table or index if the number of rows or pages locked by a single transaction exceeds the threshold level for that lock type. SQL Server dynamically adjusts the lock type and does not need any configuration. A lock of any type uses the same overhead resources, so once a lock is escalated from row or page to an index or table lock, the lower level lock is automatically released, freeing the resources.

You may wonder why a row lock would be escalated to a page or table lock if it uses the same number of resources. While it may use the same number or resources, there can be many row locks being held, one for each row being locked. So once the number of rows being locked increases to a certain point, it is more efficient in system resources to escalate the lock to one of a coarser grain—even with the loss of some concurrency.

ROW LOCKS

The smallest, or finest grain lock is a row lock. The ability to lock a single row began with SQL Server 6.5, and was available only for INSERT transactions. Insert row-level locking has been replaced by SQL Server 7's complete row-level locking. Row locking is now supported across all transactions that need to use locking at the row level.

A row lock provides the greatest level of concurrency since more users can access information in a table, but it can also be the highest in resource cost.

PAGE LOCKS

The *page lock* will lock an entire data page. A page lock can be exclusive or shared, and covers an entire 8K page, either a data page or an index page. When a UPDATE, INSERT, or DELETE transaction is about to write data to a page, it requests and holds an exclusive page lock, preventing any other transaction from writing to the page. SQL Server will promote a page lock to a table lock if the number of page locks in a table exceeds the lock threshold. Like other locks, the page lock can be shared, exclusive, or an intent lock.

TABLE LOCKS

A table lock is the coarsest lock level supported by SQL Server short of a complete database lock. SQL Server grants table locks when the server believes that a transaction will affect the entire table. Table locks can prevent lock collisions and deadlocks at the page level.

Like page locks, table locks can be either exclusive or shared. When an exclusive table lock is held by a transaction, no other transaction can access the table until the transaction granted the lock has been completed. In other words, when one transaction has an exclusive lock on a table, no other transaction can write to or read from the table until the table lock is released.

DEADLOCKS

Deadlocks are special situations where two (or more) transactions cannot proceed until the other releases a lock it is holding. Neither transaction can proceed because of the other, creating a deadlock. If a deadlock occurs, SQL Server will automatically roll back the transaction that requires the least amount of processing time, sending error message 1205 back to the client application. When this error is received by the client application, the following message is displayed:

```
Your server command (process id#%d) was deadlocked with
another process and has been chosen as deadlock victim. Re-
run your command.
```

Once SQL Server rolls back the deadlocking transaction, the other transaction is free to place a lock on the resource and complete the process it started. Client applications should always check and trap for error 1205, being sure to resubmit the transaction to the server. Of course, a well-written application will not allow deadlocks to occur in the first place. If deadlocks are frequent, recheck how you have set up the locking system in your application.

Update locks are commonly used by SQL Server to prevent deadlocks. When two transactions are both reading a page, one may obtain an update lock if it intends to change data on the page. This prevents the first transaction from escalating their shared lock to an exclusive lock until the other transaction either completes its transaction or is demoted to a standard shared lock.

> When a transaction is ready to actually write changes to a page, the update lock is promoted to an exclusive lock. The update lock also prevents *lock starvation*. Lock starvation occurs when many read transactions acquire shared locks on a page, preventing another transaction from acquiring an exclusive lock on the page. This is another form of a deadlock that SQL Server automatically prevents.

USING LOCKS WITH SELECT

You can customize how locks are used with the SELECT transaction. When lock options are stated in a transaction, they override the default lock formations. Table 11-2 lists the various options available to you.

Table 11.2 *Lock options with SELECT*

Lock Option	Description
HOLDLOCK	When selected, this option tells SQL Server to hold a shared lock until the transaction that has specified the HOLDLOCK has completed its work, instead of automatically releasing the lock as soon as the page, view, or table is no longer required.
NOLOCK	This option tells SQL Server to reject all lock requests, holding no shared or exclusive locks. When this lock option has been selected it is possible to read uncommitted transactions or data on pages that are about to be rolled back. This option is also called "dirty reads."
PAGLOCK	This is the default setting and requires SQL Server to use shared page locks.
TABLOCK	This option requires SQL Server to use shared table locks. Other users are able to read the table, but no one can update the data contained in the table until the transaction that set the TABLOCK has completed its work on the table. If used in conjunction with the HOLDLOCK option, TABLOCK will be held until the entire transaction has been completed.
TABLOCKX	This option instructs SQL Server to place an exclusive lock on the table. This lock will prevent others from reading or updating the table until the transaction has finished.
UPDLOCK	This lock option uses update locks instead of shared locks when reading a table, holding the update lock until the end of the transaction. This allows you to read data without blocking others from reading the table. By using this option you are assured that data is not changed in the table until after you have completed your transaction.

Setting Transaction Isolation Level

SQL Server allows you to set an SQL-92 isolation level. This allows you to set an isolation level that is compatible for your database needs. While the normal SQL Server serialization of transactions enables you to be sure that the information in your database remains consistent and correct, not all transactions require this level of isolation.

A lower level of isolation allows a greater degree of concurrency, but conversely may also allow a greater degree of inconsistent data. Depending on the isolation level selected, a user can select a record being updated by another user—a dirty read. SQL Server supports all four isolation levels defined by SQL-92.

- Serializable is the highest isolation level. If a transaction has locked a record, another transaction cannot read the record.
- Repeatable read is the next level. At this level a user can possibly read a record, another user can insert a record, or change the record, and then the first user would see what appears to be a phantom data record.
- Read committed is the default isolation level for SQL Server. At this level it is possible for a user to read data that has been committed, but not yet actually written, to the database.
- Read uncommitted is the lowest isolation level. At this level it is possible for a user to read data that has not yet been committed.

Table 11-3 lists the various isolation levels and the possible behaviors that may occur.

Table 11.3 *Setting the transaction isolation leve*

Transaction isolation level	Phantom data reads	Nonrepeatable reads	Dirty reads
READ UNCOMMITTED	X	X	X
READ COMMITTED	X	X	
REPEATABLE READ	X		
SERIALIZABLE			

You can set the isolation level for an entire SQL Server session by using the SET statement. The transaction isolation level specifies the default locking level for all SELECT statements during the users current session. Once you log off from the session the isolation levels return to their default settings and will have to be reset again when you log in if you require a different isolation level than the default level.

Only one option can be specified in the SET statement, and it remains the default setting for the current session unless explicitly changed.

The syntax for the SET statement is:

```
SET TRANSACTION ISOLATION_LEVEL
```

Substitute the appropriate option for ISOLATION_LEVEL: READ COMMITTED, READ UNCOMMITTED, REPEATABLE READ, or SERIALIZABLE.

Key Points

In this chapter, you have learned several techniques to ensure that your data remains consistent, while at the same time allowing the maximum number of concurrent users. Specifically, you learned:

- To use exclusive, shared, intent, and update locks on tables, pages, extents, and rows.
- How to set the lock granularity in the Server Configuration/Options dialog box.
- That SQL Server uses update locks to prevent deadlocks from occurring.
- To customize a SELECT statement for a specific locking level.
- To use the SET statement to set the transaction isolation level.

▲ CHAPTER REVEW QUESTIONS

▲ Multiple Choice:

1. *A T-SQL transaction is:*

   A. A complete set of T-SQL statements.

   B. The WHERE clause of a statement.

   C. The COMMIT TRANsaction statement.

   D. A statement that includes a BEGIN TRAN command.

2. *SQL Server normally will not allocate more than _____ percent of available memory to lock allocation.*

    A. 25

    B. 30

    C. 40

    D. 50

3. *The TABLOCKX statement does what?*

    A. Prevents anyone from reading the table.

    B. Prevents any form of a lock being placed on the table.

    C. Sets an exclusive lock on the table.

    D. Allows only shared, read locks by other users.

4. *Phantom records can be prevented through the use of:*

    A. Phantom locks

    B. Key-range locks

    C. Index locks

    D. Phantom index locks

5. *SQL Server error 1205 indicates that:*

    A. The maximum number of locks has been issued.

    B. A deadlock was reached and your transaction was rolled back.

    C. A deadlock has happened.

    D. Your transaction was selected as the victim.

▲ True or False

1. *True or False? When using implicit transactions, a new transaction begins when a new ROLLBACK statement is issued.*

2. *True or False? An intent lock will prevent another user from being granted an exclusive lock.*

3. *True or False? An exclusive lock is normally granted to a user for the time he or she is logged on the server.*

4. *True or False? Exclusive locks are automatically released on completion of a transaction.*

5. *True or False? Lock escalation is concerned with upgrading a shared lock to a more restrictive type of lock.*

Managing Database Space

As a system administrator, one of your many jobs is to ensure that SQL Server© makes optimal use of the disk space that is available to it. This includes not only being sure that there is enough disk space for SQL Server and the associated data files, but that they are distributed across the disk(s) so that recovery can be easily facilitated.

SQL Server 7 has made many significant changes to the way that databases are stored. Now, instead of storing one or more databases and their objects in database devices, each database is stored in its own set of operating system files.

MCSE 12.1   Planning Database Space Requirements

Planning the space requirements for a new database is very important. As you create a database file, you will be allocating physical disk space. You can always add additional database and log files to a database file group. If you have not adequately planned for expansion, you may quickly find that you are running out of disk space. Some database applications can quickly grow to fill even today's large disks. Another aspect of storage that should be discussed is the type of disk storage you are using—SCSI or inexpensive EIDE drives. For smaller databases, or developmental applications, you can easily use the more inexpensive EIDE drives. For very large database in a production environment, you will want to use SCSI drives. You are not limited to the current four drives as is EIDE, and you can make use of extremely large disk arrays that are simply not available otherwise.

SQL Server allocates disk space using two primary storage units:

- An 8KB page.
- The extent, composed of eight contiguous pages.

When creating a new database or allocating additional space for an existing one, you will decide not only on how large the database will be, but also how large the log file should be. When first creating a database, a rough guideline is that between 10 to 25 percent of your database's size should be allocated to the log file. If you do not specify a log size, SQL Server will automatically create a log file that is 25 percent of the total of all of the data files. Once the database has been tested and is placed into production, you should be able to more accurately assess the necessary size of the log file. Some of the factors that you will need to consider as you decide on the size of your log file are:

- The number of transactions processed between backups.
- The length of time you have set for the recovery interval.
- The average size of transactions or the amount of data updated by average transactions.
- How often very large transactions are processed.

This last point is made primarily because a poorly written transaction can potentially cause a log file to become full between backups without coming to a COMIT TRAN statement, bringing the entire database to a grinding halt.

The log file is always placed in a separate file from its database file. The reason that SQL Server locates the log file on a separate drive is so that the log file can be backed up and truncated. This allows you to keep the log backup files as up to date as possible and as small as possible, by removing the inactive part of the log—all transactions from the last BACKUP TRANSACTION statement up to the last uncommitted transaction. Previous versions of SQL Server allowed you to keep both the log and database together on the same device; you could not back up the log by itself, but had to do a full backup of the entire database. This is a much more time-consuming process than dumping just the log file. You may also want to consider placing the log file on a completely separate physical disk. This will help to ensure that you may still be able to fully recover from the failure of the database file's disk drive.

 After making any changes to the size of an existing database, be sure to back up both the database you changed, and more importantly, the master database.

Planning the Database

When you create a database, there are several parameters you supply to SQL Server, one of which is the initial size of the database files. If you do not tell SQL Server how big of a database file to create, then SQL Server will build a database file the same size as the model database. Remember that SQL Server will copy the model database and insert all of its tables into your new database. With SQL Server 7, the smallest database file that you can create is 1MB in size, with an additional 1MB for the log file. SQL Server 6.5 allowed you to create a 1MB database for use on removable diskette-based databases, but these are no longer supported.

Space for a database can be allocated across as many database files as necessary. This is often done when the file that the database currently resides on becomes full, or if you want to locate different parts of the database in different files and separate disks. Database files must exist on one of the server's local drives because SQL Server does not support database files across networked drives.

The initial default size of a database is controlled by the greater of the model database size, or the value of *database size* parameter in the sysconfigures table. For example, if your model database is 2.5MB in size, the default setting and the database size value has been set to 6, your new database will be created with a default size of 6MB, unless you specify a different value. A database cannot be created smaller than the model database. Remember, when SQL Server creates your database, it copies the necessary system tables from the model database and places them into your new database, then extends the size of your database to your specified size or to the larger of the database size value or the model database size.

The default database size value is changed using the `sp_configure` stored procedure:

```
sp_configure
'database size', 6
reconfigure
```

The reconfigure statement is required to make the changes in the sysconfigures table. Only the system administrator can use `sp_configure` with parameters and effect a change. SQL Server must be stopped and then started again for all but dynamic values to take effect. You can also increase the size of the model database so that it is 6MB in size. The recommended method is to change the database size value with `sp_configure`. This is the easiest adjustment to make, and you do not have to give over additional physical disk space for the model database.

You can also change the database size value from the SQL Server Enterprise Manager application by opening the SQL Server Properties dialog box. The database size configuration is an option available on the Database Settings tab, as shown in Figure 12-1. If you change the value of the database size, you will have to stop and then restart SQL Server before the new value will take effect.

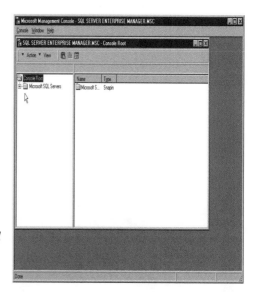

Figure 12–1 *Use the Database Settings tab in the SQL Server Properties dialog box to change the initial size of new databases.*

PAGES

Each page is composed of a 96-byte header used to store information about the type of page, current free space on the page, and the object ID of the object that owns the page. Data rows are placed one after the other immediately following the header information. At the end of every page is a row offset table. This table contains one entry for each row on the page. The row offset entry for the first data row will be the very last entry on the page.

A page is the smallest of the three units of storage used by SQL Server, and is 8KB in size. SQL Server makes use of five types of pages:

- Data or log pages. These pages are used to store the data contained in tables.
- Index pages are used to store index values.
- Text and images are stored on special pages. The data page contains a pointer, which links the page to a variable number of text/image pages that contain the actual data.
- The allocation page is the first page in each allocation unit. This page describes how the remaining 255 pages are used.
- Distribution pages contain a sample of data values contained in the table. SQL Server uses these values to determine which index to use with a query.

Each database is divided into 8KB pages; each page is assigned a logical page number beginning with 0 and increasing sequentially to the final page. This page number is part of each row ID number.

GLOBAL ALLOCATION MAP •

The Global Allocation Map (GAM) is a new type of page that is used to record information about the extents that have been allocated. Each GAM page covers 64,000 extents, or 4GB. The GAM page sets 1 bit for each extent. If the bit is set to 1 then the extent is in use, while if the bit is 0 then the extent is free.

The GAM page is the first page in any database file and is numbered 0. The next GAM will appear after 64,000 extents, or 512,000 pages. If your database grows to more than 4GB, SQL Server will add a new GAM page.

SECONDARY GLOBAL ALLOCATION MAP •

The Secondary Global Allocation Map (SGAM) page is used to record what specific extents have been allocated as mixed extents and have at least one unused page. An SGAM also covers 64,000 extents or 4GB. The bits of the SGAM are used to indicate the following: if set to 1 then the extent is used as a mixed extent and has free pages, while if the bit is 0, then the extent is either not used as a mixed extent, or it does not have a free page.

The SGAM page follows the GAM page as the second page in a database and is numbered 1. The next SGAM page will appear after 64,000 extents, and immediately after the second GAM page.

PAGE FREE SPACE •

The Page Free Space (PFS) page records information about an individual page's current usage—whether the page has been allocated and how much of the page is still free for use. A PFS page covers 8000 individual pages, or 1000 extents. Every individual page has a bitmap recording of the page, indicating if it is empty, up to 25% full, from 26 to 50% full, from 51 to 75% full, or more than 75% full.

SQL Server uses the information on the PFS page to select pages to record new data from a newly inserted row.

EXTENTS

Each extent is made up of eight contiguous pages. In earlier versions of SQL Server, the extent was the smallest unit that a table could be created from. This meant that each table covered a minimum of eight contiguous pages. In those versions of SQL Server the page was only 2KB in size, not the current 8KB. You can now create a table that is only one page, 8KB in size. SQL Server 7 allows for extents whose pages are allocated to multiple tables, and these extents are called *mixed* extents. If a table is created that will fit on a single, or anything less than eight pages, then it will be placed on a mixed extent. Once the table grows to cover eight pages, then it will be placed on its own *uniform* extent. When a new table is created, it is first assigned to either a uniform or a mixed extent, depending on the number of pages the table requires. As rows are added to the table, additional extents are also added to the table. If a table has less than eight pages, it may be allocated pages from several mixed extents.

Sizing the Log file

The size of your log file is very important to the well being of your database and information. If the log is too small, it may become full before a checkpoint is reached and the log backed up and truncated, bringing all modifications to data to a halt. If it is too large, it will unnecessarily use up valuable disk space.

Like the database file, the log file is created as a separate operating system file. The default settings give the log file a file extension of .ldf. Unlike earlier versions of SQL Server, the creation of the separate log file ensures that you can back up and truncate the transaction log as a separate step.

- Under normal database usage, SQL Server truncates or clears the log only after an incremental backup has occurred.
- By separating the log and data files of a database you can gain some additional performance advantages, especially if the files are placed on separate physical disks and/or controllers in the server.
- Recovery can be expedited and is more assured with the logs being kept separate from the data. With complete log files and incremental backups, you can be assured of recovery possibly even to the last transaction. With only full backups of all of your data, you can only recover up to the point when the last full backup was performed.

The actual size of your log files will depend on several factors:

- How often incremental back ups are performed. The more frequently incremental back ups are done, the smaller the required log file.
- The volume of simultaneous updates by multiple users. The larger the number of simultaneous updates, the larger the log file should be. If many updates are performed at once, it is possible to fill the log file, which in turn prevents all transactions from being completed.
- Numbers of long transactions. The log file can quickly become full if large amounts of data are being updated or inserted in a single transaction. Remember, the data does not get written from the log to the data rows until after a transaction has been committed. With a large, single transaction you may need to have a log file larger than the data files. It is always recommended that large transactions be broken into several smaller ones. You can then back up the log files after each.
- The normal activity level of the database. If a database has a high level of normal activity, the log file will probably need to be correspondingly larger to ensure that it does not become full before the next incremental backup and clearing of the log.

Log files can be created along with their data files with the CREATE DATABASE statement. Additional log files can be added later using the ALTER DATABASE statement. You can also, of course, use the SQL Enterprise Manager window, database Properties dialog box, and the Transaction Log tab.

Expanding a Database

Database data and log files can be expanded or additional files added to the group. This subject was covered in depth in Chapter 3. The simplest method, of course, is to allow the file to grow as needed. You can also create additional data and log files and allow a more controlled form of growth through these files. Additional files can be set so they are allowed or not allowed to grow, just as the primary data file and the log files can be set.

MCSE 12.2 **Shrinking a Database**

At times you may find that a database has not grown as you had originally anticipated and you want to recover the disk space that was allocated to the database. You cannot shrink a database so that it is smaller than the model database or to a size smaller than the space required by the current database objects. For example, if your database is 6MB and contains 5MB of actual data, you cannot shrink it so that it will fit in a 4MB database without deleting 1MB of data first. A database can be shrunk using the T-SQL statement DBCC SHRINKDATABASE or from within the SQL Enterprise Manager window.

When using DBCC SHRINKDATABASE you have four parameters that can be used or need to be set:

- The database to be shrunk needs to be specified.
- A percentage can be set. This is the percentage to shrink the database to from its current size. If the database is now 10MB, a 90% setting will shrink it to 9MB. If not specified, then the statement will free as much space as possible.
- The NOTRUNCATE option moves all pages in the freed space to the remaining part of the database and retains the freed space for the databases later use. The default setting is to recover the freed space for the operating system.
- The TRUNCATEONLY option frees all unused database space to the operating system. Data pages are not reallocated.

The syntax for the DBCC SHRINKDATABASE statement in the Query Analyzer is like this:

```
DBCC SHRINKDATABASE (pubs, 90)
```

Before shrinking a database, back up both the master and the database that will be shrunk before you actually perform the shrinking. This will ensure that you can recover your data if anything untoward happens during the process.

If you receive the message that the command completed successfully, than everything should have proceeded normally and the database will now be shrunk to the specified percentage. If you do receive error messages, be sure to check each and see what may need to be done.

You can also easily shrink a database from within the SQL Server Enterprise Manager, by simply selecting the database in the scope pane of the MMC and right-clicking on it. Select Task, Shrink Database from the shortcut menu. This will open the Shrink Database dialog box as you see in Figure 12-2. You have several options available to customize by how much a database will be shrunk, and when the process will be done.

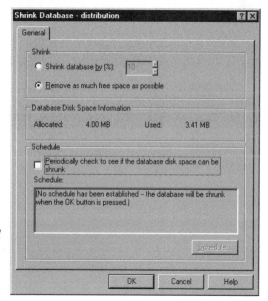

Figure 12–2 *Use the Shrink Database dialog box to select how much and when a database will be reduced in size.*

You can choose to shrink the database by a specified percentage, or to remove as much space as possible. You can also choose whether this task will be done on a schedule or only when you manually perform this task.

MCSE 12.3 Deleting a Database

One of the normal functions that you will have to routinely perform as system administrator is the deleting of unused database objects and devices. Deleting an unused object helps you to free valuable disk space on your server. You will have to set some rules and standards as to what to consider available for deleting.

Some of the reasons you may decide to delete a database could be:

- The database has been replaced by a newer, faster version of the application and all necessary data has been copied to the new database.

- The database may be used as a temporary testing or teaching database and can be deleted once this function is no longer necessary.

Deleting a database from SQL Server will also delete the database's operating system file. In previous versions of SQL Server you would not only have to drop a database device, but also delete the operating system file. To delete a database from within the SQL Server Enterprise Manager you simply have to expand the Database folder, select the database to be deleted, and right-click on it. Select Delete from the shortcut menu as shown in Figure 12-3.

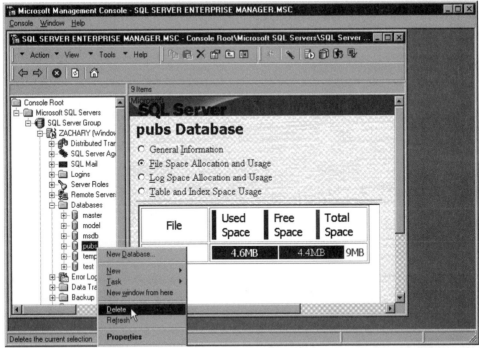

Figure 12–3 *Here you can see the pubs database about to be deleted using the shortcut menu.*

You can also use the DROP DATABASE *database_name* statement in the Query Analyzer. This T-SQL statement removes the database object and its operating system files. Unlike earlier versions of this statement, you can remove a damaged database that has been marked as suspect.

If a database has been converted from another version of SQL Server, and had been created using the DISK INIT statement, you must use the sp_dropdevice procedure to remove the database from the system tables and then delete the operating system files.

Key Points

In this chapter, you have learned to plan the size and locations for both databases and their log files. Specifically, you have learned:

- How to size both a database and its log file.
- How to expand a database and log file.
- How to shrink a database or log file.
- How to delete a database device and any databases or log files that may exist on it.

▲ CHAPTER REVIEW QUESTIONS

▲ Multiple Choice:

1. *The two primary SQL Server disk storage units are:*
    A. The 2KB page and the eight page extent
    B. Megabytes and kilobytes
    C. Data files and log files
    D. The 8KB page and the eight page extent

2. *What is the smallest set of database files that you can create?*
    A. 1.5MB
    B. 1MB
    C. 2MB
    D. 10MB

3. *If your model database is 10MB in size, and your log file is 4MB, and you want your primary data file to be 20MB, then you would set your initial data file size to:*
    A. 10MB
    B. 14MB
    C. 20MB
    D. 24MB

4. *The first page in any database is a _____ page.*
    A. Index
    B. Global Allocation Map
    C. Page Free Space
    D. Data

5. *A database that is 6GB in size will have how many GAM pages?*
    A. 1
    B. 2
    C. 64,000
    D. 768,000

6. *Each Page Free Space page records information about how many individual pages?*
    A. 1000
    B. 8000
    C. 64,000
    D. 512,000

7. *If you choose to shrink a 10MB database file by 90%, and have 5MB of data in the file, the final size will be:*
    A. 1MB
    B. 5MB
    C. 9.5MB
    D. 9MB

▲ True or False:

1. *True or False? For a very compact database, you can place the data and logs in the same file.*

2. *True or False? The database log is placed on its own log pages in the data files.*

Transferring Data

In the next two chapters you will become familiar with the subject of transferring information from one form into a new SQL Server 7 database. Chapter 13 introduces the subject of transferring information and the steps necessary to successfully plan a data transfer. Chapter 14 provides you with the details and how-to information.

Planning Data Transfers

All of you will have to transfer information from one source to SQL Server 7© at some time. More often than not it will be when you install the program and get your database ready. In many cases you will be upgrading an SQL Server 6x database application to version 7. Before planning the actual data transfer from an older version of SQL Server or from another data source, you must know not only where the data currently resides, but also what format it is now in. There are several methods of transferring information from a data source to an SQL Server database. The method you choose will depend on several factors:

- Where is the information located?
- What file format is it in?
- Are you upgrading an existing SQL Server database?
- Transfers with bcp
- Transfers with the Data Transformation Services

331

Where Is the Data Now?

Where is the information that you want to transfer into a new SQL Server database located? Is it on the same server that SQL Server 7 has been placed? Is it on another computer in the same network, a remote computer, on a tape, or other removable media? Any of these can be transferred into a new database. The different locations will make a difference in the length of time for the actual transfer and/or how accessible the information on a tape or removable media actually is. You should always understand that a tape created in one brand of type drive with a particular backup software probably cannot be read in another brand of tape drive, especially not without the same backup software loaded on the server.

A transfer over your local network can be accomplished in a relatively short time, depending on the amount of data to be moved, while a transfer from a remote site can take much longer depending on your connection and the quantity of data. If you have a large amount of data to be transferred, double or triple digit megabytes, and are trying to use a modem, I would recommend that you forget that idea and use tape. Two inexpensive tape drives would be much more reliable and faster in the long run. Transferring via modem can be a temperamental method of moving large amounts of data—lost connections, having to restart the transfer, and spending several hours of long distance phone time.

What Kind of Data?

Why would you even bother with transforming the information from one database into SQL Server 7? After all, it probably works just as well where it currently is. This may or may not be true, but more and more companies need to be able to make decisions based on information kept in all of the various databases and file formats that may be contained within the corporate information storehouse. By combining all of this information into a single database management system, you will make your own life that much easier. This is not to say that the initial transformation may not be fraught with problems and pitfalls, but in the long run you will find that you will be able to work on real projects rather than going from fire to fire just to keep everything working. The managers who must make real business decisions based on that data will also be happier because they will quickly see that the data they work with will be more current and can be delivered in a concise, usable format.

The method that you eventually choose to use for making the actual transfer of data from an existing data source into the new SQL Server 7 database will make a difference in your preparation steps and the selection of a transfer agent.

There is a wide variety of data that you can store in an SQL Server 7 database. The usual data formats—simple text, numeric, and dates—are easily stored into a database. More unusual, but becoming more common, are very long text information and images.

SQL Server 7 can easily handle large format information with its text and image datatypes. When text or image data is stored in a table, the actual data is stored on separate text and image pages. Within the data row itself are stored 16-byte pointers to the actual data. Each text or image column contains its own pointer. These pages are all stored together in the table, with the data interleaved as necessary. SQL Server 7 allows both datatypes to exist on an 8KB page together. While a user may work with a text or image as if it were a single sequential string of data, SQL Server will store it on pages that are not necessarily contiguous to each other. SQL Server 7 uses a b-tree structure, unlike earlier versions that used a linked chain of pages, making for a more efficient use of the available text and image pages.

SQL Server 7 will also allow you to take data directly from an HTML format and place it into a database. In addition, you can import, export, and transform data using OLE DB and ODBC.

MCSE 13.1   **Transforming Versus Inserting Data**

Initial preparations include whether or not you must first create a database and the necessary tables before the transfer so that you have a container to place the data in. Or can you transfer the existing data containers along with their contents. In most cases, being able to transfer and convert a database would be the preferred method.

Inserting data has been discussed throughout this book and will be covered in more detail in Chapter 14. In this module, we are primarily talking about the bulk insertion of large amounts of information. This can be done quite effectively with either the bcp application or through the Data Transformation Services (DTS).

DTS can also be used to transform data that is being imported or exported. The transformation function is a set of processes applied to the information before it is stored in a table. Transformation can mean many things—from simply inserting data into an existing table to complex data manipulation before insertion. Using DTS, you can take data in many formats and other databases and:

- Strip extraneous information
- Break up, or parse, data from a single column into two or more columns
- Combine data from multiple columns into a single column
- Calculate new values based on information from multiple columns
- Validate data before inserting it into a table
- Scrub data of inconsistent information

DTS does not move objects such as triggers, stored procedures, defaults, rules, constraints, and other user-defined objects from heterogeneous data sources to an SQL Server 7 database. A heterogeneous data source means that the information can come from a wide variety of data sources including SQL Server.

Often the services available through DTS are used to migrate information from a working database application to a data warehouse. Data stored in a data warehouse is not used for normal day-to-day transactions necessary to a business, but is used for trend analysis and archiving.

Key Points

This chapter included the following key points:

- Data source can include many different types of database and many formats.
- Information can include very long text and image formats.
- SQL Server 7 uses a b-tree format to store and find text and image information in a database.
- Transforming information may include preprocessing of the data so that it will fit into the new database.

▲ CHAPTER REVIEW QUESTIONS

▲ Multiple Choice:

1. *You can transfer information using which connections? (select all that apply)*
   A. By magnetic tape
   B. By network connection
   C. By modem
   D. By mail

2. *The DTS service can do which of the following? (select all that apply)*
   A. Remove information before inserting the remaining data into the table.
   B. Combine data from multiple columns into a single column in the new table.
   C. Validate data before inserting it.
   D. Transform one datatype into another.

▲ True or False:

1. *True or False? You are limited to transferring text and numeric data during a data transfer.*

2. *True or False? The Data Transformation Services's primary function is the bulk transfer of data from one database to another.*

3. *True or False? The bcp utility is used to copy bulk data from one database to another.*

4. *True or False? DTS is often used to transfer data from a data warehouse to a production environment.*

Methods of Transferring Data

In this chapter the primary applications included with SQL Server 7© are for the movement of information into a new database. You can use these tools to move, transform, and otherwise make information from another database ready to work with your database application.

MCSE 14.1   Using the Bulk Copy Program (bcp)

The bulk copy program (bcp) is a command-line utility included with SQL Server and is used to copy a database table to or from a file. Most often you would use the bcp utility to import data from a legacy database that you are planning to replace. You can also use it to import data from an older database that is currently being used to your SQL Server web database, enabling you to keep your web data current without revising your entire current accounting system.

You can also use the bcp utility to copy data from an SQL Server database table to an operating system file. This can then be further imported into another database. While this may not seem like the most efficient way to move data back and forth between databases, it may be your best option. Part of the bcp command line is that you must specify whether the transfer is *in* to the SQL Server table or *out* to an operating system file.

By using the bcp utility, you can quickly transfer data to or from a file and a table; it is probably your only option for transferring data to or from a non-SQL or ODBC compliant database. This is an easy way to copy data from an SQL table to an operating system file so that it can be used in another program such as a spreadsheet.

The bcp utility can import data in any ASCII or binary format so long as the field and row terminators can be described. A terminator is the character used to separate columns and rows. Column terminators are often either comma or tab characters, and these files are often called either comma or tab delimited files.

In order to use the bcp utility you must have the appropriate permissions on the file that you are copying from or to. To copy data from a file to a table you must have INSERT privileges on the table, while to copy data from a table to an operating system file you must have SELECT permissions on the table or view being used, on *sysobjects*, on *syscolumns*, and on *sysindexes*. If you are the database owner, table owner, or a system administrator, you will have these permissions; otherwise, you will not be able to copy data from the table to a file.

Most all databases can export data to an operating system file. This file can then be read and imported through the bcp utility. You can also use this utility to transfer data from an SQL Server database table on one type of processor architecture to an SQL Server database on another processor architecture. Processor architecture refers to the type of processor in your system: Intel©, Alpha©, Power PC©, or Mips©.

Making a Database Ready for bcp

Before using the bcp utility to transfer data into a table, there are two things you should do to enable the fastest possible data transfer: Set the database for select into/bulk copy (nonlogged input) and drop all indexes on the table. You can also use the bcp utility to perform logged transfers, but these will be much slower and defeats much of the purpose for using bcp in the first place.

If you are doing a bulk transfer into a table, you do not want to wait while every transaction is logged. If the table you are copying data into does not have any indexes set, then simply setting the table to bulk copy status will prevent the transactions from being entered into the transaction log. It is suggested that you dump the entire database before you allow unlogged transactions from being added to a table. This will ensure that you can recover the original database information if a problem is encountered.

If your table does contain an index on one or more columns, you may find that the transfer is much quicker if you drop the indexes on the table before using bcp. This is because any table that contains an index will automatically have all transactions logged, as they will affect the index. If the bulk copy contains many rows of new data, you may find that the transaction log will grow very large before it can be truncated. If you drop the indexes on the table and set it for bulk copy operations, you will find that the entire transfer is much quicker. Once the transfer has been completed, you can recreate the index.

Setting a database to allow unlogged bulk transfers into a table can be done from the SQL Enterprise Manager or by using the stored procedure `sp_dboption`. From the SQL Enterprise Manager you do the following:

1. Select the pubs database that contains the table into which you will be transferring data using the bcp utility. Right-click on it and select Properties from the shortcut menu, then select the Options tab on the Properties dialog box, as shown in Figure 14-1.
2. Now click the Select Into/Bulk Copy checkbox, and then click the OK button. The pubs Properties dialog box is closed, and the database is set for unlogged bulk copy transfers.
3. The next step is to drop any existing indexes on the table into which data will be transferred. Expand both the pubs database and the Tables folder, then right-click on the authors table, selecting Design Table from the shortcut menu.
4. Click the Properties button on the toolbar to display the Properties dialog box for the table and select the Index/Keys tab. Any indexes that have

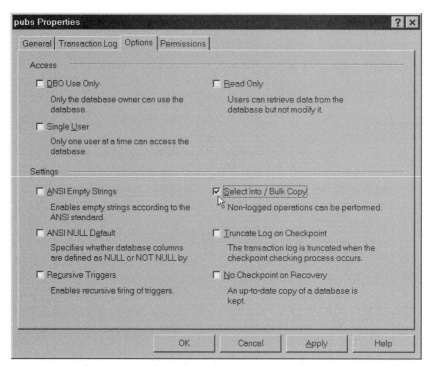

Figure 14–1 *Use the Options tab on the pubs Properties dialog box to change Access and Settings options for a database.*

been set on the table can be easily deleted from here. In Figure 14-2 you can see that the primary key index is displayed in the Selected index text box. It is easy to tell that this is the primary key by the Type indicator directly below the name text box.

5. To delete the index, click the Delete button. In the case of a primary key index, you will see the warning box displayed in Figure 14-3 telling you that all dependent indexes will also be deleted. Click the OK button here if you are actually sure that you want to remove the index.

6. Click the No button and do not delete the index at this time. You are now ready to begin using the bcp utility.

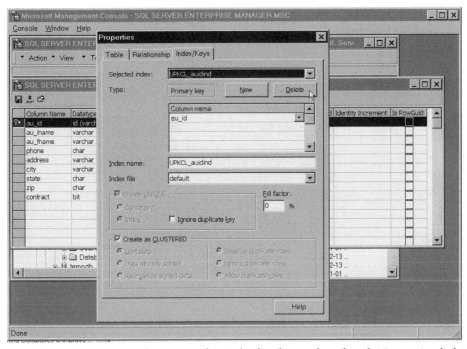

Figure 14–2 *Here you see the primary key index has been selected in the Properties dialog box of the authors table.*

If you plan to rebuild your indexes, it is highly recommended that you write down all of the information about them before you delete them. It is much easier to recreate the index if you have a written map than it is to try and remember what was related to what later.

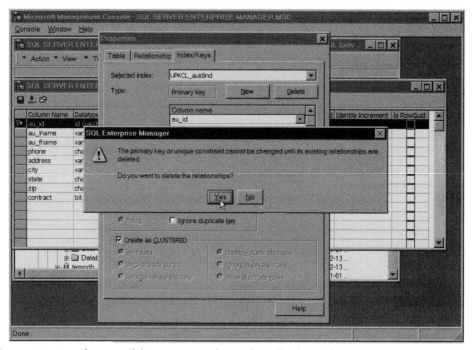

Figure 14–3 *When you delete a primary key index, all other indexes that are dependent on this index, usually foreign key indexes are also deleted.*

Creating the bcp Format File

The key to the bcp utility is the format file. This file tells bcp how to interpret a file before copying it into an SQL table, or it is used by bcp to determine how information from a table will be placed into an output file. If you have previously used the bcp utility, you have probably created a format file for that copy job. A format file should be created for each bcp job that you regularly perform. Once a format file has been created, you will not need to interactively complete all of the formatting information required by the bcp utility; it will use the format file for this data.

When copying data to an SQL database table, the format file tells bcp how to handle the data. This includes telling bcp that a column from the file is to be left blank, the datatype of each column, the column and line terminator character, and the beginning and ending rows of data.

In order to copy data from a file to a table, you must follow a few simple guidelines:

- You must supply the name of the operating system file
- The name of the database and table or view
- The direction of the data transfer, in or out of the database

In this example, you will see how a transfer works between a DOS-based database file to an SQL Server database table. This input file will require datatypes for some columns to be changed, and several fields will not be used.

1. Open a command prompt window. If you have not created a shortcut for this on your desktop, you should be able to find it by clicking the Start button and selecting Programs, Command Prompt from the menus. Type bcp at the command prompt If you have a default SQL Server directory setup, you will find bcp in the C:\MSSQL7\BINN folder. If necessary, change the folder and/or drive indicators to match your own folder structure.

2. Type the bcp command as a single line, as shown below and in Figure 14-4:

```
bcp Inventorydb..Inventory in
 F:\Mssql7\Data\Inventorydb.txt
/SZACHARY /Usa /Ppassword
```

NT will wrap your lines down to a new line if necessary, but do not press the Enter key until you have completed the entire command. Doing so will cause NT to attempt to execute as much of the command as you have entered and will result in an error message. If this happens, press the F3 key and complete the rest of the command line. The bcp command line is entered in this format:

```
bcp databasename.dbownersname.tablename (in or out)
drive and full path and filename
/Sservername /Ulogin /Ppassword
```

If you are a system administrator or the owner of this database, entering the *dbownersname* is not required. Simply type two dots, as done in the previous command line example. There are several command line switches that you can use; they are described in Table 14-1.

3. The first column from the table is displayed with a default datatype. For this column all of the four selections will be accepted as default settings,

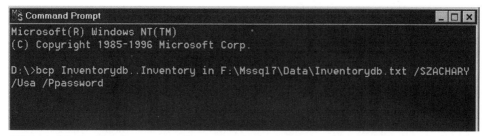

Figure 14–4 *Use the command prompt window when working with the bcp utility.*

so the Enter key will be pressed for each of the first three settings. Type "\t" for the field terminator, meaning this is a tab delimitated file.

The first line gives you the option of changing the datatype for this column now or accepting the default setting. The default setting you see in Figure 14-5 is for the column ItemID and is [char] for character. If you will remember, when this table was created, this column was given a datatype of varchar. When using the bcp utility both char and varchar datatypes will be set as char.

The next setting is for the prefix-length of the field. For most datatypes the default setting is usually the most efficient. If a value of 0 is used for a prefix length, the value stored in the field will be padded with spaces to the full length of the field as dictated in the next prompt. When importing data from, or exporting data to an ASCII file, use a prefix length of 0. For text data, a prefix length of 1 is used.

The length of field is the length of the longest value allowed for the field. When the bcp utility is converting noncharacter value to a character-based storage, it will give you a default value for field length that will be large enough to avoid truncating any data. A character-based field will be padded to its full length with spaces. A noncharacter datatype is not converted to character; it is stored in the table column in its native format and you will not be prompted to provide a length.

The final prompt is for the field terminator. The default is none. When you use a char datatype, 0 for a prefix length, and no terminator, the field values are padded with spaces to the maximum field length. This ensures that bcp or another program can correctly know where a field starts and ends. You can use any printable character as a field terminator. Commonly used characters are: \t for tabs, \n for new lines, \r for carriage return.

4. Continue with the next field, ItemName, and select all of the default settings, except for the last, changing the field terminator from none, to a tab \t.

A null terminator is not the same as no terminator. A null terminator can be indicated by using \0, and places a null terminator character at the end of the column. This is an invisible but real character, while no terminator means there is no column termination character.

 There is no problem converting a datatype from a smaller setting to a larger one, such as smallmoney to money, or smallint to int. Converting from a larger to smaller datatype will most likely cause bcp to run into an overflow situation and the information is not copied. When the datatype *datetime* is converted to a character format of less than 26 bytes, the overflow data will be truncated with no warning.

5. When you get to the next three columns that use the smallmoney datatype, you will normally not be prompted for length of field. For the file storage type enter `char` as the storage type. Since you are importing data from a tab delimited text file, all of the data will be in character fields. Select the default settings, except for field terminator, which is to be changed to a tab, as done previously (see Figure 14-5).

6. The next two fields are numeric datatypes. Numeric and decimal datatypes are virtually interchangeable, except that a decimal datatype cannot be used for a column that is an identity column. Again, type char

```
Command Prompt - bcp Inventorydb..Inventory in F:\Mssql7\Data\Inventorydb.txt /SZACHARY...

Microsoft(R) Windows NT(TM)
(C) Copyright 1985-1996 Microsoft Corp.

D:\>bcp Inventorydb..Inventory in F:\Mssql7\Data\Inventorydb.txt /SZACHARY
/Usa /P

Enter the file storage type of field ItemID [char]:
Enter prefix-length of field ItemID [0]:
Enter length of field ItemID [15]:
Enter field terminator [none]: \t

Enter the file storage type of field ItemName [char]:
Enter prefix-length of field ItemName [0]:
Enter length of field ItemName [30]:
Enter field terminator [none]: \t

Enter the file storage type of field SellPrice [money-null]: char
Enter prefix-length of field SellPrice [1]:
Enter field terminator [none]: \t
```

Figure 14–5 *You now see several column formats have been set, including one for a money type field.*

as the new datatype. Change the prefix length from 1 to 0, and accept the default setting for length of field. Be sure to change the field terminator from none to tab \t.

If you make a mistake during the creation of the format file, you will not be able to correct it at this point. In the next section of this chapter, you will learn how to edit and reuse a format file. So do not worry too much if you miss a command.

7. On the next column, make the same changes you did in step 6. On the next three columns, simply accept the default settings except for the field terminator. When you complete the last column, you will be prompted to save your responses in a format file. Press Y (Yes) to create the format file.

8. The default name for a format file is bcp.fmt; you will want to change this. This format file will be named F:\Mssql7\Data\Inventorydb.fmt, press the Enter key to save the file, as seen in Figure 14-6. If you do not provide a complete drive and path, the file will end up in the root directory of the drive you started with. This will save your responses as a new format file that can be used the next time you use the bcp utility to transfer data into or out of the Inventorydb table.

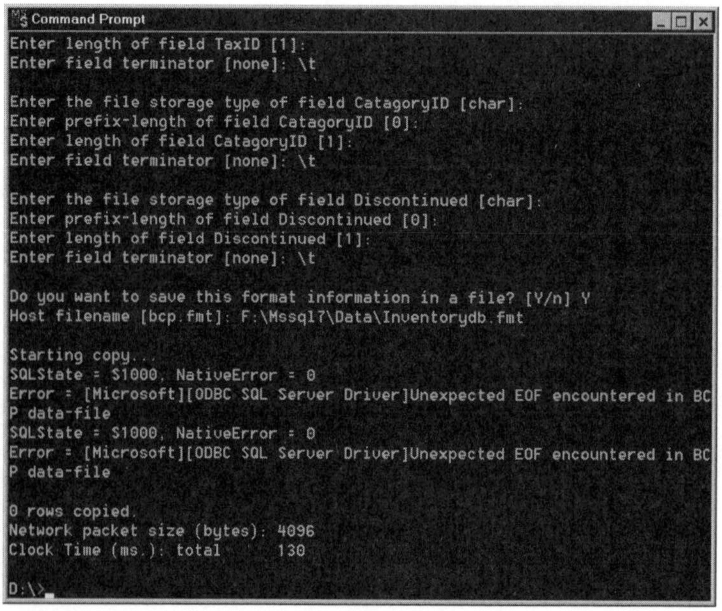

Figure 14–6 *You now see the new bcp format file has been saved. Do not worry about the error messages, they are expected and will be corrected.*

When you press Enter to save the format file, bcp will attempt to copy the data from the input file to the table. You will get an error message—this is OK and expected. In the next section of this chapter you will learn how to correct this.

There are additional switches that you can use with the bcp utility. Switch settings are case-sensitive.

Table 14.1 *bcp command-line switches*

Switch	Variable	Description
/m	Number	The maximum number of errors that are allowed before bcp will cancel the transfer. Each row that cannot be copied is ignored and counted as one error. The default setting is 10 errors.
/f	Format file name	Use this switch when using an existing format file as a copy template. A complete path is required.
/T		Forces a trusted connection to the server and database.
/e	Error file	Enter the full path and file name for the error file. bcp will place all rows it is unable to transfer here.
/F	Number	Enter the starting row number for bcp to begin the transfer. The default setting is 1.
/L	Number	Enter the ending row number for bcp to use. This is the last row that will be transferred. The default is the last row in the file.
/b	Number	Use this option to break the transfer into smaller batches. Specify the number of rows to be included in each batch. This is especially useful for very large transfers so that you do not fill the transaction log.
/n		Transfers data using the data's native datatype as the default. You will not be prompted for a datatype for each field.
/c		Selects character as the default datatype for all fields. All datatypes are converted to *char*, with no prefix, \t(Tab) as the field separator, and \n(new line) as the row terminator.
/E		Use this switch when importing data from a file with an identity value for each row. During transfer the identity value is set to 0. As the rows are inserted into the table, SQL Server assigns a unique value based on the *seed* and *increment* values specified.

Table 14.1 *bcp command-line switches (Continued)*

/t	Character	Specifies the default field terminator. This can be any printable character.
/r	Character	Specifies the default row terminator.
/i	File name	The name of the file that will redirect input to bcp.
/o	File name	The name of the file that bcp will redirect output to.
/U	Login name	Enter a valid SQL Server login name
/P	Password	Enter the valid SQL Server password for the login name being used. If you do not enter a password here, bcp will prompt for one. If you use this as the last switch in the command line with no password, bcp will use a NULL as the password.
/S	Server name	Select a specific server to connect to. This switch is required if you login from a remote computer.
/v		Display the current DB-Library version.
/a	Number	Specify the number of bytes per network packet to be sent to and from the server. Valid values are between 512 and 65535, with a default value of 4096.

Editing the bcp Format File

If the SQL Server database table and the input file do not match each other—number and order of columns—you may need to edit the format file before data can be successfully transferred. A format file can be edited in any text editor, such as Notepad. By editing the format file, you can load information from a file whose fields do not match the SQL database table. In the sample file INVNTY.DBF the columns are mismatched in both numbers and order to the table Inventory.

Often in the case of importing data into an SQL Server table, the data fields do not match the table, either in numbers of columns or in column order. This requires that you create and then edit the format file so that bcp will know how to import the necessary information, and not to include information from fields that do not exist in the table. In this example, the source file Invnty.txt has two additional columns, and has two columns in a different order than does the table Inventorydb. These two files have a format order like this:

Source: Inventorydb.txt	Destination: Inventory
Icode	ItemID
Iname	ItemName
Isell	SellPrice
Iacost	LastCost
Ilcost	AvgCost
Ionhqty	OnHandQty
Ionoqty	OnOrdQty
Ibackqty	VendorID
Ivendor	TaxID
Itax_Type	CatagoryID
ICatagory	
Iserialize	

The format file Inventorydb.fmt created in the previous section, can be edited with your favorite text editor, such as Notepad. Figure 14-7 shows the Inventorydb.fmt file open inside of Notepad.

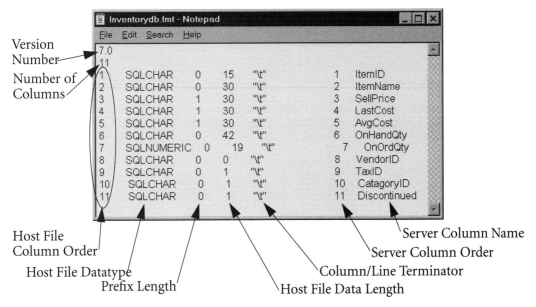

Figure 14–7 *Here the bcp format file is open in the Notepad applet and ready to be edited.*

By editing the line placement numbers and inserting additional columns to account for rows that are not included in the source file, you can easily customize the format file to accommodate the table into which you will be inserting the bulk data.

To actually use your revised format file, refer to the bcp utility you see below, being sure that you name the source file and the format file. The format file is entered following the /f switch.

```
bcp InventoryWeb..Inventorydb in
F:\Mssql\Webdb\Inventory.txt
/fF:\Mssql\Data\Inventorydb.fmt
/SZENA /Usa /Ppassword
```

If you want to do a quick check of the data to verify that it did indeed get into the table, simply open the table in the Enterprise Manager, or use Query Analyzer and a simple SELECT statement.

In addition to the bcp utility, you also have the use of the BULK INSERT T-SQL statement. This statement performs many of the same functions that bcp does, except that you cannot transfer data from an SQL Server database to a data file. The BULK INSERT statement also works within a T-SQL interface such as the Query Analyzer.

Using SELECT INTO Statements

SQL Server includes the SELECT INTO T-SQL statement that is used to move information from one table to a new table. The table into which the data will be placed cannot already exist in the database, unless you specifically drop the existing table as part of the T-SQL statement. This type of statement is often used for temporary tables so that you can easily work with a defined subset of the original data without disturbing or being disturbed by other users who are also accessing the same table. When you use a SELECT INTO statement, you can define your results set as explicitly as necessary, using any of the normal statements available to you when creating a query.

If you do not initially specify in the statement that SELECT INTO/ BULKCOPY is set for this statement, the table that is created will be either a local or global temporary table. If this is the case, you must prefix the new table name with a # pound sign. SELECT INTO/BULKCOPY can be set from the Options tab of the database's Properties dialog box in the Enterprise Manager, or by specifically setting it to on by executing sp_dboption and setting SELECT INTO/BULKCOPY to true.

In this example, the sp_dboption is used to set the pubs database into select into/bulkcopy mode. Then the SELECT statement creates the table compbus_titles and selects for all records from the titles table where the book type is popular_comp, or business. The second use of the sp_dboption is used to reset the pubs database back into normal mode.

```
EXEC sp_dboption 'pubs', 'select into/bulkcopy', 'true'
USE pubs
SELECT *
INTO compbus_titles
FROM titles
WHERE type LIKE 'popular_comp' OR 'business'
GO
EXEC sp_dboption 'pubs', 'select into/bulkcopy', 'false'
```

Figure 14-8 shows the Query Analyzer where the above query statement has been executed. Notice SQL Server checkpoints the database each time the sp_dboption stored procedure is executed. This ensures that the log files are written.

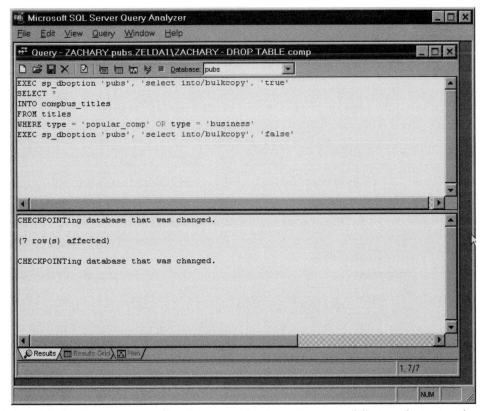

Figure 14–8 *Here you can see the above query has been run successfully. In order to view the records that have been inserted into the newly created table, simply run a SELECT query on the table.*

MCSE 14.2   SQL Server Version Upgrade Wizard

This wizard is specifically designed to help you move databases that have been built using SQL Server 6X. This wizard cannot upgrade a database created with an SQL Server version earlier than 6. With the Version Upgrade Wizard you cannot only upgrade the database and its tables and information, but objects such as:

- Server configurations. This includes information about local and remote logins, and server configuration options that can be transferred to SQL Server 7.
- Replication settings. This includes articles, subscriptions, and publications for each database selected for version upgrade. It also includes the distribution database.
- SQL Executive Settings. This will include all tasks run by the SQL Executive. These tasks and schedules will be transferred to the SQL Server Agent.

You can also select how the wizard will handle quoted identifiers, and ANSI nulls. Once you have completed the Version Upgrade wizard, entering all of the information that it requires about your SQL Server 7 database, your SQL Server 6X database will upgrade your server in this order:

- Export all selected objects from the old database.
- Shuts down the SQL Server 6X.
- Starts the SQL Server 7.
- Imports all of the objects into the new database.
- Simultaneously exports data from the old database and imports the data into the new database.

Using the Version Upgrade wizard is not difficult, but it does require some preplanning, and definitely requires knowledge of the construction of the database that is to be upgraded. Before using this wizard, you should know how your database handles quoted identifiers and uses ANSI nulls. You should also be familiar with the configuration options of the database that will be upgraded and what this wizard will not transfer. For example, any configuration options that are not supported by SQL Server 7 are not transferred, and neither are options that have changed to a setting that is not recommended. These will be set to SQL Server 7 default settings, and you will need to change them manually after the upgrade has been completed.

The Version Upgrade Wizard does not upgrade either the pubs or the model database. It is recommended that you use the pubs and model database included with SQL Server 7. If you are planning to upgrade a database

It is highly recommended that you run the DBCC utility on the SQL Server 6X database before you begin the version upgrade. This will help ensure that any database errors or corrupted catalogs or tables may be corrected and not transferred into the new SQL Server 7 database.

created with an earlier version, ensure that you have adequate disk space to perform the upgrade. If the database to be upgraded is on the same computer that you have placed SQL Server 7, you must have space for both the old and new SQL Server applications. In addition, you must ensure there is space equal to 1.5 times the existing database, plus its transaction logs. For example, if the database to be upgraded is 25MB and it has 10MB for its transaction logs, then you must have a minimum of $(25MB + 10MB) * 1.5 = 52.5MB$ of available space for the wizard to perform the upgrade. This space is used by the wizard to sort and rebuild indexes. If you are planning to upgrade an existing database, then follow these steps:

1. The Version Upgrade wizard is located in the same program group where SQL Server 7 has been placed. You can also find it in the \Mssql\Upgrade folder as `upgrade.exe`. The first screen that you will see is simply the welcome splash screen. Click the Next button to move on to the next screen.

2. In this screen you will select different options from three groups, as shown in Figure 14-9.

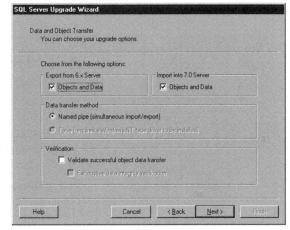

Figure 14–9 *Use this Data and Object Transfer wizard screen to choose what will be exported and then imported, the method of transfer, and how data and objects should be validated.*

- Choose whether you will export and import both objects and data, or only one or the other. If you are upgrading a working application, you will probably want to export and import both. If you have rebuilt an application completely, using SQL Server 7, you may choose to export/import data only into a new database.

- Select the data transfer method. You can use this wizard only with a named pipe connection or from data that has been saved to a tape drive. The best method is the named pipes option. This option leaves the existing SQL Server 6X database intact and gives you the fastest performance. With the previous database intact, you have the option of returning to it if a problem develops during the transfer, or run parallel systems until you are sure that the new database is working as expected.

- Choose if the objects and data that are imported will be verified and how. The first option uses DBCC to check the consistency of the database catalog, tables, and text. The second option performs through data integrity checking.

3. Once you click the Next button you will provide the necessary server logon information for both the export and import servers. You must enter the Server name for both the export and import servers, and a password for the Administrator login. You can also include any necessary command-line startup options by entering them into the text box.

MCSE 14.3   Data Transformation Services (DTS)

With the Data Transformation Services (DTS) you can import, export, and transform information between any OLE DB, ODBC, text file, and SQL Server 7. With this ability, you can easily share information with a great many other programs, and use applications such as Microsoft Excel© to analyze selected data.

DTS is used when you want to export information into a data warehouse. A data warehouse is used to archive information that is no longer needed in day-to-day transactional processes. For example, a data warehouse may contain summarized information about all transactions that occurred in years past. Instead of allowing your production database to become slower and slower as more transactions are added, you can take a prior year's transactions, summarize them, and then export them to the data warehouse. They are still available to you for analysis but in a more compact form.

What Is DTS?

DTS is a utility included with SQL Server 7 that you can use to help with the transfer of information from or to SQL Server 7. DTS supports a wide variety of formats and types of information. You can use DTS to import data from a text file, an ODBC source file, an OLE DB compatible file, to an SQL Server 7 database. This gives you a great variety of information sources that you can easily bring into a database. DTS also helps you export information from an SQL Server 7 database to another application. With this ability, you can easily share selected data with other users, and use sophisticated analysis tools, such as Microsoft Excel, to view trends and other analysis on your data.

DTS can be used to validate data that is imported into an SQL Server 7 database. Validation can include many functions, including checking data for format and consistency. DTS does not copy information such as data indexes, stored procedures, or referential integrity constraints.

Transformation functions include being able to convert information from one format to another; even more useful is DTS's ability to combine information from multiple columns to a single column, or to divide information in a single column into multiple columns. Transformation of data is especially useful when you are offloading selected data from a live transactional database to a data warehouse. Data that is being moved to the data warehouse often requires transformation so that it meets the requirements of its new function as archived data. With a data warehouse, information is no longer needed for everyday transactions, and so is converted into a more compact format that will be more useful for reports and analysis.

There are few limitations on what DTS can import or export as far as actual data is concerned. The primary source of limits on the functionality of DTS rests solely on the capabilities of the specific DBMS, ODBC, or OLE DB driver that you have to work with. For example, many databases support a single BLOB (binary large object). This limits your DTS package to exporting only a single BLOB datatype to a database. DTS does not import or export information concerning indexes, stored procedures, or referential integrity constraints.

DTS is based on an OLE DB architecture. With DTS you can import, export, and transform data from:

- ODBC data sources by using the OLE DB Provider for ODBC.
- Native OLE DB providers.
- ASCII fixed-field length, or delimited text files.

For those of you who are programmers, DTS includes COM programming interfaces so that you can create your own import, export, and transformation packages.

IMPORTING DATA WITH DTS

The simplest method of importing data using DTS is with the DTS Import Wizard. The Import Wizard is accessed from inside the Enterprise Manager application. One of the really great features of the Import Wizard is that it cannot only import information from a variety of sources, but it can build the database and its associated tables at the same time. This can be an incredible time saver—especially if you do not know the exact format of the file that you are importing. For this exercise, you will use the Inventory.txt sample file located on the CD.

1. Open the Enterprise Manager and select Tools, Data Transformation Services, Import into SQL from the menu. This will open the first of the Import Wizard dialog boxes, as seen in Figure 14-10.

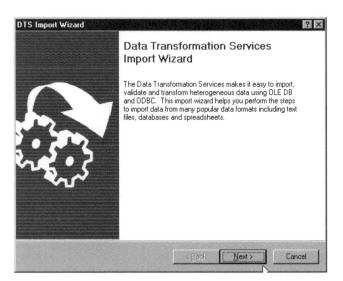

Figure 14–10 *The initial dialog box is only the first of several DTS Import Wizard dialog boxes.*

2. Click the Next button to move on to the next dialog box. Here you will select the data source. There are several types of sources that you can choose. Use the Source drop-down list box to select the type of source that you will be importing from. The choices available in the lower half of this dialog box will vary depending on your choice of a source. Basically, you are telling the Import Wizard where the source file is located, and possibly providing a password. Figure 14-11 shows that the source

file is a text file, and the file name is displayed in the text box. No passwords are required for this source type.

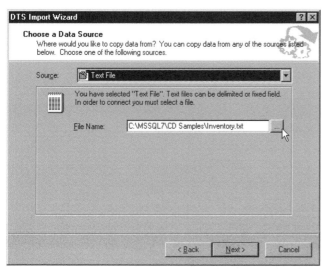

Figure 14–11 *You now see a source file has been selected, and that the necessary additional information has been entered. In the case of a text file, only the file path/name is needed.*

3. Clicking the Next button will bring you to the dialog box where you will provide the Import Wizard with information about the format of the source file. Figure 14-12 shows you the option selected for the text source file. Notice that the check box "First row has column names" has been checked. This text file has the column names situated as the first row in the file.

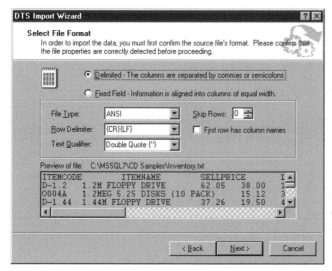

Figure 14–12 *Here you see the options selected for the text file, Inventory.txt.*

4. Click the Next button again. You now must choose the column delimiter for the text file. In this case it is the Tab character. As you can see in Figure 14-13, the column names from the file have been included in the Preview box. If you had not clicked the checkbox concerning the column names in the previous dialog box, you would have seen a generic column name/number combination displayed in this dialog box, and the real column names would be shown as the first row of data.

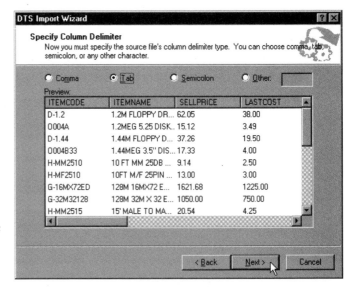

Figure 14–13 *In this dialog box you must choose the specific character that is used to delimit the columns in the text file.*

5. Click the Next button. Now you must choose a destination for the imported data. Not only can you choose whether the data is to be imported into an existing database or into a new one, but you can choose the type of server that is to receive the data. You do not have to import into an SQL Server 7 database. Here the <new> option has been selected for Database so that a new database can be created, as seen in Figure 14-14. When this is selected the Create Database dialog box is displayed. Enter a name for the database, such as "Inventory," and sizes for both the Data File and the Log File. The default setting for both is 1MB. Clicking the OK button returns you to the Destination dialog box.

6. Click the Next button. If your source file contains more than one table, you can choose to import only specific tables. You can also choose the table into which the information will be stored. Figure 14-15 displays this dialog box.

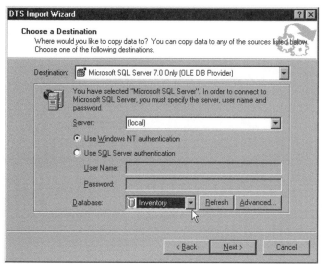

Figure 14–14 *Use the Destination dialog box to select the destination type, the server name and logon information, and select a database, or create a new one for the data being imported.*

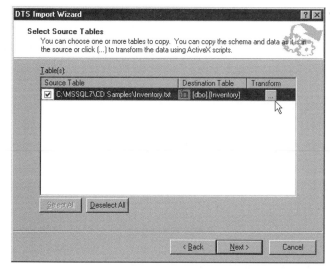

Figure 14–15 *Use the Select Source Tables dialog box to specify the tables that will be imported, and what table will receive the data.*

7. Click the … (button) beside the table name in the Transform column. This will display the Column Mappings and Transformations dialog box. In this dialog box you can specify how columns are mapped into the new or existing table. With a new database, you will also specify additional information about each column: destination column name, datatype, nullability, size, precision, and scale. Figure 14-16 shows the

completed Column Mappings tab settings, and Table 14-2 lists all of the options that have been set for this dialog box.

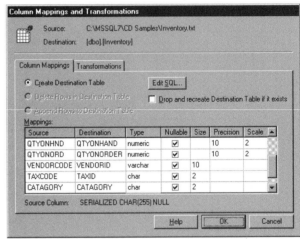

Figure 14–16 *Use the Column Mappings tab to specify the column into which data will be transferred. If you are building a new database and table, you can set all of the necessary information for the new table.*

Note You cannot select an invalid type option for the data transfer. In other words, you cannot transform text into a numeric data type.

Table 14.2 *Table options*

Source	Destination	Type	Nullable	Size	Precision	Scale
ITEMCODE	ITEMID	varchar	No	12		
ITEMNAME	ITEMNAME	varchar	Yes	35		
SELLPRICE	PRICE	money	Yes			
LASTCOST	LASTCOST	money	Yes			
QTYONHND	QTYONHAND	numeric	Yes		10	2
QTYONORD	QTYONORDER	numeric	Yes		10	2
VENDORCODE	VENDORID	varchar	Yes	10		
TAXCODE	TAXID	char	Yes	2		
CATEGORY	CATEGORY	char	Yes	2		
SERIALIZED	SERIALIZED	bit	Yes			

The Transformations tab gives you more options to control the way data is transformed during the import. Figure 14-17 shows this dialog box. You can choose the specific language used for the creation of the transformation script—the default is VBScript, but others are available. You can also edit and add to the script.

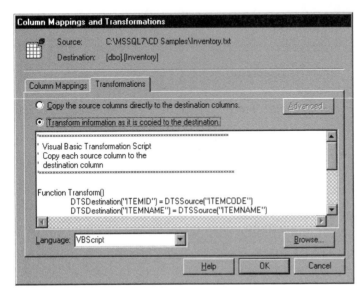

Figure 14–17 *Use the Transformations tab to make modifications to the script that will be used during the transformation.*

8. Click the OK button to continue. This will return you to the Select Source dialog box. Click the Next button to move to the next dialog box.

9. Use this dialog box to save and select how the script may be used again, as shown in Figure 14-18. Here you can choose to:

    • Run the script immediately and import the data.

    • Create a publication for replication from the script.

    • Save the script as a DTS Package to be used again. This is a good option to select if you will be using this script to update a data warehouse on an ongoing basis.

    • Schedule the execution for later.

10. Click the Next button. If you have chosen to save the package, you must provide it with a name and the server on which it will be saved, as shown in Figure 14-19, then click the Next button.

11. You have now provided all of the necessary information. Click the Finish button to complete and run the script. You will see a confirmation box and the results when completed, as seen in Figure 14-20.

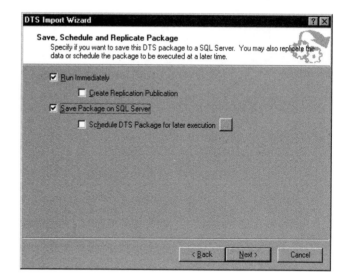

Figure 14–18   *Select the options necessary. If you want to reuse this script again, then select the Save Package checkbox.*

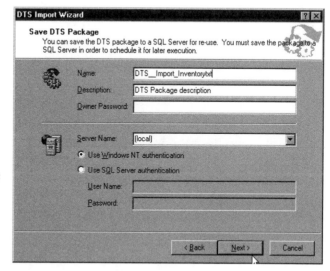

Figure 14–19   *You can accept the default settings, or give your DTS Package a name that might mean something to you later.*

12. Click the OK button on the information box, then the Done button on the dialog box. You will see your new database and/or table the next time that you expand and refresh the scope pane.

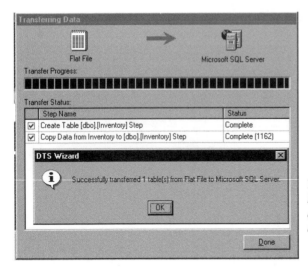

Figure 14–20 *The DTS Import Wizard has completed importing the information and placing it into a new table and database.*

You have now seen how information can be imported using the DTS Import Wizard. The details may vary depending on the data source and destination, but the techniques will be similar.

EXPORTING DATA WITH DTS

You can also use DTS to export information from an SQL Server 7 database or other source. The DTS Export Wizard will be used in this next exercise. Like the Import Wizard, the Export Wizard allows you to transfer information. In this case, it transfers out of your SQL Server database to another database, or another application. Using the DTS Export Wizard is similar to the process used with the Import Wizard, but it will be done with a slight difference in accessing the DTS Wizard. Follow the steps in this exercise to see how the Export Wizard is used to export data contained in the Northwind database to a Microsoft Access database.

1. Expand the Server that contains the database from which you will export data, and then expand the Databases. Right-click on the database and then select Task, Export from SQL on the shortcut menus. Click the Next button on the welcome dialog box.
2. The Choose a Data Source dialog box is already filled in for you when you select the database as you did in step 1. Click the Next button to continue.
3. Now you must give the Export Wizard the necessary information about the destination for your data. In the Destination combo box select `Other (ODBC Data Source)`. Enter the necessary User or System

The Export Wizard, like the Import Wizard, can also be accessed at the main menu by selecting Tools, Data Transformation Services, or using these same selections from the initial shortcut menu. You have several methods for getting to these wizards.

DSN or File DSN information into the appropriate text boxes. If you have not yet created an Access ODBC connection, you can do so now by clicking the New button. You can also select an existing database or create a new one at this point. Enter a User Name and Password if necessary for the database into which your are placing the new information. Figure 14-21 shows a completed dialog box. Click the Next button to continue.

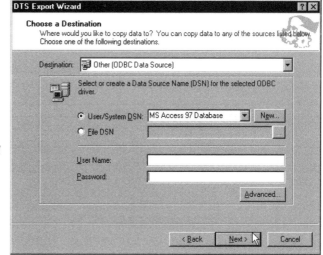

Figure 14–21 *Here is a completed Destination DTS Export Wizard dialog box. The options available in the lower half of the dialog box will vary depending on your selection in the Destination combo box.*

4. In this next dialog box you can choose whether to copy entire tables or to use a query to select specific rows and columns of data to be transferred. While you can choose to omit selected columns when you choose the first option, you cannot enter any form of criteria to select rows. When you select the first option button, you will continue with a fairly straightforward set of dialog boxes.

Choosing the query option brings you to a different series of dialog boxes enabling you to create a query for the selection of the rows and columns that will be exported. If you are familiar with using SQL statements, you can easily enter the query directly into the next dialog box that is displayed. If you are still not comfortable creating your own queries, you can continue on to the Query Builder dialog boxes. With the Query Builder you will select tables, columns, and the order in which they will be used in the query. Then you will choose a sort order for the information by selecting a table/column combination. In the next dialog box you will enter the criteria for the query or choose to select all rows. When building the criteria you can use the arithmetic operators: =, <>, <, >, <=, >=, and you can create AND/OR expressions.

Figure 14-22 shows the dialog box displayed after selecting the first option, that of copying tables has been selected, and then clicking the Next button.

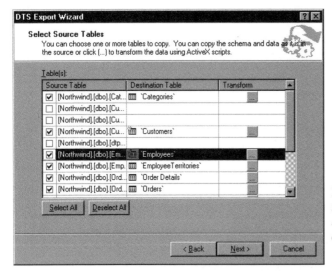

Figure 14–22 *Here you can see that several, but not all tables have been selected for copying and exporting.*

Figure 14-23 shows the criteria dialog box. In the two dialog boxes prior to this you will select tables and columns to be used in the query. You will then select the columns that will be used to provide a sort order for the results.

5. Once you have selected the tables and columns required to be exported, you will choose to run the DTS package now, save the package, or save the package and schedule it to run later.

6. Finally, click the Finish button to start the process. Figure 14-24 shows the various processes and their current status. If DTS encounters any errors, you will see an error icon and the status will be "Failed." You can double-click on a failed process and DTS will display an information dialog box telling you what went wrong. Often the problem may be

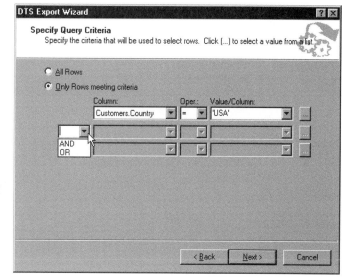

Figure 14–23 *In this dialog box you will enter the criteria to be used in the selection of rows from the tables you have selected.*

caused by the target table already existing, and you did not specify that the table should be deleted, or the records appended, or you may encounter a problem with the receiving source not being able to handle some of the data during transfer.

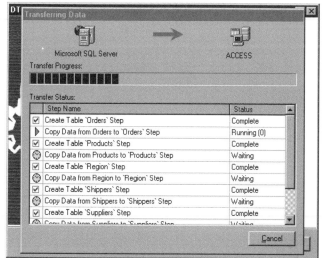

Figure 14–24 *Here you see the current processes being run by the DTS Export Wizard.*

Scrubbing and Validating Data

Validating data is something that can easily be understood—you want to be sure that the data you import into your SQL Server 7 database is valid and meets the requirements of the datatype for the column. Why and how do you scrub data? Does data gets dirty? In a way it does. Scrubbing data means that you ensure that the information is consistent.

This is especially important when you are combining information from multiple systems. Within a larger business you may easily have essentially the same information being kept on various computer systems: different databases, different operating systems, and in different formats.

For example, in a job shop company that makes a certain item to order, the salespeople refer to an item made for a particular customer by a common name, and this is how it has been entered into their database. Within the same company you also have an estimating department who has created the necessary bill of materials for this product and given it a formal name and product ID. This is what is used in their computer system. Now, how do you bring the information from both of these systems together so that one system knows that each of the others is referencing one product and not two? The answer is SQL Server 7. Through the use of the DTS data scrubbing process, the information in both systems is made to be consistent before it is brought together. If the data is not scrubbed before the two systems are combined, you will undoubtedly get analyses of your information that do not make any sense and easily lead management to poor decision making.

Another common use of the validation and scrubbing techniques available is to ensure that information is consistent. For example, one database may store address information with a spelled out state field, while another uses an abbreviated form of a state, while a third uses the two-letter USPS state abbreviation, like this:

California
Calif.
Ca
CA

All of these forms of the state, except for the last, need to be scrubbed and transformed before they can be incorporated into another database, or especially before being inserted into a data warehouse.

The scrubbing and validation of data is done as part of the data transformation that occurs within a DTS package. Data scrubbing can be done by using the DTS import and export wizards. They can be set to perform some of the validation and necessary scrubbing of information as it is imported into SQL Server or when exporting the data from an SQL Server database to another database, or a data warehouse. You can also use an ActiveX® script, executed from within a program that can make use of the DTS API, to connect to a data source and scrub and validate the information.

Creating a Data Warehouse

More and more we hear of data warehouses. What are they? A data warehouse is a special storage database used primarily for information that is not needed for everyday transaction processing. For example, you may want to place a prior year's information and summary transactions into a data warehouse. A data warehouse is created for a number of reasons:

- Can be used for a decision support system.
- Provides support for online analytical processing (OLAP).
- Gives data that is consistent.
- Data is consolidated at a single point of access.
- Information is stored in a subject-oriented view.
- Data is of a read-only nature, ensuring it does not change.
- Information is historical in nature.

Another term that is often used is the *data mart*. The primary difference between a data warehouse and a data mart is that a data warehouse would contain information for an entire organization, while the data mart will contain a subset of this information. Often the data mart contains a single department's information, and then each departmental data mart is combined into a single data warehouse.

The terminology may be different, but they are basically the same, differing primarily by scale. The data warehouse may contain information in a more summarized format than a data mart, but this will depend on its use and storage facilities.

If you have decided that your company needs to create a data warehouse or data mart, there are several things that you can do to help ensure a smooth transition. Before you actually begin the creation of a data warehouse, you will want to:

- Determine if there is a real business and user need for a data warehouse. You do not want to go to all of this effort if it is neither needed nor wanted.
- What are the technical requirements of the project? Does your IT staff have the necessary expertise or will outside help need to be brought in?

- Decide on what information is to be stored in the data warehouse, where the information is currently located, and its current format.
- Designing the database and the required infrastructure to support the data warehouse.
- Building the necessary database structure.
- Extract the information from the existing databases.
- Load the data into your data warehouse database tables.
- Design and build the OLAP infrastructure.
- Choose and create the necessary aggregations, or groups, for use in the data warehouse.
- Build and test the necessary queries and reports for the warehouse.

You may wonder why you would even use a data warehouse. Why not just offload all of the data and store it on another server and call that your data warehouse? Well, you could, but the primary use for a data warehouse is to be able to quickly extract summary information, usually for OLAP reports and decision-support systems. If you simply copy your current transactional database with all of the detail data, you will quickly find queries taking too long, and the system itself becoming overtaxed. Even though you have eliminated the everyday user queries attempting to read and update data, there is still too much data that is not stored in a format suited for OLAP and decision-support systems.

In addition, unlike the usual OLTP database that contains information in a highly normalized manner, the data warehouse is usually created in a very unnormalized fashion. While this probably does create redundant data, it ensures that queries can be run at the fastest speed possible. This is the primary function of the data warehouse—to provide support for the quickest possible information return.

A data warehouse is commonly created in what is known as either a *star* or *snowflake* schema. These formats have been found to provide excellent throughput for the queries that are run against the tables in the warehouse.

Within a data warehouse tables are divided into two types: the *fact* table and the *dimension* table. Each of these tables is used for specific purposes. It is very important that you know what data should be included from the operational database, and how this data should be divided into fact and dimension tables. It is much simpler to choose wisely now—gathering the necessary information, and placing it in a well-constructed table—then to have a data warehouse that cannot provide the information or performance that you, and your superiors, expected.

FACT TABLES

The fact table is the table that contains any of the actual data about the business transactions. Your data warehouse, and the tables it contains, is concerned only with being able to provide information that can support business decisions. This is a tool that is concerned with the fundamental business transactions that have been captured by the operational databases.

As you are combing through the various operational databases for data that should be included in the fact tables, look for the underlying business transaction. Much of the information that is captured by a relational database is recorded as the support for some operational transaction, but not for the fundamental business transaction. For example, when you record a sale there may be many peripheral transactions that attend the fundamental transaction, such as:

- Shipping transactions
- Payment transactions
- Customer information
- Product information
- Receiving transactions
- Manufacturing transactions
- Invoicing transactions

Most of these transactions do not have to be captured for loading into the data warehouse. Unless real business decisions will be based on the information, you do not need to include it.

When designing your fact tables, one of your goals will be to minimize the amount of information they will contain in each row, without the trade-off of not being able to provide the necessary data. As you design your database, you will quickly find that the fact table is the largest object that you will create. You must weigh the cost of being able to provide information quickly, against the cost of storage and how much maintenance must be given to very large tables. There are three things that you can easily do to reduce the size of your fact tables:

- Decrease the number of columns in the table. While this may sound easy, be sure that you can really do without the information before you summarily remove the column. If a column is not necessary for the OLAP analysis remove it.
- Archive historical information into a separate fact table. This would include data that is several years old and rarely included in analysis any longer. Placing this data into a separate fact table will reduce the size of the primary fact table.

- Decrease the size of as many columns as possible. Change column widths to reflect the actual data that will be stored in them. For example, change all fixed-width character and binary columns to variable lengths. Reduce the size of numeric columns. If a column is only used to hold a limited range of integers such as 1–200, then use the tinyint datatype instead of another numeric datatype. You can save a great deal of space with this simple change. Removing a single byte from each row in a table containing one million rows saves you 1MB in database space.

As you build your first fact tables, you will find that their structure goes against the grain of everything that you have done. In place of a normalized, relational database where only required data is included in a table, you will reduce this database to a single—or very few—highly denormalized tables.

DIMENSIONAL TABLES

The dimensional tables are used to describe how data in the fact table will be analyzed. If your basic fact table contains information about sales of products, then you may have several dimensional tables: Time Period, Market/ Region, Product, Sales Person. Each of these dimension tables can be used to describe and extract information from the fact table for further analysis.

While many different dimensional tables could be constructed, you want to include only those tables that will be used to analyze the data contained in the fact table. For example, you could create a dimensional table to analyze sales by customer or by payment type—but do you really need to be able to do this, or is this too much detail? This type of analysis is more often best left at the operational level of detail.

As you build your dimensional tables, they should be able to reference the fact table directly without an intervening table. While this will denormalize the database even more, it will increase your query's performance by eliminating extra joins.

THE STAR SCHEMA

The star schema is the most commonly used design for the creation of the data warehouse. This structure enables the database designer to take advantage of common queries used in typical decision-support systems. The star uses a central fact table and many dimension tables with unnormalized descriptions of the facts.

In this schema, the central fact table contains a foreign key to each dimension table. While this requires an additional column for each foreign key, it is relatively easy to manage, and the performance of complex queries will be good.

Each dimensional table contains a category of information about the fact table. Often this data is hierarchical in nature such that one column may be the child of another. For example, a date-based dimension table may be divided into year, quarter, and month. A month is a child of a quarter, and the quarter is a child of a year. Because information contained in a data warehouse is so often queried on various time periods, you may need to separate time periods into their own dimension tables. Figure 14-25 displays a very simple fact table and its associated time period dimension tables.

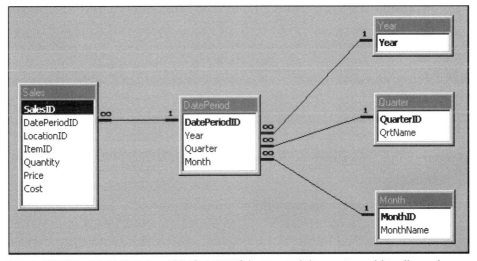

Figure 14–25   *As you can see this format of date period dimension tables allows data to be extracted by several different time periods and only requires one extra join.*

THE SNOWFLAKE SCHEMA

The snowflake schema is the next most popular schema used in the construction of data warehouses. It is a variation on the star schema. The dimension tables are created in a more normalized format. You will probably have several narrow dimension tables, instead of a few wide tables. This has the effect of some dimension tables taking on some of the characteristics of fact tables. While this does increase the number of joins, it potentially can improve some query performance due to fewer disk reads.

Key Points

In this chapter several key points have been covered on SQL Server's ability to transfer data into or out of a database. The main points include:

- Using the Bulk Copy Program (bcp) to transfer information into or out of a database table.
- Setting a database for nonlogged data copying to speed up the transfer.
- Using a format file as a template for transferring data with bcp.
- Working with the SELECT INTO statement to copy information from one table to another.
- Using the SQL Server Version Upgrade Wizard to upgrade an existing 6.X database.
- Using the DTS Import Wizard to transfer data into a database.
- Working with the DTS Export Wizard to move data out of a database.
- That data being loaded into a data warehouse may need to be scrubbed and validated by transformations.
- Building a data warehouse using DTS.

▲ CHAPTER REVIEW QUESTIONS

▲ Multiple Choice:

1. *The bcp utility is used to: (select all that apply)*
    A. Used to copy data into or out of an SQL Server database and uses the Query Analyzer interface.
    B. Used to copy bulk data into or out of an SQL Server database.
    C. Uses the ODBC interface.
    D. Uses the command line interface.

2. *A field terminator is used with bcp to determine the:*
    A. End of the file.
    B. Designates the last field in the information to be transferred.
    C. Designates the end of each field.
    D. Designates the end of each row of fields.

3. *The SELECT INTO statement is used to:*
    A. Move data from one table to a new table.
    B. Move data from one table to another existing table in a different database.

C. Move data from one table to another existing table in the same data-base.

D. Move data from one table to a temporary table.

4. *When using the Version Upgrade Wizard you can use what kind of network connection?*

A. TCP/IP

B. Multiprotocol

C. Named Pipes

D. IPX/SPX

E. All of the above

5. *Data warehouses are created for which of the following reasons? (select all that apply)*

A. Give information for decision support systems.

B. Data is updatable.

C. Data is stored as detailed records.

D. Information is historical.

6. *When building the fact tables of a data warehouse, you should consider: (select all that apply)*

A. Copying data from production tables into the fact table using bcp.

B. Not including the nonessential information.

C. Change variable length columns to fixed-length columns.

D. Reduce the size of as many columns as possible.

E. All of the above

7. *BULK INSERT has many of the same functions as the bcp utility with the exception of: (select all that apply)*

A. Can copy data from SQL Server to a data file.

B. Can copy data from a data file to SQL Server.

C. It uses the T-SQL interface.

D. It can be run from the command-line.

▲ True or False:

1. *True or False? When using bcp to copy data into a table, you must have SELECT privileges on the table.*

2. *True or False? The SELECT INTO statement is used to transfer data from one table to another existing table.*

3. *True or False? DTS is used only to transfer information from an SQL Server database to another application.*

4. *True or False? If you plan on using an ODBC connection with the DTS Export Wizard, you must create the connection before starting the wizard.*

5. *True or False? A data mart is often a departmental version of the corporate data warehouse.*

6. *True or False? Data warehouses are generally, highly normalized databases.*

7. *True or False? The Version Upgrade Wizard will not upgrade configuration options that are not supported by SQL Server 7.*

8. *True or False? The bcp utility and the BULK INSERT are functionally identical.*

Backing Up
a Database

Disaster recovery, and the preparations for it, are forms of insurance that a simple policy cannot make up for. While an insurance policy may be able to replace your physical equipment that has been damaged, there is no way for it to replace the far more valuable asset—your data. Your data and your system have several forms of protection, each with a different level of effectiveness.

Why Back Up Your Data

No matter how reliable your data hardware and software systems are, they are subject to failures. Disk drives and subsystems are mechanical in nature and at some time will fail. Even nonmechanical hardware components are subject to a variety of problems that can cause them to fail. Software systems are subject to a multitude of problems that can usually be divided into either programmatic errors or user errors. These are some of the reasons that you must provide your system with some form of backup.

Types of Failures

Computer systems fail in many ways. A system can fail due to a mechanical breakdown, power failure, natural disaster, user error, or malicious tampering. There are many more individual types of failures, but most are variations of one of these themes.

Mechanical failures of components other than disk drives are usually an inconvenience and can be easily remedied. Your server may be down until a technician can replace a part, but you will probably not lose any data if a video adapter, or even a motherboard, fails. Short of having a backup server ready to take the primary server's place, there is little to do but replace the failed parts as quickly as possible.

Power failures can be partially alleviated with UPSs, and in mission-critical situations, emergency electric generators. Otherwise, have good protection against the inevitable power surge and spikes that come with the restoration of electrical services, and wait the problem out. Most types of natural disasters fall into the power failure category. Depending upon their severity, your hardware may or may not be lost.

A comprehensive disaster preparedness plan is beyond the scope of this book, but if you want more information read Patrick H. Corrigan's book *LAN Disaster Prevention and Recovery* published by Prentice Hall PTR. For what could easily be a very dry subject, he has written a very readable and complete book on a very important subject.

There are three major categories of failures for which you can prepare. Each entail different recovery issues, and they will be discussed in this chapter.

MCSE 15.1   Client Application Failure

For some reason a client application fails, leaving uncommitted transactions in process. This can happen for a variety of reasons. The user may exit their application improperly, leaving the uncommitted transactions. A network connection may fail between the client workstation and the server, or a power failure may be localized to the client workstation. Whatever the reason, each of these failures has a common thread—a client application has unexpectedly terminated and left transactions that have not been committed or rolled back.

SQL Server uses the system of *checkpoints* and the *recovery* process to ensure that all committed transactions are written to disk and that uncommitted transactions are rolled back. Checkpoints occur under four circumstances:

- When explicitly issued by the database owner.
- As additional cache space is needed by the server.
- When the specified number of transactions has occurred.
- When the specified recovery interval has been exceeded.

When a checkpoint is issued, all dirty pages in the database are written to the disk and a checkpoint marker is then placed in the log. SQL Server then assumes at the next checkpoint that any data prior to the checkpoint marker has already been written to the disk.

When SQL Server is next restarted, the automatic recovery is started. This procedure automatically checks the logs for uncommitted transactions and rolls them back. Recovery also checks for committed transactions that were not written to the data files. These transactions are rolled forward into the data file, completing SQL Server's guarantee that a transaction that has been committed will exist in the data files, even in the event of a failure. By mirroring the transaction logs, you can help to ensure that recovery can take place even if you have a disk failure.

MCSE 15.2   Program Failure

A very similar process occurs in the event of a server program failure. The same things that can affect a client machine can also happen to the server. While the server is often better protected—with a larger battery system, tape devices, and other protections—there will be times when the server fails, leaving the potential for many committed transactions not yet written to disk and uncommitted transactions to litter the transaction logs.

The same automatic recovery process also takes care of this problem. The time to recover may take a little longer than if a single client fails, but the server will recover nonetheless. The only thing that the system administrator will have to do is to notify the users that the server is up and running again, and that they may need to check that all of their last running transactions were properly committed.

MCSE 15.3   Disk or Media Failures

Disks and media—what is meant by these two terms? Media is an all-encompassing term, which, in the computer world, refers to any form of magnetic or optical storage. Disks can mean a floppy disk, a CD-ROM disc, a magneto-optical disk, or most often—a hard-disk drive.

Disk drives, being mechanical in nature, are subject to failure over time. They may develop bad spots that can corrupt data stored there, or they can suffer catastrophic failure—a head crash. Today's hard disk drives are much more reliable than they were just a few years ago, with mean-time-before failure rates ranging into the tens of thousands of hours. If a disk fails, the system administrator will have much work to do to recover. SQL Server cannot automatically recover from this failure. How much work will depend on how much, if any, of the data is recoverable, when the last backup was performed, and whether the disk that failed contained program files, data files, transaction log files, or some combination of all of these. Whenever possible, try to separate data files and transaction logs onto different disks.

Media, often referring to tape, can also fail. A tape can be damaged by the drive mechanism, not being written properly (and so cannot be read), or damaged due to improper storage. Be sure that you test-load your backups from time to time. Loading a backup from a bad tape is doomed to fail. Be sure that you have a good backup before you really need it—testing a backup may not only save your data, but may save your job.

Be sure that you check your backup log files often so that you may be warned in the event of a backup failure. Also, know how your tapes are write-protected. When I was working for a Portland VAR we had a customer who had a disk failure, but he was not too worried as the company had been backing up their data every day since they bought the system—about six years earlier. They purchased a new disk, and one of the technicians installed, formatted, and loaded the operating system. Now it was time to begin loading data from the tapes. The restore operation succeeded, but the customer found out that the database only held transactions for the first week of operations—six years ago! The first person that performed the backups then write-protected each tape; they had never been checked or replaced! The lesson here: Be sure you check your backups.

Key Points

In this chapter a couple of key points have been discussed:

- Having a backup recovery plan provides you with protection from hardware and software failures.
- That failures can occur due to client program or hardware failures by leaving transactions in an uncommitted state.
- That a database may need to be restored because of program failures.
- Backups and backup procedures need to be periodically checked to ensure that they are indeed doing what you believe they are doing.

▲ CHAPTER REVIEW QUESTIONS

▲ Multiple Choice:

1. *Which of the following are included as one of the primary types of system failures? (select all that apply)*

    A. Acts of God

    B. Flood

    C. Client application

    D. Program

2. *What can you use to help alleviate an electrical power failure? (select all that apply)*

    A. UPS

    B. Redundant power supplies

    C. Surge suppressors

    D. Emergency generator

3. *If a client application fails, it often results in: (select all that apply)*

    A. A transaction being committed

    B. A transaction being uncommitted

    C. A transaction being declared in limbo

    D. A transaction being placed in a doubtful state

4. *The checkpoint and recovery process are used by SQL Server to: (select all that apply)*

    A. Roll back all committed transactions

    B. Write committed transactions to the database

    C. Write transaction logs to the mirrored log

    D. Roll back all uncommitted transactions

▲ True or False:

1. *True or False? A natural disaster is something that you should plan for in your Backup and Recovery Plan.*

2. *True or False? A client application failure usually results in transaction being committed that should not have been.*

3. *True or False? A checkpoint is used to write dirty pages to the disk and mark the transaction log.*

Backing Up the Database

There are many different forms of backups that you can take advantage of. In most situations, more than one type of backup is used for a server, and their costs and speeds all vary. The fastest, and most costly in hardware dollar terms, is to have a complete standby or backup server ready to take over for the primary server. A backup server must have SQL Server© running and have complete copies of all databases and system and user accounts. As backups of the log files and databases are created from the primary server, they should be immediately loaded onto the backup server. If the primary server has to be taken offline for an extended period of time, you simply have to bring the backup server online and rename it as the primary. It will then take over as of the last backup of the transaction log files as if nothing had ever happened.

Next in effectiveness is the use of a Redundant Array of Inexpensive Disks (RAID) subsystem. RAID uses several levels—0 through 5—each offering a different level of performance and recovery abilities. The level that you choose to select is based on cost, speed of disk throughput, and recovery needs.

The third level of disaster preparedness is with the use of backups. Backups are made of the transaction log and/or the database to a tape drive, or another disk drive. SQL Server supports local disk-based backups. Again, how often a backup to tape is done depends on your own recovery interval, and the time it takes for the tape drive to create the backup and then restore the backup.

The final level of protection is that of power protection. Many failures of computer hardware, and the resulting loss of data contained on that hardware, stem from the power supplied to the equipment. Be sure that your computer and all peripheral devices are properly protected with both surge/spike suppressers and uninterruptable power supply (UPS)/battery backup. Do not buy the inexpensive surge/spike bars you can buy at your local hardware or department store. These are not adequate for computer protection and should not be used. Expect a four-outlet computer-grade surge suppresser to start at about $50.00. A good UPS for a server should not only give you enough battery time to shut down the server, but should have a serial port and software that will shut an unattended server down in the event of a power failure. A mission-critical database application should also be housed in a server that is built for the job, including hot-swappable, redundant power supplies, and the same for disk drive trays. If you cannot afford to be without your data, you do not want to have to take the server down for maintenance and repairs.

MCSE 16.1 Using Backups

Making regular backups of your database is one of the surest ways to recover in the event of a system failure. It is a relatively cheap form of insurance for your business's data, and the most foolproof way to guarantee that you can restore most, if not all, of the information.

Without a backup it can be nearly impossible to recover information lost through disk failure or data corruption. You would have to go back to the physical files, if any, and reenter all of the data again. Think of how many hours and days it took to enter the information in the first place. And at the same time you are trying to reenter old data, new data is coming in. There is no excuse for not having a good tape backup device for a server. The relatively small cost more than outweighs the potential in irrecoverable business information and people-hours. Of course, the larger the database, the higher capacity tape drive you will need, and the more money you will have to spend for it.

SQL Server assigns backup responsibility to the database owner by default. The database owner, and of course the system administrator, is given the capability to use the backup and restore statements. Depending upon the size of your organization, the number of servers and disks, you may want to assign one or two people to perform backups, granting to them the db_backupoperators permission for each database they will be responsible for. The database owner and system administrator can still perform backups and restore operations.

Forms of Backups

There are three types of backups that are normally performed: the *full* backup, the *differential* backup, the *incremental* backup, and the *transaction log* backup.

- A full backup is a complete copy of all allocated pages in the database, and includes all system tables.
- The differential backup copies only changes made in the database since the last full backup was completed. This ensures that all transactions that would have made changes to the data files have been saved. Unless otherwise specified, when the transaction log is backupped, it is also truncated, making the space available once again.
- The incremental backup copies only those pages that have changed since the last backup.
- The transaction log backup copies the transaction logs, and then truncates the log files.

Note A full backup does not truncate the transaction log. Remember, if the transaction log is not truncated, it will continue to fill up with transactions, and once the transaction log is full all further transactions will be stopped.

While there are three types of backups you can perform, these backups can be accomplished on live data that is being accessed while the backup is working, or on data that is not currently in use.

Backup files are not readable by other applications. Use the RESTORE statement or the RESTORE DATABASE option on the Tools menu when working with any SQL Server backup file. SQL Server uses the Microsoft Tape Format (MTF) formatting when backing up information. This is compatible with other backups that also use MTF. If other backups being performed also use MTF, you can use the same tape media. If your backup software does not use MTF then SQL Server BACKUP will see this as a foreign format and will be unable to write its backup beside it.

OFFLINE, OR STATIC, BACKUPS

An offline backup is the preferred method of backing up. This means that there are no transactions being processed through the database while the backup is being processed. A static backup is most often done by stopping SQL Server and then restarting the server in a single-user mode. The backup is created and then SQL Server is restarted in normal mode. This process ensures that you have a complete backup of all data and system tables and transaction logs as of a single point in time.

Performing this type of backup during the middle of the workday leads to all kinds of problems, both for the system administrator and for the users. Offline backups are best done at a time when the database is not in use, usually in an unattended backup mode.

ONLINE, OR DYNAMIC, BACKUPS

Online, or dynamic, backups are done while live transactions are ongoing through the database. This method, while it does provide you with a backup of all of your data, also has some disadvantages. Users may notice some performance degradation during the backup due to the backup overhead.

When you begin an online backup, some operations are not allowed. If the backup has already started, then a user attempting to start one of these operations will receive a failure message, while if one has been started before the backup, the backup will be aborted. Operations that cannot be run at the same time as a database or transaction log backup include:

- Operations that are nonlogged such as bcp, SELECT INTO, WRITETEXT, and UPDATETEXT. These operations are nonlogged only when the Select Into/Bulkcopy option as been set.
- Creating an index on a table.
- Shrinking a database or file.
- Any file management statements such as ALTER DATABASE when either the ADD FILE or REMOVE FILE options are included.

Statements and operations such as INSERT, DELETE, and UPDATE *can* be run while BACKUP is running.

MCSE 16.2 **Creating Your Backup Strategy**

A complete backup strategy takes into account many factors. How these factors are weighed will be unique to the needs of your own business. Some of these factors include:

- How often should you back up?
- Should you use a static backup or a dynamic backup?
- Should only full backups be done?
- Would you be better served with database and transaction log backups, or with database, differential, and transaction log backups?
- What media will be used, tape or disk?
- Should backups be done manually, or can you use an automatic scheduling program?
- How often should you verify that a backup was properly completed?
- How long should backups be kept before reusing the media?
- Is the storage place for your backups secure from theft? From magnetic disturbances? From fire? Do you have on-site or off-site storage?
- Has someone been assigned to perform backups? Do they have the necessary login and passwords to perform the job?
- Do you have a backup person who has the authorization and know-how to perform backups and restores in the event the primary person is not available?

This is a short list of some of the questions every system administrator or database owner will need to consider when deciding how backups are to be done. These decisions must be made before you actually need a backup to recover from a disk failure. Not all of these questions will be answered here, but use your own answers to them as a guide.

How often a backup should be performed can be answered with the help from the answers to several questions:

- How long can you afford to be without the database and its information? If the database and its data are critical to the day-to-day operation of your business, then backups should be frequent—possibly even several times a day for transaction logs. Historical data that does not change can be backed up once. Making several copies of this backup should ensure that the data could be recovered even if one tape was bad.

- How long do you want a recovery to take? Full backups take less time to recover from than do full backups with differential or transaction log backups, but take longer to create than does a differential backup. Depending on your needs you may decide to do weekly database backups and daily differential backups, hourly transaction log backups.
- How frequently is data in the database updated? If a database is part of a heavily used online transaction processing system, it may require several transaction log backups during the day, with database backups each day. Conversely, a database with infrequent updates may only need to be backupped once a week or once a month.

The type of media to be used for backups is also very important. The fastest form of backup is to a local hard-disk backup device. But this affords you with the least security. Be sure that such backups are immediately copied to a tape device, or at the very least to another disk on a separate machine. Often backups are kept conveniently at hand so that they can be used when necessary—but this is not the safest course. If you keep backup tapes stored near the server, be sure that a copy of the backup is kept in a secure place in a different building, or even better in a secure, fireproof storage facility (bank safety deposit boxes are often used). This ensures that your data is still available to you in the unhappy event of damage to the building that houses your server. Of course, this may not be effective in the case of some form of local disaster, such as hurricanes or earthquakes that may affect the local offsite storage. Depending on your needs and budget, there are offsite storage facilities that specialize in the storage of information and archiving.

Finally, be sure that you test your backup strategy. Does it meet the needs of your business? Is the recovery time acceptable? Are the backups themselves actually working? Test your backup devices, both logical and physical, several times before relying on them, and then test them again periodically.

Creating a Backup Device

Before you can begin to back up any database or transaction log files, you must create the backup devices that will be used. Backup devices can be disk-based files or tape devices. If you want to use a tape device it must first be set up in Windows NT© before SQL Server can use it. It must also be a local tape device, one that is physically attached to the SQL Server computer. SQL Server does not support the use of a networked tape drive, but you can use a networked disk drive as a backup device.

The simplest method of creating a backup device is to do so from within the Enterprise Manager application. Follow these steps to create a backup:

1. Expand the Server Group and then the Server. Click on the Backup Devices folder in the Console Tree pane. If you have any backup devices they will be displayed in the Results pane.
2. Right-click on the Backup Devices folder and select New Backup Device from the shortcut menu to display the Backup Device Properties dialog box.
3. Type `pubsdb` in the Name text box. This will be the name of the backup file used on a disk-based backup device.

   This is optional if you are using a tape device for your backup. If you do have a tape drive(s) attached to this computer, the tape drive option button will be selected and the name of the first tape drive listed in the combo box. If you have more than one tape drive, you will be able to see them listed in the drop-down list.

4. Click the File Name option button. The name of the default folder \MSSQL7\BACKUP\ is listed. In Figure 16-1 notice how the name you entered is in step 3 above.

   If you have a different location, or drive, where you want to place your backups, then either type it into the text box, or click the ... button and select it from the dialog box that will be displayed. If your backup device will be a networked disk drive, then you must enter the fully qualified universal naming convention (UNC) name into the text box. A device name under the UNC convention is always in the form `\\SERVERNAME\sharename \folder\filename`. You can also use a mapped drive letter, if this is available.

5. Click the OK button to save your new backup device. You will have to click the OK button in the information dialog box telling you that you have successfully created the device. It will now be listed in the Results pane of the Console window.

Figure 16–1 *With the Backup Device Properties dialog box you can create a new disk-based backup device or select a tape device.*

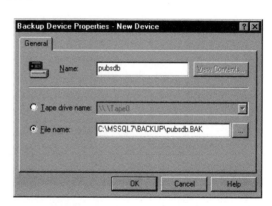

Performing a Backup

When you are ready to create your first backup you will generally do a complete database backup. A database backup is a picture of the state of the database as of the completion time of the backup. Conversely, when you do a transaction log backup it records all transactions that were written as of the starting time of the log backup. Any transaction that is logged after the log backup begins will not be included.

Like most SQL Server operations, you can create and execute a backup by using the T-SQL statements BACKUP DATABASE, or BACKUP TRANSACTIONS, or even easier by using the Enterprise Manager. The syntax for the BACKUP T-SQL statement is:

```
BACKUP DATABASE
    databasename|file-or-filegroup
TO
    backupdevicename
```

The BACKUP TRANSACTIONS statement works the same way. There are a number of additional optional parameters that you can include. You must create the backup device before it can be used. You can use the backup statement whenever necessary to create a backup or SQL Server can schedule the backup to run at a convenient time. From SQL Server Enterprise Manager you can backup selected databases, or tables within the database, like this:

1. Open the Enterprise Manager and select the server containing the database that you want to back up. Now select Tools, Backup Database from the menu and display the SQL Server Backup dialog box, as seen in Figure 16-2.
2. Select the database you want to back up from the Database combo box. For this example, choose the pubs database.
3. SQL Server enters a name automatically into the Name text box; you can change this by simply typing over it. An entry into the Description text box is optional.
4. Click the Database - Complete option button.
   - Database - Complete: This option allows you to back up the entire database selected in the above combo box.
   - Database - Differential: This option creates a differential backup of the selected database.
   - Transaction Log: This option allows you to back up the transaction log only.

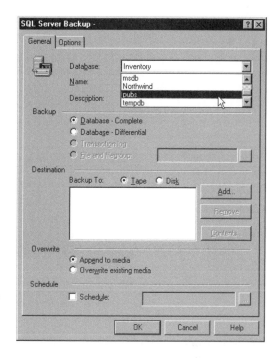

Figure 16–2 *Use the SQL Server Backup dialog box to control what databases will be backed up, what backup devices will be used, and other backup options.*

- File and filegroup: This option is used to back up a specific database operating system file or a database file group.

5. Choose the destination for the backup. Click the Disk option button to create the backup on a disk-based device, then click the Add button. In the Choose Backup Destination dialog box, as shown in Figure 16-3, click the Backup device option button, and then be sure that the device created earlier in this chapter, pubsdb, is selected in the combo box. Click the OK button when done.

If you have not yet created a backup device, you can do so here by selecting <New Backup Device> in the combo box. This will bring you to the Backup Device dialog box used to create a new backup device.

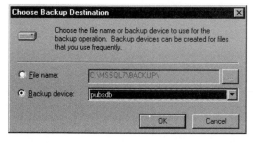

Figure 16–3 *With the Choose Backup Destination dialog box, you can select where a backup will be copied to, or create a new backup device.*

6. In the Overwrite section you have two option buttons available. Select the one that is appropriate to your situation.
   - Append to media: This option allows you to add information to an existing backup. For example, when using a disk-based device such as you have already selected, Backup will add the new data to the end of the file.
   - Overwrite existing media: This option allows Backup to write over any data already existing on the backup device. Use this option only if you know that you will not need the data that has been previously saved.

7. If you plan to schedule this backup to occur at another time, or at regularly scheduled times, check the Schedule check box.

   The default schedule for a backup is once a week on Sunday at 12:00AM. This may be fine if a complete database backup, provided additional transaction log, or differential backups are scheduled during the intervening days.

   8. To change the default schedule, click the ... button. As seeNin Figure 16-4, the Edit Schedule dialog box is displayed.

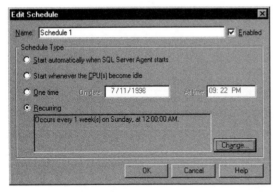

Figure 16–4 *With the Edit Schedule dialog box you can choose most of the options on how a backup will be scheduled to run.*

9. There are several option buttons available for basic scheduling features. You can choose to:
   - Start automatically when SQL Server Agent starts: This allows you to launch the backup the next time that the SQL Server Agent is started. This option may not work well for scheduling backups.
   - Start whenever the CPU(s) become idle: This option does not really apply to the scheduling of a backup.
   - One time: This option allows you to schedule the backup for a specific date and time. You must enter the date in the On date text box and the time in the At time text box.

- Recurring: This option would be the most commonly used selection for the scheduling of backup jobs.

To adjust the scheduling of a recurring backup, click the Change button. This will open the Edit Recurring Job Schedule dialog box as shown in Figure 16-5. Make the changes that are appropriate for your own scheduled backup. You may have several different backup jobs scheduled, a database backup, a differential backup, and transaction log backups.

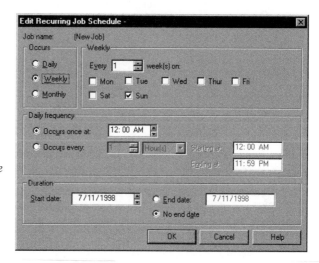

Figure 16–5 *The Edit Recurring Job Schedule dialog box is used to customize any job whose schedule is of a recurring nature. You have many options to select from.*

10. Click the OK button to return to the SQL Server Backup dialog box, then click the Options tab. As you can see in Figure 16-6, this tab allows you to set options that can be used during the creation of a backup.

- Verify backup upon completion: When checked, SQL Server will read and verify the entire backup for errors.
- Eject tape after backup: When a tape drive is used, the tape will be ejected on completion of the backup. This may help to ensure that the tape is not written over.
- Check media set name and backup set expiration: When checked, both the media set name and backup expiration date are checked before the backup begins. If a media set name has been placed on a backup device, then subsequent backups must be members of the media family and use the same media name. The expiration date check ensures that a backup will not be overwritten before its expiration date.
- Media set name: Enter the name for the media set in the text box.

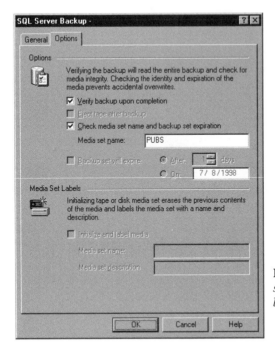

Figure 16–6 *The Options tab allows you to set various options about the behavior of a backup.*

- Backup set will expire: If checked, then you must also choose either the After option box and enter the number of days till the backup expires, or the On option button and enter the date that the backup will expire. A backup cannot be overwritten before its expiration date, with some exceptions.

- Initialize and label media: When checked, the media will be initialized (erased) and a new media set name entered onto the media. You must enter a name into the Media set name text box. The Media set description text box allows you to enter an optional description of the media set.

11. Click the OK button to begin the backup, or to execute the schedule. If you have not set a scheduled time for the backup, it will begin to run immediately.

SQL Server allows you to create a backup across multiple tape devices, though all of the tape drives must be attached to the computer where SQL Server is installed. For example, if you have a very large database that will take six hours to back up on a single tape drive, and if you have three of these drives attached to the computer, the backup could be accomplished in only two hours. When you restore this backup, you do not have to use three drives again during the restore operation. When you use multiple tape drives for a database backup, you cannot use these tapes for the backup of other information.

Heavy Duty Protection—Mirrors and RAID

This section describes additional types of disk devices, both hardware and software, that you can use to give an added dimension of protection to your data. Up to now, it has been assumed that your data and all SQL Server's devices have resided on a single disk drive. This is often true for a stand-alone PC, a small server, or a database in a developmental environment.

In a true production environment, having a single disk drive for all of your database functions is usually not seen, not to mention foolhardy. Often a single-disk system is too slow in a multiple user environment, and too dangerous, with the potential of losing the one drive to a failure.

There are several forms of additional security and protection that you can incorporate into your system, including:

- Software-disk mirroring
- Hardware-disk mirroring
- Duplexed controllers
- RAID (levels 0 through 5)

Windows NT has the ability to manage software-based disk mirroring, disk striping, and striping with parity. Within Windows NT, duplexing and mirroring are often used to mean the same thing. Generally, the difference is that duplexing refers to having two different disk controllers—one controlling the primary disks and the other controlling the mirrored disks. This ensures that a failure of one controller will not bring your server down. You can also use duplexed controllers to share I/O load between them.

Mirroring, on the other hand, refers to the technique of keeping an entire duplicate of a partition on a separate disk. As an update is performed, it is immediately copied to the mirror. You can think of mirroring as a form of continuous backup. It is highly recommended that you mirror at least your transaction logs and the master database. This can help to ensure a quick recovery time. Windows NT based mirroring implements RAID level 1.

For mirroring to work you need a minimum of two disk drives. The mirror drive should be of a size equal to or larger than the primary drive. Normally, it will be equal in size. With Windows NT mirroring, you must create partitions that are equal size. Be careful when selecting a drive to act as the mirror. Windows NT allows you to use any partition that is available for the mirror. Remember, a single disk can be partitioned into several drive-letter designations. You would not want to place the mirror on a partition located on the same physical drive. The mirror should be on a different physical drive or you lose the entire reason for having a mirrored drive or partition.

For complete details on setting up and using Windows NT mirroring, be sure to read the appropriate sections in Prentice Hall's *Core MCSE Certification Guide*, another book in this series.

RAID and Disk Arrays

RAID has been around for many years now. RAID can be either hardware or software-based. Windows NT implements a software-based RAID through the operating system. This is an effective and relatively inexpensive method of protecting your data investment. It does come at a cost of an additional overhead burden for the operating system. It is also not officially supported by the wide variety of RAID hardware solutions available. Again, read the chapters on Windows NT RAID in Prentice Hall's *Core MCSE Certification Guide* for complete details on this subject.

RAID generally comes in six levels, though there are some additional RAID levels being published by some vendors. For SQL Server, typically RAID levels 0, 1, or 5 are used.

- RAID level 0 is simple data striping. This is the highest performance RAID level because as data is written, it is written in a stripe across all of the disks in the group. Its primary drawback is that if one disk fails, then all of the information it contained is unavailable until the disk is replaced and the database restored.
- RAID level 1 is disk mirroring. This gives you the highest level of protection because all of the information on one disk is mirrored on the other. You can get good performance on read I/O, but unless you duplex your controllers, your write I/O will suffer because all of the data has to be written twice.
- RAID level 5 gives you the highest level of recoverability, but does suffer from some in throughput. This type of RAID is usually implemented on a group of five disks, four data disks and one parity disk. If any one of the five disks fails, simply replace it and the other four and the RAID software will quickly rebuild the fifth disk.

RAID devices and subsystems are the best protection you can have for your databases. But they come at a cost. RAID systems are not just expensive, they can be fantastically expensive. A good RAID system is a series of hot-swappable, redundant SCSI disk drives with duplexed controllers, and hot-swappable, redundant power supplies. This ensures that if a power supply fails, another takes over and you simply have to pull out the defective unit and replace it. The RAID box may or may not be an external unit to the rest of your server. It is a great piece of technology, and if you cannot afford to have a database go down, this is what you need.

Using Removable Media

A last method of protecting your data is to use removable media. There are many forms of removable media that you can use, and not all require the very expensive drives and media that were required just a few years ago. Some of these include:

- CD-ROM
- WORM (Write Once, Read Many) optical drives
- Rewritable, or phase-change disks
- Magnetic disks

There are now several relatively inexpensive CD-ROM recorders available on the market. Several manufacturers make popular removable magnetic disks in the 1GB and larger size. WORM and rewritable disks and drives still tend to be on the expensive side, but do provide excellent long-term archive storage.

There are several reasons that you may want to create a database and then place it on some form of removable media. A database could be marketed this way as a complete product, such as a phone listing. It can be used for long-term archiving of corporate information. A removable media database can be created for both read-only media, such as CD-ROM, or rewritable media.

There are four stored procedures that are used with databases created for use on removable media. Two are used when creating and later on, certifying a database for use with removable media. They are:

- `sp_create_removable`
- `sp_certify_removable`
- `sp_detach`
- `sp_attach_db`

The stored procedure `sp_create_removable` creates three or more files and places the necessary parts on each. This stored procedure should be run before any database development is done. The system tables are placed on one file, the transaction logs on another, while the data files are each placed in a file. Once this stored procedure is run, complete the normal development of the database, being sure to keep all of the database objects on these files. The minimum size of each file in a removable media file set is 1MB, which allows it to fit on a set of floppy disks. You can have between 1 and 16 data files, allowing you to create a removable file group with a maximum size of 16MB.

The stored procedure `sp_certify_removable` verifies that the database has been properly configured for distribution on removable media. If any errors or problems are found, they are reported and you must correct the problems before the database can be removed. Only a member of the sysadmin server role has permission to execute this stored procedure. The system administrator must be the owner of this database and all objects on it. This is because SQL Server knows that the system administrator is a known user on any server running SQL Server and they can be assured of existing on the new server.

The stored procedure `sp_detach_db` is used to detach the database from the server. Again, only a member of the sysadmin server role can execute this stored procedure.

Finally, the stored procedure `sp_attach_db` is used to attach the removable media database to the new server. This must be done before the new server can use the database. This procedure can be executed by any user who has been granted `CREATE DATABASE` permission.

MCSE 16.3   SQL Server Failover Support

Microsoft Failover Support for SQL Server is used when you require a very high degree of a server and data availability. This is not an inexpensive proposition, in terms of hardware, software, and time, but for mission-critical applications, it may be necessary.

Failover support requires the following:

- At least two physical servers. These servers must be running Windows NT Enterprise Edition, and Microsoft Cluster Server (MSCS) on their local drives.
- There must be at least one shared drive between the clustered servers. This is usually an external RAID storage device. Both nodes of the failover system must be connected to this device.
- A copy of SQL Server for each shared drive.
- A network connection linking all of the clustered servers. This is used by the MSCS software to ensure that all of the members of the cluster are in service and ready.

- The creation of one or more SQL Server virtual servers. A virtual server is what a client will attach to in order to work with the SQL Server database. The client will not be concerned with the physical server that they are connected with.

Once all of these resources have been placed in service, the client will not necessarily know which physical server they are interacting with, nor does it matter. If the current primary server fails, one of the seconday servers will automatically pickup. If a failover occurs, the clients will be required to reconnect to the virtual server. Any transactions that were in processes at the time of the failure will be rolled back and will need to be resubmitted.

SQL Server Failover comes in two configurations: Active/Passive and Active/Active.

Active/Passive: This configuration uses a single SQL Server virtual server, and copy of SQL Server on all of the shared drives, and two physical NT Servers. One of these servers is designated as the primary server and has control over the copy of SQL Server. The secondary server does not have any control until the primary either fails, or an administrator shifts control to the secondary server.

Active/Active: This configuration uses two SQL Server virtual servers, two or more copies of SQL Server on the shared drives, and two physical Windows NT Servers. The virtual servers are set up so that they are the reverse of the other. This means that virtual server 1 uses physical server A as its primary and physical server B as its secondary. Virtual server 2 uses physical server B as its primary and physical server A as its seondary.

When you set up SQL Server clustering, you must be sure that you have the appropriate network protocols running and available. SQL Server failover only is supported on the Named Pipes or TCP/IP protocols. The initial set up requires the use of Named Pipes, but support can be withdrawn once the installation is complete.

Installation of SQL Server clustering requires hardware that is on the MSCS-compatibility hardware list. The most current version of this list can be found on the Microsoft web site at: http://www.microsoft.com/ntserver/showcase. You must also supply the following configuration parameters during the installation:

The SQL Server virtual server name. In the Active/Active installation, you will need two server names.

A unique IP address for each virtual server.

The necessary subnet mask.

The drive letter designation on which SQL Server will be installed.

While you can use any hardware on the compatibility list, you should make sure that hardware that is not identical will work together before you purchase it. You also cannot combine Alpha and Intel processor nodes in the same cluster.

Key Points

There have been several key points made in this chapter:
- Backups are a relatively inexpensive form of insurance that a system administrator cannot do without.
- There are three types of backups: Database backup copies all of the information in the data files; the differential backup copies all information in the data files that have changed since the last database backup; and transaction log file backups.
- SQL Server allow the backing up of live data, with a few exceptions.
- A backup strategy should be created, maintained, and tested. If any problems are found, revise the strategy.
- Backup devices can be tape drives, disk files, and networked disk files.
- Software- and hardware-based mirror and RAID solutions can help to ensure the safety of your data.
- Databases can be created for use with removable media.
- Determine the requirements for using SQL Server failover support using Microsoft Cluster Server.

▲ CHAPTER REVIEW QUESTIONS

▲ Multiple Choice:

1. *Who can perform a database backup or restore operation? (select all that apply)*

   A. A member of the sysadmin role.

   B. A member of the db_backupoperators role.

   C. A member of the db_securityadmin role

   D. A member of the public role

2. *What function does a full backup not do? (select all that apply)*

   A. Copies the system tables in the database

   B. Copies the transaction logs

      C. Truncates the transaction logs

      D. Recovers the database

3. *Which of these backup devices are set up when you install SQL Server? (select all that apply)*

      A. Tape device

      B. Disk device

      C. Floppy device

      D. RAID device

      E. All of the above

      F. None

4. *Which of these backup devices are supported by SQL Server? (select all that apply)*

      A. A networked disk drive

      B. A local disk drive

      C. A networked tape drive

      D. A local tape drive

5. *A RAID system is best implemented on a server with how many disk drives?*

      A. Two

      B. Three

      C. Five

      D. Any number

      E. It depends on the RAID level used.

6. *Under what operating system can you install SQL Server failover support? (select all that apply)*

      A. Windows NT Server

      B. SQL Server 7

      C. Microsoft Cluster Server

      D. Windows NT Server Enterprise Edition

      E. Windows 95/98

▲ True or False:

1. *True or False? For most SQL Server production databases, an adequate level of protection against database failure can be gained through the use of a good UPS.*

2. *True or False? For most small businesses, designating the system administrator to be the sole backup operator is good protection.*

3. *True or False? SQL Server can make use of any tape drive supported by Windows NT.*

4. *True or False? Backups can be scheduled as a job through the SQL Server Agent.*

5. *True or False? Backups can be made on multiple tape drives.*

6. *True or False? You must have two physical servers, and one virtual server when installing Active/Active failover support.*

7. *True or False? When selecting servers for an SQL Server failover cluster, you cannot combine processor architechtures.*

8. *True or False? A full backup/transaction log plan and a full backup/incremental backup are functionally the same.*

9. *True or False? An incremental backup copies only data that has changed since the last transaction log backup.*

10. *True or False? A filegroup backup is the same as a database backup.*

Restoring Databases

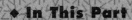
In this module, you will learn how SQL Server restores a database from a backup. This is a process that you should become very familiar with—it is inevitable that when you actually have to restore a database, there will be someone who is very unhappy with the speed of the process. You do not want to be walking yourself through the manuals.

Restoring the Database

Restoring, also sometimes referred to as loading, is the process you will take when a disk fails or a database becomes corrupt and you must restore it from a backup. This process involves determining which databases must be restored, which backups are to be used, and whether they are full backups, or differential backups; include transaction log backups as well.

MCSE 17.1   Restoring a Database

When the RESTORE command is executing, no one, including the individual who executed the command, can use the database until the restore operation is complete. Loading a database can take considerably more time than the original backup did. The reason for this is that a backup only copies those pages that have been written to. Conversely, the restore operation must read and write all of these same pages, but then initializes all of the unused pages that belong in the database. While a backup may only take several minutes to a few hours, the subsequent load of the same information can take several hours to a few days, depending on the volume of information. Unlike earlier versions of SQL Server©, you can now restart an interrupted RESTORE operation, and not have to start from the beginning—provided operation is from a removable media such as tape.

Restoring a Damaged Database

There are two different basic events that will require you to restore a backup of a database: media failure and simple data corruption. The first event, that of a system failure, will require you to restore one or more databases. The second event, that of data corruption, may be able to be taken care of by simply restoring your last backup and any subsequent transaction log, or differential backups.

When a database has been damaged and is no longer available, you may need to drop it before if can be restored. Dropping or deleting a database can be done from within the Enterprise Manager by right-clicking the database and selecting Delete from the shortcut menu. You can also do the same thing from Query Analyzer using the DROP DATABASE T-SQL statement. If a database must be deleted, you must then create the database and restore it before it can be used again.

Once the damaged database has been deleted, you can proceed with the restore process for your database and its data. This requires restoring the last full database backup and, of course, all subsequent differential or transaction log backups since the last database backup. From the Restore Database dialog box, you can choose not only what you want to restore but also where to restore. Follow these next steps to restore a database:

1. Select Tools, Restore Database from the menu and display the Restore Database dialog box. From here you can choose the database to be restored and the backup that will be used. Figure 17-1 shows the Restore Database dialog box.

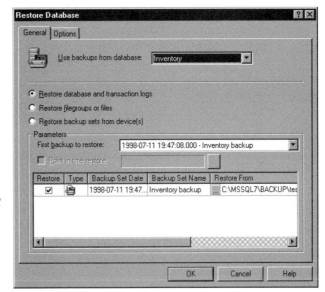

Figure 17–1 *Use the Restore Database dialog box to select the database to be restored, the backup set that will be used for the restore operation, and any other options that may be necessary for the process.*

2. Select pubs from the Use backups from database combo box.
3. Click the first option button in the next group. Depending on the option you choose, the selections in the Parameters group will vary. You have three options for the type of restore that you will now perform:

   • Restore database and transaction logs: This is the option you would normally select if you were restoring the entire database. The database will be rebuilt and the server will recognize it again. With this option selected, you also have the option to restore a database to a specific point in time by checking that box in Parameters.

   • Restore filegroups or files: This option allows you to restore a single file or a file group if you find that only that part of a database is corrupt or has been lost. You will choose a subset of the file group or the entire file group.

   • Restore backup sets from device(s): You can choose multiple backup devices for the restore operation, the type of backup set, the backup set number, and a specific backup set.

4. In the Parameters group, select the backup set to be used for the restore. If you have only one backup set, it will be selected by default.

   If you have created differential backups and/or transaction log backups, you will have the option to restore to a specific point in time by checking the Point in time restore checkbox and then entering the specific date/time in the text box.

5. Click the Options tab to choose additional settings. The options tab has several settings that you can use during the restore operation. Some of the options will not be available, depending on your selections on the General tab. Click the Force restore over existing database.

- Eject tapes after restoring each backup: This option will force a tape to be ejected upon completion of the restore operation.
- Prompt before restoring each backup: This option will display a dialog box asking you to confirm that you do indeed want a backup to be restored.
- Force restore over existing database: Use this option to force the restoration of an existing database. You must use this option if you are attempting to restore a database that currently exists. SQL Server has this option turned off by default so that you cannot accidentally overwrite a database.
- Restore as database: This option allows you to restore the database files into another database. You must select the database in the combo box beside this checkbox.
- Restore database files as: Allows you to change the physical folder and file name of the newly restored database.
- Leave database operational. No additional transaction logs can be restored: This is the same as the RECOVERY option when using the RESTORE T-SQL statement. Using this option places the database online once restore is complete and you will not be able to restore any additional differential or transaction log backups.
- Leave database nonoperational but able to restore additional transaction logs: This is similar to the NORECOVERY option. You must restore the database backup and then the differential or transaction log backups. Recovery of the database will not be performed until the last backup has been applied. The database will not be usable until this has been done.
- Leave database read-only and able to restore additional transaction logs: This option is like the STANDBY option. You can create an UNDO file so that the recovery can be undone before the database is brought online. This is useful if a transaction may have corrupted the database and you are not sure where or when the actual transaction was committed.

Figure 17-2 shows the completed Options tab in the Restore Database dialog box. You will notice that the Leave database operational option button has been checked. This is because there are not additional differential or transaction logs for this backup set.

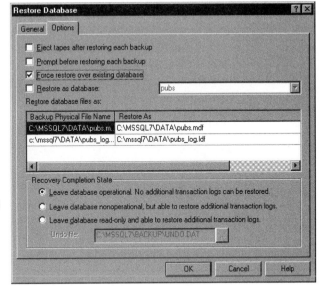

Figure 17–2 *Use the Options tab on the Restore Database dialog box to choose the necessary settings for the restore operation that you are performing.*

6. Once you have selected the necessary options for the restore operation, click the OK button to start the restoration. If you see any error dialog boxes displayed, you must make any necessary corrections and rerun restore. If no problems were encountered, then you will see a dialog box telling you that the restoration process was successful.

Restoring Transaction Logs and Differential Backups

Once you have restored a database, you can then restore all of the subsequent transaction logs. When you do restore transaction log backups, you must restore them one by one, in the order that they were backed up. If you are using differential backups, you only have to restore the last one in the series. After you have loaded the last transaction log backup, your database will be fully recovered as of the time of the last transaction backup. This is as close to live as you can get. If you have mirrored transaction log files, you may be able to recover the rest of the transactions that have been entered. You must be careful though—if one of the last transactions written caused the problem that crashed your database, then that transaction will exist as an exact duplicate on the mirrored log file.

A feature that was new starting with SQL Server 6.5 is its ability to restore a transaction log up to a specific date and time. Any transaction committed after the specified date and time will be rolled back. This option is only available when restoring transaction logs along with the database

> You cannot exclude a specific transaction during a restore or recovery. You can restore the database up to a specific point of time, but you cannot skip a transaction. This would possibly compromise the integrity of the data and is not permitted.

backup. A point in time recovery can be performed either from the Enterprise Manager Restore Database dialog box, or by using the RESTORE statement with the STOPAT option.

The point-in-time recovery option can be very helpful when you are recovering a database that may have become corrupted. For example, during the afternoon you begin to get calls from users complaining that they are getting inconsistent data from the server, and that the problem began sometime after the noon hour. Of course, since the noon hour you have had several client users continue to update data, and so you do not know exactly when the problem did begin, nor which transaction actually caused the problem. You can immediately back up the transaction log for the day's transactions, then restore the database and the transaction logs up to a point in time such as 11:00A.M. Since your users complained that the problems appeared after 12:00P.M., you can be fairly certain that your recovery will not include the transaction that caused the problem. If it does, then redo the recovery for an earlier time. Remember, you must recover the database first, and then each of the transaction logs created subsequent to the full backup used to restore the database.

MCSE 17.2   Recovering the Master Database

The recovery of the master database is a slightly different process from the procedure you use on a user database. This fact cannot be emphasized enough: When you make changes to a user database that also makes changes to the system tables in the master database, back up the master database. This is the only way that you can be reasonably assured that all of the databases, tables, and users of your database system can be recovered in the event of a failure involving the master database. The most commonly performed actions that make changes to the master database are:

- Creating, expanding, or shrinking a user database.
- Adding or dropping backup devices.
- Adding or dropping users and logins.

- Changes in server or database configuration options.
- Adding and dropping servers.

You may first notice that the master database has been damaged by an inability to start SQL Server, finding that user databases are no longer available or user logins have disappeared. The master database must be recovered from its last backup. Any alterations made after this backup must be manually reapplied. This may include adding new users and their security setups and recreating databases built after this backup. Any database created after the last backup of the master database may be able to be reattached with sp_attach_db. If this does not work, then you will need to restore the database from its last backup.

Recreating the master database can be broken down into four primary steps: Rebuild the master database using the REBUILD MASTER command-line utility; recreate a backup device; restore the latest backup of the master database; and finally, restore the msdb and model databases. Follow these steps:

1. Use NT Explorer and find the rebuildm utility that should be located in the \mssql7\binn folder. This will open the SQL Server Rebuild Master utility dialog box. Insert the SQL Server 7 CD into the drive. If the Source Directory is blank, click the Browse button to find the drive containing the installation CD.

Note The REBUILD MASTER utility will rebuild not only the master database, but also both the msdb and model databases. You will probably need to restore both of these databases from a current backup once the master database has been recovered.

2. If you selected anything other than the default settings for Character Set, Sort Order, and Unicode Collation, then click the Settings button and make the necessary selections in the dialog box that is displayed for this. When you have made the necessary selections, clicking the OK button will return you to Rebuild Master dialog box. It is very important that you select the same options that you selected when originally installing SQL Server. Figure 17-3 shows the Rebuild Master dialog box ready to begin the rebuild process.
3. Click the Rebuild button if you are ready to continue. You will not be given another chance to back out of this utility once you click the Rebuild button.

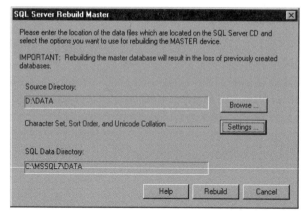

Figure 17–3 *Complete all of the necessary information for the Rebuild Master dialog box.*

The Rebuild button will not become available until after you click the Settings button and check the Character Set, Sort Order, and Unicode Collation settings. When you return to the Rebuild Master dialog box, and the other required information has been set, the button will become available.

When the process of rebuilding your databases has been completed, you will see a dialog box telling you that the rebuild was successful. If there was a problem, then the dialog box will tell you to check the error logs and try again. If you do have problems and are not able to rebuild the master database, you will have to uninstall SQL Server and then reinstall the entire program.

Again, be sure to back up the master database whenever you make any changes to your databases that are reflected in the master database. You may save yourself a tremendous amount of work trying to reconstruct it by hand.

Key Points

In this chapter you learned several key points on how to restore a database, including:

- How to restore a user database from both a tape backup and a disk-based backup.
- How to drop a defective database before restoring it from the backup.

- How to use transaction log and differential backups to restore the database.
- How to recover the master database with the Rebuild Master utility.

▲ CHAPTER REVIEW QUESTIONS

▲ Multiple Choice:

1. *A damaged database that is no longer available may need to be: (select all that apply)*

   A. Restored only

   B. Dropped before being restored

   C. Have its availability option changed

   D. Stopped and restarted

2. *The master database should be backed up so that you can fully recover it when you: (select all that apply)*

   A. Expand a user database

   B. Update data in a database

   C. Add a new user to a database

   D. Change the server configuration

3. *You can restore a database to a specific point in time when you: (select all that apply)*

   A. Use full backups of the database

   B. Do not truncate the transaction logs

   C. Use differential backups

   D. Have current transaction log backups

▲ True or False:

1. *True or False? A database can be restored to a selected point in time.*

2. *True or False? When restoring a database the transaction logs are restored first, newest to oldest.*

3. *True or False? When restoring the transaction logs, you can exclude specific transactions that may have caused the data corruption.*

Monitoring SQL Server Performance

In this next module, the subject of monitoring the performance of SQL Server and ways that can be used to improve and tweak your setup will be discussed. Performance statistics are available through the SQL Server Performance Monitor, and can be viewed real-time on a graph, or viewed later from a file. Use these statistics to find out where bottle necks occur in your database throughput, and hints on what you can do to improve the performance of your database.

Optimizing Performance

When tuning your database and application for optimal performance there are several factors that you can examine. Some of these factors are best looked at during the design phase, not after implementation. They are:

- The design of your database and application
- Query optimization
- Reducing network traffic
- Decreasing disk I/O

For performance tuning, you need to understand not only what you can do to increase performance, but the consequences of each of the actions you may decide to do. Too often, also, performance tuning involves trade-offs—what is good for one part of the database may decrease the throughput on another part.

419

MCSE 18.1 Optimizing Queries

One of the key areas to concentrate on when working on the performance tuning of SQL Server© is that your queries are properly optimized. If you have a query, or several queries, that return the data requested but do so without using the benefits of good optimization, your applications will be slower than they should be. Some of the greatest benefits when tuning SQL Server's performance are realized in:

- Building a database with a logical design.
- Creating tables designed for the specific information they are to contain, and including no extraneous data.
- Adding indexes that can be used by a query.
- Designing queries that use available indexes and return limited results sets.
- Removing indexes that slow down updates.
- Limiting the number of columns used in a query to only those that provide the required information.

Always be sure that a query makes use of an efficient index. An index is considered efficient if:

- The data in the column(s) is unique or contains relatively few values.
- The queries can use the data contained in the index column.

When a query is executed by SQL Server, the query optimizer estimates the costs involved for the various methods of execution. The query optimizer may decide that a simple table scan is the best method because an index is not available or is not part of the query. A table scan requires SQL Server to scan every row in the table, beginning with the first row, checking each against the query criteria. If a row meets the criteria, it is returned. When an index is available and the query optimizer decides that using it will involve the least cost, then the index is scanned, returning only those rows that are part of the index. Compound indexes are most useful if they are limited in the number of columns included as part of the index. Queries that scan an entire table and then return most if not all of the rows to the user are an inefficient use of network bandwidth and SQL Server's own abilities. Create queries that make use of indexes in the WHERE clause, so that only the required information is returned, versus constructing queries that return a very large data set to the client requiring additional browsing.

When building a query on a table that contains a composite index, be sure to use the first column of this index as a part of the WHERE clause for the query. If instead you build the query so that only the second or subsequent columns of the composite index are used in the WHERE clause, ignoring the first column, the optimizer will not be able to use the index. Remember that a composite index is a single index composed of several columns, not just selected columns.

Cost-based Optimization

SQL Server uses a cost-based optimizer to determine the best method of accessing information for the client application. The optimizer has been greatly improved with this version of SQL Server. The optimizer determines the best method of joining tables, and which indexes will be used. The query optimizer looks at all possible paths and chooses the one that results in the least cost. Cost is most simply put as time. The optimizer will choose the path that will require the least pages to be read, the smallest amount of I/O, and the fewest of all resources. Once it has weighed all of these factors, the plan that costs the least will be used.

There is an option that you can exercise known as the query governor cost limit option. This option has a default setting of 0 (zero), which is the same as off. If you set this to any nonnegative, nonzero value, the query governor will not permit a query plan that will take longer than the specified value to run. The value is set in seconds. This value is an advanced option under the sp_configure statement. Changes made will not take effect until you stop and restart SQL Server. Use the SET QUERY_GOVERNOR_COST_LIMIT *somevalue* statement when you construct a query if you want to ensure that a query will not run longer then the specified number of seconds.

You may wonder how the optimizer can make such decisions based on so little information. The answer is through the use of statistical information kept on each table. These statistics provide the optimizer with data on how information in the table is distributed and how its indexes are used. These statistics must be updated periodically or eventually the optimizer will be making decisions based on outdated information.

SQL Server automatically updates the statistics maintained on the tables and indexes contained in each of your databases. As data is updated and rows are added or deleted, the index statistics will be updated too. The index statistics are updated using sampling techniques, and the frequency for these updates is determined by the amount of information contained in the index and the volume of change in that data. For example, a table containing 1000 rows that has 100 rows of new data added probably will update its statistics. On the other hand, a table containing 100,000 rows that has 100 rows of new information added will probably not update the index statistics because the newly added rows are not a significant number. You can customize how often and under what circumstances statistics will be updated.

You can also update these statistics manually: This may be a very good idea after truncating and repopulating a table, bulk loading of data into a table, or a heavy period of adding and updating data contained in the table.

GATHERING STATISTICS

Statistics can be viewed for any index by running the DBCC SHOW_STATISTICS statement. DBCC is SQL Server's "DataBase Consistency Checker." Periodically checking the statistics for all or a sample of often used indexes and tables, can help you to determine if adequate statistics are being kept for your database. The DBCC SHOW_STATISTICS is used like this with the indicated parameters:

```
DBCC SHOW_STATISTICS (table_name, index_name/column_name)
```

You must specify both the name of the table where the index exists and either the name of the index or the name of the column. For example, to view the statistics for the primary key index on the Orders table in the Northwind database, follow these steps:

1. Open the Query Analyzer and select Northwind in the Database combo box, and then type:

```
DBCC SHOW_STATISTICS (Orders, PK_Orders)
```

2. Click the Execute button. The results will appear in the Results window, as shown in Figure 18-1.

As you can see in the result window, all of the statistical information contained on the distribution page for the selected index and table are displayed. The first piece of information you should notice is the date that the statistics were last updated. This will give you an indication of how good the statistics are. This example shows the statistics for a primary key index. The next values are the number of rows in the table, the number of rows sampled, and the number of distribution steps used in the index. The Density value is the key. The lower the number, the higher is selectivity and the more likely it will be used during a query. If a query were run on the Orders table, and the WHERE clause specifying that a certain OrderID value, or range of values, was to be displayed, then it would be very likely that the query optimizer would use the index.

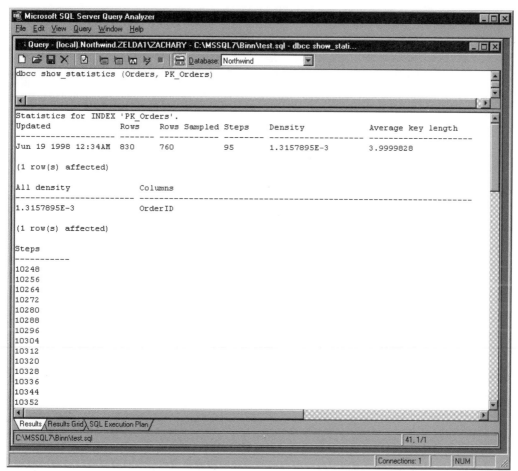

Figure 18–1   *From the Manage Indexes dialog box you can find the name of any index.*

Looking at a nonunique index, you will see a very different density statistic. Figure 18-2 shows the statistics for the CustomerID index on the Orders table in the Northwind database. Notice how much higher the density figure is than that for the primary key index shown in Figure 18-1. The *All density* statistics values display more accurate statistics of the selectivity for each column or group of columns.

The distribution pages where these statistics are kept are created when SQL Server builds the statistics for your tables. The statistics pages will be updated when you run the UPDATE STATISTICS statement. Each distribution page contains all of the statistical information for a single index.

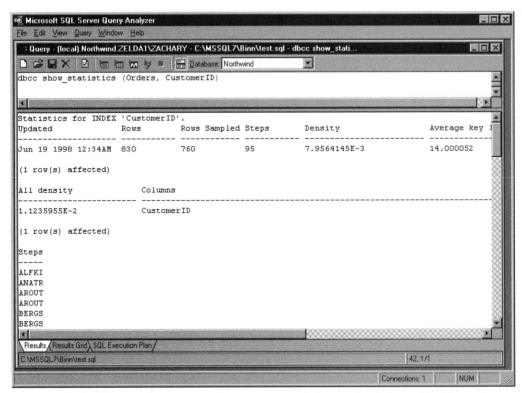

Figure 18–2 *This set of statistics is for a nonunique index on the Orders table. Notice the greater Density figure.*

UPDATING STATISTICS

SQL Server automatically updates the statistics on the indexes of your tables. This is controlled through the AUTOSTATS setting in the stored procedure sp_autostats. When set to ON, the default, statistics are automatically maintained. You can selectively turn autostats off for selected indexes or tables. The syntax for this stored procedure is:

```
sp_autostats 'table_name', 'ON/OFF', 'index_name'
```

The parameter table_name is required. If you do not use the other two parameters, then the current autostats status for all indexes on the table are listed. The next parameter is used to specify either ON or OFF for the statistics on the index specified in the third parameter, or for the entire table if you do not name an index.

You should periodically check the statistics on your tables, especially those tables through which many transactions are posted. These statistics are automatically updated each time you create or recreate an index on a table that is already populated. When you decide to manually update statistics, you can use the following T-SQL statement in the Query Analyzer query window like this:

```
UPDATE STATISTICS table_name index_name
```

The table_name parameter is required as this statement runs on the specified table. You can also run this statement from another database if you add the database/owner parameter. The `index_name` parameter is optional. When you use the `index_name` parameter, then only the statistics for the specified index are updated. Otherwise, all statistics for the named table will be updated. When these statistics are made or updated, a sampling of key values in each index is taken and the distribution of these key values is recorded. The optimizer then uses this information to help it make decisions on how a query will be optimized and then run. When this statement is executed it returns no rows or data.

Clustered Indexes

A clustered index is a special index object where the bottom or leaf pages of the index are the actual data pages. Only one clustered index can exist per table. After all, you can't have a table whose physical row order is the same as two different columns unless the columns are identical—in which case, why was the second one created?

Clustered indexes are most often used on columns whose values are grouped together; for example, a *department* column. A clustered index would then group all employees who work in the same department together within the table. This would help to speed queries that sort information by department or select records from a specific department. Often a significant increase in speed is seen because once the query finds the first matching records, the remaining matches will be found in the adjacent rows. Whenever possible, use a clustered index in the WHERE clause of a query. The optimizer will be sure to use this index and be able to maximize performance against it.

When working with a clustered index, you are not required to specify an equality in the WHERE clause. The clustered index also works very well with a query that returns a range of values. Ranges can be selected by using range operators in the WHERE clause. Range operators include:

```
BETWEEN, <, >, >=, and <=
```

The range operators are often used in expressions, which can also include AND and OR operators. For example:

```
SELECT * FROM authors
WHERE state BETWEEN 'CA' AND 'KS'
```

This query will select all rows whose values in the state column is between the values 'CA' and 'KS' inclusively. The other range operators are most often used with numeric values and data types, but can be used with alphanumeric datatype columns also.

Using Nonclustered Indexes

Unlike a clustered index, rows are not physically ordered by the index, which can result in a slower overall access to the data and a return of information from a query. Nonclustered indexes contain pointers to the data rows on the leaf pages of the index. Also unlike a clustered index, you can have as many as 249 nonclustered indexes per table. While using indexes can result in an overall increase in the speed of a query returning a results set and a reduction in the I/O cost of the query, creating and maintaining indexes adds to the server overhead.

Be sure to use indexes where they will be helpful, but do not necessarily create an index on every column and combination of columns for every table. When a nonclustered index is available for use by a query, the optimizer must choose between using the index or simply performing a table scan. When the index is used, SQL Server must read the index, which is contained on logical index pages, and then the actual data pages. When querying a smaller table, the optimizer may decide not to use the index, relying on a simple table scan. The reason behind this is that the number of page I/O operations required to read the nonclustered index pages and then the data pages becomes greater than the table scan, especially if the optimizer determines that the indexes are not useful for this query.

Creating Useful Indexes

The query optimizer determines the usefulness of an index by the selectivity of the WHERE clause in the query. This selectivity is based on an estimate of the percentage of total rows to be returned to the client. The statistics recorded on the distribution pages are used to appraise the available indexes, estimate the number of page I/Os required by using different indexes, and then select the plan which will require the fewest number of page I/Os.

You can help the query optimizer by closely examining the WHERE clauses of the queries sent to SQL Server. The WHERE clause is the primary place the optimizer looks for information about how best to perform the query. After all, this is the place you limit the query. By using a column that contains an index in the WHERE clause, you can speed the results set to the client. Alternatively, if a column is used in the WHERE clause and the query is often used, consider placing an index on this column to help the optimizer.

Another way to make your indexes useful to the query optimizer is to build *narrow* indexes. A narrow index is one that covers as few columns as possible. While a nonclustered index can include up to 16 columns, a wide composite index like this can require many I/O page reads to use the index. The query optimizer could easily decide that a table scan would be cheaper in terms of numbers of I/O page reads. A wide, composite, nonclustered index would be used if a query were constructed so that all of the columns from both the SELECT list and WHERE clause are included in the index. When this occurs, SQL Server does not have to read down to the data pages because the required information is contained on the index pages. Due to the overhead required to maintain an index like this, especially in the hope that the optimizer will use it, it is best avoided.

The speed and efficiency in using more numerous, narrow indexes will generally provide you with greater performance and a higher likelihood that the optimizer will use the indexes. Avoid creating a composite index whose first column is invariably not used as the first column in the queries WHERE clause. With careful attention to how you build indexes and then use them in queries, you can help SQL Server's optimizer increase the speed with which results are returned to the client.

MCSE 18.2   Other Performance-Tuning Factors

There are many factors that go into tuning a database and SQL Server for the best possible performance. The topic of database design has already been discussed in previous chapters. Using both the NT and SQL Server Performance Monitors can show you areas that may be improved. Other areas where you can create significant performance benefits are:

- Application Design: Creating applications that can do the job required of them without consuming unnecessary system resources, both on the client and server sides. Using the API in the correct manner for which it was intended can greatly increase the throughput of your applications.

- Server Tuning: This can include adjusting settings on both NT Server and SQL Server. One of the places to start is at the SQL Server Properties dialog box. Particularly, check the memory, processor, and connection options.

Other options available to you to help increase the performance of your SQL Server setup include understanding and using the options available with the stored procedure `sp_configure`, and properly configuring the other tools that you may use.

MCSE 18.3 Creating Full-Text Search Indexes

If you plan to use full-text search on selected columns in a table, you must set up the full-text search indexes on the columns. A full-text search index is a special index that must be populated once you have created it. It is not automatically updated as are other indexes. These indexes are created only on character-based columns.

When a search is conducted against the full-text enabled column, the Index engine conducts the search using a linguistic-oriented format. This means that the search will find all similar matches to the criteria, and can show a ranking of the found items against the original criteria. SQL Server also includes a Full-Text Indexing wizard that can help you to create the indexing catalog. You can have only a single full-text index per table, but more than one table column can be a member of that index.

Once the index has been created, you can populate the index immediately, or schedule it as a job under the SQL Server Agent. If you are creating this index on a large table, the population of the index can take a great deal of time, and would be best scheduled for a time when database usage is low. Index information is stored in a full-text catalog. This catalog is stored as part of the database file system, but can only be accessed within the context of the database. More than one table can use the same full-text catalog in a database.

When using the full-text search capabilities of SQL Server, there are several tasks that must be accomplished before it can be used. The tasks will fall in this order:

- Create the full-text catalog.
- Register the tables that will be enabled for full-text search.
- Select the specific columns in each table that will be enabled for full-text search.
- Activate the index for each table.
- Populate the index for each table.

Once a full-text index has been populated, you can repopulate the index with newly added rows by using an incremental population. The incremental population will greatly decrease the amount of time required. An incremental population will refresh the index for any column that:

- Has data that has been updated or inserted since the last population.
- Data in those tables that use a timestamp column.
- All rows that have been enabled for full-text searching since the last population of the index.

Full-text search can be created and administered through several stored procedures, or the Full-Text Search Wizard. The Full-Text Search Wizard is used like this:

1. If the Full-Text Search service is not already started, then expand the server that you want to enable full-text searches, then start it by right-clicking its icon and selecting Start on the shortcut menu.
2. Right-click the Full-Text Search icon once again, and select Tools from the menu. On the Tools sub-menu, select Full-Text Indexing to start the wizard.
3. Click the Next button on the opening dialog box. In the next dialog box you must select the database on which you want to enable full-text search. In this example, the Northwind database is selected. You must have ownership privileges to the table that you will enable if nothing else in the database. Without this, you will be unable to complete the wizard. Click the Next button to move on to the next dialog box.
4. Select the Employees table and click the Next button. This is the table on which you want to enable full-text search.
5. Select a unique index for the table from the combo box, and then click the Next button.
6. Select the character-based columns you want to use for full-text searches. In this example, the Notes field will be used. Columns are selected by either double-clicking the column name in the Available columns list, or selecting it and then clicking the Add button. Either method will mov e the column to the Added columns list. Click the Next button when you have selected all of the columns.
7. Since full-text search is only now being enabled on this database, there are not existing catalogs that you can add to. Type a name, such as NWind, for the catalog in the Name text box. The default location for full-text search catalogs is the `C:\MSSQL7\FTDATA` folder. Click the Next button.
8. You can schedule the population of the index in this dialog box. If full-text search had already been activated and scheduled, you would see

that schedule listed here. Click the New schedule button and set the schedule in the Scheduling dialog box. Figure 18-3 shows a new schedule entered. Click the Next button.

9. Use this dialog box to verify that all of the settings you require have been correctly selected. If so, click the Finish button. Otherwise, click the Back button and make the necessary corrections.

You will see an information dialog box displayed showing you the various steps that SQL Server goes through as it creates the catalog, and readies any jobs that you scheduled.

Once the catalog and index has been populated, a user will be able to run a full-text search in the Northwind database, on the Employees table, in the Notes column.

You must update the full-text search index periodically, it is not done automatically. If you have an index that needs to be repopulated frequently, then be sure that it is scheduled as a job, and that the scheduled times meet your needs.

Key Points

Several key points about optimizing the performance of your SQL Server database have been covered in this chapter.

- How SQL Server uses a cost-based query optimizer to determine what route will be taken when retrieving a result set.
- How the SQL Server uses index statistics to help the query optimizer in its determination of the cost of a route.
- How to use DBCC SHOW_STATISTICS to view and read the statistics maintained on a table and index or column.
- How to use sp_autostats to turn automatic statistics updates on or off on a specific index or an entire table.
- How you can manually update statistics on an entire table or on a specific index by using the UPDATE STATISTICS statement.
- How to create and maintain a full-text search index on selected columns and tables in a database.

▲ CHAPTER REVIEW QUESTIONS

▲ Multiple Choice:

1. *The best times to design in optimization to a database are? (select all that apply)*
   A. When designing the database tables.
   B. During selection of columns to use as indexes.
   C. After the database has been created and data loaded.
   D. After the master database has been backed up for the first time.

2. *The query optimizer bases its selection of execution plans on: (select all that apply)*
   A. Statistics based on the execution of previous queries.
   B. Statistics based on results obtained when sp_statistics_update is run.
   C. Statistics kept by SQL Server on the distribution of data in a table and its indexes.
   D. Statistics based on nonclustered indexes.

3. *Which of these options are true of a clustered index? (select all that apply)*
   A. The leaf pages of the clustered index provide pointers directly to the data rows.
   B. The bottom pages of the clustered index are the data rows.
   C. You can have no more than two clustered indexes per table.
   D. Reference the clustered index in the SELECT statement of a query.

4. *Which of these options are true of a nonclustered index? (select all that apply)*
   A. You are limited to 128 nonclustered indexes.
   B. The leaf pages of a nonclustered index contain pointers to the data rows.
   C. Reference a nonclustered index in a WHERE statement of a query.
   D. A nonclustered index is limited to a maximum of three columns.

5. *What makes a useful index? (select all that apply)*
   A. When the indexed column is referenced in a SELECT statement.
   B. When the indexed column is referenced in a WHERE statement.
   C. When the second and third columns of a four-column composite index are referenced in a query.
   D. When the first column of a four-column composite index is referenced in a query.

6. Indexes are considered to be efficient when: (select all that apply)

    A. The table has a single, wide index.

    B. The table has multiple, narrow indexes.

    C. The WHERE statement of a query references the index by name.

    D. The columns included in an index are referenced in the WHERE statement of a query.

7. When setting up a full-text search index on a table, what are some of the things that you must do? (select all that apply)

    A. That the index includes an IDENTITY column.

    B. That the index is set on character-based columns.

    C. The index in the catalog is populated.

    D. That a database is enabled for full-text searching.

    E. All of the above.

▲ True or False:

1. *True or False? An index can be placed on a table that will actually slow down a query.*

2. *True or False? A query will always use any available index on a table.*

3. *True or False? The time a query takes to execute can be dynamically set with the sp_configure statement.*

4. *True or False? A clustered index is created when you create a composite index of two or more adjoining columns.*

5. *True or False? You are limited to a maximum of 249 nonclustered indexes.*

6. *True or False? A user with SELECT permission on a table can set up full-text searching on that table only.*

7. *True or False? The query governor option is used to slow a query down so to not saturate the capacity of the network.*

Automating Tasks

In this module you learn to automate many of the everyday tasks involved in the administration of SQL Server. Many tasks can be set up as a job and then scheduled to be run as needed. The most common objects that are run in schedules are jobs and replication. In the case of a data warehouse, you may also schedule DTS packages to be run at scheduled times. Jobs may include many different things such as backups and other administrative tasks. In the next two chapters you will learn how this is done.

The SQL Server Agent

The Microsoft SQL Server Agent Service© is the key to how any job, task, replication task, and alerts are handled throughout the SQL Server system. The Agent service works in either a single or multiserver configuration. Jobs can be scheduled to run at specific times. If any errors occur, then an alert can be sent via e-mail, or pager, net send to a specified individual(s).

435

The Role of the SQL Server Agent

SQL Server Agent's primary role is to act as the buffer between various SQL Server activities that must interact directly with the NT Server. When a job is scheduled, the SQL Server Agent service handles the activities involved with the job. Jobs and activities can be managed for single servers or for a multiserver environment.

In a single server environment, SQL Server Agent service simply manages all jobs, alerts, and the operators who need to be notified. Alerts will be discussed in detail later in Chapter 20. Jobs are defined and then scheduled. When a job is scheduled, then it becomes the SQL Server Agent's responsibility to ensure that the job runs as defined at the scheduled time. If any notifications are part of the job, then those are also done. The multiserver environment will be discussed later in this chapter.

MCSE 19.1   ## Setting Up the SQL Server Agent Service

The SQL Server Agent service is set up during the normal installation of SQL Server. The Agent service must be running before you can begin to automate some of your administrative tasks. The SQL Server Agent runs as a Windows NT© service, and must have appropriate security permissions in order to do the work that is assigned to it. When you first create the SQL Server Agent service during the installation process, you must assign it to a security account. Your options include:

- System account: This is the built-in Windows NT account for the local system administrator. This account is always a member of the Administrators Windows NT group and, as such, is also a member of the SQL Server sysadmin role. Use this account only if SQL Server Agent does not ever need access to networked resources on another Windows NT Server.

- This account: This option enables you to select a specific account that the SQL Server Agent service will use when running a task. The Windows NT domain account that you choose must be a member of the SQL Server sysadmin role.

If you have either not yet set up an account for SQL Server Agent, or you want to change the NT security account from a system account or to a different account, you can do so in one of the following two ways:

- You can use the Service applet in the NT Control Panel. Simply select the SQL Server Agent service and change the account in the Service dialog box.
- You can also change the service startup account from within the SQL Server Enterprise Manager application.

If you already have the SQL Server Enterprise Manager application open, then changing the SQL Server Agent startup account takes only a few mouse clicks and is done like this:

1. Right-click on the SQL Server Agent icon and select Properties from the shortcut menu. This will display the SQL Server Agent Properties dialog box as you can see in Figure 19-1.

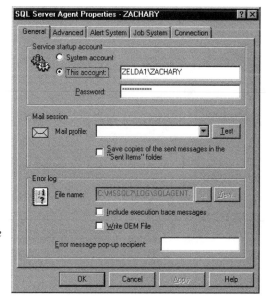

Figure 19–1 *With the SQL Server Agent Properties dialog box you can change the service startup account, among many other options.*

You can also open many of these properties dialog boxes by clicking the Properties button on the toolbar. This can eliminate the shortcut menu step.

2. Be sure that you are on the General tab of the Properties dialog box. Make any necessary changes to the Service startup account. Clicking the System account option button allows you to set the SQL Server Agent service as a system account for the local server. If you choose the This account option button, you must specify the *domain\accountname* and password in the appropriate text boxes.

3. Click the OK button to save your changes and return to the SQL Server Enterprise Manager application. Your changes will not take effect until you stop and restart the SQL Server Agent service.

The SQL Server Agent service can be stopped and started here in the Enterprise Manager application. Simply right-click on the Agent icon and select Stop from the shortcut menu. Once the service has been stopped, you will see that the icon changes and shows a small red square on it; you can now display the shortcut menu again and click on Start. The new account is now in control of SQL Server Agent service.

Another setting that you may want to ensure is set to ON is the auto restart option. This can be set in the Properties dialog box under the Advanced tab. Just check the checkbox for the "Auto restart SQL Server Agent if it stopped unexpectedly" option. This will ensure that the SQL Server Agent service will automatically restart when SQL Server is stopped or your Windows NT server crashes suddenly. When the server is brought back up and restored, the service will be started. Provided there are no other problems, your jobs will continue normally at their scheduled times.

MCSE 19.2   The SQL Server Agent Error Logs

The SQL Server Agent service maintains its own error logs. They can be viewed by using a text editor, such as Notepad, and are stored in the folder \MSSQL7\LOGS. The Agent logs are all named *Sqlagent*. Like the normal SQL Server errorlog files, a total of ten logs are maintained. The current log is SQLAGENT.OUT, and the subsequent logs are SQLAGENT.1, SQLAGENT.2, ..., SQLAGENT.9. The log with the largest numbered extension is the oldest log. As a new log file is created, the oldest is dropped, and all of the others are renamed.

You can also easily view the SQL Server Agent logs from within the Enterprise Manager application. View your most current log like this:

1. Right-click on SQL Server Agent and select Display Error Log from the shortcut menu. As you can see in Figure 19-2, the error log is displayed in its own dialog box.

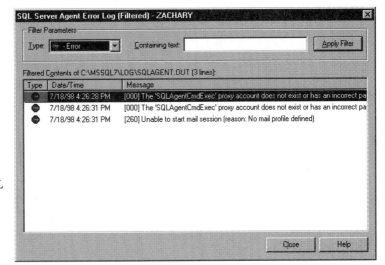

Figure 19-2 *Use the SQL Server Agent Error Log to view the current error log.*

2. Notice that the log is filtered by default, showing only log items that are typed as Error. Click the button on the Type combo box and select the All Types option. You can now see all events that have been logged since the SQL Server Agent service was last started.

You can filter the log events for specific text by typing it into the Containing text text box and clicking the Apply Filter button. Any events that contain the text you enter will be displayed.

MCSE 19.3 **Multiserver Administration**

In a multiserver environment one server is set as the master server, while all others in the group become target servers. The letters MSX designates master servers, while target servers are designated as TSX. All servers can run their own jobs and schedules, or you can define each job once on the master server and then enlist the target server to run the job. The target server runs the job as configured and scheduled, then reports back to the master server. Figure 19-3 illustrates how the master server talks to each target server. There is no connection between the two target servers—at least as far as SQL Server Agent is concerned.

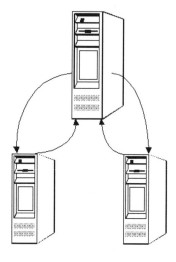

Figure 19–3   *In this illustration, the master server talks to each target server, sending them jobs, and then the target servers report back to the master server on the success or failure of the job(s).*

The following basic steps are used to create a master/target server for the Agent to work through.

1. Verify the security settings for both the SQL Server and the SQL Server Agent service on all target servers. Each must be a member of the Windows NT domain accounts.
2. Create the master server operator, MSXOperator, on the master server.
3. Start SQL Server Agent service on the master server.
4. Enlist the target servers.
5. Create the jobs and select the target server(s) to run the job.

A master server must be running in a Windows NT Server environment. Target servers can be created from SQL Servers that are operating in other environments, such as Windows 95/98, or Windows NT Workstation.

Target servers are enlisted when they become part of the master server group, and they defect when they are removed from the group. A target server can be enlisted by a single master server at any one time. All members of a master/target group must be using the same version of SQL Server. In order to remove a multiserver group, you must first defect all of the target servers from the master server.

Creating the Multiserver Group

In order to create a multiserver group, you must first ensure that the servers you plan to enlist as targets, and the master server, are members of an NT domain security account and not simply members of the local system account. Once this has been done, you can continue with the creation of your group.

1. Right-click on SQL Server Agent for the server that will become the master server, and select Multi Server Administration from the shortcut menu. Then select Make this a Master, from the next menu.

> You can also open this wizard by selecting the server that will become the master and then choosing Tools, Wizards from the menu. Then, in the Select Wizard dialog box, expand the Management option and select Make Master Server Wizard.

2. Click the Next button. In this dialog box MSXOperator is created, and the various avenues for sending notifications is created. As you can see in Figure 19-4 two types of notifications have been set up: One via e-mail and another to a user via net send. If you have access to a pager system, this can be used for automatic notifications. Click the Next button to move on to the next dialog box.

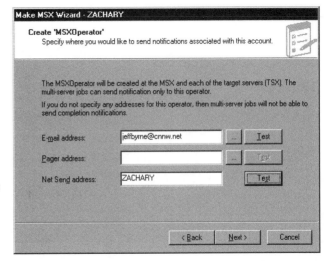

Figure 19–4 *Use the Create MSXOperator dialog box to create the methods that SQL Server Agent will use to notify the master server operator of any alerts.*

3. Select the servers that will be targets for the jobs assigned by the master server. Place a checkmark beside each server that you want to use as a target server. When you have selected all of the servers that you want to include, click the Next button. You can adjust properties, or register a server, by clicking the appropriate button. Figure 19-5 shows a server selected.

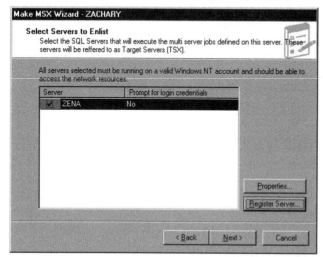

Figure 19–5 *Use this dialog box to enlist a server as a target.*

4. This next dialog box is used so that you can enter a description for each target server. This is an optional step. If you have many target servers, a short description of their function, where they are located, et cetera, may help you to keep straight what jobs should be assigned to each of the target servers. Click the Next button.

If the wizard encounters any errors with the target server connections, you will see a new dialog box telling you what errors were found and what you need to do to correct them. One of the more common errors is that one or more of the servers is running as a service using the System Account security account. This account does not allow the server to connect to networked resources. You must use an account that is a domain user account.

5. If you have not encountered any errors, you will see a dialog box that shows you the server that will become the master, and all servers that will be enlisted as targets. When you click the Finish button the wizard will start this task, as shown in Figure 19-6.

6. When the wizard has completed setting up the master server and all of the target servers, you will see a confirmation dialog box telling you that "SQL Server 'SERVERNAME' was successfully made an MSX." Click the OK button.

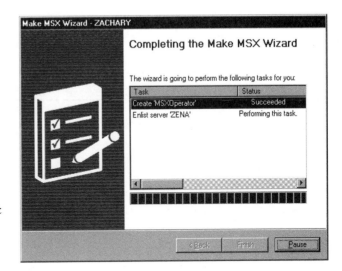

Figure 19–6 *This dialog box shows you what operations the wizard will perform when you click the Finish button.*

You will now see that the SQL Server Agent in the master server has had its designation changed to read SQL Server Agent (MSX) indicating that it is the master server Agent. You will also see that the Agent in the target server has changed to read SQL Server Agent (TSX: MASTER_SERVER_NAME). Once this has been completed, you will be able to create jobs and alerts and then assign them to all of your target servers, or only to selected servers. You may very well not want all of the servers to perform all of the jobs, as some may not be appropriate to some servers.

As your company continues to grow, you will probably add new SQL Servers to your enterprise. Some of these servers may work as stand-alone servers, while others may work as part of a group. You can easily add new target servers to the multiserver group. You do not have to recreate the master/target group that you just created to add a new server as a target, you can simply add the new target server.

By right-clicking on the master SQL Server Agent and selecting Multi-Server Administration from the shortcut menu, you will notice that the next menu has changed. Instead of the options to Make a Master Server, or Make a Target Server, you have the option to Manage Target Servers, or Add Target Servers.

When you need to add a new target server, just select the Add Target Servers option and follow along with the wizard. The dialog boxes that you will work with are very similar to those you just completed.

The Manage Target Servers option enables you to manage the target servers. This is where you will assign jobs and tell the target servers who, when, and how to send alert messages. The Target Servers dialog box is divided into two tab windows: Target Server Status and Download Instructions.

- Target Server Status: This tab gives you information about the current status of the target servers. You will see the server name, the local time for the target server in its own time zone, the local time the target server last polled the master server, the number of unread instructions, and the current status. The status of a target server can be OK, offline, or blocked. Offline would indicate that the server is not available for some reason, while blocked indicates that the target has not polled the master server in the last three polling intervals.
- Download Instructions: This tab allows you to download instructions to a specific target or to all target servers. You can choose all, or a specific job, to download. The tab also shows the name of each target server, the operation that was downloaded, the name of the object that is affected by the instruction, the date/time the job was posted for downloading, the date/time the job was downloaded to the target. You will also see the current status of the downloaded instruction. If there was a problem with the download, an error message will be displayed.

Figure 19-7 shows the Target Server Status tab of the dialog box. The other options available on this tab include:

- Force Poll: Use this option to force a target server to poll the master server. If you find that a target has a status of blocked, you may want to force it to poll the master. If it is still not able to perform this function, then you should investigate further. You may have some type of network problem that needs attention.
- Force Defection: You can force the defection of a target from the master server. This is especially useful if a target is not easily accessible or may be compromised.
- Post Instructions: This button allows the master server to post instructions to the selected target servers.

Figure 19-8 displays the Download Instructions tab. The options available to you on this tab include:

- Delete: This button allows you to delete the selected download instruction. Be sure that you have the correct instruction selected and the correct target server selected. If you delete the wrong instruction, you may have to rebuild it completely.
- Clear: Use this button to clear the status of an instruction that downloaded with errors. This will allow the target to attempt another download of the instruction.

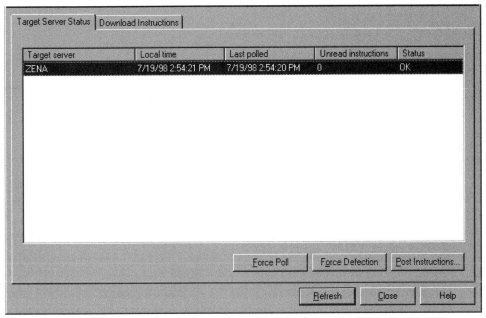

Figure 19–7   *The Target Server Status tab allows you to view the status of your target servers, and to perform some administrative tasks.*

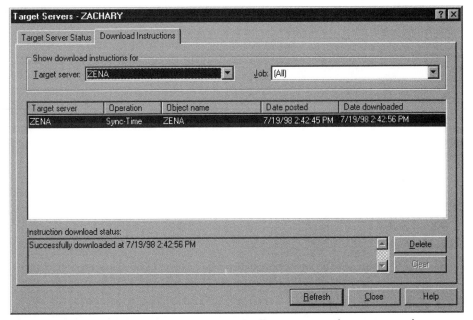

Figure 19–8   *The Download Instructions tab allows you to select targets and instructions for download.*

Defecting a Target Server

Defecting, or removing, a target server from a master server is a very simple task. There are several reasons that you may want to defect a server from the group.

- You may want to physically remove a server.
- The server may now be performing a different function.
- You may want to change the name of the server.
- The security of a target server has been compromised.
- You may want to move the server to a different master server.

A target server can defect from a master server, or the master can force the defection of any target server.

To force the defection of a target server by the master server, simply open the Target Servers dialog box, as discussed in the previous section of this chapter, and click on the Target Server Status tab. Select the target to be defected, then click the Force Defection button. You will see a confirmation dialog box; click the Yes button to continue with the process.

From the target server, you can easily defect from a master server by right-clicking on the SQL Server Agent on the target, then selecting Multi-Server Administration on the shortcut menu, and then Defect from MSX. You will see a new confirmation dialog box. Click Yes to defect the target. The checkbox Force defection is available for you to use if the master has become damaged or is permanently unavailable to the target. Without this option, the target would not be able to release its status as a target of a specific master server and, as such, would not be able to enlist with another master server.

Key Points

In this chapter you learned the following key points about setting up the SQL Server Agent and assigning a server to the role of master server, and others, as target servers:

- The role of the SQL Server Agent.
- How to set up an appropriate security account for the SQL Server Agent to use on startup: Use a valid domain user account when the SQL Server Agent must have access to networked resources.
- How to view the SQL Server Agent error logs.
- How to create a multiserver group to simplify the administration of jobs throughout an enterprise.

- How to use the Make Master Server Wizard to select the master server, create the MSXOperator accounts and enlist the target servers.
- How to add new target servers.
- How to manage target servers from the master server.
- How to defect target servers from the master server.

▲ CHAPTER REVIEW QUESTIONS

▲ Multiple Choice:

1. *The primary job of the SQL Server Agent Service is to: (select all that apply)*

   A. Manage jobs within SQL Server.

   B. Ensure that replication tasks are completed.

   C. Act as the interface between SQL Server tasks and jobs and Windows NT.

   D. Ensure that operators are notified of events.

2. *When setting up the security account for SQL Server Agent you can use: (select all that apply)*

   A. Any valid SQL Server User account that is also a member of the SQL Server sysadmin role.

   B. The system account as a Windows NT service.

   C. Any valid Windows NT domain account that is also a member of the SQL Server sysadmin role

   D. The SQL Server Agent does not require a security account.

3. *How are master and target servers designated by the SQL Server Agent? (select all that apply)*

   A. A master server is designated (master).

   B. A master server is designated (MSX).

   C. A target server is designated (target).

   D. A target server is designated (TSX).

4. *A master server can use which operating system? (select all that apply)*

   A. Windows NT Server

   B. Windows NT Workstation

   C. Windows 95/98

   D. Windows for Workgroups

5. *When would you want to defect a server from a group? (select all that apply)*

   A. When the name of a server is changed.

   B. When a server is to be placed in a different group.

   C. When a server has become compromised.

   D. When a server is to be made a master server.

▲ True or False:

1. *True or False? The SQL Server Agent Service is a key component for jobs and replication tasks.*

2. *True or False? The SQL Server Agent Service requires a valid Windows NT security account.*

3. *True or False? The SQL Server Agent will automatically restart after a system failure by default.*

4. *True or False? You must use the SQL Server Agent log reader to view the error logs.*

5. *True or False? In a multiserver environment, target servers are managed from the master server.*

Creating and Using Schedules

As you have learned earlier in this book, the SQL Server Agent Service© is used to support scheduling of tasks as jobs. In this chapter you will learn how jobs are created and then scheduled to run at a set time.

MCSE 20.1   Defining a Job

In order to schedule a job, you must first create, or more properly, define, the job. Jobs can be defined that will automate many common administrative tasks that you might otherwise have to do "by hand." The main components of a job definition are:

- A job name
- The category of the job
- The name of the job owner
- A description of the job
- The steps necessary to complete the job
- Any success or failure actions
- The job schedule
- Who is notified in the event of the success or failure of the job

Why would you want to bother with creating and scheduling jobs? Many of the functions of the SQL Server system administrator can be very repetitive and occur at regularly scheduled times or intervals. By defining and scheduling these types of jobs, you can free some of your time to tasks that may require more of your abilities. There are also many tasks that are not done on a regular basis, but still need to be done frequently. You can create a job that can be executed when needed. This is especially helpful for a job that you must do infrequently, but is somewhat complex. Instead of writing out a procedure of all of the steps involved in the job, you can create the job and then run it. An example of such a job is a year-end closing procedure.

If you are using a master/target server configuration, then you may want to define all of your jobs on the master server and download them to the targets.

Starting a Job Definition

One of the most commonly automated tasks is the creation of a backup job and schedule. This task is normally done at very regulated intervals, and there is no good reason for you to spend your time running back to the server to start and monitor a backup job. To see how a backup job is defined, follow these steps:

1. Right-click on the server where you want to define the job. Select New, Job from the shortcut menus. This will display the New Job Properties dialog box.

2. Enter a name for your job in the Name text box. A name is limited to a maximum of 128 characters and must be unique to the server on which it originated. If your job originates on a master server, the target server could have a job that uses the same name defined as a job too. When the master server job is downloaded to the target, both jobs remain valid names and defined jobs.

3. Select a category from the Category combo box. When you install SQL Server, twelve local job categories are created. The default is [Uncategorized (Local)] for local jobs. If your server is a master server, a default master server category is also created–[Uncategorized (Multiserver)]. Choose Database Maintenance for this job definition.

4. When the Enabled checkbox is checked the job will run at its scheduled time. If you want to test the new job first, remove the checkmark.

5. Select the owner of this job. Only a member of the sysadmin role can define and own jobs. Enter a description for the job in the Description box. This is a good place to fully describe what the job is supposed to do. You are limited to 512 characters.

6. The Target local server option button is selected by default. The Target multiple servers option button and the Change button are not available if the server you are using is either a stand-alone server or a target server. Figure 20-1 shows the completed New Job Properties dialog box and the General tab.

If your server is a master server and you plan to download this job to a target, then click the Target multiple servers option button. Then click the Change button. You will see the Change Job Target Servers dialog box. Use this box to select the target servers who will use this job.

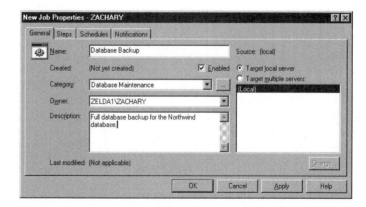

Figure 20–1 *Use the General tab of the New Job Properties dialog box to set up the initial information for a new job definition.*

Defining the Steps of a Job

You cannot save a job definition until it has a minimum of one step. The steps of a job are the sequence of events that the job will perform while it runs. Job steps can be a series of T-SQL statements, a saved SQL query, operating system commands, an Active Script, or a set of replication commands. Here, you will continue with the example of defining a backup job.

1. Click the Steps tab to continue with the job definition.
2. Click the New button to open the New Job Step dialog box and be sure that the General tab is selected. Type a name for the step in the Step Name text box.
3. You can choose from among several different types of commands that will be run in the Type combo box. Select Transact-SQL Script from the combo box.
4. Change the database from master to Northwind in the Database combo box. This is the database that will be affected by the action performed in this step.
5. If you already had a prepared SQL query saved, you could click on the Open button and select it from the Open File dialog box. The query saved in the file would be run for this step. This allows you to create and test your query before including it as a step and is an excellent idea. Enter the following query into the Command text box, as seen in Figure 20-2. This query of course will only succeed if you have already created the Backup Device Northwind_FBK.

```
USE NORTHWIND
GO
BACKUP DATABASE NORTHWIND
TO Northwind_FBK
```

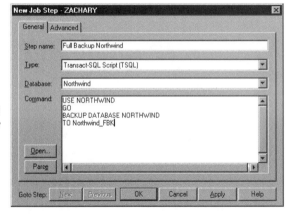

Figure 20–2 *From the General tab on the New Job Step dialog box you can create very complex steps for a job using T-SQL statements, or other types of scripting.*

6. Click the Parse button to verify the syntax of your statement, then click the Advanced tab button.

7. The first option here allows you to place the output of this step into a specific file. If you have such a file, then enter the name in the Output file text box. The View button allows you to view an existing output file. You also have the option to Overwrite an output file with new data, or to Append the output to the existing file.

8. Click the Append output to step history. Since this is a simple backup statement, the output will only list the files that are backed up and how long it took to do so. You also have the option to run this step as another user by selecting the user name in the Run as user combo box.

9. This next section of the dialog box is where you specify what happens after the success or failure of a step. In the On success action combo box, select the option "Quit the job reporting success."

You also have the option to continue to the next step. In the case of a backup job, if you were backing up several databases at the same time, you may have to back up the master database, continuing until all of them have been backed up.

10. If the first attempt to perform a step fails, you can force SQL Server Agent to attempt the run the step again by specifying how many times in the Retry attempts box. The default setting is 0 retries; if the step ends in failure the system will not attempt the step again. If you want the step to retry again, specify the Retry interval in the next box. This is set at minutes.

11. Finally, choose the action to be performed on failure of the step. Like a successful action, you can choose to continue on to the next step, or report the failure and quit the job.

Depending on the job you are defining, you may choose to quit the job. After all, if the next step requires that the previous step is successful, then there is no reason to go on to the next part of the job. If the job is not really step dependent, such as a series of backups, then simply allow the job to continue on to the next step. If this is the last step in a series, you would not choose to continue to the next step option.

Figure 20-3 shows the completed Advanced tab of the New Job Step dialog box. Notice the Next and Previous buttons. If you were working with a multiple step job, you could quickly switch between steps and make any necessary adjustments to another step.

12. Click the OK button to save the step and return to the New Job Properties dialog box.

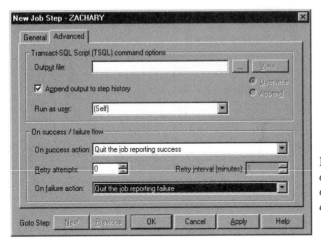

Figure 20–3 *Use the Advanced tab of the New Job Step dialog box to set output options and what a step will do on success or failure.*

Figure 20-4 shows the new step having been inserted into the New Job Properties dialog box. If you were working with a multiple step job, you can use the up and down Move step arrows to shift a steps position in the group.

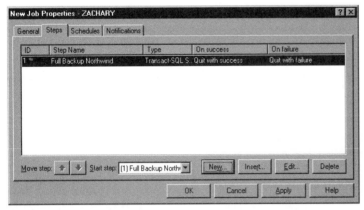

Figure 20–4 *A new step has been inserted into a new job definition.*

MCSE 20.2 Creating Schedules

Once you have defined a job, you can choose to save it immediately and then go on to a different task. Alternatively, you can go ahead and create a schedule for the job as the next step in the job definition.

A job can be scheduled to run once—on a certain day of the week, after a certain number of days, hours, et cetera. You can set a job to start when the

SQL Server Agent service is started, in response to an alert, or when the CPU is idle for a certain period of time. In case you aren't sure, this last option in particular is not a good choice for scheduling backups.

You are not allowed to run two instances of a job at the same time. For example, if a job is running as scheduled, you cannot start the job manually. SQL Server Agent would refuse the second instance of the job. Jobs are enabled by default. If you do not want a job to run as scheduled, you must disable the job. When a job is disabled, it cannot be started from a schedule. It can still be started from either an alert, or from a user-issued command.

To continue with the job started in the previous section, follow these steps to create a schedule for the backup job.

1. Click the Schedules tab button on the New Job Properties dialog box. If this were a multiserver job, the name of the currently selected target server would be listed in the combo box at the top of this part of the dialog box. The current time for the target server is also shown. This can be very helpful when deciding how some jobs should be scheduled.

2. Click the New Schedule button, displaying the New Job Schedule dialog box. This is essentially the same dialog box you will see when creating or editing any other schedule.

3. Enter a name for this specific schedule. In this case, we will call it `Database Backup - Northwind`. You are limited to a total of 128 characters for the schedule name. You can disable the schedule for this job by removing the checkmark from the Enabled checkbox. Choose one of the four option buttons that makes the best sense for the job you are scheduling. The default option is Recurring and will be left as is for this job.

4. Because the Northwind database is a very heavily used database, and updates are frequent, we are going to set this job to run more often then the default of once a week. Click the Change button to display the Edit Recurring Job Schedule dialog box. This is the same dialog box you would use to change any other recurring schedule.

5. Click the Daily option button. This will schedule the backup for every day of the week. If your business was not open on Saturday and Sunday, you may want to use a Weekly schedule and then select the specific days of the week.

6. Selecting the Daily option gives you the option to choose what interval of days you want to use. One day is the default and it will stand as is. In the next section, Daily frequency, you can choose to run the job once a day at a set time, or at specific intervals throughout the day. Leave the option button Occurs once selected, and change the time from 12:00 A.M. to

If you decide to schedule a job for a set of specific days of the week, be sure that you select the right days. For example, if you decide to back up your server at 1 A.M., and want to back up each day's work, and you are closed on Saturday and Sunday, then you would want to schedule the backup for Tuesday through Saturday—not Monday through Friday. Scheduling Monday through Friday would leave all of your Friday data unprotected until 1 AM on Monday morning.

1:00 A.M. Select the time based on your own shop and when is the best time for a backup or other job to run. Some businesses run a set of daily reports that are created and printed at midnight for the previous day. So you would want to run the backup just after, or before, that time.

7. You can choose the duration for the job. If the job is one that you want to run for a specific period of time, you can select a starting and ending date for the job. Once the ending date is reached, the job will no longer be scheduled to run. The default option of No end date works well for a backup job. Figure 20-5 shows the current recurring schedule.

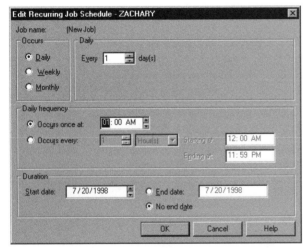

Figure 20–5 *Use the Edit Recurring Job Schedule dialog box to specify when a job should be scheduled to recur again.*

8. Click the OK button to return to the New Job Schedule dialog box. As seen in Figure 20-6, the schedule listed in the Recurring box now reflects the current schedule.

9. Click the OK button to return to the New Job Properties dialog box. As seen in Figure 20-7, the new schedule has been inserted into the list.

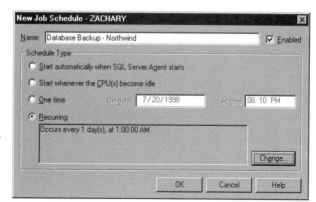

Figure 20–6   *Here you can see the new schedule for the backup job listed in the New Job Schedule dialog box.*

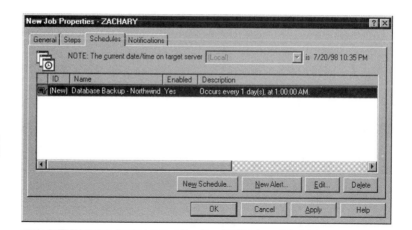

Figure 20–7   *Now the new schedule is inserted into the New Job Properties schedules.*

Using Notifications on a Job

When a job has been completed, either successfully or unsuccessfully, you may want to be notified, send a message to another operator, or write an event to the Windows NT application log. Any or all of these things can be done after a scheduled job is completed. Follow these next steps to set up notifications for the backup job.

1. Click the Notifications tab button on the New Job Properties dialog box. Notice that there is already one box checked. By default, the SQL Server Agent will write an entry to the Windows NT event log if the job fails. The options here are very similar to those you have already seen in Chapter 19, when notifications were set up for the MSXOperator.

2. Click the Net send operator checkbox. If you have not yet set up an operator account, you will be prompted to create a new operator. Click the Yes button to create a new operator.

3. The General tab of the New Operator Properties dialog box is used to set up an operator, while the Notifications tab is used to choose which alerts the operator will receive notifications about, and how they will be sent. Enter a name for the operator.

4. Choose from any or all of the three notification options: E-mail name, Pager e-mail name, and Net send address. After you select the notification avenues you want to use, you can test them by clicking the Test button beside the option. Figure 20-8 shows the pop-up net send test message.

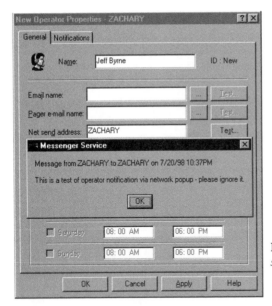

Figure 20–8 *Here you see the successful sending of the Net send test message.*

The Pager on duty schedule is only active if you have selected a Pager e-mail name as a notification method. If you do use this option, setting the schedule is as simple as checking off the days this operator works, and the times when they are available for notifications.

5. The Notifications tab shown in Figure 20-9, allows you to check those alerts that the operator you are now creating needs to be notified of, and how the notification should be sent. Simply place a checkmark in the box for each alert this operator is responsible for, and in the column for the type of notification. If you have set up this operator with all three

Check your notification avenues by using the Test buttons. It is much better to find out now than to find out in a month that you have to set up an operator's Pager e-mail name when an operator does not receive a critical message. You know where the fingers will be pointing once this comes to light!

types of notification methods, you can have the SQL Server Agent send a message by e-mail, pager, and net send to the same operator to be trebly sure that they get the message. Click the OK button to save this operator and return to the New Job dialog box.

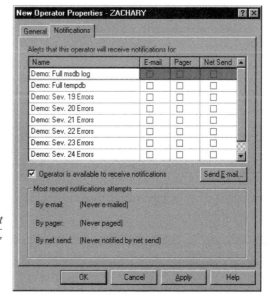

Figure 20–9 *From the Notifications tab in the New Operator Properties dialog box you can select those alerts that the operator should be notified of, and how the notification should be sent.*

6. Choose the type of notification in the combo box beside the operator. You have three options available:

- Upon successful completion: This option will notify the operator that the job was completed successfully. In the case of a backup, the operator may know that they need to go and change the tape.
- Upon unsuccessful completion: This option notifies the operator that a problem occurred and prevented the job from completing successfully.
- Whenever the job completes: This option notifies the operator of either the success or failure of the job.

Figure 20-10 shows the completed Notifications tab on the New Job Properties dialog box.

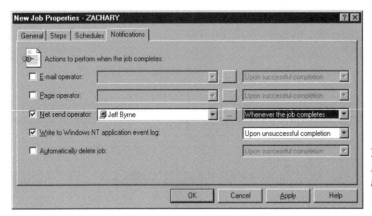

Figure 20–10 *Once the Notifications tab is complete, the job is ready.*

7. Click the OK button to save your new job definition. The job is now ready and scheduled to run at the specified time without further intervention.

The job has now been scheduled and when it has completed, either successfully or with failure, a notification will be sent via net send to the operator. Figure 20-11 shows the SQL Server Agent error log with the entries for this job after running successfully. An error log does not necessarily contain only error messages.

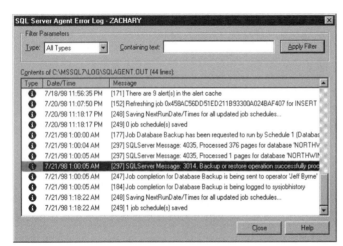

Figure 20–11 *Here you can see the SQL Server Agent Error Log with the information entries concerning the backup job just created.*

If you want to see all of the detail for a particular log entry, simply double-click it and the SQL Server Agent Error Log Message dialog box will pop up with the entire text of the log entry.

Troubleshooting Scheduling

As with any networked service, there are always a variety of things that can potentially go wrong with an SQL Server Agent schedule or job. If you receive an alert message indicating that a schedule or job is having a problem, first check the error log for as many details as you can get. Break the problem down into manageable segments:

- Is the problem with the schedule or the job?
- Has the job run successfully in the past?
- Verify each of the steps of the job?
- Did the job fail at a particular step?
- Did someone change the system clock or time zone?
- Is the SQL Server Agent service not properly logged in?
- Has the SQL Server Agent login account changed?
- Is there a physical network problem?

As you can see, there are many things that you can check to begin to eliminate the possible problem areas. If either Windows NT or SQL Server has not failed, and no immediate hardware problems are evident, start with the error logs and see what they can tell you. Be methodical, and do not let someone standing over your shoulder push you into a solution that may cause other problems down the road.

Stopping a Scheduled Job

If you find that you need to stop a job from running as scheduled, you can do so quite easily. From within the SQL Server Enterprise Manager you can stop a job with just a few mouse clicks. Simply expand the SQL Server Agent that manages the job you want to stop. Then expand the Jobs folder and select the job in the scope pane of the Enterprise Manager window. Right-click the job and select Stop from the shortcut menu. When you are ready to allow the job to run again as scheduled, do the same thing and select Start from the menu.

You can change the time a job is scheduled by opening the job's Job Properties dialog box. Select the Schedules tab, to choose the specific schedule that you want to change and click on the Edit button. You can now change the schedule using the same set of dialog boxes you used to create the schedule.

Using a Stored Procedure

There are several stored procedures involved when working with a job. You will find that it is simpler to use the Enterprise Manager to manage jobs, but you can start, stop, and delete a job using stored procedures. You cannot schedule a job with a stored procedure.

- `sp_add_job`: This procedure is used to create a job and its first step. You must provide the job with a unique name. You can set some notification options at this time.
- `sp_add_jobstep`: This procedure is used to add additional steps to an existing job.
- `sp_update_job`: Use this procedure to change job attributes such as—job name, whether enabled or disabled, and notification levels.
- `sp_stop_job`: This procedure is used to stop a job from executing on a schedule.
- `sp_delete_job`: Use this procedure when you want to delete a job.

MCSE 20.3   Using Alerts

Alerts are actions that SQL Server Agent takes when a specific event occurs. The SQL Server Agent reads the Windows NT application event log and fires an alert when it finds an event that it has been told to respond to. Events can include different items: a specific error or an error of a specified severity. Events can also include database administrative functions, such as notifying an operator when a transaction log or database file is getting full.

When an event fires an alert, the alert can trigger several different responses, such as:

- They cannotify an operator that the event has occurred.
- They can start a job to remedy the event.
- They can forward the event to the NT application event log on another server.

When an event meeting any of the circumstances below is written to the NT application event log, an alert can be triggered:

- A sysmessage error with a severity of 19 or higher.
- Any information, warning, or error with a severity level of 110, 120, or 130 from the server.

Under Windows 95/98, SQL Server Agent uses the SQL Server Profiler trace to support the alert system. Alerts are more limited under these operating systems, and cannot be forwarded, nor is an SNMP trap supported.

- Any event written from a RAISERROR event and using the WITH LOG clause.
- When a user defined event message is created or modified using sp_altermessage.
- Any event that was logged from xp_logevent.

Setting Alerts

Creating and setting alerts is very much like creating a job and can be done during the same process. One of the option buttons available on the New Job Properties dialog box is a New Alert button. Alerts can also be defined before or after a job is created, but you must define the alert before SQL Server Agent cannotify an operator that an event occurred.

Alerts can be set to fire when a defined event occurs. An event can be of many different types:

- A specified text string in the application event log.
- An event occurring in a specific database.
- When an event with a certain error number occurs.
- If a certain category of events is registered.
- If an event above a specified severity level occurs.

You can also create an alert that will trigger only when a certain series of events occur. Alerts can be created from within the Enterprise Manager by following these steps:

1. Expand the SQL Server Agent on the server where you want to set the alert. Right-click on the Alerts icon and select New Alert from the short-cut menu. The New Alert Properties dialog box will be displayed.
2. Enter a name for the alert. The alert name is limited to a maximum of 128 characters. The ID number for a new alert is set at "New."
3. There are two options for the Type of event. The default "SQL Server event alert" is the normal setting for any alert except those that are concerned with performance events.

4. Check the Enabled checkbox if you want the alert to be enabled. This is the default option.

5. As you can see in Figure 20-12, you have several options available for an Event alert definition. The options available to you here include:
   - Error number: The alert will be triggered when the specified event number is found in the application event log.
   - Severity: The alert is triggered when the selected category of event occurs.
   - Database name: If the event specified by Severity is found and occurs in conjunction with the selected database, the alert is fired.
   - Error message contains this text: When the event specified by Severity is found, and the event message contains the specified text, then the alert is triggered.

For this part of the example, select the Error Number option box, then click the (…) button. You will now see the Manage Server Messages dialog box.

Figure 20–12 *With the New alert Properties dialog box you can set up your own alerts in response to selected events.*

6. From the Search tab of the Manage Server Messages dialog box you can select a specific message, or a find all messages, that meets your search criteria. Click on the "023 – Fatal Error: Database Integrity Suspect" message in the Severity list box, then click the Find button. As you can see in Figure 20-13, there are six messages that have a severity level of 23.

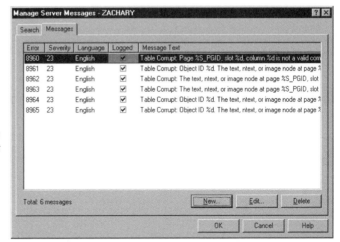

Figure 20–13 *From the Manage Server Messages dialog box you can select a specific message as the event to search for, or a group based on severity, for messages that have specific text.*

You can see that all messages with a severity level of 23 concern table corruption and would be something that the SQL Server System Administrator would want to be notified about. You could also have searched for all messages with the text "backup" in them and you would have found 54 event messages. You can also create a new event message or edit an existing one.

7. Click the OK button when you have the criteria you require for your alert set and the messages selected that meet it. In this case, click the Cancel button to simply return to the New Alert Properties dialog box.

8. Click the Severity option button and then select "023 - Fatal Error: Database Integrity Suspect" from the combo box. Figure 20-14 shows the completed dialog box.

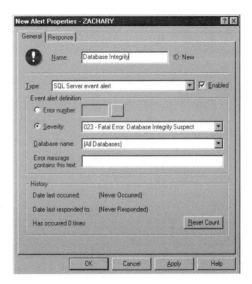

Figure 20–14 *A new alert has been created that will trigger some response.*

In the next section of this chapter you will see how a response is created for the alert.

Alert Responses

Creating the alert is only half of the job. Once SQL Server Agent finds the indicated event in the application event log, what is it supposed to do? This is the response. A response can be a simple notification to an operator via e-mail, pager, or a net send message. You can designate an alternate operator in case the primary is not available. A response can also be that the SQL Server Agent begins another job to attempt to remedy the problem.

Before the alert is really effective at doing anything, you must tell SQL Server Agent what the response to the alert event is supposed to be. Continue with the example begun in the previous section of this chapter.

1. Click the Response tab of the New Alert Properties dialog box.

   You can now choose to execute another job, raise an SNMP Trap (this is only available if you have SNMP already set up), or notify an operator. You can choose to do any or all of these, and depending on the type of alert and event, you may need to have SQL Server Agent begin another job and send a notification to an operator. The operator notification can inform them both about the event that triggered the alert, and that another job was starting in response.

   To start a new job in response to the alert, click in the Execute job checkbox, and then select the specific job in the combo box beside it. You can also click the (...) button to browse for the job that you want to run in the Job Properties dialog box. You can also create an operator here by clicking the New Operator button.

2. This alert will simply notify an operator. You have several options in how the notification is sent, the transmission method, and what information is included along with the notification.

   • Place a check mark in the box beside the operator to be notified, and in the column for the type of notification.
   • You can choose to send the text of the alert error along with the notification by checking the appropriate box under the operators list.
   • If you want to send an additional text message to the operator, type it in the list box at the bottom of this dialog box.
   • For alerts that are recurring, you can choose a delay between responses by choosing how much delay to allow in minutes and seconds.

   Figure 20-15 shows the completed Response tab. This alert is ready to be saved and run when the NT application event log shows this event.

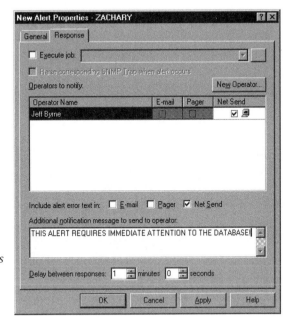

Figure 20–15 *The response for the alert has now been created, and the alert will be available to SQL Server Agent.*

Using a Stored Procedure with Alerts

There are several stored procedures that are used in administering alerts. As with jobs, you will quickly find that using the Enterprise Manager is the simpler of the methods. All of these stored procedures must be run from the msdb database. The procedures include:

- `sp_add_alert`: This procedure is used to create a new alert. You will need to be able to provide all of the necessary information for the new alert.
- `sp_add_notification`: This procedure allows you to add a notification to an operator(s) to the alert.
- `sp_update_alert`: Use this procedure to update the information contained in an alert.
- `sp_delete_alert`: This procedure will delete a selected alert.

Removing an Alert

In the previous section, you saw that an alert can be deleted using the `sp_delete_alert` stored procedure, but, of course, this can be just as easily done from within the Enterprise Manager.

Simply expand the server and SQL Server Agent where the alert exists. Expand the Alerts icon and you will see the list of alerts in the details pane. Right-click the alert to be deleted and select Delete from the shortcut menu. You will need to confirm the deletion in another dialog box; the alert is then removed from the database.

Key Points

In this chapter you have learned several key points about jobs, schedules, and alerts, including:

- How to define a job so that you can automate many of the everyday tasks of administering SQL Server.
- Jobs defined under the SQL Server Agent of the server are to be used in or under the master server agent.
- A job can consist of a minimum of one step and can have as many as needed.
- Notifications can be set for either success or failure of a job.
- Jobs can be set to run once, as scheduled, when the CPU is idle or when the SQL Server Agent service starts.
- Notifications can be sent to selected operators via e-mail, pager e-mail, and through net send.
- How to create an alert that can be triggered by SQL Server Agent when an event is written to the NT application event log.
- You can choose the type of response that SQL Server Agent will perform when an alert is triggered.

▲ CHAPTER REVIEW QUESTIONS

▲ Multiple Choice:

1. *If you want to test a job before it is scheduled, you would do what when creating the job?*

   A. Click the Schedule Later button.

   B. Remove the check from the Enabled checkbox.

   C. Set the scheduled time to run to 00:00.

   D. Remove the check from the Start Schedule checkbox.

2. *When can a job be scheduled to run? (select all that apply)*

   A. When scheduled.

   B. When SQL Server is started.

   C. When the CPU is idle for a set period.

   D. In response to an alert.

3. *When a job has been disabled, it can only be run when: (select all that apply)*

   A. Its scheduled time is reached.

   B. A user issues a command for the job.

   C. An alert is issued that would start the job.

   D. Not until it has been enabled.

4. *Notifications can be sent on: (select all that apply)*

   A. Successful completion of the job.

   B. Job failure.

   C. When prompted by an operator.

   D. When scheduled.

5. *An alert can trigger many different responses, including: (select all that apply)*

   A. Start a job.

   B. Log the event in the NT system event log.

   C. Log the event in the NT application event log on another server.

   D. Notify an operator.

▲ True or False:

1. *True or False? A job that will be downloaded to a target server must be created on the master server.*

2. *True or False? You can run multiple instances of a job.*

3. *True or False? If a job is scheduled to run, you can still run it manually.*

4. *True or False? A job can be scheduled with the stored procedure sp_sched_job.*

5. *True or False? You must create all operators who will be notified by an alert before you begin to create the alert.*

6. *True or False? An alert is only triggered when in the case of a database error.*

Publishing Data on the Web

As the Web gets bigger and bigger, more of you are being called upon to get your company on the Web, or to link an existing Web site more closely with your company database. There are many good books published that go into this subject in depth. This chapter will provide you with an overview of the subject, and how to use the Web Assistant Wizard.

Your Data and the Web

More and more businesses want to use the World Wide Web as a showcase to their company for product and service information and for online e-commerce. Each of these needs can require information from, or connections to the data contained in the various company databases.

There are a variety of ways that you can allow company data to be presented on a web site, and still maintain the security level that you need.

MCSE 21.1   The Web Assistant

The simplest method of publishing data to a web page is through the SQL Server Web Assistant Wizard©. This feature allows you to create Hypertext Markup Language (HTML) documents, also called web pages, from information available in the databases on your server. These web pages can be viewed with any HTML browser. Using the Web Assistant with databases created with an earlier version of SQL Server will result in errors and a web page that will not work. The Web Assistant is really a front-end for the stored procedure sp_makewebtask. This stored procedure can be run from any platform supported by Windows NT©. Two more stored procedures are used when generating HTML documents: sp_runwebtask and sp_dropwebtask. These three stored procedures have the following uses:

- sp_makewebtask is used to create the task that will produce the HTML document. This is the stored procedure that is run through the Web Assistant interface.
- sp_runwebtask is the stored procedure that actually creates the HTML document. When you run this stored procedure, it runs the task specified in the parameters.
- sp_dropwebtask is used to drop a previously created web task. You can specify either the task process name or the output file name when using this stored procedure.

The Web Assistant can be used to generate an HTML file as a one-time-only or regularly scheduled server task. The Web Assistant can make use of SQL Server procedures, queries, and extended stored procedures, enabling you to create a web page that makes use of the most current information available at almost any time.

Using the Web Assistant is a very simple method for creating a web page with information from your database. Some uses for this could be:

- Creating a web page where customers can browse through the items or services you supply and the prices for them.
- Building a web page on which your salespeople can view available inventory.
- Making a web page that can display updatable spec sheets for your products.

The Web Assistant is used like this:

1. Expand the server from which you want to create the web page and right-click on the Web Assistant Jobs icon. Select the New Web Assistant

Remember, you can set this task to run as often as necessary. Each time the task runs again, all of the information displayed on your web page is updated with the most current information contained in your database. This has the potential to save a company many thousands of dollars in printing and postage costs. Consider how many color flyers and spec sheets are printed, mailed, and thrown away each year, and how many of these same flyers and spec sheets are out of date by the time they come back from the printer. You can have a completely up-to-date flyer and spec sheet on your web page that the customers can print for themselves if they want a copy, and they have the satisfaction of getting current information about your product.

Job option from the shortcut menu. This will open the welcome Web Assistant dialog box, click the Next button to open the next dialog box.

2. Select the Database from which you will be drawing information for the web page, as seen in Figure 21-1. Choose the pubs database and click the Next button.

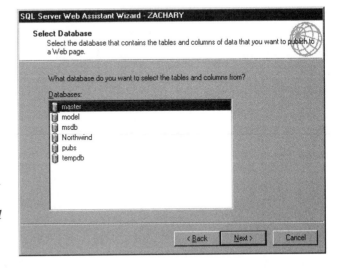

Figure 21-1 *In this wizard dialog box you will select the database on which the web page information will be based.*

3. Now you must enter a name for this Web Assistant job. Be sure that you give the web job a name that will mean something later on. Often you will string these jobs together, creating one page after the other in a series. You also will choose between the one of three option buttons displayed. Figure 21-2 shows the options available to you.

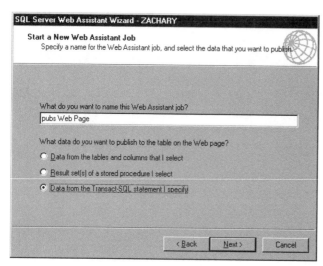

Figure 21–2 *Enter the name for the Web Assistant Job and choose how information will be drawn from the database.*

Your selection of an option button in this dialog box will determine the next two dialog boxes that you will be working with. The three option buttons that you must choose from include:

- Data from the tables and columns that I select: This option allows you to select a table and the columns where the rows that will be displayed on the web page will come from. You will then be given the option of creating a query that will be used to select the rows to include.
- Results set(s) of a stored procedure I select: This option allows you to select a stored procedure that will be used to select rows for display.
- Data from the Transact-SQL statement I specify: Use this option when you want to create a more complex query and/or a query with table joins. You can also execute stored procedures from within your query. Figure 21-2 shows the selections made for this example.

4. Click the Next buttonand enter the following query statement into the text box. Figure 21-3 shows the completed statement.

```
SELECT au_lname, au_fname, title
FROM authors a, titleauthor ta, titles t
WHERE a.au_id = ta.au_id
AND ta.title_id = t.title_id
ORDER BY au_lname
```

5. Click the Next button and open the next dialog box. Now you must choose when the task you are creating will be run and create the web page. You have five options to select from:

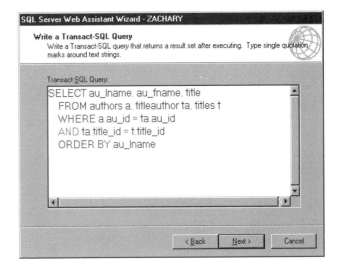

Figure 21–3 *The completed query has been entered into the text box provided in the dialog box.*

- Only once, when I complete this wizard: This option runs the task as soon as you have finished using the wizard and only the one time. The script is not saved with this option.
- On demand: The task is run whenever you choose to execute it.
- Only once, at the following time: Allows you to save the script and run it at a scheduled time and date.
- When the SQL Server data changes: Runs the script each time data is changed in the table, columns, or rows that are used in the script.
- At regularly scheduled intervals: This option allows you to schedule this as a normal job.
- Generate a Web page when the wizard is completed: This checkbox is active only when the last four options boxes above are selected. When checked, the web page will be initially created when the wizard is completed, and then scheduled or run as indicated.

It is not recommended that you use the fourth option, "When the SQL Server data changes" on a heavily updated table. You may find that all of your server resources are being used to update the table, and then to update the web page. A script that uses such a table can be scheduled to run several times a day if necessary. This should be more than adequate for most web pages.

Choose the last option and be sure that the checkbox is selected. This will create the web page when you complete this wizard, and will also allow you to schedule the job as necessary. Figure 21-4 shows the completed dialog box.

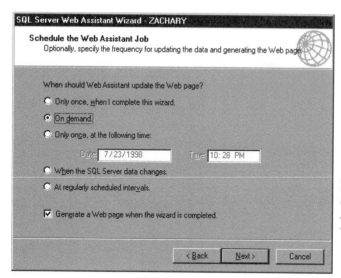

Figure 21–4 *Use this dialog box to choose when and how often the script will run to create an updated web page.*

6. Click the Next button to move on. Now you can create the schedule for the new job as shown in Figure 21-5. Remember, that you can always adjust the schedule later if you find that it is either too frequent, or not often enough.

7. Click the Next button, and choose where you will save your web pages. The default location is the `C:\MSSQL7\HTML` folder. You can use this folder as a temporary storage location, and then move all of the web pages to the web server.

Figure 21–5 *In this dialog box you will create a schedule for the new web page job to use.*

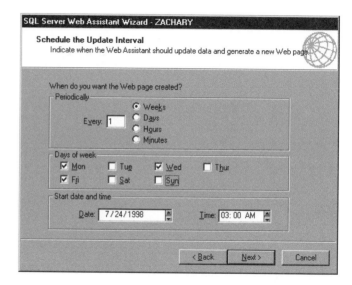

8. Click the Next button again. You will begin formatting your web page. You can choose to step through the wizard and format your HTML code now, or if you have a template set up for your web site, you can choose to use it in the second option. Leave the default first option selected.

9. Click the Next button. Enter a title for the new web page in the first text box. In the second text box enter a title for the table that will display the results of your query. The third text box allows you to select a font size for the table title. Click the + (plus) or - (minus) buttons to increase or decrease the size of the font. The checkbox allows you to include a time and date stamp on the web page. This gives an easy indicator to someone viewing your web page of when the page was last updated. Figure 21-6 shows the completed dialog box.

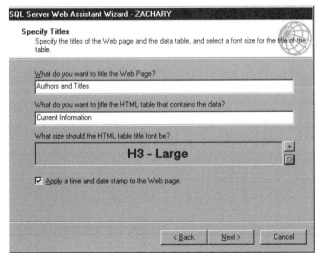

Figure 21–6 *Here, the titles for the web page have been completed.*

10. Click the Next button. In this dialog box you will select the attributes for the columns and the rows displayed. First, you can choose to display column names or not for the columns that will be included in the output. The second option is to choose the characteristics of the font that will be used on the table data: Fixed, Proportional, Bold, or Italic. Finally, select whether to include border lines around the table. Figure 21-7 shows the completed dialog box.

11. Click the Next button. Now you have the option to include hyperlinks to other web pages or sites on the new page. You can include a single link, or a list of links drawn from a table with a query.

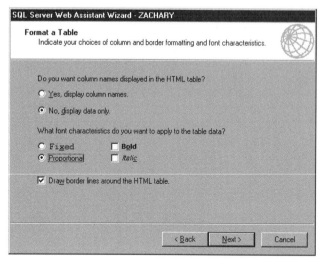

Figure 21–7 *Apply the attributes that are appropriate for your company's web page.*

12. Click the Next button. Now choose whether to limit the number of rows returned, or to allow all rows that meet the criteria to be returned. If you choose to limit the number of rows, then enter that number in the text box provided. Next, choose to limit the number of rows that will be displayed on a page. If you simply allow all rows to be returned, then the page will be allowed to scroll through the information. Otherwise, the viewer can click on a next or previous hyperlink to view additional rows. Figure 21-8 shows this dialog box.

13. Click the Next button. Here, at the final dialog box, you can choose to write your SQL statement to a file. If it is a very complex statement and/or

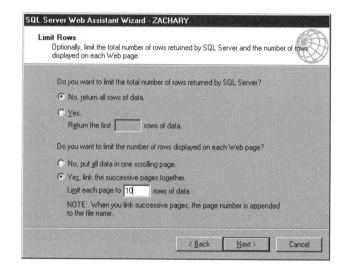

Figure 21–8 *Here, this web page allows all rows to be returned and limits the rows on each page to 10.*

you plan to use it in other applications, then by all means save the query by clicking the Write Transact-SQL to File button. This will only save you time later; if you find that you do not need the query, you can delete the file. You will need to provide the saved query a name and choose a folder for it to be placed in. Click the Finish button to create the web page.

If your web page is created successfully and there was nothing wrong with your query statement, then you will see a dialog box telling you that the Web Assistant completed the task. In Figure 21-9 one of the pages of the Web Assistant output is shown.

Notice the title entered is displayed on the title bar of the window, and the table title is also shown. You can view additional pages of output by clicking the First, Previous, and Next hyperlinks that were automatically inserted for you.

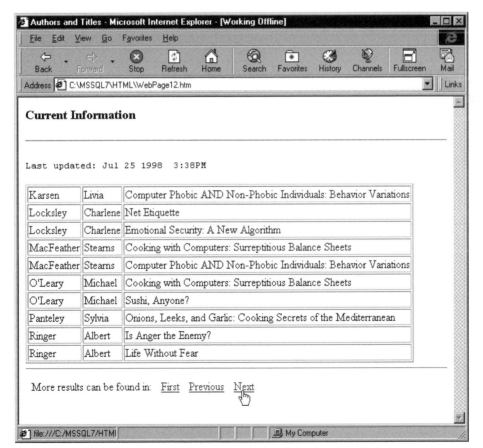

Figure 21–9 *Now you can see the web page output displayed in the browser.*

Key Points

In this chapter you learned several key points about the creation of a web page using information pulled out of a table.

- How to use the Web Assistant Wizard to select a database and tables.
- How to select specific tables and columns with the Web Assistant.
- The Web Assistant acts as a front-end for the stored procedures sp_makewebtask and sp_runwebtask.
- The third stored procedure sp_dropwebtask simply drops an existing web task. You can do the same thing by selecting the task in the Enterprise Manager and deleting it.
- How to use the Web Assistant to format your web page or to apply a web template for formatting information.

▲ CHAPTER REVIEW QUESTIONS

▲ Multiple Choice:

1. *When does the Web Assistant generate the HTML pages from your database? (select all that apply)*

   A. Once, when you have finished using the Web Assistant.

   B. On a scheduled basis as a task.

   C. Only when someone accesses your web site.

   D. Whenever you click the Generate button.

2. *While using the Web Assistant you can select from among several data sources for the information to be included on a page, and they include: (select all that apply)*

   A. A Transact-SQL statement.

   B. A DB-Library data source.

   C. An ODBC data source.

   D. Results set from a stored procedure.

3. *You can use a _____ to give your web site a consistent look.*

   A. Format file

   B. Template file

   C. HTML file

   D. Corporate image

4. *When creating a web page, you can limit the number of rows displayed on a page: (select all that apply)*

    A. All rows are always displayed.

    B. Can be limited to a specified number of rows.

    C. Always limited to 10 rows per page.

    D. Always limited to 12 rows per page.

▲ True or False:

1. *True or False? The Web Assistant can be used with any database created with SQL Server version 6 and above.*

2. *True or False? The Web Assistant can be used to create a complete web site across multiple databases.*

3. *True or False? You can base the selection of information on a query.*

4. *True or False? It is highly recommended that a web page based on a table that is frequently updated with new information, allows SQL Server to update the web site as changes are made.*

5. *True or False? Once you create a web page with the Web Assistant, you cannot reset the standard body font without recreating the page.*

6. *True or False? Hyperlinks to other pages cannot be set from the Web Assistant.*

Beginning Replication

Replication at its simplest means to duplicate the table schema, data, and/or stored procedures from a source database to one or more destination databases. Each of these databases will usually reside on different servers.

Replication Basics

Replication is the process of duplicating information from one database and placing it in another
database. SQL Server's© ability to replicate information began with version 6.0, and has been further enhanced in versions 6.5 and now with 7.0.
The duplicated data can include a table schema
and the data contained in the table, or it may also
include stored procedures. Replication can also
use queries to control what data is duplicated and
sent on to the receiver database.

MCSE 22.1   **Replication Models**

The terms normally used for the databases involved in the replication process are the *source* database and the *destination* database. The source database is the information provider. All of the replicated data comes from the source. The destination database is the information receiver. You may have multiple destination databases, and they may even receive different data. The destination databases are usually located on different servers. These servers may be located in the same room, same building, city, state, or country.

Replication is often used to coordinate the information stored by each outlying office. For example, your corporate headquarters is located in Los Angeles, and you have offices located in Chicago and New York. Each evening the server in Chicago dials in to the corporate server and synchronizes its information with the main server. Then the New York server does the same thing.

Within SQL Server, replication works on a publish and subscribe model. A database or table that will participate as the source database is published. Databases and servers who receive a publication are subscribers. Between the publisher and subscriber is the distribution database. When information is replicated, it is published and forwarded to the distribution database. The distribution database may be located on the same server that published the information, or it may be located on a different server. Figure 22-1 illustrates this.

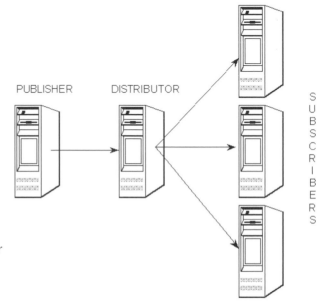

Figure 22–1 *The Publisher replicates data and places it in the Distributor database. From there the data is transferred to the Subscriber servers. The Publisher and Distributor may be on the same server.*

PUBLISHER   DISTRIBUTOR   SUBSCRIBERS

Publisher

The publisher in the replication process is the source SQL Server. A publisher publishes selected data for others to subscribe to. A publication is a metaphor for the data that is replicated from the source database. All replicated data has a single publisher—the server that originally published the information. This is true even if a subscriber server later updates the data and republishes it to another subscriber.

The publisher server decides what information will be published from what databases. When publishing data, you have complete control over choosing the information to be replicated. You can select the columns that will be included, and use a query to select the rows that will be replicated. You even have control over who may or may not subscribe to the information that you publish. This is done by publishing the publication as either unrestricted or restricted.

The publication that you create is further subdivided into *articles*. An article is the basic unit of a publication and consists of the actual data or stored procedures that are included into the publication. A publication can be composed on one or more articles, and new articles can be added to an existing publication.

Subscriber

The Subscriber is the SQL Server that receives a publication. A subscriber can choose to subscribe to any unrestricted publication. When you choose to subscribe to a publication, you may either receive updates at certain intervals, or you may choose to send for the current publication. This is the basic difference between push and pull subscriptions, which will be discussed in greater detail later in this chapter.

Depending on the type of information that is received in a subscription, you may or may not be able to update the information. A subscription can be either a read-only replica, or a full-working copy.

Replicated Data

Data is replicated as articles and publications. These are then sent from the publisher to the distribution server, and then on to the subscribing servers. Information can be replicated a single time, or scheduled as a job so that the data is updated on a schedule. Depending on the type of information that is replicated and the subscribers that you have, you can choose the appropriate replication schedule for your publication.

ARTICLES

The article is the smallest unit of a publication. An article consists of the data from a table that has been marked for replication. An article can also include, or consist only of, stored procedures. Any single table can have multiple articles defined on it. An article will contain a defined set of data from the table. The article may cover the entire table or only a small portion of it.

Articles can be defined such that only specific columns are included. This is also called *vertical partitioning* of the table. This is the simplest form of partitioning of information. You simply select the specific columns to be included in the publication.

You can also use queries to choose the specific rows that will be included in the article—this is also called *horizontal partitioning* of the table.

Articles can be both vertically and horizontally partitioned. This gives you very good control over the data that is published from your database.

PUBLICATIONS

A publication is created from one or more articles. The publication is the object that is normally replicated between a publisher and a subscriber. This helps to ensure that a subscriber receives all of the information that they should. If they were to receive only one article from a publication, the subscriber would probably end up with a database that is incomplete.

In earlier versions of SQL Server, a subscriber could subscribe to just a specific article from within a publication. This required a greater degree of administration of the replication process than it should. With SQL Server 7.0, article subscription is not supported except for backward compatibility. It is highly recommended that you change any subscriptions now calling a specific article to publication subscription.

The main problem with allowing article subscription is that when you create a publication it is often composed of related pieces. You expect that the publication will be used intact and that it is updating selected components on the subscriber's database. If the subscriber only pulls in one article, they are getting only part of the updated material. For example, you may create a publication composed of updates to the products, employee, and customer tables. This publication is supposed to update the databases for all of the outlying offices with the most current information. If the Chicago office decides that they only want to subscribe to the products article, they would not receive the updated information about customers and employees. They may then not know that the sales manager for the company has been promoted, and that some customers have had their credit limits raised, while others are on credit hold. They are working with outdated data that may cause a multitude of problems.

SUBSCRIPTIONS

Setting up a publication and the articles contained in them is only the first half of the process. Once that has been completed, you must then set up the subscriptions. The subscription is what actually starts the replication process. The publication only tells SQL Server what is to be included.

Push Versus Pull

Replication/subscriptions can work in one of two directions: pushed from the source or pulled from the destination. Any publication can be either or both a push or pulled subscription. You can easily have some servers that receive a subscription as a push, while others pull it from the publisher.

Push subscriptions are begun from the publishing server. A push subscription can be done either as a near real-time transaction process or on a scheduled basis. Pushing a subscription using a near real-time format places significant processor overhead on to the publishing server. Be sure that your system has enough system resources to handle this additional transaction process. This is a good method for transactional processes where each subscribing server needs the most current data possible. In order for the publishing server to push a subscription to the subscribing server, it must have adequate permissions on that server. This usually means access to the sysadmin permissions.

The alternative to pushing is pulling a subscription. A subscription that is pulled is one that is requested from the subscriber side. The subscriber sends a request to the publishing or distribution server asking for an updated copy of the publication. This method is often used when there are a large number of subscribers in different time zones, or with mobile users. This gives the subscriber the option of determining when is the best time to update and synchronize their database.

MCSE 22.2   Types of Replication

There are three basic replication models supported by SQL Server. Each gives you different capabilities that you can make use of as you create your replication application.

- Snapshot replication: This form of replication takes a picture of the published data as of a point in time.

- Transactional replication: This type of replication can replicate either data or stored procedures.

- Merge replication: This type of replication synchronizes changes in both a source and destination database.

You do not have to use one type of replication exclusively in an application. You may find that some information lends itself to a transactional replication, and other information can use the snapshot replication. You are not limited to a single form of replication. You can enhance all of the replication models by using vertical and horizontal partitioning of the information.

There are several Agents that work in conjunction with replication. Often, your replication application will use two or more of these Agents:

- Merge Agent: This Agent tracks changes that occur after the initial merge has been accomplished. Every merge publication has its own merge Agent. The merge Agent is connected to both the publisher and subscriber and updates both. If the subscription is a push subscription, the Agent resides on the Publisher, while Agents that manage pull subscriptions reside on the Subscriber.

- Snapshot Agent: This Agent usually runs under the SQL Server Agent and on the Distributor server. It prepares the publication schema and records the initial data files and any stored procedures, then stores the snapshot on the distributor. All information about synchronization between publisher, distributor, and subscriber is then recorded.

- Distribution Agent: This Agent usually runs on the Distributor and connects to the Subscriber. The exception is pull subscriptions for either snapshot or transactional publications, where the Agent resides on the Subscriber and connects to the Distributor. Push snapshot and transactional publications that are set up to run synchronization when created have their own Distribution Agents; otherwise, they will share an Agent between any publisher/subscriber pair. The Distribution Agent normally runs under SQL Server Agent.

- Log Reader Agent: This Agent is used in conjunction with transactional publications. It moves all transactions marked for replication from the Publishers transaction log to the distribution database. Each database that uses a transactional publication has its own Log Reader Agent that resides on the Distributor.

Snapshot Replication

The snapshot replica is a complete picture of the publication as of a specific point in time. This is a relatively simple form of replication and requires much less processor overhead than other types of replication.

The snapshot replica does not require the continuous monitoring of transactions in the database. Once the replica has been done, that is it. Any new transactions added to the database do not exist. One of the primary drawbacks to this type of replication is that it can require a great deal of network bandwidth. If the replica contains a large amount of information, then all of that data is transmitted to the destination database. The snapshot works best for data that does not change frequently, or when there is not a large amount of data.

For example, tables that contain information about shipping codes, invoice term codes, or employee data, generally do not contain a lot of data, nor do they change frequently, and as such are excellent candidates for snapshot replication.

Snapshot replication is done with the cooperation of two replication Agents: the Snapshot Agent and the Distribution Agent.

Transactional Replication

The transactional replication publication can be used with either tables or stored procedures. Publishing table data is much like other forms of replication, but the ability to publish stored procedures is very powerful.

Whenever a published stored procedure is executed on the Publisher, the fact of its execution and the parameters passed to it are recorded and then forwarded to the Subscribers to the publication. When the publication with the stored procedure information is received by the Subscriber, the stored procedure along with its parameters is executed on the Subscriber. This enables you to pass only the instructions that make the changes instead of each INSERT, DELETE, or UPDATE statement that makes up the transactions. When the Subscriber receives this information, then it will execute the stored procedure using the same parameters and make the necessary changes to the data contained in the publication affected by the stored procedure.

Transactional replication records all changes made in the transaction log of a database that concerns the data included in an article. The changes are forwarded to the Distribution database and then on to the Subscriber where they are applied one by one. These changes can be updated to the Subscriber continuously with a good network connection, or at scheduled intervals.

Note

Caution is required when using transactional replication with stored procedures. If you create an article that is horizontally partitioned such that there are different rows at the Publisher and the various Subscribers, then the stored procedure may result in different results at the Subscriber than at the Publisher. Using stored procedure transactional replication requires a very good working knowledge of both your data and stored procedures.

A transactional publication can be pushed from the Publisher side, or pulled from the Subscriber side. A pull subscription is often used in the case of a mobile user or for an office without a persistent network connection.

The transactional publication makes use of the Snapshot Agent, the Log Reader Agent, and the Distribution Agent. You may think that the Snapshot Agent would not be used in a transactional publication. The Snapshot Agent is used to create the initial starting point for each Subscriber. Without the initial snapshot of the database, there is no initial database to which the transactions will be applied.

Merge Replication

Merge replication is used when both a Subscriber and the Publisher are able to update the data in a publication. The server that creates a merge replica is the Publisher of that publication. Once the publication has been subscribed to by another server, the Publisher does not necessarily take precedence over a Subscriber when there is a conflict with a data update. You determine the criteria by which these conflicts are resolved. Data updates are propagated in both directions: from the Publisher to the Subscriber and the Subscriber to the Publisher. Updates do not move from Subscriber to Subscriber.

When you create a merge publication, SQL Server makes three changes to the base table. These changes are made so that updates to the table data can be tracked at both ends.

- A unique column is identified. If the table already contains a column that uses the uniqueidentifier datatype and the ROWGUIDCOL property, then this column will automatically be used. If this column does not exist, then SQL Server will add a ROWGUID column to the table. This column is added to the table when the Snapshot Agent executes the publication for the first time, or when the article is activated when created.
- Next, SQL Server installs a set of triggers used to track changes to the data contained in each row and/or column. These triggers are used to

capture all changes made to the table data, and then records the changes in a set of merge system tables. These triggers are created when the Snapshot Agent for the publication is run the first time or when the article is created. A different set of triggers is created to track changes by row or by column. These triggers do not interfere with other triggers that may already have been created on the table.

- Two system tables are created that are used to support tracking data changes, synchronization, data conflict, resolution, and reporting. The two tables—`Msmerge_contents` and `Msmerge_tombstone`— track all updates, inserts, and deletes to the information contained in a publication.

Merge replication uses the Snapshot Agent and the Merge Agent. The Snapshot Agent creates and manages the initial snapshot of the publication and ensures that each Subscriber has a good starting point when they subscribe to a publication. The Merge Agent then takes care of tracking all data changes that need to be synchronized between the Publisher and the Subscriber.

Key Points

In this chapter there are several key points that have been covered including:

- Defining what replication is and how the source and destination databases are used.
- Publications can be either restricted or unrestricted.
- Publications are composed of one or more articles.
- Articles contain the actual data or stored procedures contained in the publications.
- A Publisher is the database and server that creates a publication.
- A Subscriber is the database and server that receives a publication.
- The Distributor coordinates the publications by storing and forwarding publications as needed.
- The Distributor can be a separate server from the Publisher, or may reside on the same server along with the Publisher.
- Data published from a database can be vertically or horizontally partitioned.
- Vertical partitioning means that only selected columns of data are included in the publication.
- Horizontal partitioning means that only selected rows of data are included in the publication.

- Publications can be pushed from the Publisher to the Subscriber or pulled from the Subscriber.
- The Snapshot replica model gives you a view of the publication as of a single point in time.
- The Transactional replica model copies the INSERT, DELETE, and UPDATE statements that make changes to the information contained in a publication and then forwards these changes to the Subscriber where they are then applied in order.
- The Merge replica model allows both the Subscriber and the Publisher to make changes to data in a publication and then updates both ends with the changes. Conflict resolution is based on criteria that you must set up.
- Several specialized agents are used in conjunction with replication: the Snapshot Agent, the Merge Agent, the Log Reader Agent, and the Distribution Agent.

▲ CHAPTER REVIEW QUESTIONS

▲ Multiple Choice:

1. *From what database does information come from?*
   - A. A replication database
   - B. A distribution database
   - C. A subscribing database
   - D. A publishing database

2. *Which database receives a publication?*
   - A. A replication database
   - B. A distribution database
   - C. A subscribing database
   - D. A publishing database

3. *Which type of replication allows a publication to be updated by a Subscriber?*
   - A. A Transactional replica
   - B. A Merge replica
   - C. A Subscribing replica
   - D. A Snapshot replica

4. *Which agent process is charged with ensuring that transactions affecting data in a publication are recorded?*

   A. The Transaction Recorder Agent

   B. The Log Reader Agent

   C. The Distributor Agent

   D. The Transactional Replica Agent

5. *Which agent is in charge of ensuring that all Subscribers have an initial starting replica?*

   A. The Initialization Agent

   B. The Synchronization Agent

   C. The Snapshot Agent

   D. The Log Reader Agent

6. *One form of replication requires substantially less processor overhead and it is:*

   A. Transactional replication

   B. Merge replication

   C. Single publisher replication

   D. Snapshot replication

▲ True or False:

1. *True or False? Each time the Snapshot Agent runs, it creates a copy of all transactions that have been recorded since the last time it ran.*

2. *True or False? A publication that uses horizontal partitioning selects data only from tables at the same horizontal level.*

3. *True or False? A publication that uses vertical partitioning selects data only from specific columns in a table.*

4. *True or False? The Log Reader Agent records all transactions and forwards them to the Subscriber to apply to their publication.*

5. *True or False? Transactional replication can include stored procedures.*

Planning a Replication Strategy

In this module, you will be concerned more with the nuts and bolts of replication. You will see how replication is set up and when the different replication models are best used. Replication is normally between corporate and branch offices, or from the branch to the corporate office. SQL Server 7 now allows for replication between other database sources and over the Internet.

TWENTY-THREE

Planning and Setting Up a Replication Strategy

Replication is one of the more fascinating subjects covered in this book. With replication you can connect multiple servers together and share all or part of a database. Data can also be replicated to a wide variety of other servers—not just SQL Server databases. All earlier discussions in this book have been primarily centered on the sharing of information between a server and its clients. Now we will see how information is shared among servers.

MCSE 23.1   Planning Replication

There are many factors that have to be taken into account as you are planning your replication schema. As you begin the tasks of planning and setting up your replication schema, you will not only need to know where information resides in your databases, but also on what servers the databases reside, and who needs access to what information. Also, how will information be replicated, when should replication take place, and are new subscribers permitted? Are some or all publications restricted? What kind of network connection is available? Are you using the Internet as a replication transport?

During the planning phase of your replication, you should be able to answer these and many other questions about how data will be moved between servers.

What Information Needs to be Replicated

There may be a great deal of data contained in a database. Do you need to replicate all of it or just a portion? If only a part, what part, and do all subscribers need the same information, or can they do their job just as well with only a subset of the data? As you begin to look at the information contained in your database, you will find that some of it is location specific. What is applicable to the office in San Francisco is not necessary for the Atlanta office. As you find these types of divisions in your data, this is where you will partition the information. The more that you can partition the information that is included in a publication, the faster the replicated publication can be sent, and the less network bandwidth will be required to send it. This, of course, requires the usual balancing act from you as the system administrator—the more complex the partitioning of a publication, the longer it will take to create it, and the more server resources it will take during the initial replication process. Depending on the type of replication selected, many of the same resource requirements may be required during updates.

The specific data that should be replicated will depend completely on your own business needs, the needs of the users who subscribe to the publications, available bandwidth, available disk space, and the security available to you over your network connections.

Choosing a Replication Model

In Chapter 22 you learned about the three primary replication models supported by SQL Server©: Merge, Transactional, and Snapshot replication. You can mix and match each of these models within your replication application. You are not stuck with a single model.

You will quickly find that for some information the snapshot model will work quite well. The data does not change frequently, or the Subscriber does not need access to up-to-the-minute data. For example, price information, customer data, or employee data may all be successfully published using a snapshot model. Often, users who only require information for decision support applications can make very good use of snapshot publications.

The transactional replication model works very well for Subscribers that need access to near-on-line information. Each time that a transaction is processed on the Publisher that affects a row in a publication, the Log Reader Agent copies the transaction and stores it on the Distributor database. When the Subscriber is updated, all of the transactions are applied in the same order as on the Publisher, ensuring that the replica is synchronized with the original. This is a good model for information that needs to be updated almost immediately at the Subscriber side. If you have a good network connection between Publisher and Subscriber, this can mean only a few minutes between a transaction being applied on the Publisher and the same transaction being applied on the Subscriber.

The merge model is used when both the Publisher and Subscriber need to be able to update information in the database. This is the most complex model because it requires you to create a method of conflict resolution. Conflicts arise when a change is made to the same row on both the Publisher and a Subscriber. You must be able to provide the rules that govern which update will take precedence, or if one is applied, then the other, or some other method of resolution.

You may find that you will want to use different replication models with the same basic information. For example, you may want to use a Merge model for all of the branch offices for order entry information. At the same time, you have an independent salesperson who replicates data while he or she is traveling. You may want to use a Snapshot model so that they have all of the current information, but they do not need to use a Merge.

When to Replicate

There are several considerations to take into account when you are deciding what time replication activities will be performed by the Publisher. When you choose to replicate is a function of many factors, but it can be reduced to three primary factors for the following reasons:

The type of replication you have decided to use

1. Snapshot replication is most often used for publications that have a low latency requirement and can be replicated on an as-needed basis.
2. When using Merge replication, you may decide to allow synchronization on a specific schedule, or when a certain number of transactions have been written to a replica or the original publication.
3. Transactional replication is more often replicated. Depending on the nature of the particular publication, you may choose to replicate this data immediately, or every hour, or as needed for your own business practices.

The Subscriber's need for concurrency

1. You would use Snapshot replication when there is not a need for a high level of concurrency between Publisher and Subscribers. This would be a good replication method for information that does not change frequently. This is not to say that you cannot use Snapshot replication for higher concurrency information.
2. With Merge replication, you would want to adjust the frequency of updates in either direction, depending on the particular publication. If you were to use a Merge replication with a database that needed near online transactional updates, then you would need to allow updates almost continuously.
3. Using Transactional replication works well for most databases that need near online transactional updates, but only from the Publisher to the Subscriber. You do not get the option of two-way updates.

Network connections between Publisher and Subscriber

1. When using Snapshot replication you can use a wide variety of network connections with considerable success. The sticking point becomes the amount of actual data that needs to be replicated. If you are moving relatively small publications, you can use simple modem connections. With larger publications, you will need to be able to use more permanent connections.
2. The considerations are similar using Merge replication. How much data needs to be transferred and how often?
3. Transactional replication will more often require the need of a high-speed, permanent connection between Publisher and Subscriber.
4. A low-speed modem connection is only suitable for relatively small amounts of data and intermittent connections. A permanent, high-speed network connection can be used for large amounts of data and fast transfers.

Site Autonomy

The term *site autonomy* refers to the independence of any particular site. A server that can do its normal work without requiring a connection to another site is autonomous. A server that uses merge replication often has site autonomy, because it can update the Publisher with its new information later. It does not depend on a transaction being processed by the Publisher and then replicated back to the Subscriber. Of course, a server may be autonomous for some publications and not so for others. A server that uses a two-phase commitment for a transaction has no site autonomy. This type of commitment will be discussed in the next chapter.

Between these two extremes lie the other two forms of replication that have been discussed: Snapshot and Transactional. Snapshot is considered to render a greater degree of site autonomy than does transactional replication for the simple reason that it usually means that the entire publication can be sent and then the connection closed. The publication may be read-only, but the Subscriber can perform its normal work without having to refer back to the Publisher for updates. Transactional replication, on the other hand, generally means that the Publisher updates the Subscriber on a more or less constant basis.

Who Can Subscribe?

Who can subscribe to your publications can be left totally unrestricted, enabling anonymous users to access a publication, or you can restrict a subscription to a list of authorized subscribers. As you create a new publication using the Publication Wizard, you will have two opportunities to restrict a publication:

- The first opportunity is the option to allow anonymous subscribers or to restrict the subscription to only known, enabled subscribers. A subscriber is one who is known to the Publisher and that has the proper security mode for this publication.
- The second opportunity is when you are prompted for the Access List for the publication. You have the option to use the Publisher's access list, or you can create a customized list for the publication.

The stored procedures used in setting up subscriptions and their security status are `sp_addsubscription` and `sp_changesubstatus`. The parameter used for security status is the `@status=` parameter.

MCSE 23.2   Setting Up Your Servers

The primary steps to set up replication and publication on your servers are covered in this and the next section of this chapter. Build your replication framework of servers, then the articles and publications that will travel on it.

When you create the Distribution server, SQL Server adds three new jobs to the schedule:

- Subscription cleanup: This job is added to the Publisher and is used to delete the initial Snapshot files after a specified period of time.
- Transaction cleanup: This job is added to the Distributor and is used to delete transactions that have been replicated to the Subscribers.
- History cleanup: This job is added to the Distributor and deletes replication history data after the specified time period has elapsed.

Setting Up a Publisher and Distributor

The Distributor and Publisher are the first part of the replication framework that needs to be created. Depending on your network, you may have several Publishers, each responsible for their own set of publications. A single Distributor can handle the synchronization needs of many Publishers. The Distributor is created first. This can be done at the same time that you create the first Publisher. Creating the Distributor or Publisher takes only a few minutes through the Enterprise Manager and is done like this:

1. Open the Enterprise Manager and select the server that you want to use as the Publisher.
2. Select Tools from the menu, then choose Replication, Configure Publishing and Subscribers. This will start the Publishing and Distribution Wizard. You can use this Wizard to create and configure Publishers and Distributors. Click the Next button.
3. Since this is the first Distributor/Publisher server, select the first option button, "Yes, use servername as the Distributor," as seen in Figure 23-1, then click the Next button.
4. Click the "Yes, let me customize the settings" option button so that you can see the next several dialog boxes. If you select the second option button, the Wizard will bring you to the finish dialog box immediately.

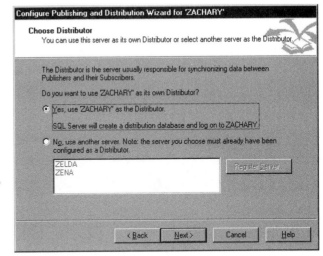

Figure 23–1   *Use this dialog box to choose a Distributor server for a Publisher. You can also create a new Distributor.*

Figure 23-2 shows the available options and what the default settings look like in the list box. Click the Next button to move on to the next dialog box.

5. You can now enter the name for your Distributor's database, and where the database will be stored. The default options are shown in Figure 23-3. Make any necessary changes for your own Distributor and click the Next button.

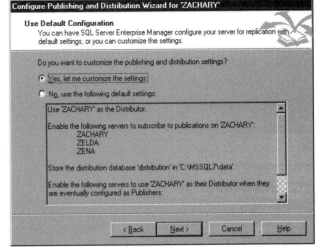

Figure 23–2   *In this dialog box you can choose to use a set of default settings for your Distributor, or you can customize those settings in the next few dialog boxes.*

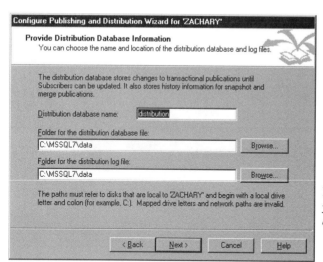

Figure 23–3 *With this dialog box you can customize the Distributor's database name and location.*

6. Now you will select the servers that will be allowed to Publish on this Distributor. You can always add Publishers later. A server must be registered in SQL Server Enterprise Manager before you can enable it as a Publisher. In Figure 23-4 you see that the server ZACHARY is enabled as a Publisher. Click the Next button to move on.

7. In this dialog box you select the databases that are enabled for publishing. You also choose the type of replication that can be done. Click the checkbox in the Trans column if you want to be able to use Transactional or Snapshot replication. Click the checkbox in the Merge column

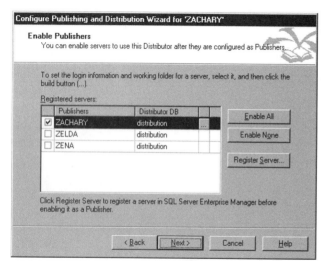

Figure 23–4 *From this dialog box you can choose the servers that are enabled as Publishers to this Distributor. You can add more Publishers later.*

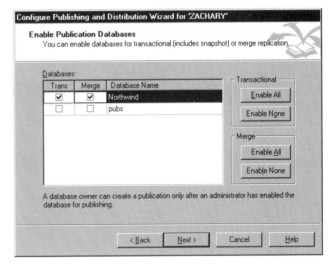

Figure 23–5 *Use this dialog box to select the databases enabled for replication, and choose the type of replication that can be used.*

if you want to enable Merge replication. In Figure 23-5 you see that all replication types have been selected for the Northwind. Click the Next button to move to the next dialog box.

8. You can now select servers to be Subscribers to publications held on this Distributor. In Figure 23-6 you see that all three registered servers have been selected by default. You can register a new server if needed by clicking on the Register Server button. If you do not want a server to be able to subscribe to publications on this Distributor, remove the checkmark beside the server name.

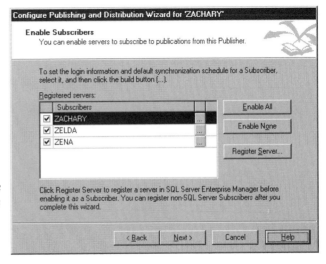

Figure 23–6 *In the Enable Subscribers dialog box you will choose those servers that can subscribe to the available publications.*

Only SQL Server Subscribers can be configured as Subscribers at this first pass of the Wizard. You can configure non-SQL Server Subscribers later by using the Wizard for a second time.

9. Click the build (...) button beside any of the server names in order to set login information and set up a synchronization schedule for the Subscriber. Figure 23-7 shows the General tab options, while Figure 23-8 displays the Schedules tab.

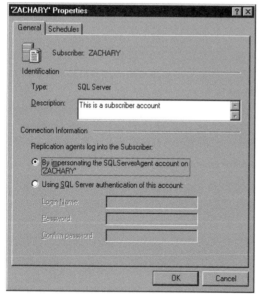

Figure 23–7 *Use the General tab options for connection/login information.*

You have several options available to you on the General tab. You can enter a short description of the Subscriber server in the Description text box. Then you can choose how the replication agents will log onto the Subscriber. They can log on by impersonating the SQL Server Agent account, or you can specify an account. If you choose to specify an account, it must be a member of the sysadmin role.

Use the Schedules tab options to make changes to the default schedules. You can create schedules for the Distribution Agents and the Merge Agents. These are two different schedules. By default, the Distribution Agents are set

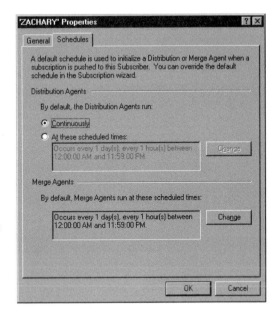

Figure 23–8 *The Schedules tab gives you the option to create customized schedules for the Distribution Agents and Merge Agents.*

to run continuously, while Merge Agents run once an hour. To change the Distribution Agent schedules you must first check the At these scheduled times option button, and then the Change button. To change the Merge Agents schedule, simply click the Change button.

10. If you have made any changes to the Schedules, or General tab options, then click the OK button to save them, otherwise click the Cancel button to return to the Wizard dialog box, and click the Next button to move on to the next dialog box.

11. You can verify the actions that are about to take place by reading the configuration options in the text box in this last dialog box. If you are satisfied with the results, then click the Finish button. If you want to make some adjustments, click the Back button until you get to the appropriate dialog box to make the necessary changes. Figure 23-9 shows the completed dialog box.

You will now see an information box displayed checking off the processes as they are completed. When you see another dialog box indicating success, click its Close button. If any problems are encountered you will see a failure listed. Be sure to check the error logs for more information on the failure.

One of the more common problems that you may encounter is that a logon account does not have the correct privileges—in other words, it is not a member of the sysadmin role.

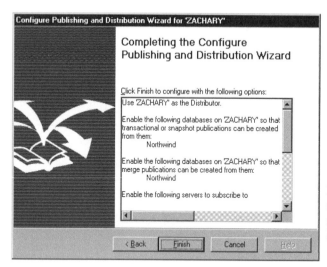

Figure 23–9 *Read through the configuration description to ensure that all of your options have indeed been recorded.*

Setting Up Subscribing Servers

Once you have set up the Distributor and a Publisher, creating a new Subscriber takes only a few moments. Since the Publisher server controls access to its own publications, you create/add Subscribers from the Publisher side of the equation. Create Subscribers like this:

1. Select the Publishing server that you want to add a Subscriber to the console tree.

2. Select Tools from the menu, then select Replication. Notice the new options now available on the next submenu, and the change in the Configure option. Select Configure Publishing, Subscribers, and Distribution from this menu.

   From this dialog box you can make many changes to your publication/replication schema. You have five tabs available to you:

   • Distributor: Here you can add a New or Delete a distribution database. You can also change the Publisher's password from this dialog box. When the Properties button is clicked, the Properties dialog box is displayed for the selected distribution database. From there you can see what servers are authorized Publishers to this Distributor, and you can view or change how long transaction records and replication performance history are stored. The Agent Profiles button opens another dialog box that you can use to view and edit the profiles used for each off the replication agents. To change an agent profile, simply select the profile to change in the Agent Profiles list box and then click the Profile Details button. Another dialog box is opened where you can edit and view the detailed settings for the selected Agent profile. If you want all of the Agents to use the selected profile, then check the box at the bottom of the dialog box before clicking the Apply button.

- Publishers: On this tab you can enable or disable servers from being able to publish to the Distributor. You can also register a new server by clicking on the Register Server button and completing the next dialog box. Clicking the build (…) button for a selected Publisher allows you to edit some of the properties and the security account of the Publisher.

- Publication Databases: From this tab you can enable or disable databases from being used in publication.

- Subscribers: On this tab you can enable or disable servers as Subscribers to publications on this Distributor. You can also add new subscribers to the replication schema by clicking the New Subscribers button. This will bring up the Enable New Subscriber dialog box. From here you can choose an SQL Server subscriber, an ODBC data source, or an OLE DB data source as subscribers. Depending on the option button you select, you will see another dialog box listing the available servers, DSNs, and OLE DB linked servers.

- Publication Access List: Here you can add or remove logins for pull and updatable subscriptions on this Publisher. The Access List authorizations can be applied to all publications, or to an individual publication.

3. Click the Subscribers tab, as shown in Figure 23-10. You can enable any currently registered SQL Server as a Subscriber. They will then be able to subscribe to any of the publications from this Publisher, except for those publications that have a restricted Publication Access List.

At this time you would be able to add a new Subscriber that is not a registered SQL Server. By clicking the New Subscriber button you will be presented with a new dialog box with three option buttons. Once you select the appropriate option button for the type of Subscriber that you want to add, you will see another dialog box where you can select the new Subscriber.

If you are using an ODBC Subscriber, you must first create the ODBC Data Source Name in the ODBC applet in the Control Panel before you will be able to select it here. An OLE DB data source must be set up as a Linked Server before you will be able to choose it here.

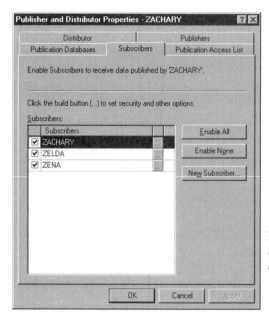

Figure 23–10 *From the Subscribers tab on the Publisher and Distributor Properties dialog box you can add new subscribers.*

MCSE 23.3   Replication and Synchronization

Once you have your Publishers, Distributors, and Subscribers created there are still a few more objects to be created. You have created the infrastructure, but not the objects that will travel on it—you still need publications and articles.

Creating Articles and Publications

The creation of articles and publications is primarily a matter of deciding what information is available, the location of the tables, selecting the data needed, and who is authorized to receive the publication.

The easiest method of creating articles and publications is from within the Enterprise Manager. Articles are the basic component of a publication. Every publication contains at least one article, but may have many articles. Generally, articles contained in a publication should be related to each other. For example, you may have a publication that contains articles from your inventory or product tables and another publication that has data about customers or suppliers.

Within the Enterprise Manager you have access to the Create Publication Wizard if you are a member of the sysadmin role. If you are the owner of the database that you want to base a publication on, then you can have a member of the sysadmin role enable the database for publication for you. You will be able to use the Create Publication Wizard to select the types of subscriptions that will be permitted, how a publication is initially synchronized, and the data format published to a Subscriber.

To create an article and publication, do the following:

1. Expand the Server Group that includes the Publisher and then select that Publisher server.
2. Select Tools from the menu, then Replication, and then Create and Manage Publications. You will now see the Create and Manage Publications on *Servername* dialog box.
3. Select the database from which you will base an article and publication; here the Northwind database has been selected for publication. Click the Create Publication button to start the Create Publication Wizard and open its first dialog box.
4. Click the Next button on the Welcome dialog box. Now select the type of publication that best meets the needs of your application. For example, if you need to allow for both a Publisher and Subscriber to be able to update data, then select the Merge publication option button. As you can see in Figure 23-11, the Snapshot publication has been selected for this example. Click the Next button to move on.
5. Now specify what types of Subscribers will be using the publication. If all of your Subscribers are on SQL Server, the publication will be written in a native format. If you will have some Subscribers that are not on

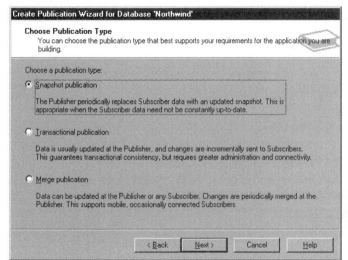

Figure 23–11 *Use this dialog box to select the publication type that is most appropriate to your needs.*

SQL Server, then the publication will be written in character mode. When you have made your selection, click the Next button.

6. Now select the tables and other objects that will be part of this publication. In Figure 23-12 you see that the Products and Categories tables have been checked. Each of these tables will become an article.

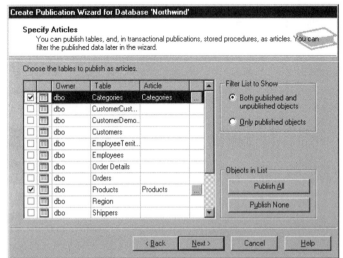

Figure 23–12 *Select the objects to include as articles in your publication.*

If you are creating a Merge publication and you want your Subscribers to be able to update and add new data into the tables, you must be sure that you include all of the reference tables. For example, the Orders table has a foreign key constraint on the fields EmployeeID and ShipperID going to the primary keys of the Employees and Shippers table, respectively. When an order is entered into the Orders table, the values entered into each of these fields are referenced to the table containing the primary key. If you do not include these referenced tables, then an INSERT will fail. An UPDATE on an existing row would not fail.

There are four buttons, in two groups, available to you in this dialog box.

- Filter List to Show: This group allows you to either view all objects or only those objects that have been previously used in a publication. This affects the display of objects in the list box.
- Objects in List: The first of these buttons allow you to quickly select all of the objects in the list. The second allows you to unselect all currently chosen items.

7. Click the build (...) button beside the Products table. You will see the Options for Article dialog box. Figure 23-13 shows the General tab for

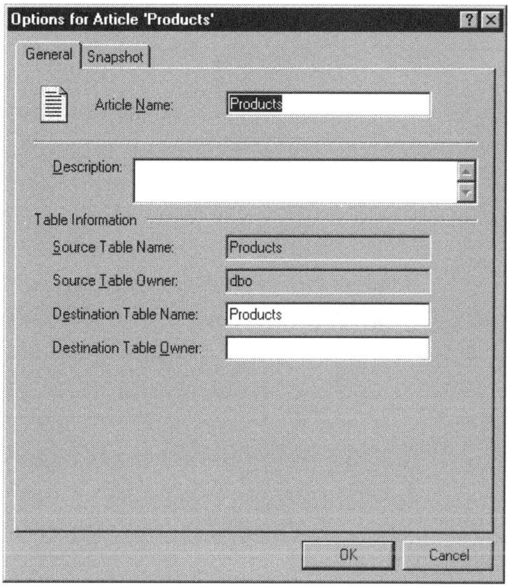

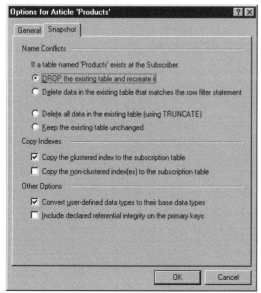

Figure 23–13 *Use the Options for Article General tab to set the article name, the destination table name, and owner.*

this dialog box, while Figure 23-14 shows the Snapshot tab. Both figures show their default options.

From the General tab you can set the name for the article and provide a short description of what the article contains. You can also set the name of the table at the destination and the table owner.

Figure 23–14 *The Snapshot tab is used to select Indexes to copy, how conflicts with existing tables are handled, and how user-defined data types are converted, and whether to declare referential integrity on primary key columns.*

There are three option groups on this tab. The first, Name Conflicts, allows you to choose how the Snapshot Agent will handle a conflict in table names. This usually occurs after the first snapshot replication. The first time replication occurs, the table is created and populated. Each subsequent time, a conflict is found because the table the agent is trying to create and populate already exists. You can select only one of these options.

The second option group lets you select the indexes that will be included during replication. You can choose to not copy any indexes by removing all checkmarks. You can also choose either one or both of the options: replicate only clustered indexes or all nonclustered indexes.

The last group consists of two independent options. You can chose to convert user-defined data types to their base data type. This option is often used when you are not sure that the user-defined data type exists on the Subscriber. The other option allows you to declare referential integrity on the primary key columns.

8. Click the Next button to move to the next dialog box. Now you can name your publication and give it a short description. When entering the publication name, you cannot use spaces. Click the Next button.

9. In this next dialog box you can choose to publish the entire table articles. This is the default option. Choosing this option will bring you to the final dialog box. Selecting the first option button will allow you to place data filters on the articles. This enables you to publish only selected rows and columns. Select this first option and click the Next button.

10. You have two options in this dialog box. The first option brings you to the set of dialog boxes that enable you to filter the article for rows and columns. The second option skips the filter dialog boxes. Choose the first option and click the Next button.

11. With this dialog box you can select specific columns to be included in each article. Click on the Products article and you will see the list of columns displayed in the right list box. Remove the checkmark from the columns SupplierID, and ReorderLevel, as seen in Figure 23-15. These columns are not necessary for an outside office and do not affect the functionality of the application.

12. Click the Next button. In the Filter Table Rows dialog box you can create a query that will filter the individual rows in the table, and include only rows that filter through into the article.

By clicking the build (...) button for the article that you want to include a row filter, you will see a new dialog box displayed. Create the filter by completing the WHERE clause for the filter. The WHERE clause is used to filter the rows.

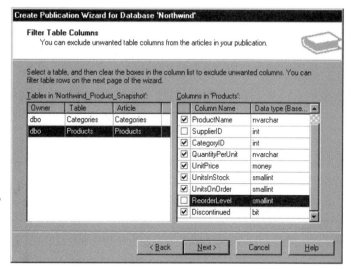

Figure 23–15 *The Filter Table Columns dialog box allows you to choose specific columns to be included in the article.*

13. Click the Next button. Here, you can choose to create this publication as an updatable subscription. An updatable subscription is one that allows changes to be made at the Subscriber side, but only if they can be simultaneously committed at the Publisher side. This uses a two-phase commit function and Microsoft Distributed Transaction Coordinator. Be sure that the No option is selected, and then click the Next button.

14. Now you can choose to allow or not allow anonymous Subscribers. An anonymous Subscriber is a special pull subscription, and the Subscriber keeps the subscription synchronized with the Publisher. You may want to use anonymous subscriptions if you have a large number of subscribers. The Distributor normally keeps performance data, and the Publisher keeps Subscriber data for each registered Subscriber. Using anonymous Subscribers avoids the overhead associated with recording all of this information for every Subscriber. Click the Next button.

15. This next dialog box is used to set the Snapshot Agent schedule. This is the schedule used by the Snapshot Agent to create the special files containing the publication schema and data. These files are used by new Subscribers as their starting point. You can alter this schedule by clicking the Change button and using the Edit Recurring Job Schedule dialog box. Click the Next button.

16. Now select a Publication Access List. You can use the default setting of the Publisher's List, or you can create a customized list for this specific publication. Click the Next button.

17. This is the final dialog box. You can review the settings that you have made in the list box. If you are not happy with the options you have selected, then click the Back button until you come to the dialog box where you can change your selection. Otherwise, click the Finish button.

If the Create Publication Wizard has any problems in creating your publication, it will display a dialog box indicating the error. You can go back and correct the appropriate settings. Otherwise, a dialog box telling you that the publication was created successfully will be displayed, and you will see the new publication listed, as shown in Figure 23-16.

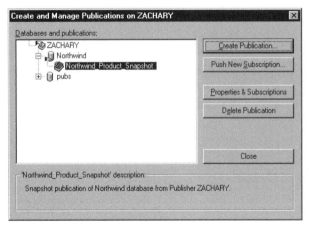

Figure 23–16   *You can see the new publication listed in the Create and Manage Publications dialog box.*

By using the Create and Manage Publications dialog box you can push subscriptions to Subscribers, edit the properties and subscription lists, or delete a publication entirely.

Key Points

There have been many key points discussed throughout this chapter. Replication can be as simple or as complex as you want to make it. Some of the points that were discussed include:

- Partitioning information can cut down on the amount of network bandwidth required for replication and the amount of time needed to replicate the data from the Publisher to the Subscriber.
- You can use the specific replication model that best suits the information that is being replicated, even for a specific Subscriber.

- The decision of when to replicate is a function of the replication model selected, the network connection available, and the Subscribers concurrency needs.
- The replication model selected will determine the autonomy of a specific Subscriber. A site's autonomy may be different for different aspects of the replication application.
- You can allow for anonymous Subscribers, or allow only those Subscribers on the Publisher's Access List.
- An Access List can be created for an individual publication, restricting Subscribers to a select few.
- Replication can be easily set up and managed from the Tools, Replication menus.
- When setting up replication, you can use the Wizards to create both a Distributor and Publisher server. SQL Server Subscribers can also be added during this process.
- Once the Distributor and Publisher have been set up, you can create Subscribers from non-SQL Server sources. This will enable you to share data between many different heterogeneous sources.
- Finally, you must create the articles and publications that will be published. Use the Create Publication Wizard for the simplest method of setting up a publication.

▲ CHAPTER REVIEW QUESTIONS

▲ Multiple Choice:

1. *You want to set up replication so that multiple branch offices can update data at the central server. If all databases are updatable, what replication model should be used? (select all that apply)*

   A. Updatable Replication

   B. Transactional Replication

   C. Snapshot Replication

   D. Merge Replication

2. *What Agent is used to read the Publishers data and transfer it to the Distributor database? (select all that apply)*

   A. Snapshot Agent

   B. Distributor Agent

C. Log Reader Agent

D. Synchronization Agent

3. *What three cleanup jobs are added when a Distributor is created? (select all that apply)*

A. Subscription, Transaction, and Snapshot

B. Transaction, History, and Merge

C. History, Subscription, and Transaction

D. History, Replication, and Transaction

4. *What is the best replication mode for a mobile user? (select all that apply)*

A. Transactional

B. Merge

C. Snapshot

D. Mobile

5. *What replication model is least likely to be used for a mobile user? (select all that apply)*

A. Transactional

B. Merge

C. Snapshot

D. Mobile

6. *Branch offices that update the corporate server is an example of:*

A. Single publisher to single subscriber

B. Multiple publisher to single subscriber

C. Single publisher to multiple subscriber

D. Multiple publisher to multiple subscriber

7. *Branch offices that maintain synchronization between each other and the corporate server are an example of:*

A. Single publisher to single subscriber

B. Multiple publisher to single subscriber

C. Single publisher to multiple subscriber

D. Multiple publisher to multiple subscriber

8. *A sales manager receives a weekly sales update from all of her outside sales people is an example of:*

    A. Single publisher to single subscriber

    B. Multiple publisher to single subscriber

    C. Single publisher to multiple subscriber

    D. Multiple publisher to multiple subscriber

9. *When the distributor and the publisher are not in the same server, this is an example of:*

    A. A publisher and distributor

    B. A remote distributor

    C. A networked replicator

    D. A shared workload

Managing Replication and Distributed Transactions

You have replication setup and running, you have created your Publishers, Distributors, and enabled your Subscribers—now you must manage this entire system. In this final chapter, the tools available to you for monitoring replication will be covered, as will replication in a heterogeneous environment.

Replication Management

Replication and distributed transactions are a very complex topic and can require a considerable amount of time and expertise to manage properly. As you learned in the previous chapter, with replication your remote users can maintain a copy of the data that they need to have access to, update data, and return the changes to the Publisher. Depending upon the needs of the remote users and your network connections, your final choice of distributing information will be dependent on several factors:

- What kind of access do the remote users need?
- Do they need to be able to update live information?
- Are they using information only for decision support?
- What kind of connection do they have to the current corporate server?

Answers to these and other questions will enable you to make decisions about what type of support the remote users require. If they need to be able to access current information and update it from their remote location, then you can create a system using the Microsoft Distributed Transaction Coordinator (MS DTC), whereby transactions can be committed between the two databases. If they simply require information for decision-support processes, or do not need to have online data transactions, then simply replicating the database, or portions of it, and providing it through the publish/subscription process, will work quite well.

MCSE 24.1 Distributed Transactions

What is a distributed transaction? Any transaction that involves SQL Server's replication, publishing, and subscribing process can be considered a distributed transaction if the transaction affects two or more servers. A simple read-only snapshot replication would not be considered a distributed transaction because actual transaction can only be done at the publisher side. A transaction that makes use of Microsoft DTC to coordinate transactions across a network would be a distributed transaction. Most often a transaction is distributed from businesses' branch offices that may be located in different places in a campus environment, in different cities, or in different countries. Distributing data through replication may involve only SQL Server databases, or it may involve other replication partners.

You need to create an application that will allow a transaction to span across more than one server. This is not an uncommon occurrence. For example, a customer presents a check for cashing at their bank at branch 1. The same bank at branch 2 maintains their account. Branch 1 must communicate with branch 2, informing them that they are about to cash this check. Branch 2 must inform branch 1 that the customer does have the funds for the check and that it is OK to cash. Branch 1 then will cash the check and inform branch 2 that their end of the transaction is complete and that the customer's account needs to be reduced accordingly. This is a very simplistic example of a distributed transaction across two servers, one in branch 1 and the other in branch 2.

Two-Phase Commit

The two-phase commit transaction is a transaction that updates, inserts, or deletes data on more than one server, often in different locations. The transaction is one that can normally be broken down into at least two parts, but you do not want the first half of the transaction to be committed without being sure that the second half is also committed.

Earlier, an example of a banking transaction was given. A customer goes to the bank to cash a check. While this seems to be a relatively straightforward transaction, it can suffer from timing problems if the transaction is not committed on all servers involved with the transaction, in the event of a failure to the bank's computer hardware, software, or communications.

SQL Server works with MS DTC to coordinate transactions such as the two-phase commit. MS DTC uses a *two-phase commit* to ensure that all SQL Servers involved in the transaction are in agreement about what is happening. In other words, MS DTC ensures that all of the servers agree that each part of the transaction has been committed, and if they are not in agreement then the transaction is rolled back by all servers involved. This is the crucial part of a two-phase commit: All stations must commit each part of the transaction or none of it can be committed. SQL Server also supports transactions that are managed by transaction managers using the X/Open XA specification for distributed transaction processing. In the two-phase commit transaction, SQL Server works as a resource manager to MS DTC's job as the transaction manager.

Definitions

In order for a transaction to fit within the definition of a two-phase commit transaction, it must meet the ACID properties.

- *Atomicity*: The entire transaction must either be committed or aborted. When the transaction does commit, then it commits throughout the entire transaction. If it aborts, then it aborts through the entire system, changing nothing. At any point, either the server or the application can abort the transaction.
- *Consistency*: The transaction must ensure that consistency is maintained throughout the system.
- *Isolation*: One transaction is isolated from another incomplete transaction. This has often been called *serializability*, whereby transactions cannot perform updates at the same exact point in time.
- *Durability*: When a transaction is committed, it will have been committed throughout the system and will remain even if there is a system failure in one part.

The transaction must be consistent within SQL Server's frame of reference. SQL Server acts as a resource manager for the transactions that are being processed on it. MS DTC manages transactions that are processed through multiple resource managers. MS DTC will create the transaction object that brackets the transaction and monitors its progress as it moves from one resource manager (server) to another. As this movement is being accomplished, MS DTC carries out the two-phase commit protocol, ensuring the transactions remain atomic and durable.

How the Two-Phase Commit Works

The two-phase commit requires a great deal of coordination between SQL Server, as the resource manager, and MS DTC, as the transaction manager. MS DTC must ensure that all resource managers have received the necessary information to process the transaction, that they are ready to do so, and that each server does in fact commit the transaction. If there is a failure at any point in the communication, then all resource managers must abort the transaction and roll it back.

When a resource manager comes online, it notifies the local MS DTC that it is available. When a transaction arrives from an application, the local resource manager enlists in the transaction and notifies MS DTC. MS DTC keeps track of all resource managers that have enlisted in the transaction.

When the application asks that the transaction be committed, MS DTC initiates the two-phase commit protocol. This begins with MS DTC asking each resource manager, in this case SQL Server's, if they are ready to prepare to commit the transaction. In Figure 24-1, you can see how information flows from the application to transaction manager to the resource managers.

Once the request to prepare to commit the transaction has been sent to the various transaction managers, they must take the necessary steps to ensure that the transaction can be rolled back if it is aborted. If any one of

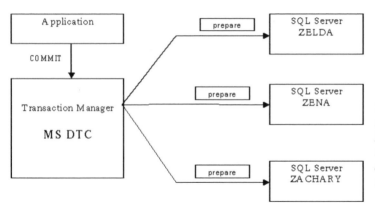

Figure 24–1 *Each of the three SQL Servers that have enlisted in this transaction are asked if they are prepared to commit the transactions.*

the servers is not prepared to commit this transaction, it will send a message back to MS DTC that it is not prepared and the transaction will be aborted. If all of the servers do state that they are ready to commit the transaction, they wait for MS DTC's decision to commit or abort the transaction. In Figure 24-2 you see that each of the enlisted servers has sent a message back to MS DTC that they are prepared to commit the transaction.

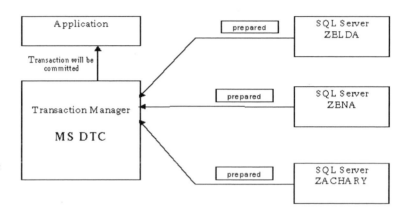

Figure 24–2 *The transaction has been committed to the application and all servers have informed MS DTC that they are prepared to commit the transaction.*

If the decision to commit the transaction is made then MS DTC will send a commit distributed transaction statement to all of the servers involved with the transaction. Figure 24-3 shows this being done.

At this point, MS DTC does not know if all of the resource managers did indeed commit the transaction, and it waits for a message from each server that the transaction was successfully committed or not. During this time period, MS DTC is in doubt of the transaction's outcome: Have all the

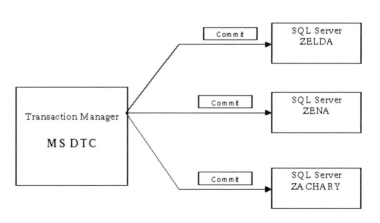

Figure 24–3 *MS DTC makes the decision to commit the transaction and tells the resource managers to go ahead and commit the transaction.*

resource managers committed the transaction? With a resource manager located in a different city, or even country, there can be occasional periods of communication delay. During this period when MS DTC is in doubt of the transaction's commitment state, a lock is maintained on the information that is to be modified by this transaction. This ensures that the transaction remains isolated from other transactions, which may try to update information in a doubtful state. Since MS DTC must track what happens with the transactions it is managing, even in the event of a failure by a resource manager, it maintains a log of all transactions it is managing. This log can be used to recover a failed commit attempt by one of the resource managers in the case of a failure. Figure 24-4 shows that all of the transactions have been committed and the fact reported back to MS DTC. This ensures that a transaction that is committed by MS DTC can be committed by all resource managers, or will be rolled back by all.

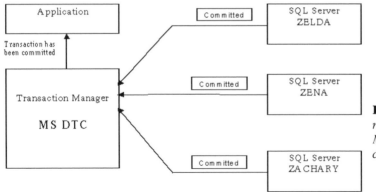

Figure 24–4   *Each of the resource managers informs MS DTC that they have committed the transaction.*

Once all of the resource managers have reported to MS DTC that they have successfully committed the transaction, the process is complete.

Configuring MS DTC

MS DTC is easy to install and set up. There are two versions of MS DTC that come with SQL Server:

- Full MS DTC service for an SQL Server database server.
- MS DTC client utility for use on the client side.

Install MS DTC on the client side only if the client application resides on the client's computer and the client application must call to a C or C++ BEGIN TRANSACTION statement. MS DTC will catch this statement and create the transaction object, sending the transaction onto the server containing the MS DTC service. Otherwise, simply install the full MS DTC service on the server. When using MS DTC on the server, distributed transactions must use the T-SQL statement `BEGIN DISTRIBUTED TRANSACTION`. This tells everyone that this transaction will require resources other than only those residing on the local server.

Problem Areas

Transactions that remain in doubt for long periods of time can cause systems to become bogged down at many points, waiting for resolution. They also will cause MS DTC to lock data that other applications may need to have access to.

MS DTC provides the operator with the ability to force a resolution to these conflicts. The system administrator can force a transaction to either commit on the available resource managers or to abort. The resource manager/server that was the cause of the in-doubt status will be brought up to date on the transactions status when it comes back online—either committing or rolling back the transaction.

Nodes involved in the two-phase commit transaction are considered parent and child in the transaction. The node that passes the transaction to another node is considered the parent to the other. When a transaction is placed in an in-doubt status, look to the parent node to determine the outcome of the transaction.

- If the transaction is not displayed in the MS DTC window of the parent node, the transaction has been aborted. You can safely abort the transaction manually on each child node downstream from the parent.
- If the transaction is displayed in the MS DTC window of the parent node, but with Only Failed to Remain to Notify status, then the transaction has been committed by the child nodes. Manually commit the transaction on the parent node. All further upstream parent nodes will be notified and will then commit and forget the transaction.
- If the transaction has a status of In Doubt on the parent node, look at the MS DTC window in the parent immediately upstream from this node. Continue to examine each parent further upstream until you find a parent node where the transaction has been aborted, and therefore does not show in the MS DTC window, or is shown in the Only Failed Remain to Notify status, which indicates that the transaction has committed. If the transaction is shown to have aborted, then manually abort the transaction on all child nodes downstream

from that point. If the transaction was committed, then manually commit the transaction on all of the child nodes downstream.

When the transaction is in the Only Failed Remain to Notify status, it indicates that the transaction has been committed, but that one of the child nodes downstream has failed to notify the parent node that they have completed their task. The only way to determine which of the child nodes has not notified the parent is by examining each child node manually. You must look for an in-doubt transaction with the same global identifier as the Only Failed Remain to Notify transaction on the parent node. As you locate each child node with this transaction, force each to manually commit the transaction. When this has been completed through the entire stream of child nodes, go back to the first parent node and force it to forget the transaction.

Note   Be cautious with the use of the Forget option. Do not use it until you have completely resolved all of the child nodes downstream of the parent. Doing so may leave a transaction that has not been committed or aborted properly.

MCSE 24.2   **Heterogeneous Replication**

SQL Server can act as either a Publisher or Subscriber to other data sources. A heterogeneous data source is any nonnative SQL Server data source. Many other SQL databases can be used as heterogeneous data sources, as can applications such as Microsoft Access. By working within the Microsoft SQL Server framework, other data sources can become Publishers or Subscribers. Many of the normal transactional replication services are available to non-SQL Server Publishers and Subscribers, including:

- Use of SQL Server Enterprise Manager to administer and monitor replication between servers and clients.
- Using programmable SQL-DMO objects to both monitor and administer replication.
- Use of the SQL Server Distribution Agent for forwarding transaction to all Subscribers.
- Use of the Replication Distributor Interface, a COM interface for storing replicated transactions.

Snapshot replication can be created for use with heterogeneous data sources through the use of the SQL Server DTS services.

Another method of replication used with DB2 databases is the Host Data Replication (HDR). HDR supports both vertical and horizontal filtering, and allows for data replication, and the synchronization of updates back to the database. When using HDR against the host database, the data flows like this:

- Data is replicated from the Host to SQL Server.
- Data is updated, inserted or deleted on SQL Server.
- The databases are synchronized and data returned to the mainframe.

One of the primary applications of this type of replication is the ability to replicate a subset of the data for decision support applications. You will find that some mainframe databases may extend to the limits imposed by SQL Server, or at least the practical limits imposed by your hardware. By replicating only a data subset, you can easily manage the information within SQL Server. When working with large data sets such as those in mainframe applications, you may want to use HDR to subset information for division or department level production databases. Again, this enables you to use SQL Server work with an easily manageable data set.

MCSE 24.3   **Monitoring Replication**

In order to maintain your replication in top form you will need to monitor the application. There are a number of monitoring tools available to you within SQL Server to monitor the performance of replication. Replication monitoring is available from the Distributor server. Whenever a server is enabled as a Distributor, the monitoring tools are also activated. You must be a member of the sysadmin role in order to use the monitoring tools. In order to monitor the various Replication Agents, they must be scheduled through the SQL Server Agent. The replication monitoring tools will not work unless you also have the SQL Server Agent running.

Performance Monitoring Tools

The replication and performance-monitoring tools allow you to view many different statistics for each replication agent. The agent monitors can be used to view current statistics so that you can see what is happening in real-time, or you can view the history of a specific agent.

From the SQL Server Enterprise Manager you can use the replication monitor to:

- View a list of Publishers, their publications, and the subscriptions to each of the publications supported by the Distributor.
- Monitor the current and historical statistics for scheduled agents.
- Create alerts for selected replication events.

Once replication has been set up and started, you can view SQL Server replication messages from within the Microsoft NT Event Viewer. The Replication Monitor is accessed from within the SQL Server Enterprise Manager application. Expand the Distributor server and you will see a new object has been added, the Replication Monitor. By expanding the Replication Monitor you will see three entries: Publishers, Agents, and Replication Alerts.

The Publishers object can be expanded to reveal a listing for each server that publishes to this Distributor. By expanding the Publisher you will see a listing for each publication that they have placed with this Distributor. Click on a publication and you will see the details of the publication listed in the result pane, their names, Subscriber information, type of replication, its status, the last action, and other details about the publication. As you can see in Figure 24-5, there are two entries in the result pane for the Northwind_Product_Snapshot publication. The first is the actual snapshot publication, while the second is the Distributor information about a Subscriber to the publication. Right-clicking on a publication will display a shortcut menu with various options depending on the type of object you have selected.

Right-clicking on the publication and selecting the Agent History option will display the Agent History dialog box as shown in Figure 24-6. Here you see that the detail list has been filtered to show only those sessions that occurred within the last two days. You can change the filtering to include all sessions, those within the last 24 hours, two days, seven days, or those with errors.

You can also view additional details about each of the sessions that have been recorded by selecting a specific session and then clicking the Session Details button. This will bring up the Session Details of Snapshot Agent dialog box. The actual name of this dialog box will depend on the specific Replication Agent. Figure 24-7 shows the session details for one of the Snapshot Agent sessions. The session details a list all of the commands that go into creation of the publication. If this publication is continuously generated, such as a transactional publication, clicking on the Refresh List button will display the most current information. If any errors occur during the creation of the

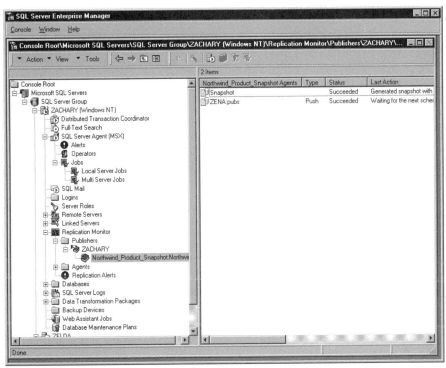

Figure 24–5 *In the results pane of the Enterprise Manager you can see the detail information about a selected publication.*

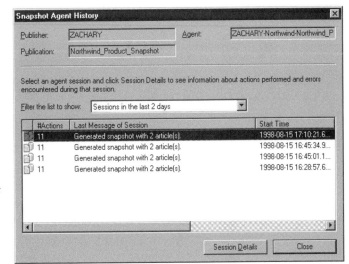

Figure 24–6 *In the Agent History dialog box you can view information about history of this agent's actions. Scroll across the list box to see additional details.*

publication, you can view the details of the errors by clicking the Error Details button.

You can view details for the Distribution Agent in the same manner.

Note   Whenever errors occur during the creation of a publication, or while it is replicated from the Publisher to Distributor, or while sending from the Distributor to the Subscriber; it will be indicated by a red circle with an "X" displayed inside of it. This indicator will be prominently displayed on the Replication Monitor icon and on down to the actual detail record for the error. This enables you to see that an error has occurred and to quickly drill down to the problem.

Troubleshooting Replication and Viewing Error Logs

When problems are noticed with replication, the first thing that you can do is to view the error logs and find out what failed. The replication error logs are very easy to find. SQL Server makes it simple to see that problems have occurred during the replication of a publication, or in the transfer of a subscription from Distributor to Subscriber. In Figure 24-7 you see that errors have occurred during the replication of a publication.

The Replication Monitor easily shows you that an error has occurred, and by expanding both the Publishers and Agents folders, you can quickly see in which publication the error occurred within the Publisher drill-down. The Agent's drill-down shows you which Agent reported the error.

Double-clicking the publication, and then again on the specific piece of the publication displaying the error indicator, will display the Error Details dialog box, as you can see in Figure 24-8.

The same information can be displayed by viewing the errors from the other end and going into the error log through the Agents folder. As you can see in this dialog box, the error that occurred was that the Agent was not able to drop the Categories table before replication because a field is referenced in a Foreign Key constraint. This error means that you will need either to revise the database at the Subscriber side to edit the publication so that it doesn't require the dropping of the table before replication, or to replicate to a different database at the Subscriber.

Once you know what process failed and you can take steps to correct the problem. You may need to reinitialize a publication in order for one of the Subscribers to synchronize with the publication. This is a simple matter

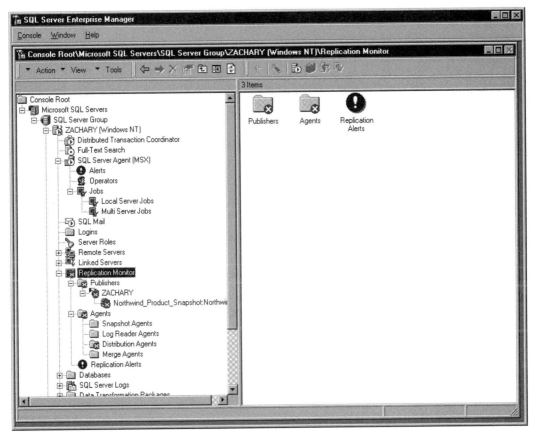

Figure 24–7 *Notice the error indicators, the red circles with the "X" displayed inside. You can easily follow the error chain in this view.*

of selecting the publication in the Create and Manage Publications dialog box and opening the Properties & Subscriptions dialog box from there. On the Subscriptions tab is a Reinitialize button and a Reinitialize All button. The first allows you to reinitialize the selected publication, and the second allows you to reinitialize all publications.

As with troubleshooting any SQL Server process, be methodical. Use the error logs and check that all of your network connections are working and that you can communicate between each of the replication partners—Publisher to Distributor and Distributor to Subscriber. Check databases for mode problems, DBO Use Only, or Single-User modes, or that a database has not been marked as damaged.

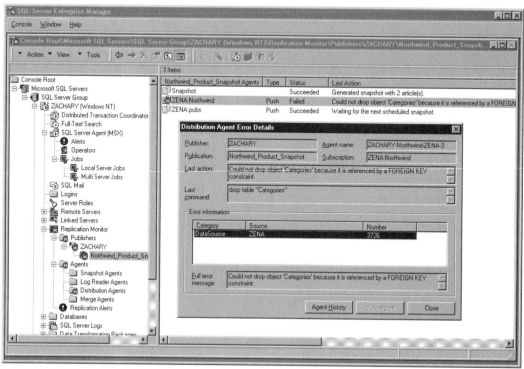

Figure 24–8 *Use the Error Details dialog boxes to view information about a specific error.*

Key Points

In this chapter, there have been several key points made:

- Microsoft Distributed Transaction Coordinator (MS DTC) is used to coordinate a distributed transaction between multiple servers.

- The Two-Phase Commit process is used to ensure that a distributed transaction is either applied across all servers enlisted into the transaction or is rolled back by all.

- The two-phase commit is divided into two parts, the prepare to commit, and the commit transaction phases.

- SQL Server supports transaction managed by any transaction manager that uses the X/Open XA specification for distributed transaction processing.

- Heterogeneous replication involves at least one SQL Server and any numbers of other replication partners. Other databases can participate in SQL Server's replication as Publishers or Subscribers.
- Replication monitoring tools are available on the Distributor server. They can be used to monitor the Publisher, Distributor, and Subscriber processes.

▲ CHAPTER REVIEW QUESTIONS

▲ Multiple Choice:

1. *When is MS DTC not used to coordinate a transaction?*

    A. When the transaction is between two SQL Servers.

    B. When the Publisher is a version 7 SQL Server, and the Subscriber is a version 6.5 SQL Server.

    C. When the Subscriber is a heterogeneous data source.

    D. When the transaction is between two databases on the same SQL Server.

2. *The two phases of the two-phase commit are:*

    A. Notification of Commit and Actual Commit

    B. Prepare to commit and commit

    C. Ready and Go

    D. Subscriber prepared and commit

3. *A two-phase commit transaction must be:*

    A. Committed by all SQL Servers

    B. Committed by all servers

    C. Committed by all enlisted servers

    D. Committed by all officer servers

4. *A heterogeneous data source is:*

    A. Any data source that is not homogenous

    B. Any database other than Microsoft SQL Server

    C. Only OLE DB data sources

    D. Any Microsoft SQL Server data source other than the originator

5. *Replication monitoring is done from the:*
    A. Replication server
    B. Publisher server
    C. Distributor server
    D. Subscriber server

6. *When an error occurs during replication, it is displayed on the console tree as a:*
    A. Red text
    B. A flashing ERROR message
    C. A red "X"
    D. A red circle with an "X" inside

7. *What can you do when using Host Data Replication? (select all that apply)*
    A. Synchronize data between SQL Server and DB2.
    B. Create horizontal subsets from SQL Server to DB2.
    C. Create vertical subsets from DB2 to SQL Server.
    D. Process data at SQL Server.
    E. All of the above.

▲ True or False:

1. *True or False? Replication Agents must be scheduled through SQL Server in order to be monitored.*

2. *True or False? The application that originates a distributed transaction keeps track of all resource managers that are part of the transaction.*

3. *True or False? An Only Failed to Remain to Notify status means that a child node downstream has not notified the parent node that they have completed a transaction.*

4. *True or False? MS DTC is required when a heterogeneous data source is involved in replication.*

5. *True or False? You would use HDR replication to create a data subset from SQL Server to a mainframe application.*

Answers to Chapter Review Questions

▲ CHAPTER ONE

▲ Multiple Choice

1. C
2. C
3. D
4. D
5. E
6. A

▲ True/False

1. *True*
2. *True*
3. *False*
4. *False*

▲ CHAPTER TWO

▲ Multiple Choice

1. D
2. B
3. B
4. C

5. C
6. B
7. D
8. E
9. D
10. C
11. B

▲ True/False

1. *True*
2. *False*

▲ CHAPTER THREE

▲ Multiple Choice

1. C
2. B
3. E
4. A
5. D
6. A
7. D
8. C
9. A, C, D

▲ True/False

1. *False*
2. *False*
3. *False*
4. *False*
5. *True*

▲ CHAPTER FOUR

▲ Multiple Choice

1. D
2. B
3. B
4. C
5. E
6. C
7. C
8. E
9. B

▲ True/False

1. *False*
2. *False*
3. *False*
4. *False*
5. *False*
6. *False*
7. *True*
8. *False*

▲ CHAPTER FIVE

▲ Multiple Choice

1. B,C
2. A
3. B
4. C
5. B
6. B
7. E

8. A, D
9. C
10. B, C
11. B, D

▲ True/False

1. *False*
2. *False*
3. *False*
4. *True*
5. *True*
6. *False*

▲ CHAPTER SIX

▲ Multiple Choice

1. C
2. D
3. C
4. C
5. B
6. C
7. C
8. A

▲ True/False

1. *False*
2. *False*
3. *True*
4. *True*
5. *False*

▲ CHAPTER SEVEN

▲ Multiple Choice

1. B
2. A, B, C
3. C
4. C
5. A
6. D

▲ True/False

1. *False*
2. *False*
3. *True*
4. *True*

▲ CHAPTER EIGHT

▲ Multiple Choice

1. A,B
2. A, B
3. B, C
4. B
5. B
6. C
7. A, B, D
8. B
9. C
10. D
11. A, D

▲ True/False

1. *True*
2. *True*
3. *False*
4. *False*
5. *True*
6. *False*
7. *False*
8. *True*
9. *False*

▲ CHAPTER NINE

▲ Multiple Choice

1. B, C
2. C

▲ True/False

1. *False*
2. *False*
3. *False*
4. *False*

▲ CHAPTER TEN

▲ Multiple Choice

1. C
2. A, B, C, D
3. A,C
4. C
5. A, C
6. C

7. B

▲ True/False

1. *False*
2. *True*
3. *True*
4. *False*

▲ CHAPTER ELEVEN

▲ Multiple Choice

1. A
2. C
3. A, C
4. B
5. B, D

▲ True/False

1. *True*
2. *True*
3. *False*
4. *True*
5. *False*

▲ CHAPTER TWELVE

▲ Multiple Choice

1. D
2. C
3. C
4. B
5. B

6. B

7. D

▲ True/False

1. *False*

2. *False*

▲ CHAPTER THIRTEEN

▲ Multiple Choice

1. A, B, C

2. A, B, C, D

▲ True/False

1. *False*

2. *False*

3. *True*

4. *False*

▲ CHAPTER FOURTEEN

▲ Multiple Choice

1. B, D

2. C

3. A, D

4. C

5. A, D

6. B, D

7. A, C

▲ True/False

1. *False*
2. *False*
3. *False*
4. *False*
5. *True*
6. *False*
7. *True*
8. *False*

▲ CHAPTER FIFTEEN

▲ Multiple Choice

1. B, C, D
2. A, D
3. D
4. B, D

▲ True/False

1. *True*
2. *False*
3. *True*

▲ CHAPTER SIXTEEN

▲ Multiple Choice

1. A, B
2. C, D
3. F
4. A, B, D
5. E
6. D

▲ True/False

1. *False*
2. *False*
3. *False*
4. *True*
5. *True*
6. *False*
7. *True*
8. *True*
9. *False*
10. *False*

▲ CHAPTER SEVENTEEN

▲ Multiple Choice

1. B
2. A, C, D
3. C, D

▲ True/False

1. *True*
2. *False*
3. *False*

▲ CHAPTER EIGHTEEN

▲ Multiple Choice

1. A, B
2. C, D
3. B
4. B, C
5. B, D

6. B, D
7. B, C, D

▲ True/False

1. *True*
2. *False*
3. *False*
4. *False*
5. *True*
6. *False*
7. *False*

▲ CHAPTER NINETEEN

▲ Multiple Choice

1. C
2. B, C
3. B, D
4. A
5. A, B, C, D

▲ True/False

1. *True*
2. *False*
3. *False*
4. *False*
5. *True*

▲ CHAPTER TWENTY

▲ Multiple Choice

1. B

2.   A, C, D

3.   B, C

4.   A, B

5.   A, C, D

▲ True/False

1.   *True*

2.   *False*

3.   *True*

4.   *False*

5.   *False*

6.   *False*

▲ CHAPTER TWENTY-ONE

▲ Multiple Choice

1.   A, B

2.   A, D

3.   B

4.   B

▲ True/False

1.   *False*

2.   *False*

3.   *True*

4.   *False*

5.   *False*

6.   *False*

▲ CHAPTER TWENTY-TWO

▲ Multiple Choice

1. D
2. C
3. B
4. B
5. C
6. D

▲ True/False

1. *False*
2. *False*
3. *True*
4. *False*
5. *True*

▲ CHAPTER TWENTY-THREE

▲ Multiple Choice

1. D
2. C
3. C
4. C
5. A
6. B
7. D
8. B
9. B

▲ CHAPTER TWENTY-FOUR

▲ Multiple Choice

1. D
2. B
3. C
4. B
5. C
6. D
7. A, C, D

▲ True/False

1. *False*
2. *False*
3. *True*
4. *False*
5. *False*

INDEX